CRIMINAL JUSTICE IN AMERICA
1959–1984

APPLIED SOCIAL SCIENCE BIBLIOGRAPHIES
(General Editor: H. Russell Bernard)
Vol. 2

GARLAND REFERENCE LIBRARY
OF SOCIAL SCIENCE
Vol. 271

APPLIED SOCIAL SCIENCE BIBLIOGRAPHIES

General Editor: H. Russell Bernard

CRIMINAL JUSTICE IN AMERICA
1959–1984
An Annotated Bibliography

John D. Hewitt
Eric D. Poole
Robert M. Regoli

GARLAND PUBLISHING, INC. • NEW YORK & LONDON
1985

Library of Congress Cataloging in Publication Data

Hewitt, John D., 1945–
  Criminal justice in America, 1959–1984.

  (Applied social science bibliographies ; vol. 2)
(Garland reference library of social science ; vol. 271)
  Includes indexes.
  1. Criminal justice, Administration of—United
States—Bibliography.   2. Criminal justice,
Administration of—United States—Abstracts.   I. Poole,
Eric D., 1950–   . II. Regoli, Robert M.   III. Title.
IV. Series.   V. Series: Garland reference library of
social science ; v. 271.
Z5703.5.U5H48   1985   [HV9950]   016.364′973   84-48386
ISBN 0-8240-8813-1 (alk. paper)

Cover design by Larry Walczak

Printed on acid-free, 250-year-life paper
Manufactured in the United States of America

CONTENTS

GENERAL EDITOR'S FOREWORD

There is some confusion about what "applied social science" is. From my perspective, applied social science may show up in three activities: advocacy, management, and research. Social scientists are quite often these days called on to work as advocates for constituent groups: mental health patients, recipients of public housing, ethnic minorities, and so on. Other trained social scientists make their careers in the day-to-day management of programs that deliver public services. Social scientists in advocacy and in management are generally *consumers* of social research, while others are *producers* of research. Applied social research is *the conduct of social research in the context of someone else's need to make a data-based decision (or to justify one) about the distribution of some resources* (day care centers, food stamps, salary raises, etc.). This effort includes such things as "needs assessments," "social impact assessment," and "evaluation research."

Thus, applied social science as I conceive it takes in a wide variety of activities. "Applied Social Science Bibliographies" series has been designed to cover all these activities and to meet the needs of new researchers in a particular field. Scholars confronting for the first time such topics as the ones treated in this volume run into thousands of titles very quickly. Where to begin?

The compilers in this series have been selected because they have already gained considerable expertise in their fields of study; they have read through the thousands of titles; and they know "where to begin." There is a major literature on most of the topics covered here. The new researcher on, say police, should not expect to find an exhaustive bibliography but rather a view of *essential* literature on the topic. Researchers will find this annotated work a highly useful starting point. They may work backward from the bibliographies contained in the works that are cited here. Or they may work forward in time by using the Social Science Citation Index to see who has cited, since 1969, any of the works annotated in this volume. In fact, all compilers in this series were asked to keep this last technique in mind as they selected works for their bibliographies. They were asked to "choose works that, for better or for worse, were likely to be cited by other researchers in the field."

H. Russell Bernard
Gainesville, Florida

PREFACE

This collection of selected abstracts—covering the literature on police, courts, and corrections in the United States from 1959 through 1985—is a singularly important work for criminal justicians. Nowhere is the scholarly literature scattered more widely in disparate books, monographs, journals, and other periodicals than it is in criminal justice. While the distinterested observer may see such bibliographic diversity as a sign of vigorous and flourishing scientific health, the individual investigator, the practitioner, and the student often find the mechanics of pursuing knowledge inconvenient, time-consuming, and frustrating, with the results realized not commensurate with the time and effort invested. Reports of research and other scholarly productions about criminal justice concerns have often been criticized for the failure to build upon already established bases of knowledge and information. A prominent cause for the failure lies in the difficulty in identifying the relevant literature. This annotated bibliography is intended to help remedy this situation.

The abstracts are wide-ranging and comprehensive in their coverage and have been prepared so as to give the reader the greatest amount of pertinent information in the shortest possible space. One is not only able to grasp the essential content of a particular publication, but also, if a researcher, to form a reasonably valid estimate of its methodological strengths and weaknesses, and if a practitioner, to apprehend crucial applied concerns and implications of the work being described. In short, the abstracts provide readers with a succinct summary of the work in sufficient detail to enable them to make their own evaluation of its relative merits and utility. Further, the abstracts are organized and indexed in such a manner that facilitates ease and efficiency of use.

The prodigious growth of the published works in criminal justice has created a need for access and dissemination of knowledge about issues and policies, research and evaluation, and practices and programs—a need which this guide to the literature meets. If any note of caution to users of this volume is necessary, it is this: the fact that more abstracts appear for some topical areas than for others does not mean that these areas are more salient or relevant to the field. It simply means that some topics are more often written about. This caveat is intended to prevent misinterpretation and to emphasize that the collection of abstracts simply reflects something about the published literature. Indeed, it is hoped that this volume is but the first in a series of continuing cumulative efforts to organize and present theoretical developments, research, and practical applications in criminal justice. The usefulness of such works, both to the scientific community and the applied professions, ultimately rests in their ability to serve not only as places of record but also as catalysts for innovation and creative thought that transcend traditional disciplinary and occupational boundaries. Our ideals are lofty, and so should be our goals.

The successful completion of a project of this magnitude necessitates the assistance of many individuals other than those named on the title page. Our deepest appreciation is extended to Suzanne Sergott, Karen Crow, Tracie Goodman, and Stephanie Hatch of Ball State University for their kindly assistance and commitment throughout the project. Our spouses—Avis, Zoe, and Debbie—aided us in our work and often made what seemed like an arduous ordeal manageable. We thank them for their support, encouragement, and understanding.

Finally, there are the three of us. We have been friends since our days as graduate students at Washington State University, and we remain friends today. At every step of the way we have worked together, and, thus, our contributions can only be judged to be equal. Each of us played various roles in the project, yet we never viewed any one role to be more crucial to the project's completion than was some other. Thus, as we have in our previous collaborative works, we have listed our names alphabetically.

JDH
Muncie, Indiana

EDP
Auburn, Alabama

RMR
Boulder, Colorado

December 1984

INTRODUCTION

This system of criminal justice in America is neither monolithic nor consistent. It was not designed or built at one time. Upon the basic philosophic principle that a person may be punished by the state if, and only if, an impartial and deliberate process proves the person has violated a specific law, layers upon layers of institutions and procedures have accumulated. Some have been carefully constructed and others improvised. Some have been inspired by principle and others by expediency. The entire system represents an adaptation of the English common law to America's peculiar structure and government, which allows each state and, to a certain extent, each local community to construct institutions that fill its special needs. Every village, town, county, city and state, in effect, has its own criminal justice system, and there also is a federal one. All of them operate somewhat alike, but no two of them are identical.

In a constitutional democracy, a criminal justice system involves a process whereby society seeks to enforce standards of conduct deemed necessary to protect individuals and the community. It operates by apprehending, prosecuting, convicting, and sentencing members of the community who violate those legal proscriptions as determined by duly sanctioned constitutional and statutory processes. Action taken against convicted offenders is designed to serve mixed purposes: punishment, incapacitation, deterrence, and rehabilitation. What most significantly distinguishes this system from an authoritarian or arbitrary one is the form and extent of protections afforded individuals in the process of determining guilt and imposing punishment. Our system of justice deliberately sacrifices much in efficiency, simplicity, and effectiveness to preserve local autonomy and to protect the individual.

The criminal justice system has three separately organized

parts—the police, the courts, and corrections—and each has distinct tasks; yet, these parts are by no means independent of each other. What each one does and how it does it directly affect the work of the others. The courts must deal, and can only deal, with those whom the police arrest. The corrections component involves those delivered to it by the courts. How successful corrections keeps and treats offenders determines whether they will once again become police business and influence future judicial sentencing. Police activities are subject to court scrutiny; some are determined by court decisions. Hence reform or reorganization in any part or procedure of the system changes other parts or procedures. The criminal justice process, the method by which the system deals with individual cases, is not a hodge-podge of random actions but a progression of events. Some of them, like arrest and trial, are highly visible; and some, like prison disciplinary and parole hearings, occur out of public view.

In the following sections we present a simplified overview of the administration of justice in America. We shall focus our attention on major decision points, as well as some underlying assumptions of criminal justice processing.

To a considerable degree, individual police officers make law enforcement policy because their duties constantly compel them to exercise personal discretion—in deciding what kind of conduct constitutes a crime, whether an offense is serious enough to provide statutory or constitutional basis for arrest, and what specific crime it is. Moreover, every police officer, in effect, is an arbiter of social values, deciding whether invoking formal sanctions is the best way to deal with a situation from the standpoint of both society and the individual. Finally, the manner in which an officer works is influenced by practical matters, such as the legal strength of the available evidence, the willingness of victims to press charges and of witnesses to testify, the temper and norms of the community, and the time and information at the officer's disposal.

In contrast to the police, the magistrate before whom a suspect is first brought usually exercises less discretion than the law allows—in inquiring into the facts of the case, in setting the amount of bail, and in appointing defense counsel. Congested court calendars are a major reason for insufficient inquiry into the facts of an arrest. Insensitivity to the rights of the accused may account for a judge's being too little concerned about the appointment of counsel. And the belief that requiring money bail is the best way to keep a defendant from committing more crimes before trial may be an inducement to set high bail as a routine matter.

The prosecutor—the key figure in processing cases—exercises wide discretion. He wields almost undisputed sway over the pretrial progress of most cases. He decides whether to press a charge or drop it; determines the precise charge against the defendant; and, when the charge is reduced (as happens in about two-thirds of the cases), the prosecutor is usually the official who reduces it. When the prosecutor reduces a charge, it is typically because "plea bargaining" with the defense attorney has taken place. The issue at stake is how much the prosecutor will reduce the original charge or how lenient a sentence will be recommended, in return for a plea of guilty. It is problematic how many bargains reflect the prosecutor's belief that a lesser charge or sentence is justified and how many bargains simply result from the pressures of congested dockets.

Another critical point in the criminal justice process that depends on the exercise of official discretion is the pronouncement of sentence by the judge. Judges are usually given broad latitude to fit the sentence to the individual defendant. The skill with which they act is heavily influenced by the time available, access to probation information on the defendant's character, background, and problems, and the correctional alternatives.

Finally, theory and practice are widely apart in corrections, largely because the correctional apparatus is the most isolated part of the criminal justice system. Not only is it isolated physically, but also its officials do not have everyday working relationships with police, prosecutors, and court officials. Its practices are seldom governed by any but the most broadly written statutes and are almost never examined by appellate courts. It is often used as a rug under which disturbing problems and people can be swept as well as a scapegoat for system failures reflected by rising crime and recidivism rates. Though treatment and rehabilitation are viewed as legitimate goals of corrections, custody and security are actually its major tasks. Two-thirds of the people being "corrected" on a given day are on probation or parole; yet the one-third in prisons or jails consume four-fifths of correctional money and the attention of nine-tenths of correctional personnel. The most crucial discretionary decision-making in corrections involves the question of parole—how much of the maximum sentence must an inmate serve. This is an invisible determination that is seldom open to attack or subject to review. Often it is made in haste, without sufficient information, without adequate parole machinery that can provide adequate supervision, and without appeal. These factors tend to make paroles a matter of arbitrary or capricious judgments.

Overall, informal administrative procedures have tended to supplant formal traditional ones in the actual working of the criminal justice system. The transformation of America from a relatively homogeneous rural society into a heterogeneous urban one has presented the criminal justice system with a variety and volume of cases exceedingly difficult to handle by traditional methods. In this milieu of turmoil, the American criminal justice system must address its major challenge and question: Justice for whom? Closing the gap between the theory and reality of the administration of criminal justice may be possible to some extent through the development of responsive mechanisms and relationships that support and enhance day-to-day operations of all the components of the system. Regardless of the varied organizational responsibilities involved, the system should function as a continuum—from pre-apprehension surveillance to post-correctional programs—if success in terms of societal and individual needs is to be achieved.

This stress on system should not be interpreted as an argument for a monolithic criminal justice structure in which all components are directed by a single operating head. Such a proposal is antithetical to democratic precepts and to the constitutional doctrine of separation of legislative, executive, and judicial powers. In addition, this focus should not be viewed as an ill-disguised effort to effect a massive shift in responsibilities and duties from local to state or federal jurisdictions. Much of the system required in criminal justice processing must operate at the community level, under local control, and with a high degree of community involvement and support.

The need for a more systematic approach does imply that a highly mobile and interdependent society no longer will tolerate standards of criminal justice that vary widely in terms of the protection afforded, the caliber of justice meted out, the success of rehabilitative efforts, and the costs incurred. It does imply that expenditure patterns and resource allocation for police services must be balanced against resource commitments for legal services, courts, and correctional activities regardless of the source of the expenditures. It does imply that criminal justice services must be available and accessible in all communities in accordance with their needs, not their fiscal capacities. Finally, a strong emphasis on system implies that its components—police, courts, and corrections—should function in ways that are mutually supporting and harmonious. Police cannot provide protection if court dockets are clogged and if correctional services achieve only the mandated goals of incapacitating and punishing offenders who will eventually be released to free society. Courts cannot render even-handed, constructive justice if police fail to provide adequate evidence, and if judges are without readily available disposition resources. And corrections cannot correct offenders who are harassed or brutalized by police, held interminably in detention limbo, or processed by an insensitive court.

A fundamental purpose of a criminal justice system in a democratic society is to preserve social order—hence the basis of individual liberty and social progress—through just laws, protective surveillance and apprehension, impartial and speedy adjudicatory processes, and effective correctional services. To provide a vantage point from which to assess the status and operation, as well as possible reforms, of America's criminal justice system—we have organized our annotations of the literature covering the police, courts, and corrections, respectively, into four sections: (1) history, (2) organization, (3) processes, and (4) issues.

CHAPTER 1

LAW ENFORCEMENT - HISTORY

1 Belknap, M. R. "The Mechanics of Repression: J.
   Edgar Hoover, the Bureau of Investigation and the
   Radicals, 1917-1925." CRIME AND SOCIAL JUSTICE, 7:
   49-58, 1977.

   Arguing that American democracy is riddled with
repression, Belknap believes that those groups that
question the policies or threaten the position of the
United States' rulers have found themselves under attack.
This is true regardless if the group studied existed as
long ago as in the Jeffersonian Republican era (the
1790's) to the Black Panthers of the 1970's. Belknap
believes that nothing in American history better
illustrates this point than the early anti-radical
operations of the Justice Department's Bureau of
Investigation and the related rise to power of J. Edgar
Hoover. He concludes by saying the way to reform the FBI
or CIA is not by trying to destroy them, but rather to
reform the system within which they exist.

2 Bowsky, W. M. "The Medieval Commune and Internal
   Violence: Police Power and Public Safety in Siena,
   1287-1355." AMERICAN HISTORICAL REVIEW, 73 (1): 1-17,
   1967.

   A dearth of cross-cultural, historical literature on
policing exists. This article   broadens our understanding of policing, generally. The paper reports on police
power and public safety in a Tuscan city-state from the
late thirteenth century through the mid-fourteenth
century. Problems of protecting the community from law-
breakers are discussed. Bowsky identifies various
strategies implemented for detection, apprehension, and
detention of alleged offenders.

3 Brodt, S., D. Hoover, and J. D. Hewitt. "Policing
   Middletown: 1880-1900." JOURNAL OF POLICE SCIENCE AND
   ADMINISTRATION, 11 (2): 237-243, 1983.

   This paper focuses on changes in law enforcement and
crimes charged in Muncie, Indiana, in the last part of
the nineteenth century. It outlines the social context
of Muncie from its inception to 1900, focusing on
factors such as population, physical growth, industrial-
ization, and community attitudes.   The nature and
extent of criminal activity also is documented as shown
by those crimes charged in the county court. The factors
leading to the creation of a professional police force in

1893 are exposed along with a description of law enforcement practices that predate the police department. The kind of police system that was created also is discussed. The impact of the police on the community composes the final section of the paper. In a short epilogue, the consequences of the Muncie experience for present-day police forces are considered.

4   Carte, G. "August Vollmer and the Origin of Police
    Professionalism." JOURNAL OF POLICE SCIENCE AND ADMIN-
    ISTRATION, 1 (3): 274-281, 1973.

        Carte presents a historical account of the operational philosophy of the police executive who was most responsible for the professionalization of police-- August Vollmer. This account of Vollmer's career permits a more thorough understanding of the influence Vollmer had on contemporary police organizations and their philosophy. Vollmer emphasized efficient law enforce- ment, aggressive street patrol, and honesty. These issues remain controversial among police leaders.

5   Douthit, N. "Police Professionalism and the War
    Against Crime in the United States, 1920's-30's." Pp.
    317-333 in G.L. Mosse (ed.), POLICE FORCES IN HISTORY.
    Beverly Hills, CA: Sage, 1975.

        Most studies of police professionalism have been written by sociologists and political scientists. They approach the problem of police professionalism almost entirely in terms of interrelationships between police and other parts of the criminal justice system. Douthit adds an interesting twist to this line of thinking by recognizing the historical roots of police professionalism. This paper investigates the factors that influenced police thought during the 1920's and 30's and that have helped to define professionalism as it is viewed today. The essay concludes with a discussion of the degree J. Edgar Hoover's actions affected police professionalism, especially his position on the "war against crime."

6   Ferdinand, T. N. "From a Service to a Legalistic Style
    Police Department: A Case Study." JOURNAL OF POLICE
    SCIENCE AND ADMINISTRATION, 4 (3): 302-319, 1976.

        This paper provides an account of the long-term development of the American police. Studies of this sort are rare. Yet, Ferdinand reports on one such investiga- tion, that of the Rockford, Illinois Police Department. Data are presented from 1878 to the present that include the number of arrests, officers at each rank, the amounts

budgeted for various police expenditures and more.
Ferdinand's paper offers insight into the structural
development of the Rockford Police Department over a 90
year period.

7 Gazell, J. "O. W. Wilson's Essential Legacy for Police
   Administration." JOURNAL OF POLICE SCIENCE AND ADMINI-
   STRATION, 2 (4): 365-375, 1974.

    In this tribute to Wilson,   Gazell writes that
Wilson was August Vollmer's most successful student. As
chief of several departments, Wilson's primary objective
was to implement and improve on Vollmer's ideas. Gazell
cleverly synthesizes Wilson's position on police operations as they relate to organizational theory, which
includes police administration and the use of scientific
methods of policing through adapting new technologies.
Gazell also discusses those external factors that affect
police operations. Among those discussed are community
relations, civil liberties, and organized crime.

8 Greenberg, M. A. "Auxiliary Civilian Police: The New
   York City Experience." JOURNAL OF POLICE SCIENCE AND
   ADMINISTRATION, 6 (1): 86-97, 1978.

    The origins of auxiliary police are examined. As it
is for most other police forces, the auxiliary force
follows a pyramidal and semi-military organizational
pattern. Ranks serve to maintain social as well as role
boundaries. Roles are officially defined by rank from
auxiliary commander down to officer. No auxiliary officer has any authority over regular police officers.
Based on participant-observation, the dynamics of power
in the auxiliary force are studied. In most instances
auxiliaries adhere to the chain of command and positions
of authority are maintained. Higher echelon auxiliaries
are limited in their substantive power, and the real
power tends to be localized at the precinct level. A
regular police officer under police precinct commander is
assigned as a coordinator to each auxiliary precinct,
where s/he is responsible for hiring, promotion, advice,
and instruction. Usually through tacit agreement these
duties are performed with varying degrees of authority by
both the police coordinator and the auxiliary precinct
commander. While auxiliary commanders have a degree of
internal authority, their public authority is limited by
rules regarding citizen arrest and citizen use of force.
Further, the auxiliary may not be assigned to plain
clothes or hazardous duty and is generally unarmed. In
the event of crime, the auxiliary is to seek aid from the
regular police. It is concluded that, with increasing
police professionalization and demands for community

control/involvement, utilization of auxiliary patrol
forces will probably increase.

9   Grimshaw, A. D. "Actions of Police and the Military in
    American Race Riots." PHYLON, 24 (3): 271-289, 1963.

    Grimshaw discusses anti-riot activities by external
forces of control--the police and the military, and of
municipal agencies. This paper identifies two theses of
work on racial social violence. The first is that racial
social violence has resulted from the reactions of the
dominant group (whites) to assaults upon the accommoda-
tive structure by the subordinate group (blacks). The
second thesis is that background factors of prejudice,
discrimination, and social tension are present in all
Northern urban centers with black populations sufficient
to allow the development of situations characteristic of
"violence-proneness." Grimshaw discusses the nature and
scope of data that are necessary to test these theses.

10 Haller, M. H. "Civic Reformers and Police Leader-
    ship: Chicago, 1905-1935." Pp. 39-56 in H. Hahn
    (ed.), POLICE IN URBAN SOCIETY. Beverly Hills, CA:
    Sage, 1971.

    Haller tells us that police work is shaped by
political forces. Haller notes that police officials and
reformers in Chicago in the period 1905-1935 discovered
they shared a common desire to control crimes against
property. Consequently, many technical and administrative changes were made that were intended to improve
their crime fighting capabilities. The net result of
these changes was an increase in crime rates. But this
also proved problematic. Police began diverting attention
from the needs of ethnic neighborhoods. The police mission changed from providing community services to combat-
ing crime.

11 Haller, M. H. "Historical Roots of Police Behavior,
    Chicago 1890-1925." LAW AND SOCIETY REVIEW, 10 (2):
    303-323, 1976.

    Haller offers an in-depth look at the Chicago police
department at the turn of the century. Haller explains
police behavior outside the context of legal norms. Between 1890-1925, Chicago police perceived their responsibilities from diverse but overlapping perspectives. From
this vantage point, Haller accounts for the police perspective on a number of issues: recruitment and control,
police and courts, crime control, public morals, and
police violence.

12 Harring, S. L., and L. M. McMullin. "The Buffalo
    Police, 1872-1900: Labor Unrest, Political Power, and
    the Creation of the Police Institution." CRIME AND
    SOCIAL JUSTICE, 4: 5-14, 1975.

        This paper presents a systematic account of a police
    agency in the United States. This paper differs from
    others in that it uses a Marxist perspective to explain
    the development of police in Buffalo, New York. This
    paper offers a preliminary analysis of the development
    of the Buffalo police department in the context of the
    political and economic struggles that occurred between
    1872-1900. Harring explains why the Buffalo police sys-
    tem expanded just after the Civil War, the changes it
    underwent during the past decades, and links the social
    backgrounds of key city officials to these changes.
    Harring concludes by calling for additional query into
    the role of power elites in the development of the police
    and of the function the police in capitalist industrial
    societies.

13 Harring, S. "The Development of the Police in the
    United States." CRIME AND SOCIAL JUSTICE, 5: 54-59,
    1976.

        Harring challenges the traditional belief that
    cities in the United States developed as dangerous and
    violent places. Assumptions like these have led histor-
    ians to conclude that the development of the police
    institution was a natural consequence of violent crime
    and disorder of city life. Harring does not believe
    conditions were quite this way. Rather, Harring believes
    that to understand police in the United States generally
    requires examining capitalist industrial society. This
    essay is a criticism of earlier work and an extension.
    Harring concludes that traditional analyses of the police
    institution fails to consider the role of power rela-
    tions, economic interests, and class conflict in communi-
    ties as they relate to the development of a police
    institution. Once these dimensions are understood, then
    attention can turn to the police institution itself--its
    structure and policies. Harring's piece is outstanding
    because it challenges existing accounts of the develop-
    ment of police and presents an alternative. Harring is
    able to tie Marxist theory of capitalist development and
    class struggle to the police system.

14 Johnson, B. C. "Taking Care of Labor: The Police in
    American Politics." THEORY AND SOCIETY, 3 (1): 89-
    117, 1976.

        Johnson offers a Marxist account of American police.
    Johnson sees the police as the natural center of

attention when it comes to providing a critical approach
to the criminal justice system. The police are the
system's gatekeepers. Johnson provides an account of
American policing by discussing separate events and by
identifying limitations of existing theoretical models.

15 Liebman, R., and M. A. Polen. "Perspectives in
    Policing in Nineteenth Century America." SOCIAL
    SCIENCE HISTORY, 2 (3): 346-360, 1978.

    Changes in the character of American policing
between 1820 and 1920 are discussed. Three perspectives
for the rise and reform of urban police are considered:
social disorganization, politial process, and class
conflict. Liebman and Polen select studies
representative of each perspective and evaluate their
utility in explaining changes in policing. The authors
conclude that research on policing should broaden its
definition of policing and include an accounting of the
political circumstances of a period. By moving in this
direction, new interpretations of historical events will
evolve.

16 Miller, W. R. "Police Authority in London and New
    York City, 1830-1870." JOURNAL OF SOCIAL HISTORY, 8
    (2): 81-101, 1975.

    Miller compares the first modern full-time police
force created in London with the first force outside the
British Empire, New York City. Miller demonstrates the
effect of various political and social developments on
the principles and practices of police authority. He
concludes by saying that London's police force was
characterized by impersonal authority while New York's
was grounded in personal authority.

17 Murphy, P. V. "The Development of the Urban Police."
    CURRENT HISTORY, 70: 245-273, 1976.

    Murphy provides a brief history of urban police. He
examines policing in the cities and on the police
department as an urban service agency. Murphy begins
with a glance back and examines the origins of American
police. He discusses and criticizes ideas of early
police reformers--August Vollmer, Bruce Smith, O. W.
Wilson, and Herbert Jenkins. Murphy concludes with a
presentation of current police issues and offers some
insights for the future. Foremost among these is that
police managers teach the public that as long as
social and economic ills flourish, so will crime.
Moreover, the public must understand that even the best-
equipped police agency is limited in what it can do.

Murphy believes crime has its roots in social and
economic conditions--like poverty--that the police cannot
affect.

18   Parks, E. L. "From Constabulary to Police Society:
     Implications for Social Control." CATALYST, 5: 76-
     97, 1970.

     Parks identifies the link between law, crime, and
the police. She argues that the history of social
control in the United States is the history of transition
from "constabulary" to "police society." This shift gave
the United States a proliferation of criminal laws,
enforcement officials, criminal courts, and prisons, none
of which was designed to protect the general welfare of
society, but rather to protect the lifestyle of the
wealthy. Parks contends that the establishment of the
police   made possible a new conception of law and order
whereby   more effective control of citizens became
possible.   Parks argument is that the growth of the
police was necessary for both law and crime.

19   Price, B. R., and S. Gavin. "A Century of Women in
     Policing." Pp. 399-412 in B. R. Price and N. J.
     Sokoloff (eds.), THE CRIMINAL JUSTICE SYSTEM AND
     WOMEN. New York: Clark Boardman, 1982.

     This is a historical account of women in policing.
The authors discuss the contemporary situation.   Price
and Gavin conclude that females in policing are still
not accepted by male officers. They explain that while
sexual integration has been slow, sex role stereotyping
continues to exist and the police organization also
reflects stereotypical views. In other words, police
organizations are shaped by the social structure and
reinforce stereotypes found within it.

20   Richardson, J. F. "Police in America: Functions and
     Control." Pp. 211-224 in J. Inciardi and C. Faupel
     (eds.), HISTORY AND CRIME: IMPLICATIONS FOR CRIMINAL
     JUSTICE POLICY. Beverly Hills, CA: Sage, 1980.

     The functions of American urban police, their modes
of control, and how these have changed over time, are the
topic of this paper. Richardson traces the evolution of
American police from the early 19th century. This
period was characterized by mutually autonomous groups of
salaried watchmen, elected constables, and marshals who
had been appointed by mayors. It was because of the
abuse generated from these social arrangements that the
bureaucratic police department was formed. The
principal function of this impersonal police organization

was crime control, not order maintenance. Richardson
argues that caution should be exercised when identifying
the functions of American police. He states that the
actual roles of police are affected by many factors,
including the officer's view of the world.

21   Robinson, C. D. "The Mayor and the Police: The Poli-
     tical Role of the Police in Society." Pp. 277-316
     in G.L. Mosse (ed.), POLICE FORCES IN HISTORY.
     Beverly Hills, CA: Sage, 1975.

     Robinson investigates the relationship between the
mayor and the police in large American cities. He shows
how the police shield the mayor from responsibility
arising out of long-time neglect of city problems.
Foremost among these problems are conditions found in
ghetto communities. The essay investigates only
Chicago.

22   Smith, B. "The Police Problem." Pp. 1-9 in B. Smith
     (ed.) POLICE SYSTEMS IN THE UNITED STATES. New York:
     Harper and Row, 1960.

     Smith explores the consequences of police control
by partisan political machines that exploit them for
their own purpose. According to Smith, this occurs
world-wide and police lack popular support to change
the condition. Smith's discussion of partisan
political control remains popular today and will be an
issue police executives always will face.

23   Spitzer, S., and A. T. Scull. "Privatization and
     Capitalist Development: The Case of the Private Pol-
     ice." SOCIAL PROBLEMS, 25 (1): 18-29, 1977.

     Spitzer and Scull study the relationship between
private policing and capitalist economic systems.
Spitzer and Scull argue that the emergence and transformation of private policing can only be understood in
terms of the larger movement toward the extension of
capitalist control over labor processes and the rational-
ization of production. They identify three stages in the
development of private policing: policing as piece-
work, policing in the industrial age, and policing under
corporate capitalism.

24   Walker, S. "The Urban Police in American History: A
     Review of the Literature." JOURNAL OF POLICE SCIENCE
     AND ADMINISTRATION, 4 (3): 252-260, 1976.

        Walker asks questions that have no answers.   He
     proceeds to discuss what is known and what is based more
     on implicit assumption than on scientific evidence.
     Walker believes that much more research on police history
     is needed. This is documented by presenting evidence
     on several popular themes. Walker shows that the history
     of police literature fails to adequately address the
     issues presented. Walker argues that for an understand-
     ing of police to emerge, the police must be studied in
     terms of the broader context of the history of justice
     in the United States.   It makes little sense to study
     the police apart from other components of the criminal
     justice system.

25   Walker, S. "The Origins of the American Police-
     Community Relations Movement: the 1840s." CRIMINAL
     JUSTICE HISTORY: AN INTERNATIONAL ANNUAL, 225-246,
     1980.

        Walker examines the origins of the first police-
     community relations programs.   Only limited aspects of
     these programs, however, are considered. Walker asks:
     What circumstances brought the first programs into being?
     Why did they appear at this time? What were the factors
     within policing and in the external social environment
     that facilitated their creation?   What was the orienta-
     tion of the first programs?   What was the substantive
     content and what assumptions about race relations and
     police work did they reflect? What contribution, if any,
     did these initial programs make to improving the future
     of police-race relations? Walker answers each question
     through specific incidents.   He concludes that the
     police-community relations programs that emerged during
     and after the riots in the 1960s were similar in content
     to the ones of the 1940s.

26   Watts, E. J. "Police Priorities in Twentieth Century
     St. Louis." JOURNAL OF SOCIAL HISTORY, 14 (4): 649-
     673, 1981.

        Watts tests the notion of police priorities as they
     are embedded in arrest statistics. Watts focuses on
     groupings of offenses, which he calls order maintenance
     arrests that include drunkenness, disorderly conduct, and
     vagrancy. He found that over time changes in order
     maintenance arrests reveal important alterations in
     police behavior, at least in St. Louis. He then matches
     shifts in police practices to three periods of major
     reform in St. Louis's police department as well as with

two structural factors--the number of police and arrest
activity. Watts also compares patterns uncovered in St.
Louis with those found elsewhere. His study shows that
both theory and quantitative analysis of data must be
sensitive to police response to categories of crime,
rather than only to arrest rates. Also, data analysis
must consider changes in police structure and the nature
and scope of the reporting system that is being used.

27   Watts, E. J. "St. Louis Police Recruits in the Twen-
     tieth Century." CRIMINOLOGY, 19 (1): 77-114, 1981.

     Professionalizing the police has been a goal of
police reformers for many years. Watts gives police
professionalism a historical perspective, arguing that
not until after World War II did the "giant" police
forces alter their entrance requirements. Watts notes
that criminologists have not undertaken research
necessary to document the diachronic dimension of police
recruitment. Using data derived from St. Louis, Watts
shows marked shifts in the education, ethnicity, race,
military experience, age, and length of residence of
recruits. But, changes in entrance standards affected
only changes in age and length of residency. More important is that these developments did not disturb
continuity or the social background of police recruits.
In other words, like their predecessors, officers in the
1970s, were predominantly married males with blue-collar
backgrounds, with unstable occupational records, and a
history of previous arrests.

28   Watts, E. J. "The Police in Atlanta, 1890-1905."
     JOURNAL OF SOUTHERN HISTORY, 39 (2): 165-182, 1973.

     This early paper by Watts examines the origins and
evolution of the Atlanta Police Department. The organization, structure, and recruitment patterns are examined
as well as the relationship of the newly formed police
agency to the Atlanta community.

29   Weiss, R. "The Emergence and Transformation of
     Private Detective Industrial Policing in the U.S.,
     1850-1940." CRIME AND SOCIAL JUSTICE, 9: 35-48, 1978.

     Weiss examines the origins of private policing be-
tween 1850 and 1940 in the United States. He presents a
Marxist explanation arguing that to understand private
policing, scholars must appreciate the need for an obed-
ient working class in capitalist societies. The paper
traces the development of private policing by posing an
argument regarding surplus value and labor discipline and
laissez-faire capitalism. A good historical presentation

is made of Pinkerton's Protective Patrol. Weiss concludes
by requesting that additional research be conducted,
stating that research is needed to determine those other
instances where the state has permitted extra-governmen-
tal violence on behalf of corporate profits.

30 Young, S. "Historical Development of Selected Police
    Performance Measures." Pp. 1-14 in R. Larson (ed.),
    POLICE ACCOUNTABILITY. Lexington, MA: D. C. Heath,
    1978.

    Young gives a historical analysis of performance
factors used by police and the roles these measures
play.   Young traces the historical importance of three
types of evaluative criteria now being used to measure
police performance effectiveness: response time, patrol
frequency, and workloads.

CHAPTER 2

LAW ENFORCEMENT - ORGANIZATION

31 Angell, J. E. "Toward an Alternative to the Classic
   Police Organizational Arrangements: A Democratic
   Model." CRIMINOLOGY, 9 (2): 185-206, 1971.

      Angell explains how the police can operate more
democratically without being less efficient. Angell
criticizes the bureaucratic model, wherein dysfunctional
byproducts of the classical organizational style
develop: routinization of operating procedures, career
routes, and decreased incentives. Employees' status
becomes a function of their jobs and hierarchical position, not their contribution to the achievement of police
organizational goals. Angell summarizes difficulties in
the application of the rational and theoretically efficient Weberian model, noting that the entire theory of
bureaucracy was predicated upon an authoritarian social
order and that the democratic values of the United States
are betrayed by the bureaucratic demand for impersonal
employee/client and employer/employee relations. Angell
sees this organizational model discouraging mature and
independent decision-making.

32 Angell, J. E. "Organizing Police for the Future: An
   Update of the Democratic Model." CRIMINAL JUSTICE
   REVIEW, 1 (2): 35-39, 1976.

      Angell expands the democratic model he developed
previously and calls for modifications in the police
organizational structure by instituting participatory,
community-based, collegially controlled policies. He
discusses methods to improve upon the democratic model
and explains the likely impact of these on organizational
arrangements and on police performance.

33 Antunes, G., and E. I. Scott. "Calling the Cops:
   Police Telephone Operators and Citizen Calls for
   Service." JOURNAL OF CRIMINAL JUSTICE, 9 (2): 165-179,
   1981.

      The range of calls for police service by citizens is
the focus of this paper. Data were derived from twenty-
one police agencies. Some 26,000 calls for service were
classified. The findings suggest that most citizen calls
involve the provision of information (or assistance),
nuisance abatement, traffic problems, or the regulation
of personal disputes. Only about twenty percent of all
calls involve predatory crime. Most important, however,
is the police operator's response. Typically, operators
promised to dispatch a unit. Antunes and Scott conclude
with a discussion of the implications of their findings.

34 Baggett, S., and M. Ernst. "From Research to Application: Development of Police and Older Adult Training
   Modules." POLICE CHIEF, 44 (2): 51-54, 1977.

   The development and operation of two training
programs designed to increase the reporting of crime by
senior citizens are discussed. The programs evolved from
the findings of previous research on the motivations for
reporting by this age group. A 1975 Dallas survey of 466
persons over age 55 revealed that crime victims who had
not reported crimes were the least likely to feel a part
of the police/judicial system. In addition, these people
generally believed that the police would not act on the
crime, that the crime was not important enough to bother
the police, or that they did not have enough information
for the police. As a result of these responses, a 2-
hour, in-service, recruit training package was designed
that focused on increasing the police officers' awareness
of the special needs of older adults. A second program
was aimed at increasing the senior citizens' awareness of
their role in the criminal justice system and at correct-
ing false perceptions about the role of law enforcement.

35 Baker, B., and W. Danielson. "Recruitment." Pp. 59-68
   in O. G. Stahl and R. Staufenberger (eds.), POLICE
   PERSONNEL ADMINISTRATION. Washington, D.C.: Police
   Foundation, 1974.

   Baker and Danielson describe the needs of police
organizations to recruit people from all backgrounds who
have the abilities to perform police work. The article
discusses conditions of effective recruitment that include the impact of standards, job alterations, actual
selection procedures, recruitment planning, and advertising techniques.

36 Barbour, G. P., and S. M. Wolfson. "Productivity Measurement in Police Crime Control." PUBLIC MANAGEMENT,
   55 (4): 16-19, 1973.

   The difficulties in measuring productivity for agencies such as the police, the need for accountability of
the police, and 12 productivity measurement indicators
for police activity are discussed. The most useful approach to the complexities of measuring police crime control activity is the collection and analysis of a variety
of indicators, as no single productivity measurement
function is a measure of productivity. The authors offer
12 measurement indicators, 5 that can be used immediately
and 7 that require supplemental information. These indicators include crime rate; clearance rate; and arrest,
clearance or population served for police employee, or
per thousand dollar expenditure. Measures requiring

additional data include crime rates and clearance rates
based on victimization survey data, percent of arrests
that lead to convictions, percent of arrested surviving
court of limited jurisdiction, average response time for
calls of service, and percentages of the population expressing lack of feeling of security or satisfaction with
police service.

37 Bard, M., and B. Berkowitz. "Training Police as Spe-
    cialists in Family Crisis Intervention: A Community
    Psychology Action Program." COMMUNITY MENTAL HEALTH
    JOURNAL, 3 (4): 315-317, 1967.

       The major purpose of training police in family
crisis intervention involves the utilization of innovative crime prevention and mental health techniques.
There is evidence, claim Bard and Berkowitz, that police
already are involved in mental health roles and need
programs to enhance their skills at handling domestic
violence. Moreover, the program developed here is among
the most widely used of those available by police across
America.

38 Barnabas, G. "Profile of a Good Police Officer." LAW
    AND ORDER, 24 (5): 32,34,36,38,40,42,44, 1976.

       A test was developed for police applicants in
Wichita to predict successful training and performance in
compliance with equal employment opportunity and affirmative action laws. The test measures personality
parameters, adjustment under stress, vocational interests, and the standard intelligence, vocabulary, oral
comprehension and clerical efficiency tests. The test
was highly efficient in predicting applicant success.

39 Becker, T. M. "The Place of Private Police in Soc-
    iety: An Area of Research for the Social Sciences."
    SOCIAL PROBLEMS, 21 (3): 438-453, 1974.

       A type of police that have escaped inquiry is
private police.   Little is known about the nature or
extent of this kind of police work. Becker examines
private police within the general context of policing in
order to identify the factors that should be considered
when developing a research design. The origins, growth,
and functions of private police are discussed. Further,
Becker explores the degree of regulation occurring in the
industry. These components are analyzed within a conceptual framework that taps the interrelationships between
the "public" and "private" sectors of policing.

40 Bernstein, D. "Police Volunteers." POLICE MAGAZINE,
   13: 17-26, 1977.

     Bernstein describes the use of police volunteers in
various localities. There are some 350,000 people who
help catch criminals, supervise parades, and assist law
enforcement agencies in other ways. Most go without
pay. This article explains how much training volunteers
have, whether they are armed, and their other duties.
The effectiveness of volunteers is examined, as well as
the type of praise and criticism they have received. The
need for standards is discussed.

41 Blumberg, A. S., and A. Niederhoffer. "Police and the
   Social System: Reflections and Prospects." Pp. 2-21 in
   A. Niederhoffer and A. S. Blumberg (eds.), THE AMBIVA-
   LENT FORCE: PERSPECTIVES ON THE POLICE, 2nd Ed. New
   York: Dryden Press, 1976.

     Some causes of police ambiguity and frustration,
their historical background, and prospects for the future
of the police are examined. Sociologists view crime as a
normal product of society. Everyone violates the law,
but few are prosecuted. Like other bureaucracies, the
police force is anxious about its productivity and related budgetary grants; public order and commonplace
offenses serve as the requisite statistical data bolster-
ing law enforcement budgets. Society expects police to
perform effectively within two models of justice--the due
process model, where protection of the rights of the
accused is foremost; and the crime control model, where
concern is with efficiency and production in day-to-day
operations. The police are the most visible element of
the criminal justice system and are held responsible for
any negative features of the end product of that system.
In many cases, police perform more important judicial
functions than do judges, particularly in deciding whom
to arrest. A system of external review is necessary to
control and reduce possible harmful consequences of
police discretion. Many police officers feel that there
is one universal solution to their problems--profession-
alization. Problems that could result from this are
discussed.

42 Bostick, R. J. "Small Department Training-Management."
   POLICE CHIEF, 42 (1), 19-21, 1975.

     After reviewing the need for police training in
small departments, Bostick reviews the financial,
developmental, and administrative problems that must be
solved to provide the training. He notes the imbalance
between the training activities and expenditures of
medium to large police departments and small police

departments. The significant growth in population and
crime rates in small cities and rural areas are cited as
justifications for increasing the training in small
police departments. The obstacles to small police
department training also are reviewed, and include
limited financial resources and high turnover rates.
Possible solutions to these problems are discussed and
consolidation of smaller departments, state funding of
all police training, and development of research studies
to determine training needs are policies that are
advanced.

43 Bourdeaux, P., J. C. Pisa, G. L. Carson, and C.
   Schroeder. "Model of Burglary Patrol Allocation."
   JOURNAL OF POLICE SCIENCE AND ADMINISTRATION, 5 (2):
   179-184, 1977.

     This article describes the history and status of the
feasibility of using mathematical models to allocate
police stakeouts at high-risk burglary locations. The
study was undertaken in response to a request by the
Baton Rouge Police Department to determine the optimal
allocation of stakeout personnel to small areas. The
authors developed modeling techniques within existing
data files for deployment of manpower by ranking areas
according to the likelihood of criminal occurrence for
purposes of maximizing the number of burglaries interrupted in progress. These efforts supported specialized
units that patrol in civilian clothes and private automo-
biles and are not engaged in normal patrol activity. The
allocation model and ranking procedures developed are
further enhanced by the method's relative insensitivity
to forecasting error and simplicity of maintenance and
calculation.

44 Brief, A., R. Aldag, and R. Wallden. "Correlates of
   Supervisory Style Among Policemen." CRIMINAL JUSTICE
   AND BEHAVIOR, 3 (3): 263-271, 1976.

     These authors investigated the relationship between
supervisory style and police behavior. A sample of
patrol officers were given a questionnaire that tapped
supervisory behaviors that affect friendships, mutual
trust, respect, and rapport between managers and subordinates. The authors conclude that police officers respond differently to the factors measured when compared
to workers in other occupations.

45 Burpo, J. H. "Improving Police Agency and Employee
   Performance Through Collective Bargaining, Part 1."
   POLICE CHIEF, 41 (2): 36-38, 1974.

   Collective bargaining is a two-way process. Public
employers should begin to make management demands on
police unions like unions make demands on management.
One term of management bargaining demands is to improve
the police agency's productivity and to improve individual employee performance standards. However, this either
has not been recognized or has been put to limited use.
Union resistance to programs geared toward improving
agency or employee performance can be eliminated or reduced by management negotiators placing these programs on
the bargaining table and negotiating them into the
collective bargaining contract.

46 Burpo, J. H. "Improving Police Agency and Employee
   Performance Through Collective Bargaining, Part 2."
   POLICE CHIEF, 41 (4): 30,32,34,36, 1974.

   Productivity bargaining is the negotiation and implementation of formal collective bargaining agreements
stipulating changes in work rules and practices in order
to achieve increased productivity and reciprocal worker
gains. New York City's successful experience with this
technique for reducing employee - union resistance to new
programs that improve overall performance involved a 4-
phase program--reduction of unit costs, improvement of
personnel resources deployment, improvement of government
processing procedures through the use of computers, and
development of new technologies. Problems with bargaining over productivity programs which should be foreseen
by management negotiators include its subjectivity to
change through union negotiating initiatives, the
possible need to make program adjustments, and the program's subjectivity to the grievance procedure. Kalama-
zoo, Michigan, also applied the principles of
productivity bargaining to the improvement of individual
employers by negotiating an annual firearms qualification
policy for all police officers.

47 Buzawa, E. S. "The Role of Race in Predicting Job
   Attitudes of Patrol Officers." JOURNAL OF CRIMINAL
   JUSTICE, 9 (1): 63-78, 1981.

   Do black and white police officers see their occupations differently? Relying on data derived from Detroit
and Oakland, Buzawa tests for attitude differences. Not
only did she find variation between blacks and whites,
but also noted significant differences between Detroit
and Oakland police. Findings from this research suggest

the importance of specifying both occupation and work-related variables in future studies.

48 Campbell, V. "Double Marginality of Black Policemen: A Reassessment." CRIMINOLOGY, 17 (4): 477-484, 1980.

Police scientists see black officers as occupying a problematic position. This article explores the extent black officers are victims of "double marginality," a concept which describes the double bind black officers are in. Double marginality results from the expectations held of them as a black person and as a police officer. Data were derived through questionnaires mailed to 1050 black police officers; a 90 percent response rate (N=947) was achieved. The author found "double marginality" to have little explanatory power in accounting for variation in either black officers' perceptions of public involvement in police affairs or black officers' perception of police authority.

49 Cawley, D. F. "Managers Can Make a Difference: Future Directions." Pp. 23-56 in A. W. Cohn (ed.), THE FUTURE OF POLICING. Beverly Hills, CA: Sage, 1978.

Cawley argues that for social scientists to understand police management they must study four areas. First, the success police managers have enjoyed in the preceding five years should be studied. Second, social scientists should investigate the failures police executives have encountered. The third and fourth areas of concern are the internal and external problems police managers face. Cawley believes that police administrators must carefully examine themselves and their role. Police leaders must be stronger, flexible, and able to make hard decisions in the areas of resource allocation, workloads, procedural policymaking, and criminal investigations.

50 Chwast, J. "Value Conflicts in Law Enforcement." CRIME AND DELINQUENCY, 11 (2): 151-161, 1965.

Believing that the social and personal values of police officers influence the quality of service they deliver, Chwast says that we must be clear about our values. The article begins with a discussion of the nature of police values and then considers the impact of conflicting values on police behavior.

51 Conser, J. A. "Case for State Mandated Minimum Selection Standards for Police Officers." PUBLIC PERSONNEL
   MANAGEMENT, 7 (2): 135-142, 1978.

   The issue of whether it is necessary to establish
standards for police officer selection is addressed, and
reasons for the establishment of state-mandated standards
are summarized. The National Advisory Commission on
Criminal Justice Standards and Goals recommends that all
states have legislation that establishes a state commission empowered to develop and enforce minimum mandatory
standards for the selection of police. Other organizations that advocate the establishment of minimum
mandatory standards are the President's Commission on Law
Enforcement and Administration of Justice, the Advisory
Commission on Intergovernmental Relations, and the
National Council on Crime and Delinquency. Recommendations to aid in the establishment of standards offered
focus on development and enactment, content and issues,
enforcement, and basic training followed by probation.

52 Decker, S. H., and R. L. Smith. "Police Minority
   Recruitment: A Note on Its Effectiveness in Improving
   Black Evaluations of the Police." JOURNAL OF CRIMINAL
   JUSTICE, 8 (6): 387-394, 1980.

   One justification given for recruiting minority
personnel is to improve the relationship between police
and minority communities. This study explores the relationship between minority recruitment and black citizen
attitudes toward the police. The findings show that the
minority police per capita variable was modestly related
to perceptions of police by black citizens.

53 Doig, J. W. "Police Policy and Police Behavior:
   Patterns of Divergence." POLICY STUDIES JOURNAL, 7
   (Special Issue): 436-442, 1978.

   Doig analyzes the problem of persuading police "who
continually confront pressure to act in ways contrary to
organization objectives to adhere to the enterprise of
its higher goals." Doig discusses the difficulties
police executives face when trying to restrict police
behavior that is not consistent with the department's
policies. Doig identifies the barriers that prevent
control of police activities by the chief in the assessment of recruitment, training, peer socialization, reward
and penalty structures.

54 Eisenberg, T., and J. Murray. "Selection." Pp. 86-100
   in O. G. Stahl and R. Staufenberger (eds.), POLICE
   PERSONNEL ADMINISTRATION, Washington, D.C.: Police
   Foundation, 1974.

   This article addresses the issue of choosing police
candidates for employment. The authors discuss the
theory underlying selection in the context of the practical everyday realities of police personnel administration. They report on a few police selection programs and
offer realistic alternatives for the selection of police
personnel.

55 Farmer, D. J. "Police Productivity." OVERVIEW, 1 (1):
   18-20, 1973.

   The basic approach for improving police productivity
in any agency should begin with the establishment of an
appropriate operational and personnel environment. Beyond this, planning should be undertaken involving,
first, the identification of low productivity areas and
the development of improvement measures. The increased
use of civilians and preventive patrol is an example of
such measures. Second, the planning should consist of
the application of modern management techniques, such as
participatory, that emphasize objectives and goal orientations.

56 Farmer, D. J. "Fact Versus Fact: A Selective View of
   Police Research in the United States." POLICE JOURNAL,
   49 (2): 104-113, 1976.

   Farmer reviews the literature in the areas of police
patrol, program performance measurement, anti-corruption
management, and criminal investigations. Research is
discussed that shows that police patrol is not effective
in preventing crime and promoting public feelings of
confidence, and that police response time is usually not
related to crime outcome. Traditional evaluation measures, such as crime and clearance rates, are inaccurate
and distorting. Studies of police investigative techniques have indicated that police spend an unwarranted
amount of time on cases with little likelihood of being
solved. These are said to be indicators of future areas
of concentration for police administrators.

57 Fox, V. "Sociological and Political Aspects of Police
   Administration." SOCIOLOGY AND SOCIAL RESEARCH, 51
   (1): 39-48, 1966.

   Fox sees the administration of police agencies as a
vital part of political sociology, because it represents

the tangible authority necessary to secure social order. He also examines the role of police in a democratic society. Fox feels social scientists should be concerned with the study of police administration in order to more fully understand police authority as it relates to theories and practices of social control.

58 Fyfe, J. J. "Administrative Intervention on Police Shooting Discretion: An Empirical Examination." JOURNAL OF CRIMINAL JUSTICE, 4 (4): 309-324, 1979.

Ever since America witnessed episodes of police brutality at the 1968 Democratic convention, the study of police violence has become important. This article examines policy in America's largest police department--New York City. Using data that included all reported New York City police firearms discharge and serious assaults on police between 1971-75, Fyfe examines the effects of guidelines and procedures on shooting frequencies, patterns, and consequences.

59 Goldstein, H. "Administrative Problems in Controlling the Exercise of Police Authority." JOURNAL OF CRIMINAL LAW, CRIMINOLOGY & POLICE SCIENCE, 58 (2): 160-172, 1967.

Goldstein states the difficulties of imposing controls on a police officer's misuse of authority-- difficulties that arise because there are no criteria for judging individual actions. Goldstein lists the strengths and weaknesses of various controls and insists that while external controls of police authority are needed, these controls must be coordinated with controls that are imposed by the department itself. External controls alone will not work; they must be integrated with department policy.

60 Goldstein, H. "Higher Education and the Police." Pp. 283-306 in H. Goldstein (ed.), POLICING IN A FREE SOCIETY. New York: Ballinger, 1977.

Goldstein offers an overview of the relationship between two social institutions--the police and higher education. He traces the relationship from its inception to analyzing arguments supporting the trend to raising questions about the usefulness of higher education for police. Besides presenting the shortcomings of current programs of police higher education, Goldstein provides recommendations for change and discusses how higher education will affect future police leadership styles.

61 Goodall, R. "Management by Objectives: A Conceptual
   Application for Police: Part I." POLICE JOURNAL, 47
   (1): 178-186, 1974.

   The author contends that management by objectives
(MBO) provides a clear statement of the organization's
goals and objectives, resources, and constraints. MBO
prescribes a technique for turning objectives into
programs, formulating work activities for department
members and determining the utilization of resources
needed to fulfill the objectives. The MBO method will
provide a statement of action that police officers and
police executives can pursue to achieve their goals.

62 Greene, J. R. "Organizational Change in Law Enforcement." JOURNAL OF CRIMINAL JUSTICE, 9 (1): 79-91, 1981.

   Police agencies are not static; they are changing
structues. Greene identifies those factors that are associated with the introduction of a structure-changing
strategy in police agencies. Data were derived from six
specialized police units in Michigan. The results show
that factors like domain consensus, dependence and influence relationships, and the perceptions of threat
affect organizational change.

63 Greene, J. R. "Changes in the Conception of Police
   Work: Crime Control Versus Collective Goods." Pp.
   233-256 in K. N. Wright (ed.), CRIME AND CRIMINAL
   JUSTICE IN A DECLINING ECONOMY. Cambridge, MA: Oelge-
   schlager, Gunn, and Hain, 1981.

   The changing nature of the police function is the
focus of this work. As the municipal economy has wors-
ened, there has been an increased demand for accountability. The police are being asked to prove their effectiveness. Since the police have been unable to curb
crime, much less control it, the police are reexamining
their crime control function. As a result, Greene believes that police work is becoming defined more in terms
of collective goods and not crime control. As such, we
can expect additional structural and process changes
within police agencies as municipal resources become more
scarce.

64 Gylys, J. A. "Pricing System and the Allocation of
   Contractual Metropolitan Police Services." CRIMINOLOGY,
   13 (1): 21-32, 1975.

   Problems of a market pricing system for the allocation of metropolitan police services are discussed, and a
model dealing with allocation of centralized police

services among two political units is presented. It is
suggested that a market pricing system will permit, up to
a certain output level, a solution of the problem of
allocating contractor's police services among metropolitan political areas. However, when low levels of
criminal activity are achieved through additional police
inputs, the market mechanism will have a tendency to
break down because the marginal increases of police services will not be able to elicit the expected decreases
in crime. A model dealing with allocations of centralized services among two political units is presented in
which the contractor's output, a county sheriff's office,
is quantified in terms of probability for a resident of a
given political area to become a victim of crime during
some fixed period of time. Thus, relatively greater
outputs will be reflected in falling probabilities of
becoming a victim.

65 Hahn, H. "A Profile of Urban Police." LAW AND CON-
   TEMPORARY PROBLEMS, 36 (4): 449-466, 1971.

     Hahn provides a description of urban police. While
many issues are discussed, four are noteworthy: the
police recruit, police socialization, police and the
community, and police discretion. Within each area,
subareas are identified and discussed. Hahn's paper
provides a framework for culling hypotheses about urban
police. His argument is that police officers possess
several attributes that differentiate them from the
general public and other occupational groups.

66 Halpern, S. "Police Employee Organizations and
   Accountability Procedures in Three Cities: Some Reflections on Policy-Making." LAW AND SOCIETY REVIEW,
   8 (4): 562-582, 1974.

     Halpern examines the role of police associations in
formulating and implementing policy affecting police
accountability programs in three cities. In his study of
Baltimore, Philadelphia, and Buffalo, Halpern reports and
analyzes the role of police labor leaders. Halpern
focuses on two areas of attempted regulation of police
internal departmental policy. Accountability of police
is defined in terms of accounting for police behavior
when it is called to the attention of department superiors. How police employee organizations strategically
affect the outcome of the review process for police
misconduct in the three sites is well presented. It
illustrates the power police employee organizations have
in protecting the safeguards of police officers' rights.

67 Hennessy, J. J. "Management of Crime: PPBS and Police
   Management." POLICE CHIEF, 39 (7): 62-67, 1972.

   The importance of a planning, programming, and
budgeting system (PPBS) as a realistic and useful alternative to more traditional methods of police administration management is discussed. In a PPBS and management-
by-objective system, the control of crime is systematically analyzed, programmed, and budgeted. The analysis
is based on statistical information available regarding
resources and areas of crime control need. The importance of establishing goals and achievable objectives is
useful in that it forces the decision-maker to select and
define duties and activities to be performed. When these
actions are subjected to cost-effective analysis
application they can be viewed in terms of direct and
indirect costs. Measuring effectiveness in terms of cost
when weighed against other competing goals accomplishes
the need of planning and eventually total system integration.

68 Hillen, B. F. "New York City Police Department's Investigative Case Management System: An Impact Study."
   JOURNAL OF POLICE SCIENCE AND ADMINISTRATION, 7 (4):
   400-425, 1979.

   Hillen focuses on the impact of the New York City
police department case management system (CMS) used for
criminal investigations. The CMS is designed to increase
input by and feedback to the investigator's supervisor.
Quality investigations achieved by early supervisor input
and control of investigation; establishment of a depart-
ment-size standardized investigative system and documented individual case folders for cases receiving input
beyond usual initial investigation. To examine the system's quality improvement of criminal investigations,
evaluators statistically analyzed data on the robbery,
burglary, and sex crimes squads and on three selected
precinct investigation units' cumulative arrest and
clearance rates for January through March 1974
(presystem) and January through March 1975 (system in
use). The findings show that the CMS has had modest
success in reaching its objectives and that it appears to
produce an effective investigative aid. The apparent key
to success rests on the conscientious effort and involvement of the investigative supervisors. Their leadership
qualities and comprehensive application of the system's
management procedures will determine the degree of overall improvement in criminal case investigations.

69 Hirsch, G. B., and L. J. Riccio. "Measuring and Improving the Productivity of Police Patrol." JOURNAL OF POLICE SCIENCE AND ADMINISTRATION, 2 (2): 169-184, 1974.

Parameters are proposed for measuring patrol output and suggestions are given for improving police patrol efficiency and productivity. Only the function of apprehending criminal offenders is analyzed here, but parallels are drawn to other primary patrol functions--the deterrence of crime and the provision of noncrime services. A more accurate indicator than number of arrests is needed. The quality of arrests can be considered if, for instance, only those arrests that lead to conviction are counted. This way to measure arrests is more in line with the goal of police patrols--the maintenance of community safety and well-being. Suggestions for improving patrol productivity include reducing time spent in court, reducing vehicle downtime, taking reports over the phone, and reducing excessive time spent on calls.

70 Hochstedler, E. "Testing Types: A Review and Test of Police Types." JOURNAL OF CRIMINAL JUSTICE, 9 (6): 451-466, 1981.

Hochstedler reviews the literature on police types and compares the major types she found. She concludes with the suggestion that the types reflected in the literature contain four major distinct categories. She goes on to test the existence of these generic types and finds little support for the notion that the generic types exist in reality.

71 Holzer, M. "Police Productivity: A Conceptual Framework for Measurement and Improvement." JOURNAL OF POLICE SCIENCE AND ADMINISTRATION, 1 (4): 459-567, 1973.

Aspects of police productivity measurement and enhancement are discussed with attention to input and output measures and catalysts for productivity improvement. Productivity in law enforcement organizations, as in other public and private organizations, is the relationship between inputs and outputs. Indices of police productivity are the ratios of outputs, such as arrests, to inputs, such as capital and labor. Resource inputs available to police organizations are measurable in terms of the common denominator of dollars or units of time in the case of labor resources. Thus, the major obstacles to judging police productivity are measures of output, not input. The bases for police productivity indices are: (1)internal output, which ranges from internal investigation to clerical, transportation, and training;

(2)external output, which can be defined as the end
products of the organization (i.e., those goods and services rendered for use outside the organization itself);
and (3)effectiveness of output--the utility, social benefit, impact, or client satisfaction derived from the
external outputs.

72 Hoover, L. T. "Planning-Programming-Budgeting Systems: Problems of Implementation for Police Management." JOURNAL OF POLICE SCIENCE AND ADMINISTRATION,
   2 (1): 82-93, 1974.

     Hoover discusses the problem of implementation and
suggests alternative methods of planning-programming-
budgeting systems (PPBS) for police departments. Hoover
offers procedures for establishing organizational objectives and illustrates how various PPBS programs relate to
alternative objectives.

73 Horney, J. "Citation Arrest: Extending the Reach of
   the Criminal Justice System." CRIMINOLOGY, 17 (4):
   419-434, 1980.

     Horney studies the utility of a police officer
issuing a citation in a potential arrest situation. Only
recently has this alternative been available. Horney
assesses the effect of having a citation policy on arrest
rates. Data came from Omaha, Nebraska; a quasi-experimental, interrupted time series design was used. The
results were straightforward. The predicted increase was
only found for one offense, assault. Horney concludes
with a discussion of the implications of the findings for
using citations.

74 Hudzik, J. K. "College Education for Police: Problems
   in Measuring Component and Extraneous Variables."
   JOURNAL OF CRIMINAL JUSTICE, 6 (1): 69-82, 1978.

     Hudzik identifies some of the methodological prob-
lems encountered when studying college education and
police. He reviews existing research and concludes that
much of what is reported to be known comes from poorly
designed studies. Specific problems are identified and
discussed. Hudzik suggests that subsequent research on
"college education" at least be sensitive to five
factors: (1) college attended and coursework taken, (2)
whether the college is a 2-year, 4-year, or graduate
university, (3) number of full-time students, (4) whether
the instruction is residential or commuter, and (5) extent of student-student interaction out of the classroom.

75 Hughes, J. "Training Police Recruits in the Urban
   Ghetto." CRIME AND DELINQUENCY, 8 (2): 176-183, 1972.

        Inservice training for police is an important factor
in the development of officers who, in their interactions
with the community, need to be knowledgeable of the
subcultures they serve. Hughes describes his experiences
as a social worker who trained police recruits to work in
an urban ghetto. Hughes emphasized the acculturation
needs of officers who were recruited outside of the urban
area as well as the internal conflicts of black police
who were from the city. The training focused on the
behavior of juveniles and was directed at helping the
officers discover, identify, and practice effective handling of youth.

76 Igleburger, R. M., and J. E. Angell. "Dealing With
   Police Unions." POLICE CHIEF, 38 (5): 50-55, 1971.

        Many states now require local governing bodies to
collectively bargain in good faith with police employees.
Police executives must be realistic in dealing with police employee organizations. Ingleburger and Angell call
for the adoption of new policies and the development of
needed skills in handling labor organizations if they
intend to maintain managerial control over the department. The paper concludes by offering police executives
strategies for effective relations, all designed to increase administrative effectiveness.

77 Jones, E. T. "The Impact of Crime Rate Changes on
   Police Protection Expenditures in American Cities."
   CRIMINOLOGY, 11 (4): 516-524, 1974.

        Jones analyzes the effects a city's crime rate has
on the annual budgetary expenditure for police. Jones
found little evidence of a relationship between crime
incidence and appropriations to police departments on a
yearly basis. He also considers other factors that may
be of significance in determining police protection and
expenditures that account for departmental budgets.

78 Juris, H., and P. Feuille. "The Impact of Police
   Unions." Pp. 385-397 in A. Niederhoffer and A. S.
   Blumberg (eds.), THE AMBIVALENT FORCE: PERSPECTIVES ON
   THE POLICE, 2nd Ed. New York: Dryden Press, 1976.

        Juris and Feuille report on the results of a major
study designed to learn more about police unions. The
full report discusses data on the whole spectrum of
labor-management relations.   The authors identify their
methodology and the specific areas that were explored.

Juris and Feuille believe that the most salient impact of
police unions has been the creation of a new system of
governance in the police agency to which police management is adapting.

79 Kaplan, E. H. "Evaluating the Effectiveness of One-
   Office Versus Two-Officer Patrol Units." JOURNAL OF
   CRIMINAL JUSTICE, 7 (4): 325-355, 1979.

   Kaplan develops and tests a model designed to evaluate one- versus two-officer patrol staffing. Kaplan
presents the pros and cons of each. After testing various
models, the author reports the following: (1) doubling
the number of available units in a beat increases the
expected area coverage by less than twice, (2) the probability of officer-specific injury is about the same for
both patrol staffings, and (3) percentage increases in
absolute visibility are the same as percentage increases
in patrol frequency.

80 Katsampes, P. "Participation in Policing." POLICE
   CHIEF, 41 (12): 60-65, 1974.

   Katsampes proposes a democratic organizational model
that would permit line officers to participate in the
decision-making process of their community. The traditional police bureaucratic, hierarchical structure, with
a chain of command from chief to patrol is inadequate for
resourceful and innovative ideas to be initiated.
Katsampes sees line officers assuming responsibility for
developing new programs and improvements in the areas of
crime prevention, and new enforcement techniques in the
areas they work. He argues that participation in management decisions would allow police to implement their
ideas into action. Katsampes' participatory model emphasizes open communication, relies on concensus decision-
making, and recognizes that officers have the need for
self-expression of ideas, feelings, and for occupational
autonomy.

81 Kerstetter, W. A. "Police Participation in Structured
   Plea Negotiations." JOURNAL OF CRIMINAL JUSTICE, 9
   (2): 151-164, 1981.

   Kerstetter examines police participation in pretrial
settlement conferences for felony plea negotiations.
Data were produced during the testing of pretrial settlement conferences conducted in Dade County. The most
striking finding was that police were active in the
discussions and they affected discussion outcomes. Moreover, police behavior was affected by the presence of
either the victim or the defendant.

82 Kuykendall, J. L. "Styles of Community Policing."
   CRIMINOLOGY, 12 (2): 229-240, 1974.

   Kuykendall describes police agencies as having distinctive philosophies of policing the community. He
utilizes Wilson's predominant policing styles by analyzing the approach of police in order-maintenance and law
enforcement situations. Kuykendall notes that styles of
policing also can be developed by analyzing police practices in relation to their impact upon the community.
The basis for the four policing styles discussed here are
the reactive-proactive emphasis given to various combinations of positive and negative methods, or counselor and
enforcer roles stressed by the department.

83 Kuykendall, J. L. "Toward an Integrated-Professional
   Model of Administration of Justice Education." JOURNAL
   OF CALIFORNIA LAW ENFORCEMENT, 10 (3): 103-109, 1976.

   Kuykendall reviews previous efforts on the identification of curriculum models for law enforcement. Based
on features of these models, a new curriculum model
called the "integrated-professional" model is outlined.
Synthesizing the curriculum models found in law enforcement education literature, Kuykendall proposes five basic
curriculum types: technical, integrated professional,
mixed professional, studies, and general mixed. These
curriculum types range from purely technical to purely
abstract instruction. The integrated professional model,
considered to be the most appropriate for police involves
instruction in both theoretical and practical aspects of
law enforcement. The objectives of this curriculum model
are discussed, and a detailed outline of the courses and
levels appropriate for this type of curriculum is
provided.

84 Kuykendall, J. L., and R. R. Roberg. "Mapping Police
   Organizational Change." CRIMINOLOGY, 20 (2): 241-256,
   1982.

   Kuykendall and Roberg discuss changing police organizations. Suggestions offered are presented in the form
of a model for "mapping" organizational change. They
describe mechanistic and organic model constructs and
relate them to both continuum and matrix change perspectives and a change problem-intervention strategy
typology. They use the matrix and typology constructed
to "map" the change process associated with team
policing.

85 Leahy, F. J. "Budgets--More Than a List of Items and Figures-- Planning Program Budgeting System." POLICE CHIEF, 35 (7): 16-18,20-22,24-27, 1968.

The planning, programing, budgeting system (PPBS) is a technique to help police administrators do a better job. Its uniqueness is that it combines planning, programming, and budgeting functions in a systematic manner, and it utilizes cost-benefit and cost-effectiveness analyses and operations research to improve decision-making processes. It is a four-step system requiring, first, a careful specification and analysis of department objectives; second, an analysis of the output of a program in terms of the objectives; third, the measurement of the total costs of a program, not just for 1 year, but for several years ahead; and fourth, an analysis of alternative ways to achieve the objectives and the selection of the alternative or combination of alternatives that is best.

86 Lewin, D., and J. H. Keith. "Managerial Responses to Perceived Labor Shortages: The Case of Police." CRIMINOLOGY, 14 (1): 65-92, 1976.

During the early 1970's, expansion of police manpower was common. Often, such responses were a reaction to a perceived shortage. Lewin and Keith challenge this notion and argue that claims of police shortages are exaggerated and are artificial. Relying on official statistics, they show that police managers and police officials possess only limited direct control over police wages. Thus, to overcome police labor shortages requires the manipulation of police manpower utilization. The authors conclude that police managers must formulate their labor market and employment policies in recognition of the linkages among wage determination, external labor market, manpower practices and collective bargaining in the production of police services.

87 Lundman, R. J., and J. C. Fox. "Maintaining Research Access in Police Organizations." CRIMINOLOGY, 16 (1): 87-98, 1978.

Producing data about police activity is not easy. This paper outlines some pitfalls and general problems associated with maintaining research access in police agencies. Data for the project were derived from a fifteen month study of police-citizen encounters. Among the problems faced are difficulties in communicating and gaining acceptance from line-officers, developing a mutually acceptable field role, and threats of premature termination. The authors offer solutions to these problems. Some solutions include specific and repeated efforts to inform line-officers of the research and emphasis of the occupational features of the participant-as-observer role.

88 Maciejewski, J. "Team Policing Improves Teamwork."
    POLICE CHIEF, 42 (7): 54-57, 1976.

    A description of the development and implementation of a police manpower deployment system which allows for the provision of specialized services without diminishing the effectiveness of regular patrol or requiring additional personnel is presented. Specialized juvenile, police-community relations, and crime prevention units were formed by grouping the three functions into one section and cross-training the personnel in all of the tasks involved. All regular uniform patrol officers were then graded according to experience, training, special skills, and productivity. The officers were grouped into four closely matched units or teams, each headed by a patrol sergeant, and were allocated to twenty of the twenty-one 8-hour shifts. A fifth unit comprised of specialists, detectives, and administrative personnel was formed to cover the remaining shift. This system is evaluated according to its effect on specialization, lines of supervision and command, training, and morale. It is concluded that the introduction of this system increased productivity, improved the lines of communication and morale, and has given the department a good community image since, because of cross-training, there is always someone available for community relations, work with juveniles, or crime prevention.

89 Mark, J. "Police Organizations: The Challenges and Dilemmas of Change." Pp. 356-366 in A. Niederhoffer and A. S. Blumberg (eds.), THE AMBIVALENT FORCE: PERSPECTIVES ON THE POLICE, 2nd Ed. New York: Dryden Press, 1976.

    Mark proposes organizational and administrative changes that could be implemented by police managers to help them be more effective. Mark sees police agencies as being fragmented and recommends that they consolidate and regionalize. By doing this, Mark claims the monitoring of national police standards would decrease, improved cost effectiveness would result, and more career opportunities would present themselves.

90 Marx, G. T. "Alternative Measures of Police Performance." Pp. 15-32 in R. Larson (ed.), POLICE ACCOUNTABIL-
ITY. Lexington, MA: D. C. Heath, 1978.

   The development of performance measures that are
comprehensive and easily understood is a difficult task.
Marx discusses the need for police to develop a variety
of measures of police effectiveness as they directly
relate to the goals and expectations the public has of
police. Marx suggests using performance measures that
utilize a reward system tied to the types of police
activity valued by police managers and the public. He
concludes by assessing the utility of several approaches
to the measurement of performance evaluation and with a
discussion of the types of reforms that are needed to
produce effective policing.

91 McClellen, J. E. "Changing Nature of Police Manage-
     ment." LAW AND ORDER, 26 (5): 18-21,25, 1978.

   Unionization, professionalization, equal opportunity
and affirmative action hiring, and provision of community
services make the police manager's job complex. Despite
a desire to adhere to traditional modes of behavior,
police managers must be prepared to accept changes.
Unionism in the public work sector is a hotly contested
issue. It is suggested that unionism can be avoided by
developing a system of open communication, application of
good supervisory skills, equitable grievance procedures,
emphasis on career development, and a progressive management environment. Equal opportunity employment and affirmative action policies are an important aspect of
police personnel administration. Acceptance of these
policies, coupled with enlightened management, can prevent adverse public or employee charges against police
administration.

92 McCreedy, K. R. "The Changing Nature of Police Man-
     agement: Theory and Transition." Pp. 59-86 in A. W.
     Cohn (ed.), THE FUTURE OF POLICING. Beverly Hills,
     CA: Sage, 1978.

   Because police departments have traditionally adopted a paramilitary style of organization and management,
police executives are selected more because of operational exigencies than because of their managerial expertise.
But future police managers must be committed to active
and proactive modes of change, for the functions of
police managers will be performed in very complex social
and political environments. Future police executives see
their position in relation to the total system of ongoing
social arrangements rather than simply to their police
organization.

93 McDonough, L., and J. Monahan. "The Quality Control
of Community Caretakers: A Study of Mental Health
Screening in a Sheriff's Department." COMMUNITY MEN-
TAL HEALTH JOURNAL, 11 (1): 33-43, 1975.

The authors discuss the importance of screening
police candidates for mental health purposes. They argue
that there has been an increasing awareness of just how
complex the police role has become. The selection of
persons who can meet the rigorous criteria of community
caretaker is called for. The authors conducted a study
of applicants for a police agency that included a battery
of psychological tests and a psychiatric interview. The
results were matched against on-the-job behavior and the
authors identified factors that were related to job failure. It was concluded that no mental health screening
procedure can predict "good" or "bad" police officers,
but such tests can identify areas of concern and pinpoint
special talents desireable of new police personnel.

94 Mehay, S. L. "Intergovernmental Contracting for Municipal Police Services: An Empirical Analysis." LAND
ECONOMICS, 55 (1): 59-72, 1979.

Municipal governments can improve their efficiency
and lessen their budgetary problems by contracting for
public services with private firms. Contracting for
public services is a common practice for such services as
sanitation and street maintenance. Injecting competition
into the provision of services yields important economic
advantages, as contrasted with local governmental monopo-
lies. Also, as economies of scale are introduced, contracting from a large-scale provider permits government
oversight of cost-effective operations. In the Lakewood
plan of intergovernmental contracting, Los Angeles County
has contracted to provide police services to 30 other
municipalities. Data on police services indicate that
contract cities experience a significantly higher violent
crime rate than do independent cities, and that cost per
officer is higher in contract cities. A regression model
for police services reveals that contract cities have
significantly lower patrol manpower levels than do independent cities. However, with the absence of reliable
policing standards, it is difficult to determine whether
contract cities are "underpoliced" or independent cities
are "overpoliced." Although tax benefits may accrue to
cities using contracting, the correspondingly higher
crime rate may make the contracting less beneficial.

95 Miller, J., and L. Fry. "Measuring Professionalism
   in Law Enforcement." CRIMINOLOGY, 14 (3): 401-412,
   1976.

   More and more, social scientists who study work and
occupations are turning their attention to police. One
area that has received much attention is police professionalism. Miller and Fry measure professionalism among
officers in three small police departments. Using the
Snizek (1972) revision of Hall's (1968) professionalism
scale, Miller and Fry identify certain difficulties they
experienced with the measure. This paper brings forth
the sensitivitiy of scales and warns against some of the
problems of using a scale designed for one occupation on
some other.

96 National Commission on Productivity. "Barriers to
   Productivity Improvement in Law Enforcement." Pp. 65-
   70 in National Commission on Productivity, OPPORTUNI-
   TIES FOR IMPROVING PRODUCTIVITY IN POLICE SERVICE.
   Washington, D.C.: National Commission on Productivity,
   1973.

   The National Commission on Productivity undertook a
study of the services provided by the police. This
selection from the Commission's report identifies the
impediments that are responsible for the lack of innovative programs on the part of police organizations that
affect police service productivity. The particular
issues discussed analyze such factors as impediments to
change, apprenticeship programs, police officer attitudes
toward organizational change, lateral entry, financial
management, and commitment of police managers toward
innovative programming. Recommendations are outlined by
the Commission for methods which should alleviate barriers to productive change as well as guidelines that
suggest methods for maintaining successful programs.

97 Nolan, J. T. "Managing The Police Demand." POLICE
   CHIEF, 45 (2): 70-74, 1978.

   Managing the demand for police services through
communication, investigation, patrol, and the split force
concept is the focus of this article. To respond to the
demand for police services, it is necessary to allocate
manpower effectively and to increase productivity. It is
assumed that efficiency will be better served by varying
the level of communication response. Four levels are
stipulated: immediate personal response, delayed personal response, telephone adjustment, and service at a
police facility. For the majority of complaints received, dispatchers have three response levels available:
(1) complaint can be resolved by the telephone, (2)

complainant can be advised to respond to the police
facility for assistance, and (3) personal service can be
rendered if the caller demands it, if any potential for
further violence exists, or if the dispatcher feels that
an officer must be at the scene. Police department
management must realize that the entire police force
contributes to the success of criminal investigation.

98 Pence, G. "Program-Planning-Budgeting System." POLICE
    CHIEF, 38 (7): 52-57, 1971.

The Dayton (Ohio) Police Department uses a planning,
programming, and budgeting system (PPBS) that uses mathematical analysis, data processing, and independent collective estimates to identify problems and suggest
solutions based on management by objectives (MBO) and
management by exception concepts. Police planners are
encouraged to consider ways they can allocate their
limited resources to meet the public's greatest and most
immediate needs. By utilizing a systematic problem-
solving methodology, a team of specialists can identify
problems and generate cost-effective decision-making information. The methodology, a program structure, budget
concepts, and problems of defining measurable objectives
are discussed.

99 Pfister, G. "Outcomes of Laboratory Training for
    Police Officers." JOURNAL OF SOCIAL ISSUES,31 (1):
    115-121, 1975.

Description and evaluation of the effects of a volunteer Seattle police program involving training in sensitivity, community service, working with youth groups,
and interpersonal relations. The study was conducted
with 48 officers participating in an intensive 6-day
communication orientation workshop and 26 other officers
as a control group. The Edwards Personality Inventory
was administered pre- and post-test to both groups. Questionnaire responses obtained before and after the program
from residents who had nonadversive (no arrest, no citation) contact with officers in both groups were obtained.
The experimental officers were reported by residents
after training as significantly more warm and sincere,
behaving more as coworkers, and leaving the citizens
feeling generally satisfied with the contact. Controls
were reported as communicating little understanding, as
treating the citizen more like a case than as an individual, and generally leaving the citizen feeling
frustrated.

100 Pizzuto, C. S. "The Police Juvenile Unit: A Study in
    Role Consensus." Ph.D. Dissertation, Brandeis Univer-
    sity, 1967.

    Pizzuto's examination of departments serving cities
of 50,000 to 100,000 population in Massachusetts revealed
that juvenile officers and administrators often agreed
about the kinds of juvenile programs police should adopt.
He found they agreed on the need for police-community
agency liaison, informal probation for offenders, police-
sponsored delinquency programs, and juvenile counseling
services. They also agreed that juvenile officers should
help administrators in establishing juvenile processing
policy. Despite their agreement, Pizzuto noted that
there still existed a divergence between opinion and
performance; actual performance of duties deemed important by both groups was sometimes different than that
established in department policies. Officer discretion
apparently often overrules department guidelines.

101 Poole, E. D., and R. M. Regoli. "Changes in the Pro-
    fessional Commitment of Police Recruits: An Explora-
    tory Case Study." JOURNAL OF CRIMINAL JUSTICE, 7
    (3): 243-248, 1979.

    The effect of the initial socialization process on
professionalism is the focus of this study. Police recruits were surveyed at two points in time about their
degree of professional commitment. Data suggested that a
significant decline in commitment occured between the
test periods. The research demonstrates the effect of
the initial socialization process and suggests ways police administrators can minimize the effect of early
socialization on professionalism.

102 Quarles, C. L. "Police Manpower Alternatives." LAW
    AND ORDER, 25 (5): 44,46-50, 1977.

    Quarles examines the reasons for using sworn and
non-sworn police personnel. There are numerous manpower
alternatives to the use of sworn police officers working
within every division of the police department. These
important considerations should be made by every police
department to determine where civilians or nonsworn officers may be used. The benefits, where professional standards are promulgated, are dollar savings, the increased
availability of police officers to their primary task,
and increased productivity in law enforcement and in the
specialized auxiliary services because the best people
are working in their own area of expertise. Morale,
motivation, and productivity are at their highest level
when the best people are placed in the positions for
which they are qualified. The use of nonsworn personnel

should always be made with the broadest bases of police
efficiency, effectiveness, and economy as the primary
consideration.

103 Reams, J. E. "Automated Criminal Records Systems for
    Small Departments." POLICE CHIEF, 43 (10): 54-56,
    1976.

    Discussion of factors to be considered when small
police agencies decide to unite and implement a multide-
partmental information processing system. Topics
addressed include chain of command and policies, psychological impact, system growth, communications problems,
presentation of material to line officers, and improper
use of shared information. Future trends are also considered.

104 Reams, R., J. L. Kuykendall, and D. Burns. "Police
    Management Systems: What is an Appropriate Model?"
    JOURNAL OF POLICE SCIENCE AND ADMINISTRATION, 3: 475-
    481, 1975.

    The authors analyze a model police agency to deter-
mine its management style and the characteristics of
developing an ideal police management system. Reams and
his co-researchers present four management styles. They
are the exploitative authoritative, the benevolent authoritative, the consultative, and the participative
type. Each particular system is characterized by differences in leadership, communication, motivation, decision-
making, interaction, influence, goal setting, and
control. The authors discuss which of the four systems
is most beneficial for police and identify the necessary
conditions that must exist to utilize the ideal
management type.

105 Regoli, R. M., and D. G. Jerome. "Recruitment and
    Promotion of a Minority Group Into an Established
    Institution: The Police." JOURNAL OF POLICE SCIENCE
    AND ADMINISTRATION, 3 (4): 410-416, 1975.

    The policies and practices of police departments in
major United States cities are examined to determine
trends in the hiring and promotion of black officers.
Reasons for the underrepresentation of blacks on police
forces are examined. These include discriminatory hiring
practices, the inability of blacks to pass white-oriented
written entrance examinations, and reluctance of blacks
to join police forces. The need for special efforts in
recruiting blacks is discussed, and examples of several
recruiting programs are provided. Among these are the
training of blacks through community service officer or

police cadet programs, and advertising campaigns designed
to encourage blacks to join the force. Patterns of black
promotion and black representation on police forces are
considered in the final section. The data show that
blacks are underrepresented on police forces throughout
the United States and once hired, they are not promoted
as quickly.

106 Rhodes, W. R. "Behavioral Science Application to
    Police Management." POLICE CHIEF, 37 (5): 46-50,
    1970.

    Behavioral science theories about employee motiva-
tion are presented along with suggestions for implementation of participative management to increase
productivity. To critics of police productivity it seems
that police are unwilling to put forth any more than
minimum effort, even though they are well paid and have
good fringe benefits and job security. The problem can
be explained by a "hierarchy of needs." As soon as one
human need is satisfied, another appears. After physical, safety, and social needs are fulfilled, people are
free to concentrate on ego needs. If people are content
with present attainments, they lack personal goals and
become frustrated and unmotivated: a situation which
causes problems for administrators. Police managers must
realize that today's police officers do not have to worry
about their physical or social needs. They feel an
increasing need to assert their individuality, and administrators must gear management control to the needs of
officers. Two basic administrative viewpoints on employees are summarized: one is based on the assumption that
the average human being has an inherent dislike of work
and will avoid it if possible; the other arises from the
belief that the expenditure of physical and mental effort
in work is as natural as play or rest.

107 Rusinko, W. T., K. W. Johnson, and C. A. Hornung.
    "The Importance of Police Contact in the Formulation
    of Youth's Attitudes Toward Police." JOURNAL OF
    CRIMINAL JUSTICE, 6 (1): 53-68, 1978.

    Building on studies that assess the effects of con-
tacts with criminal justice agents for juveniles, Rusinko
et al. examine types of contact as determinants of
attitudes toward authority figures. Data were collected
through questionnaires administered to nearly 1200 ninth
grade students in Lansing, Michigan. Several items in
the questionnaire assessed the nature and extent of the
youth's previous experience with police. Analysis of
these data lead to the conclusion that positive contact
with police was most predictive of positive attitudes
while negative contact generated negative attitudes.

Finally, the effects of negative police contact were most
significant for white youths who reported infrequent
deviant behavior, and had little or no positive contact
with police. Policy implications of the findings are
discussed.

108 Scaglion, R., and R. G. Condon. "Determinants of
    Attitudes Toward City Police." CRIMINOLOGY, 17 (1):
    485-494, 1980.

    Improving police-community relations is something
police administrators are concerned about. This study
had four aims: (1) to identify variables having a direct
effect on attitudes toward police, (2) to determine the
significance of each variable (3) to examine causal
relationships among these variables, and (4) to discuss
implications of the findings. Data were derived from a
survey of attitudes among 273 citizens representing four
neighborhoods in Pittsburgh. Results were that personal
history is a more significant determinant of general
attitudes towards police than were socioeconomic factors.
The conclusions were that positive styles of policing
will significantly affect police-community relations and
that programs stressing officer-citizen interaction will
have the highest probability of success.

109 Sherman, L. W., and the National Advisory Commission
    on Higher Education for Police Officers. "Higher
    Education and Police Reform." Pp. 18-38 in L.
    Sherman et al., THE QUALITY OF POLICE EDUCATION. San
    Francisco: Jossey-Bass, 1978.

    Sherman et al. examine the relationship between
advanced schooling and police performance. They argue
that while the need for educating police is firmly rooted
in police ideology, the kind of police education early
reformers proffered has been forgotten. The consequence
of this is that the realities of police education today
are inconsistent with that earlier vision. Sherman and
his associates discuss what is being done and why it
will fail.

110 Sherman, L. W., and M. McLeod. "Faculty Characteris-
    tics and Course Content in College Programs for
    Police Officers." JOURNAL OF CRIMINAL JUSTICE, 7
    (3): 249-267, 1979.

    A study of the "sociology of criminal justice," the
focus of this research is on variations in the conceptual
abstraction of course content in college-level courses
for police officers. Data were derived from forty-eight
programs via self-report questionnaires. Salient

LAW ENFORCEMENT

findings included: (1) faculty education level is related (positively) to book abstraction level; (2) faculty criminal justice agency experience and percentage of part-time faculty are negatively related to abstraction level; and (3) institutional characteristics and student vocational orientation work to specify the observed relationships.

111 Skogan, W. "Efficiency and Effectiveness in Big City Police Departments." PUBLIC ADMINISTRATION REVIEW, 36 (3): 278-286, 1976.

Skogan defines the concepts of efficiency and effectiveness in terms of their relationship between inputs and outputs for police organizations and their costs. Deriving data from a large sample of cities, Skogan assessed the impact of numerous factors that are likely to maximize efficiency and effectiveness. He presents evidence that certain organizational reforms and innovations do enhance performance by police.

112 Symonds, M. "Policemen and Policework: A Psychodynamic Understanding." AMERICAN JOURNAL OF PSYCHO-ANALYSIS, 32 (2): 163-169, 1972.

Symonds focuses on the consequences of police work for individual officers. The goal of this paper is to increase the communication between police and the public about police behavior. The paper is qualitative. Data were derived from the author's experiences as a psychiatric consultant in a medical unit of the New York City Police Department.

113 Townsey, R. D. "Female Patrol Officers: A Review of the Physical Capability." Pp. 413-426 in B. Price and N. J. Sokoloff (eds.), THE CRIMINAL JUSTICE SYSTEM AND WOMEN. New York: Clark Boardman, 1982.

Police organizations sometimes act as though females are not strong enough to be line officers. This line of thinking, coupled with attitudes about the role of females generally, has lead to their underrepresentation on police departments. Townsey (1) provides an overview of women in policing, (2) shows that women are as capable as men for line-officer positions, (3) questions the validity of existing physical capability tests as they relate to police performance, and (4) offers recommendations for nondiscriminatory agility tests. While Townsey is not opposed to agility tests, she objects to the tests currently being used because their relationship to police performance variables is unknown. It is toward developing tests with criterion-validity that she moves.

114 Van Mannen, J. "Observations on the Making of Po-
    licemen." HUMAN ORGANIZATION, 32 (4): 407-418, 1973.

    Van Mannen studies a much neglected area of police
research--the "making" of police officers. While much
police research exists on the description of police and
their "on stage" performance, Van Maanen's article examines the occupation from the "backstage." He begins by
constructing a paradigm for understanding the police
recruit's initiation into the organizational setting.
The paradigm includes four discrete stages: pre-entry,
admittance, change, and continuance. Van Mannen concludes by speaking to police reformers. Somewhat pessi-
mistically, Van Mannen contends that given the police
role, real change is only illusionary.

115 Waldron, H. A. "Management by Objectives: Principles
    for an Integrative Manager." POLICE CHIEF, 44 (5):
    76-78, 1977.

    Waldron presents a review of modern management phi-
losophies and a discussion of the problems and benefits
associated with implementing these strategies in police
departments. He notes that the theory of management by
objectives rests on a philosophy that emphasizes integration between external manager-control and individual
self-control. Under this system, management must believe
that employees can best reach their own personal goals
and needs by working for organizational goals, and must
allow employees to participate in goal setting. Also
discussed are the worker's needs, as described by
Maslow's policy of job enrichment and Herzberg's philosophy on job satisfiers and dissatisfiers.

116 Webster, J. A. "Police Task and Time Study." JOUR-
    NAL OF CRIMINAL LAW, CRIMINOLOGY & POLICE SCIENCE,
    61 (1): 94-100, 1969.

    Few studies have examined police activity. Webster
offers an account for one area of police activity, the
patrol division. Deriving data from a city ficticiously
called Baywood, Webster reports the results of a detailed
analysis of the work day of patrol officers. Estimates
are given for the amount of time spent in a variety of
activities, including traffic, crimes against persons and
property, administration, and social service. Webster
concludes by saying police organizations are among the
most poorly managed organizations in society.

117 White, S. "A Perspective on Police Professionalism."
    LAW AND SOCIETY REVIEW, 7 (1): 61-85, 1972.

     The idea that better training and more educated
personnel will improve police performance is the subject
of White's paper. She provides a structure for discussing past efforts at professionalizing police and
discusses three aspects of professionalism: a critical
analysis of the professionalization model, a typology of
police roles, and suggestions for using the typology in
policy research.

118 Wilson, J. Q. "Dilemma of Police Administration."
    PUBLIC ADMINISTRATION REVIEW, 28 (5): 407-417, 1968.

     Wilson takes the position that police work is much
like a craft occupation that generates individual solutions to organizational problems. Wilson's view is discouraging for reformers who call for massive modifications in police management practices and organizational
change to remedy police ills. According to Wilson, the
dilemma for police executives is wanting to reduce crime
and not knowing how. Wilson also notes the dual role of
police as law enforcers and as community peacekeepers.
Playing these two roles sometimes results in conflicting
role expectations, that is, officers experience role
stress.

CHAPTER 3

LAW ENFORCEMENT - PROCESS

119 Arthur, G. L., P.J. Sisson, and C. E. McClung.
"Domestic Disturbances: A Major Police Dilemma, and
How One Major City is Handling the Problem." JOURNAL
OF POLICE SCIENCE AND ADMINISTRATION, 5 (4): 421-429,
1977.

The Columbus, GA, family crisis intervention program
is described and evaluated. The community-related goals
of the program were to reduce the number of recalls in
domestic conflicts, to increase both the quantity and
quality of referrals to social service agencies, to
reduce the incidence of family violence and homicides, to
reduce the number of injuries to police and citizens, and
to advance the public image of the police officer's role
in the community. Interdepartmental goals included
increasing officers' repertoire of responses in conflict
management, effecting attitudinal changes, increasing
sensitivity to and understanding of the elements in
family conflict, enhancing officers' application of
acquired skills, increasing multicultural awareness, and
increasing officers' understanding of their own feelings.
The effectiveness of the program was evaluated in terms
of community feedback, departmental reports, and trainee
feedback. Positive program outcomes include improvements
in knowledge and attitude among officers, an increase in
the number of referrals made to community agencies, and
positive response from the public.

120 Badalamente, R. V., and C. E. George. "Training
Police For Their Social Role." JOURNAL OF POLICE
SCIENCE AND ADMINISTRATION, 1 (4): 440-453, 1973.

Social work of the police role, with a proposal for
a training program designed to equip police for more
effective performance of that role, is the focus of this
article. The authors present a job analysis and discuss
training objectives, including the traits, knowledge, and
skills required to be effective in the social work role
of the police. In order to specify the means of meeting
these objectives, characteristics of police applicants
are reviewed. This section discusses some of the
psychometric measurement techniques used to study the
police. The final material considers available training
methods and comments on performance evaluation. Training
is delivered in the classroom, in T-groups, encounter
groups, and sensitivity training. The authors conclude
with a fourteen point recommendation on police selection
and training.

121 Barton, W. H. "Discretionary Decision-Making in Juve-
    nile Justice." CRIME AND DELINQUENCY, 22 (4): 470-
    480, 1976.

    Barton reviews the results of studies dealing with
the influence of demographic, criminal history, and
social variables on decision-making during police
handling, presentence reporting, and court dispositions.
The social distribution of youths who engage in
delinquent behavior is not exactly the same as that of
youths who come into contact with the juvenile justice
system. Thus, a certain amount of discretion
characterizes the decisions made at various points within
the system. This review suggests that as a youth
penetrates further into the juvenile justice system,
factors other than the present offense become
increasingly important to decision-makers. It also
appears that, once apprehended, females fare worse than
males. However, extreme caution is urged in generalizing
from the studies that were reviewed since they differed
in time, place, methodology, and scope.

122 Bennett, R. R., and R. S. Corrigan. "Police Occupa-
    tional Solidarity: Probing a Determinant in the
    Deterioration of Police/Citizen Relations." JOURNAL
    OF CRIMINAL JUSTICE, 8 (2): 111-112, 1980.

    Police-citizen relations affect the administration
of justice. To the extent police and citizens are
suspicious, distrust, and fear one another, relations
between them deteriorate. This study examines the
determinants of social isolation and occupational
solidarity among police. Data were derived from sixty-
one police officers from a medium-sized, midwestern
police department. The findings suggest that police
reduce their tendency to rely on aggressive enforcement
techniques. Policy implications of this and related
findings are discussed.

123 Berk, S. F., and D. R. Loseke. "Handling Family
    Violence: Situational Determinants of Police Arrest
    in Domestic Disturbances." LAW AND SOCIETY REVIEW, 15
    (2): 317-346, 1981.

    Data were drawn from 262 official police reports
concerning domestic disturbances. The propensity of
police to make arrests is examined through a variety of
exogenous variables, such as whether the disturbance
occurred between legally married spouses, whether the
female called the police, whether both principals were
present with police, whether the male had been drinking,
and whether there were signs of property damage or
injury. These recorded incident characteristics were

subjected to multivariate analysis, which revealed four
variables to be significant to police arrest decisions.
Significant positive influence was exerted by the female
victim's refusal or agreement to sign a citizen's arrest
warrant. When both principals were present at the point
of police intervention, the female's allegation of
violence and drinking by the male also increased the
likelihood of arrest. The probability of arrest
decreased if the female had made the initial call for
help.

124 Bernstein, D. "Police vs. Child Abuse: Protecting
    the Victim Comes First." POLICE MAGAZINE, 1 (5): 58-
    63,1978.

    A Tucson police detective's efforts to combat child
abuse by establishing a child abuse unit and by improving
police relations with medical personnel and social
workers is described. The child abuse unit trys to
convince parents to obtain counseling, resorting to
arrest and prosecution only for repeat offenders and in
cases involving serious injury. The officers' consider
the pressures that may have led to abuse and avoid
putting parents on the defensive. Their approach has
earned them the respect of physicians and child welfare
agency personnel, who now make special efforts to
cooperate in police investigations of abuse cases. A
committee of physicians, social workers, lawyers, and
police meets monthly to discuss new approaches to dealing
with child abuse. All Tucson hospitals have established
child abuse teams. In addition, the citizens of Tucson
have donated funds for two shelters, where parents can
leave their children when they feel inclined to abuse
them. Consideration is being given to expanding the
child abuse unit to encompass other kinds of domestic
violence.

125 Bittner, E. "Police Discretion in Emergency
    Apprehension of Mentally Ill Persons." SOCIAL PROB-
    LEMS, 14 (3): 278-292, 1967.

    The focus of this research is the rules and
considerations underlying the exercise of discretion in
emergency apprehension. Data were derived from field
work notes covering ten months of observation of a large
west coast city, and on psychiatric records of the
hospital receiving all police referrals. The most
salient conclusion of this study was that structure and
means contained in these practices determine who will be
referred to the hospital on an emergency basis.
Moreover, external characteristics of the case were not
relevant to the decisions; their import always was media-

ted by practical considerations of what can and needs to
be done.

126 Black, D. J., and A. J. Reiss, Jr. "Police Control
    of Juveniles." AMERICAN SOCIOLOGICAL REVIEW, 35 (1):
    63-77, 1970.

    This paper presents findings on citizen and police
detection of juvenile deviance and on the sanctioning of
juveniles through arrest. Data were derived from thirty-
six observers who rode with police officers in one of
three cities--Boston, Chicago, and Washington, D.C. A
total of 5,713 incidents were observed; 281 encounters
included juveniles. Only the latter data are examined
here. Findings from this research are numerous; some
are: (1) most police-juvenile encounters are initiated by
citizens, (2) the probability of arrest is very low, (3)
police sanctioning is related to citizen complaints, and
(4) while blacks have a higher arrest rate, it should not
be concluded that police are racist.

127 Bonovitz, J.C., and J. S. Bonovitz. "Diversion of the
    Mentally Ill into the Criminal Justice System: The
    Police Intervention Perspective." AMERICAN JOURNAL OF
    PSYCHIATRY, 138 (7): 973-976, 1981.

    To test the hypothesis that police would arrest
disruptive but non-dangerous individuals to expedite
their removal from the community, the outcomes of all
incidents involving a mentally ill individual during a 5-
month period between 1975-1979 were reviewed. Data
showed that mental illness-related incidents increased
227.6 percent from 1975-1979, whereas felonies increased
only 5.6 percent and the total number of incidents
excluding these catagories decreased by 9 percent. A
total of 62 (25 percent) of the 248 incidents involving
mentally ill individuals neither met the dangerousness
criteria of the State's Mental Health Procedures Act nor
fell within the penal category. Another 62 calls did
meet the Act's dangerousness criteria and involved
individuals for whom emergency commitment proceedings had
been initiated, committed patients who had eloped from
the State hospital, and self-destructive and assaultive
individuals. The police referred all but 1 of the 10
individuals charged with violence against persons to the
local mental health center for evaluation. The remaining
92 incidents (42 percent) involved mentally ill
individuals whose behavior constituted grounds for arrest
on such charges as disorderly conduct, terroristic
threats, harrassment, defiant trespassing, or indecent
exposure. The data do not support the hypothesis that
the noncommittable mentally ill are being arrested and
jailed as an expedient means of removing them from the
community.

128 Breslin, W. J. "Police Intervention in Domestic Law
    Enforcement Confrontations." JOURNAL OF POLICE
    SCIENCE AND ADMINISTRATION, 6 (3): 293-302, 1978.

    This overview covers the legal problems peculiar to
the handling of domestic confrontations, court decisions
applicable to these issues, the need for written police
policies, and police guidelines. Following a discussion
of the difficulties of gathering data on the extent of
domestic violence, a summary of possible police
intervention policies is given. To date most police
departments have had a policy of nonarrest in domestic
confrontations, but new pressures from women's groups
have made it necessary to reexamine these policies. The
handling of domestic disputes is made more difficult by
the doctrine of marital unity under common law, a view
still upheld by many courts. It is noted that family
court is designed to promote family unity, not to
prosecute an offender.

129 Chaiken, J. M., P. Greenwood, and J. Petersilia.
    "The Criminal Investigation Process: A Summary Re-
    port." POLICY ANALYSIS, 3 (2): 187-217, 1977.

    This article provides an assessment of the Rand
Corporation's national study of the criminal
investigation process in municipal and county police
departments. The authors examine the report's
methodology, findings, and policy implications. The
article provides a comprehensive overview of the Rand
study and is recommended as a starting point for persons
studying criminal investigations.

130 Culver, J. H. "Television and the Police," POLICY
    STUDIES JOURNAL, 7 (Special Issue): 500-505, 1978.

    TV portrayal of police is inaccurate and misleading,
contributing to a gap between the public's perception of
policing and the reality of police work. Some of the
more glaring inaccuracies include an overemphasis on
violence, an overemphasis on technological sophistication
in solving crimes, the inconsequential role of citizens
in helping the police, the unwavering success of the
police in apprehending criminals, and overestimation of
violent street crime which justifies the reaction of
police. The socialization of new recruits within a
department is frequently ignored, because it lacks action
priority. Furthermore, the role and function of police
is portrayed as consisting entirely of fighting crime,
while real police are deluged with calls for assistance
of a noncriminal nature. Police corruption is viewed in
most TV scripts as a manifestation of individual failing

rather than the conditioning of institutionalized corruption. The internal and community politics actually involved in police management are frequently ignored in the TV police world, including the politicalization of departments, the consequences of police unions, and police activity in a political capacity in the selective enforcement of laws. Non-Anglos are not cast as central figures or as officers in supervisory capacities; women are rarely portrayed as equals with male officers.

131 Ferdinand, T. N., and E. C. Luchterhand. "Inner-City Youths, the Police, the Juvenile Court, and Justice." SOCIAL PROBLEMS, 17 (4): 510-527, 1970.

    Ferdinand and Luchterhand examine how an officer's perception of what the courts will do affects the likelihood of referral of a juvenile to court. They found that crimes against the person had lower rates of referral than did crimes against property. An examination of the dispositions by the juvenile court showed that juveniles referred for violent personal crimes received more severe dispositions than did those referred for property crimes. The authors speculate that police reluctance to send an offender to juvenile court reflects their attempt to give the youth the full benefit of the doubt, especially in cases where the risk of receiving a harsh disposition is great.

132 Fisher, C. J., and R. I. Mawby. "Juvenile Delinquency and Police Discretion in an Inner-City Area." BRITISH JOURNAL OF CRIMINOLOGY, 22 (1): 63-75, 1982.

    Since passage of the 1969 Children and Young Persons Act, the cautioning rate has dramatically increased for officially recorded juvenile offenders. The survey covered all juvenile offenders, including those under the age of criminal responsibility, who lived in the area and were detected for offenses between March 1977 and March 1979. In all, 254 different juveniles were included in the study, but because some were handled on separate occasions, the data refer to 293 cases. The survey found that minor offenses predominated, with shoplifting accounting for over one-third of the cases. Only one-sixth of the offenders were female, and approximately three-fifths of the juveniles were first offenders. A total of 7 of the juveniles were under age, 117 were aged 10-13, and 167 were aged 14-16, with 2 apparently over age (17 years old). The police decision to recommend a caution is related to both social conditions within the offender's home and the offender's attitude.

133 Fyfe, J. J. "Administrative Interventions on Police
    Shooting Discretion: An Empirical Examination,"
    JOURNAL OF CRIMINAL JUSTICE, 7 (4), 309-323, 1979.

    The data cover the years 1971 to 1975. In 1972, the
New York City Police Department issued restrictive
administrative shooting guidelines. Former statutory
"Defense of Life" and "Fleeing Felon" justifications for
officer shooting at felons were augmented with further
stipulations requiring the minimum force necessary to be
used in all police-suspect encounters. Warning shots
were prohibited if innocent bystanders could be harmed.
Data also were analyzed for geographic distributions of
shooting incidents, arrests for felonies against persons,
and reported murder and non-negligent manslaughter.
Analysis shows that the guidelines do appear to result in
fewer deaths and injuries to both police and suspects.
Before the new rules, 3.9 suspects were injured and 1.6
were killed per week by the police; afterwards, figures
fell to 2.3 and 1, respectively. Deaths and injuries to
on-duty police also declined, injuries from 4.4 to 2.5
per week, and deaths from 1 every five weeks to 1 per ten
weeks. Further, the reduction in shootings was most
prevalent among the most controversial shooting
incidents: shootings to prevent or terminate crimes.

134 Galliher, J. F. "Explanations of Police Behavior: A
    Critical Review and Analysis."   SOCIOLOGICAL
    QUARTERLY, 12 (3): 308-318, 1971.

    Why police behave as they do is a question that
social scientists have asked for many years. Still,
answers have not been found. Galliher reviews the
dominant themes running through the published materials
that explore the topic. Six approaches to the study of
police behavior are discussed: psychological, immediate
situation, role conflict, subcultural, organizational,
and socio-cultural. After discussing each, shortcomings
are discussed. That is, existing perspectives pay no
attention to the influence of class conflict on law
enforcement. This orientation is the one Galliher
promotes. This paper is valuable on two counts. It
offers a good review of literature through 1970, and it
is an early critical (or "neo-Marxist") writing.

135 Galliher, J. F., L. P. Donovan, and D. L. Adams.
    "Small-Town Police: Trouble Tasks." JOURNAL OF
    POLICE SCIENCE AND ADMINISTRATION, 3 (1): 19-28,
    1975.

    Reports on research designed to assess the popular
image of the role of rural police as well as the limited
related literature by the utilization of interviews of

small-town officers. The image anaylzed is that of the
Chief of Police who as an indolent, unarmed combination
social worker- philosopher seldom arrests anyone, and, as
a result, is well-liked by all local citizens. A total
of 310 police officers in 74 communities of less than
50,000 population in Missouri were interviewed.
Interview questions focused on the officers' perceptions
of their most critical community problems, including
citizen demands for assistance, the services performed in
the local community, and the source(s) of citizen
opposition and support. Police involvement in the
smallest communities (under 5,000) centered around
control of traffic and adolescents. In larger
communities, there was more concern with handling family
disturbances, watching known criminals, and with
communicating with the public. Nightly checking of
business doors to see if they are locked ("rattling
doorknobs") was listed as a police service which took up
a significant portion of time. Support for local
enforcement came from local groups such as fraternal
orders and government bodies.

136 Goldman, N. THE DIFFERENTIAL SELECTION OF JUVENILE
    OFFENDERS FOR COURT APPEARANCE. New York: National
    Council on Crime and Delinquency, 1963.

    This study focuses on variations between specific
offenses in cases drawn from four communities. The
variations for the four combined cities ranged from no
referrals for trespassing to 100 percent referrals for
robbery and assault. Those offenses in which all
contacts resulted in referral generally involved very
small numbers. For example, in all four communities
there were only ten robbery arrests and two arrests for
assault. Goldman also observed several offense-related
factors that affected the likelihood of referral other
than the legal nature of the offense. The degree that a
juvenile offense approached adult criminal conduct was
considered an important cue in understanding the nature
of the offense. Cases involving the use of a gun or
burglar tools, strong-arming, careful planning, or other
professional attributes signified to the police the need
for immediate referral to juvenile court. Also, if the
police viewed the juvenile offense as motivated by
"meanness or spite, rather than mischief or play," then a
more severe disposition was considered necessary.

137 Guidone, P. F., and J. Gervasio. "Directed Deterrent
    Patrol: The Small Department's Approach." POLICE
    CHIEF, 45 (2): 35-37, 1978.

    The optimum use of police department resources,
especially in small departments, is discussed, and the

experience of south central Connecticut in directed
deterrent patrol is reported. The widely used police
procedure of random patrolling is not always the most
efficient and does not always make the most productive
use of manpower resources. Police organizations, both
large and small, must explore all avenues toward
maximizing the productivity of their existing resources.
The innovative patrol methodology employed in police
departments of south central Connecticut is directed
deterrent patrol. This form of patrol has as its core
the replacement of random patrol with a planning system
that directs patrol units to target areas at specific
times in accordance with crime data assessment. In each
department, a planning team has been formed to include
representation from all organizational levels. The south
central Connecticut patrol project has integrated crime
analysis into operational planning to affect all
available patrol resources. While the planning team has
overall responsibility for the project, functions of
operational planning are the responsibilities of
individual squads. The ability to plan and make
decisions is conditioned on access to a valid, timely,
and continuous supply of data. The task of data
collection in a small department must be an ongoing
effort in order to provide the planning team with
accurate and timely crime and workload information.

138 Hayden, G. A. "Police Discretion in the Use of Deadly
    Force: An Empirical Study of Information Usage in
    Deadly Force Decision-Making." JOURNAL OF POLICE
    SCIENCE AND ADMINISTRATION, 9 (1): 102-107, 1981.

     A device known as the "information board" was used
to analyze police deadly force decision-making. Three
cases were given to a sample of 50 police selected
randomly from a large northeastern city and its suburbs.
After familiarizing themselves with the cases, each
subject was asked to select, in the order of their
perceived importance, those information topics regularly
used to decide whether the situation possessed a low,
medium, or high chance of requiring a response involving
the use of deadly force. Findings show that police
generally do not consider all the information available
to them and rank substantial amounts of that information
as unimportant in deciding whether to use deadly force.
Also, the decision on the use of deadly force is shown to
be a highly individualistic one, where personal judgment
and small amounts of information play an important role
in decision-making. No significant correlation was found
between officers' decision and their prior use of force,
physical size, work community, age, years of experience,
education, or marital status. Results suggest that
officers consider information on the suspect's

characteristics as unimportant, while attention is given
to the nature of the act initiating their response.

139 Hepburn, J. R. "Race and the Decision to Arrest: An
    Analysis of Warrants Issued." JOURNAL OF RESEARCH IN
    CRIME AND DELINQUENCY, 15 (1): 54-73, 1978.

    The analysis covers 28,238 arrests and introduces
controls for type of offense, age, sex, and racial
composition of neighborhoods. Nonwhites are more likely
than whites to be arrested under circumstances that will
not constitute sufficient grounds for prosecution; i.e.,
proportionately fewer arrests of blacks than of whites
are upheld by the subsequent issuance of a warrant by
the prosecutor's office. The race of the offender is a
particularly important factor in the decision to arrest
with less than sufficient evidence when the nonwhite
arrest occurs in a heavily nonwhite area. The data also
show that females are more likely than males to be
arrested under conditions in which a warrant is not
subsequently issued, particularly for stereotypically
"female" crimes such as shoplifting. The findings are
lend support to the labeling and conflict perspectives on
police-civilian interactions. The former suggests that
existing stereotypes of criminal or potentially criminal
persons include a racial component. The latter maintains
that those most likely to be criminalized are those with
relatively little power.

140 Hobenstein, W. F. "Factors Influencing the Police
    Disposition of Juvenile Offenders." Pp. 138-144 in
    T. Sellin and M. E. Wolfgang (eds.), DELINQUENCY:
    SELECTED STUDIES. New York: John Wiley, 1969.

    Hobenstein identified which factors were most
predictive of disposition decisions from a sample of 504
delinquency events resulting in injury to persons or
property loss or damage in Philadelphia in 1960. The
data revealed no systematic racial bias by the police in
their handling of juvenile offenders. There was only one
exception: in those cases where the offense was minor and
where the offender had only one or two previous arrests,
blacks were arrested 78 percent of the time and whites
were arrested 22 percent of the time. But such
situations were rare, representing only 18 of the 504
events studied.

141 Hudson, J. R. "Police-Citizen Encounters That Lead
    to Citizen Complaints." SOCIAL PROBLEMS, 18 (2):
    179-183, 1970.

    Encounters between police and citizens are sometimes
tense and violent. This paper explores those factors in
police-citizen encounters that best predict outcomes.
Data for the study came from complaints of alleged police
misconduct filed by citizens with the Philadelphia Police
Advisory Board. Included among the characteristics
describing these encounters are circumstances under which
the interaction began, the citizen's social status, and
the social context of the incident. Data revealed that
certain combinations of these factors seem likely to lead
to tense encounters, strained relations, and subsequent
altercations.

142 Hyman, M. M. "Ascertaining Police Bias in Arrests for
    Drunken Driving." QUARTERLY JOURNAL OF STUDIES ON
    ALCOHOL, 33 (1): 148-159, 1972.

    This study was conducted to determine the degree to
which police arrested minority group persons for
behaviors for which Anglos would go free. Multivariate
analysis found that minority persons from poor areas were
more likely to be involved in alcohol-related accidents
than Anglos from more affluent neighborhoods. It found
that younger males were involved in more accidents than
older males. So few females were involved that
comparison was not possible for this group. Blood
alcohol concentrations increased with age until about age
45-50, then decreased. However, concentrations were
higher among poor minority persons arrested than among
Anglos arrested. It was concluded that the reason more
poor minority young males are arrested is that they are
involved in more alcohol-related accidents.

143 Johnson, W. T., R. E. Petersen, and L. E. Wells.
    "Arrest Probabilities for Marijuana Users as Indica-
    tors of Selective Law Enforcement." AMERICAN JOURNAL
    OF SOCIOLOGY, 83 (3): 681-699, 1977.

    Marijuana arrest data for July through December
1970, were obtained from police records in Cook County
(Chicago), Ill., Douglas County (Omaha), Neb., and
Washington, D.C. Marijuana use estimates were obtained
in sample surveys conducted in the same jurisdictions.
Arrest probabilities were then determined for the
following groups: males and females; white-collar
workers, blue-collar workers, and students; blacks and
nonblacks; and persons under age 25 and over age 25. The
analysis shows that arrest probabilities are higher for
males than for females and higher for blue-collar workers

than for others in all jurisdictions. In two jurisdictions, younger persons have higher arrest probabilities than older persons. In one jurisdiction, arrest probabilities are higher for blacks than nonblacks. The plausibility of differential enforcement and differential visibility explanations for observed arrest probability variances is explored by examining data on the circumstances of marijuana arrests and on the characteristics of law enforcement activities preceding the arrests. Both interpretations appear to be consistent with the data. The social location of marijuana use (i.e., the context and manner in which it is used) and suspicion cued by certain sociodemographic characteristics of marijuana users are equally tenable explanations of arrest probability differentials.

144 Klein, M. W. "Labeling, Deterrence, and Recidivism: A Study of Police Dispositions of Juvenile Offenders." SOCIAL PROBLEMS, 22 (2): 292-303, 1974.

Juvenile delinquency recidivism rates were compared for nine police departments showing high rates of juvenile diversion and nine departments which had low diversion rates to determine the effects on labeling. It was found that police departments with high rates of juvenile diversion did not yield different recidivism rates from those with low diversion rates unless comparisons were made between first offenders and multiple offenders. Then, the two sets of departments differed substantially: high diversion departments had lower subsequent recidivism rates for first offenders than for multiple offenders, while low diversion departments did not exhibit these differences. It is stated that the emergence of differences in multiple, but not in simple, recidivism among high diversion, but not among low diversion, departments supports both labeling theory and a deterrence approach in interaction with departmental and offender variables. There also is a suggestion that the effects of delinquent stigmatization are cumulative with each arrest, supporting Lemert's secondary deviance conception, at least among first offenders in high diversion departments.

145 Klein, M. W., S. Rosensweig, and R. Bates. "The Ambiguous Juvenile Arrest." CRIMINOLOGY, 13 (1): 78-89, 1975.

Many of the 49 California police departments these authors studied gave little guidance to their juvenile bureaus. The chiefs considered juvenile matters to be of little interest and gave them less attention. This "policy" permitted the operation of independent juvenile bureaus and officers within formally structured

departments. Many juvenile officers felt that they could
develop approaches to juvenile processing independent of
or even in opposition to the standardized departmental
procedures.

146 Klockers, C. B. "Dirty Harry Problems." ANNALS OF
    THE AMERICAN ACADEMY OF POLITICAL AND SOCIAL SCIENCE,
    452 (November): 33-47, 1980.

    Policing places its practitioners in situations in
which good ends can be achieved by dirty means. When the
ends to be achieved are urgent and unquestionably good
and only a dirty means will work to achieve them, police
officers face a moral dilemma. In such situations in
policing, called Dirty Harry problems after the 1971 film
by the same name, the danger lies not in becoming guilty
of wrong, but in thinking that one has found a way to
escape a dilemma which is inescapable. Dire consequences
result from this misunderstanding. Police officers lose
their sense of moral proportion, fail to care, turn
cynical, or allow their passionate caring to lead them to
employ dirty means too crudely or too readily. The only
means of assuring that dirty means will not be used too
readily or too crudely is to punish those who use them
and the agency which endorses their use.

147 Krohn, M. D., J. P. Curry, and S. Nelson-Kilger. "Is
    Chivalry Dead: An Analysis of Changes in Police Dis-
    positions of Males and Females." CRIMINOLOGY, 21
    (3): 417-438, 1983.

    This study is an attempt to examine the effect of
sexual stereotyping on treatment by the criminal justice
system. In this study, it is suggested that police
respond to female offenders in a paternalistic manner.
This line of thinking is explored by examining the
relationship historically. Data for the study were
derived from following the criminal careers of three
birth cohorts in a north central city. The authors
conclude that there have been changes in the disposition
of police contacts that reflect redefinition of sex roles
and official reactions to female offenders may partially
account for increases in female crime rates.

148 LaFree, G. D. "Official Reactions to Social Problems:
    Police Decisions in Sexual Assault Cases." SOCIAL
    PROBLEMS, 28 (5): 582-594, 1981.

    LaFree adds to a growing body of knowledge that
identifies three competing models of police descretion:
legal, extralegal, and change. These models were tested
on 905 sexual assault complaints to police in a large,

midwestern community over six years. The most important determinants of arrest were charge seriousness and felony screening. Suspects received more serious dispositions when: (1) the victim identified them, (2) the victim would testify, (3) the incident included sexual penetration, (4) charges were more serious, and (5) a weapon was used. Extralegal variables exerted less of an effect. Reorganization of the police agency did not affect arrest and felony filing rates.

149 Lundman, R. J. "Routine Police Arrest Practices: A Commonwealth Perspective." SOCIAL PROBLEMS, 22 (1): 127-141, 1974.

Police departments are viewed as serving the public at large (Commonwealth perspective). Lundman shows the extent to which routine police arrest practices suggest police abuse of the societal delegated privilege to exercise non-negotiable coercive force. A participant observer design was used to select data. Seven trained persons travelled with police on a random time basis. Specifically, however, this paper only examines encounters for public drunkenness. As such, the sample is small (n=195) compared to the number of encounters observed (N=1,978). Significantly higher arrest rates were associated with offense conspicuousness, offender powerlessness, and offender disrespect. The most striking conclusion was that police abuse this societal delegated privilege. It is problematic, therefore, to conclude that police subscribe to a Commonwealth perspective, at least for encounters for public drunkenness.

150 Lundman, R. J. "Organizational Norms and Police Discretion." CRIMINOLOGY, 17 (2): 159-171, 1979.

Criminologists believe that police officers routinely violate norms emphasizing the consistent or equitable treatment of citizens. In this study, which focuses on traffic law violators, it is suggested that police discretion is a function of relations between organizational norms and employee concerns with autonomy. If officers are constrained to act by reference to organizational norms, then police discretion results in a disproportionate number of citations for minority, lower class, and disrespectful persons. Data were derived from a participant observer study covering fifteen months. The findings are based on 293 traffic law violation encounters. The main finding was that police decision-making in the context of traffic law violations is a function of relations between organizational norms and employee concerns with autonomy as was predicted.

151 Lundman, R. J., R. E. Sykes, and J. P. Clark. "Police
    Control of Juveniles: A Replication." JOURNAL OF
    RESEARCH IN CRIME AND DELINQUENCY, 15 (1): 74-91,
    1978.

    The analysis encompasses police response to 200
calls in which the alleged violator was present and under
18 years of age. The data are analyzed and compared with
data from an earlier study in the following areas:
detection of juvenile deviance; seriousness of juvenile
deviance; arrest rates; legal seriousness and arrest;
citizen preference and arrest; race and arrest; evidence
and arrest; and demeanor and arrest. The 1970 data
support the following conclusions: most police encounters
with juveniles arise in direct response to citizen
requests; most encounters are for matters of minor legal
significance; the probability of arrest is low for
juveniles who have encounters with police; that
probability increases with the legal seriousness of the
alleged offense; police sanctioning of juveniles reflects
the preferences of citizen complainants in field
encounters; the arrest rate is higher for black youths
than for white youths; the presence of situational
evidence linking a juvenile to a deviant act is an
important factor in the probability of arrest; and the
probability of arrest is higher for youths who are
disrespectful toward the police.

152 Monahan, T. P. "National Data on Police Dispositions
    of Juvenile Offenders." POLICE, 14 (1): 36-45, 1969.

    Relying on FBI arrest rate statistics from 1965-66,
Monahan found variation in the percentage of juvenile
offenders across communities, regions, and states.
Controlling for state and region, he found that urban-
rural differences accounted for much of the variation in
reported rates. The lowest percentage of minors were
arrested in rural areas. Police in both large cities and
rural areas were more likely to take court action against
juveniles than were police in medium-sized cities.
Police in large cities handled a proportionately higher
volume of juvenile cases. Although a lower percentage
were sent to court from large cities than from rural
areas, a higher percentage were petitioned in larger
cities than in medium-sized cities.

153 Mooney, M. C. "Immigrant and Colonial Models of
    Police-Community Relations: An Inquiry." JOURNAL OF
    POLICE SCIENCE AND ADMINISTRATION, 6 (2): 222-231,
    1978.

    Using historical research, the prevalent immigrant
mode of police-community relations is examined and

compared to the colonial model as it has been applied to police interaction with racial minorities. The popular concept of the immigrant model of police-community relations views the white immigrant as having moved quickly within a two-generation span into the dominant society, while under the colonial model, racial minorities like Blacks, Hispanics, and Native Americans have remained subject to the dominant white majority through the use of police control. These two model concepts are examined in the study of the immigrant community of Paterson, NJ, between the years of 1890 and 1920. A new model of police-community interaction is proposed for minority groups who are exploited. In such cases, overt attempts by such minorities to secure rights are challenged through the use of police, who adopt a combative stance toward them.

154 Moyer, I. L.   "Demeanor, Sex, and Race in Police
    Processing." JOURNAL OF CRIMINAL JUSTICE, 9 (3):
    235-246, 1981.

    This paper assesses the processing of females by police, and adds to the police-citizen encounter literature. The article reports the results of a study that took place between September-December, 1978. Questionnaires were completed by 282 police officers/detectives in a large southeastern state. Police officers indicated that their decisions are not contingent on the sex and race of offenders. The factors that influenced police officers' reactions most were the nature of the offense and the alleged offender's demeanor.

155 Muir, W. K. "Power Attracts Violence." ANNALS OF THE
    AMERICAN ACADEMY OF POLITICAL AND SOCIAL SCIENCE, 452
    (November):   48-52, 1980.

    Often police officers are called to restore order to situations where one of the parties is fighting to avenge himself (or his family) and to establish the family as persons who will not be passively victimized. In these circumstances, police officers are not likely to be successful when they intervene nonviolently. If a crowd is watching, the avenging party may only be able to save face by attacking the officers. A citizen's reputation for implacability and vengeance may be vital to preserving his safety after the officers have left the scene. A police officer who attempts to restore order at the expense of a citizen's honor leaves the citizen no recourse but to attack. The only nonviolent solution is for police officers to redefine the crowd's acceptance for the proposition that the superior form of vengeance

is legal prosecution of offenders, which can wreak more
havoc in the lives of perpetrators than can beatings.

156 Piliavin, I., and S. Briar. "Police Encounters with
    Juveniles." AMERICAN JOURNAL OF SOCIOLOGY, 70 (2):
    206-214, 1964.

    Piliavin and Briar studied the relationship between
demeanor and police dispositions of juveniles. Observing
juvenile officers in a large metropolitan police
department over nine months, they concluded that the
police had access to little information about juvenile
suspects when they decided their fate. Dispositional
decisions were based largely on character cues which
emerged from the interaction between the officer and the
youth, including the juvenile's age, race, grooming,
dress, group affiliation, and demeanor. According to the
police, demeanor was a factor influencing their decision
for 50-60 percent of the juvenile cases they processed.

157 Pope, C. E. "Post-Arrest Release Decisions: An
    Empirical Examination of Social and Legal Criteria."
    JOURNAL OF RESEARCH IN CRIME AND DELINQUENCY, 15 (1):
    35-53, 1978.

    The data are from a crime-specific burglary
program. Six law enforcement agencies were involved.
The analysis takes into account the significance of the
apprehended offender's age, race, and sex, the number of
crime partners involved in the incident, the distance
from the offender's residence to the burglary victim's
residence, and the offender's criminal history. When
legal factors are disregarded, age, sex, and race
influenced police decisions to hold burglary arrestees
with priors for trial. However, when legal criteria are
considered, these factors do not influence post-arrest
decisions. Burglary arrestees with prior records are
more likely to be held than are arrestees without
records. Arrestees who are under supervision at the time
of their arrest are more likely to be held than others.
However, a prior record for burglary is not an important
determinant of the hold/release decision.

158 Powell, D. D. "Race, Rank, and Police Discretion."
    JOURNAL OF POLICE SCIENCE AND ADMINISTRATION, 9 (4):
    383-389, 1981.

    Subjects were 171 police officers selected from an
urban and three suburban police agencies in northwest
Indiana. Subjects were categorized by three regions:
Region 1, consisting of 58 officers (28 minority) from a
predominantly black urban community; Region II,

consisting of 57 officers (2 minority) from a predominantly white urban community; and Region III, consisting of 56 officers (all white) selected from three different all-white suburban communities. Among the officers selected from each region were supervisors holding the rank of sergeant. A self-administered questionnaire was used to measure differences in the use of discretion. Data showed that the police of the black urban community demonstrated the highest overall use of discretion and were more punitive toward white offenders than blacks. The police of the predominantly white urban community and all-white suburbs were more punitive toward black offenders than whites. The findings also showed that line officers were significantly more punitive toward black offenders than white ones, but the reverse was true of police supervisors.

159 Reiss, A. J., Jr. "Discretionary Decision-Making and Professionalization of the Police." Pp. 47-61 in S. G. Chapman (ed.), POLICE PATROL READINGS, 2nd Ed. Springfield, IL: Charles C. Thomas, 1970.

Different situations in which a police officer must exercise judgment are reviewed, and the need for professionalism as a basis for police authority is presented. Professional duties of the police officers, such as handling physical or verbal abuse; dealing with emergency situations or large numbers of persons; and controlling those not directly concerned in an action, such as family members or crowds of witnesses, are discussed. Reiss says that the dilemma for police is to balance moral and quasi-legal concerns on law enforcement and on catching criminals with the concerns for civil rights and legal requirements on police methods. Professionalization of police is advanced as a solution to this problem.

160 Sanders, W. B. "Police Occasions: A Study of Inter-action Contexts," CRIMINAL JUSTICE REVIEW, 4 (1): 1-13, 1979.

In contrast to studies of police discretion that examine individual behavior, Sanders locates the interaction context through the dimensions of social occasion. Goffman defines a social occasion as an affair, undertaking, or event bounded by time and place within which many situations and gatherings form, dissolve, and reform. Occasions are not as permanent or as structured as the larger social organizations from which they arise. To test the relationship between occasions and police mobilization, data were gathered over a 5-month period. Two hundred ninety one police mobilizations were observed in a small city's police department. Observation schedules were developed for recording data; occasions on the schedule were given these dimensions: loose, open, scheduled, unscheduled, closed, tight, and focused and unfocused. Forms of interaction were hypothesized to be dependent on the social occasion in which the police and citizens found themselves. Findings verified that loose and open occasions were more likely to lead to police intervention since they were occasions when feelings could get out of hand and antagonism could erupt. There also was a significant relationship between the type of occasion and of police intervention, thus leading to speculation that crime and disorder are related to forms of social occasions in specific dimensions.

161 Scharf, P. L., R. Linninger, D. Marrero, R. Baker, and C. Rice. "Deadly Force: The Moral Reasoning and Education of Police Officers Faced with the Option of Lethal Legal Violence." POLICY STUDIES JOURNAL, 7 (Special Issue): 450-454, 1978.

Critical to any understanding of the police officer's assessment of the "deadly force" dilemma is a theory of legal decision-making. Kohlberg's (1977) theory of moral judgment posits six stages of moral development that evolve sequentially in all societies regarding the relationship of law to the individual and society. Twenty-four police officers were randomly selected from two California police departments to test the hypothesis of an association between the stage of moral reasoning and the decision on a hypothetical use of force dilemma. Descriptive analysis showed an apparent association between an officer's moral stage and the decision made on the "shooting dilemma." While no officers were in stage six, ones at stage five reasoned from a philosophical position that the taking of anyone's life was a final resort that would occur in extreme circumstances, and the saving of lives of all persons should be paramount.

162 Schubert, F. A. "Enforcing the Blue Laws: Police Discretion and the Rule of Law." CRIMINAL JUSTICE REVIEW, 4 (2): 65-78, 1979.

During the 1976 Christmas season many Massachusetts retailers violated Sunday Closing Laws by opening their stores. They sensed that public opinion was behind them. They also knew that a justice of the Supreme Judicial Court, while refusing to enjoin the Laws' enforcement, had said he thought the law was unconstitutional. The Governor and Attorny General openly disagreed over whether the police should enforce the law. In the midst of this turmoil were the State's police chiefs who had to formulate local enforcement policy. A questionnaire was mailed to each of the 310 police chiefs to determine what policy they had taken towards enforcement, the reason for the police response, and who had communicated with the chief in the decision-making process; 44 percent of the questionnaires were returned. Chiefs experiencing violations reported exercising broad discretion and did not uniformly comply with the statutory enforcement mandate. The chiefs who prosecuted violators also reported that they became involved because of their own initiatives and not because of citizen requests. The results also indicated that chiefs made few communications with nonpolice persons prior to making their policy decision. These results suggest that wider input should be made into the process by which chiefs decide enforcement policy.

163 Schubert, F. A. "Police Policy and Rulemaking: The
    Need for Definition." JOURNAL OF POLICE SCIENCE AND
    ADMINISTRATION, 9 (3): 261-271, 1981.

    Police departments have not regulated police discretion because police administrators who attempt to often find themselves in direct contradiction with local statutes and ordinances. Other reasons are ambiguity as to who is in charge of policy-making (the police chief or the mayor) and lack of administrative support. Wide disagreement exists regarding the nature of police rules and policy, although procedures pertaining to the manner in which activities are performed have been more consistently defined.

164 Shannon, L. W. "Types and Patterns of Delinquency
    Referral in a Middle-Sized City." BRITISH JOURNAL OF
    CRIMINOLOGY, 4 (1): 24-36, 1963.

    Shannon analyzed 4,554 records of police-juvenile contacts in Madison, WI, between 1950-1955 by dividing them into zones consisting of groupings of school districts. He observed differences in court referral rates from zone to zone, but said that the differences were not significant. He noted that juveniles engaging in comparable types of delinquent behavior received similar police dispositions.

165 Sharp, E. P. "Street-Level Discretion in Policing:
    Attitudes and Behaviors in the Deprofessionalization
    Syndrome." LAW AND POLICY QUARTERLY, 4 (2): 167-189,
    1982.

    Two hypothesized consequences are examined: police officer alienation from the citizenry and police officer disaffection with the department. Both attitudinal data (from a survey) and behavioral data (from observations) are used. The data support the hypothesis that disaffection with the department is a consequence of the discretion-constraint clash, but no support of alienation from the citizenry was found. Instead, the data suggest that officers back away from discretion in situations where the public is perceived to be hostile and where supervisors reinforce that perception by monitoring police-citizen encounters.

166 Shimota, K. L. "Study of Police Services to Children in a Rural Wisconsin County." JOURNAL OF CRIMINAL LAW AND CRIMINOLOGY, 56 (2): 257-259, 1965.

The methods, findings, and recommendations of a study of police services for children and juveniles in rural Sauk County, WI, in the early 1960's are summarized. The study was conducted at the request of the Sauk County sheriff and a juvenile court judge. The study team interviewed the administrators of all police departments and junior and senior high schools in the county, as well as welfare department case-workers who provided services to the juvenile court. The team paid close attention to police investigative, discretionary, and recordkeeping practices. The following problems were identified: (1) lack of police protection services to children; (2) inadequate police investigations, questionable dispositions, and poor recordkeeping in cases involving allegedly delinquent children; (3) a lack of communication and standardized procedures among law enforcement, school, social service, and court agencies; and (4) a need for in-service police training in child protection and delinquency prevention.

167 Siegel, L. J., J. R. Greene, and D. C. Sullivan. "Decision Games Applied to Police Decision-Making: An Exploratory Study of Information Usage." JOURNAL OF CRIMINAL JUSTICE, 2 (2): 131-146, 1974.

These authors examine the nature of the decision-making process of police in an arrest-nonarrest situation and conclude that police use different amounts and types of information to arrive at the same decision. A variety of information possibilities were provided to a sample of police as they made arrest-nonarrest decisions in simulated encounters with citizens. In selecting information for decision-making, the nature of the offense was considered most frequently. The attitude of the offender also was an important determinant, and the offender's attitude also influenced the amount and type of information subsequently used.

168 Stoddard, E. "Organizational Norms and Police Dis-
    cretion: An Observational Study of Police Work with
    Traffic Violators." CRIMINOLOGY, 17 (2): 159-171,
    1979.

    Stoddard offers an explanation for "blue-coat
crime." He explains police corruption in terms of an
informal social system whose norms and practices are at
variance with legal statutes. In fact, within the police
subculture, illegal behavior is referred to as the
"code." He concludes that misbehavior among police has
more to do with the informal "code" than aberrations of
individual officers.

169 Sullivan, D. C., and L. J. Siegel. "How Police Use
    Information to Make Decisions: An Application of
    Decision Games." CRIME AND DELINQUENCY, 18 (3): 253-
    262, 1972.

    Sullivan and Siegel used a decision game technique
with a group of 24 officers who were asked to select
items of information they thought were necessary to
decide whether to arrest. The hypothetical case involved
a juvenile who was drunk and belligerent. On the
average, the officers selected five pieces of information
before making a decision. Race was not among them.
Given the opportunity to examine additional pieces of
information and reconsider their decisions, only one
officer added the offender's race. While some officers
may have played the decision game as they believed they
ought to rather than as they would have actually behaved,
the results suggest their sensitivity not to consider
race as a factor in their decisions.

170 Sundeen, R. A., Jr. "A Study of Factors Related to
    Police Diversion of Juveniles." Ph.D. Dissertation,
    University of Southern California, 1972.

    In interviews with the chiefs of 47 police
departments in California, Sundeen found that most chiefs
could not specify disposition policies. Resorting to
impressions gained through the interview process, Sundeen
offered a rough cataloging of departmental policies
relating to juvenile processing: 27 departments favored
"counsel and release," 16 departments judged each case on
its merits, and 4 departments preferred referrals to
juvenile court.

171 Swanson, C. R., Jr. "Influence of Organization and
    Environment on Arrest Policies in Major United States
    Cities." POLICY STUDIES JOURNAL, 7 (Special Issue):
    390-398, 1978.

     The research is based on the premise that variation
in law enforcement activity cannot be explained solely by
differing crime rates among cities. Equation factors
were derived from the theory that the activity of an
organization is largely derived from whether it is an
open system or a closed one. To examine variation in
arrest policies, data were collected from 40 U.S. cities
with populations from 300,000 to 1,000,000. The focus of
the study was on explaining arrest variation for certain
misdemeanor or Part II UCR crimes, since previous
research suggests an inverse relationship between the
seriousness of a crime and the exercise of police
discretion. Arrest data for a number of Part I offenses
also are included. Independent variables used were crime
environment, political culture, region, and economic
interests. Organizational independant variables used were
centralization, specialization, professionalism,
community relations orientation and task orientation.
While there are some exceptions, indicators of a city's
crime environment are positively related to arrest rates,
with percent nonwhite population being the best
predictor.

172 Sykes, R. E., and Edward E. Brent. "The Regulation
    of Interaction by Police: A Systems View of Taking
    Charge." CRIMINOLOGY, 18 (2): 182-197, 1980.

     Police officers are taught to "take charge" of
police-citizen encounters. But exactly how often is left
unstated. Sykes and Brent pay attention to the processes
of interaction within encounters from which taking charge
is accomplished. They conceptualize the process of
taking charge and examine data that was part of a long-
term study on police-civilian interactions. The findings
show that authority is maintained in most cases by subtle
means. Officers dominate encounters primarily by
definitional, and only secondarily by imperative,
regulation. Coercive regulation is rare.

173 Talarico, S. M., and C. R. Swanson, Jr. "Policing
    Styles: Notes on an Empirical Synthesis of Wilson and
    Muir." JOURNAL OF CRIMINAL JUSTICE, 8 (5): 327-334,
    1980.

     James Q. Wilson's VARIETIES OF POLICE BEHAVIOR and
William Muir's POLICE: STREETCORNER POLITICIAN are
classic police studies. Talarico and Swanson examine a
component common to both works--police styles. Data were

derived from police in eighteen departments through self-
report questionnaires; a 72.2 percent of the 900
potential respondents returned the survey instrument
(N=650). The results of the study were that style
congruity is critical for line officers.

174 Terry, R. M. "The Screening of Juvenile Offenders."
    JOURNAL OF CRIMINAL LAW, CRIMINOLOGY & POLICE
    SCIENCE, 58 (2): 173-181, 1967.

    In a study of 9,023 juvenile dispositions in a
midwestern city, Terry hypothesized that police would
take into account the number of individuals involved, the
degree of involvement with offenders of the opposite sex,
and the degree of involvement with adults. The data
supported only the last prediction. Juveniles who were
involved in offenses with adults were arrested more often
than juveniles who acted only with other juveniles. Part
of this relationship is the result of the age of the
juvenile offenders. Older juvenile offenders are more
likely to be arrested, and juveniles who commit offenses
with adults tend to be older.

175 Thomas, C. W. "Exercise of Discretion in the Juvenile
    Justice System." JUVENILE AND FAMILY COURT JOURNAL,
    32 (1):   31-50, 1981.

    Recent U.S. Supreme Court decisions have demanded
greater regularity and procedural formality in the
juvenile justice system, which is characterized by broad
discretionary powers. However, their impact has fallen
only on adjudicatory stages of processing. The police,
however, screen juveniles at the intake stage, combining
legal and extralegal decisions, and continuing the
discretionary processing of children in trouble at the
prehearing stage of the system. There is a need to
distinguish between the proper use of discretionary
powers in the juvenile justice system and their abuse.
There is no evidence that dispositional decisions at the
intake level are improperly made on the basis of such
variables as the social background or demographic
characteristics of the offender, the personality of key
decision-makers, or the structural organization of police
and intake departments. However, individual police and
intake officials cannot insure that their decisions are
consonant with administratively promulgated policies and
standards, since such standards do not exist.

176 Visher, C. A. "Gender, Police Arrest Decisions, and
Notions of Chivalry." CRIMINOLOGY, 21 (1): 5-28,
1983.

Whether females receive preferential treatment when
they come into contact with criminal justice agents is a
topic criminologists have pondered. This paper examines
preferential treatment during arrest. The data show that
chivalry does exist for women who display appropriate
gender behaviors and characteristics. Older, white
females are less likely to be arrested than are younger,
black or hostile females. Moreover, at the arrest stage,
female property offenders receive no leniency, and some
evidence suggests that offenses against property weigh
more heavily in arrest decisions for females than they do
for males.

177 Waegel, W. B. "Case Routinization in Investigative
Police Work." SOCIAL PROBLEMS, 28 (3), 263-275, 1981.

The study was performed during 9 months of
participant observation in a police detective division.
In the police department studied, detectives are required
to produce a formal investigative report within 2 weeks
after a case is assigned. In addition, detectives feel
under pressure to produce an acceptable level of arrests
to enhance their chances of remaining in the detective
division and gaining promotion. Under these constraints,
the officers resort to categorization schemes that typify
cases as routine or nonroutine. Should a case fall into
a generally familiar type, it does not receive a vigorous
or thorough investigative effort. These are reserved for
extraordinary cases falling outside the recognized
patterns. It is this process of investigative police
work that largely determines what criminal incidents will
be treated as suspended cases and which ones will be
investigated and to what extent.

178 Weiner, N. L., and C. V. Willie. "Decisions by
Juvenile Officers." AMERICAN JOURNAL OF SOCIOLOGY,
77 (2): 199-210, 1971.

Weiner and Willie study dispositional decisions by
juvenile officers in Washington, D.C. and Syracuse. They
found no evidence of racial bias. In an analysis of
6,099 youths processed by juvenile officers in
Washington, D.C. during 1963, they observed that while
police in the field had greater contact with black youth
compared with white, the disposition process appeared to
be even handed--38 percent of the police encounters with
black youths were referred to juvenile court and 34
percent of those with whites were referred. Their
examination of records of 1,351 juveniles with whom

police had contact in Syracuse in 1969 produced similar results.

179 Wheeler, S., E. Bonacich, M. R. Cramer, and I. K. Sola. "Agents of Delinquency Control: A Comparative Analysis." Pp. 31-60 in S. Wheeler (ed.), CONTROL- LING DELINQUENTS. New York: John Wiley, 1968.

The authors administered a set of questions to police officers, probation officers, and juvenile court judges to determine their perception of delinquent acts and their selection of dispositions. While the police resisted sending children to court, they felt that most of the cases they did refer deserved institutional confinement. Probation officers and judges, in contrast, more often favored court referral in handling the offenders, but were more reluctant to have them incarcerated.

180 Wilbanks, W. L. "The Insertion/Diversion at the Juvenile Police Level." Ph.D. Dissertation, State University of New York--Albany, 1975.

In 1973, Wilbanks administered a questionnaire to officers in 13 police departments in Florida, New York, and Texas and to officers attending a training seminar in Louisiana to study the effects of officers' perception of departmental policy on case decisions. Court referral recommendations for nine hypothetical cases ranged from 29 percent to 85 percent. However, he found that disparity in case dispositions within departments was not explained by differences in officers' policy perceptions. The most important predictors of case disposition were the personal beliefs of the officers. Wilbanks noted that 41.4 percent of the officers said they relied on their own points of view rather than departmental policy when a conflict occurred between the two.

181 Wiley, M. G., and T. L. Hudik. "Police-Citizen En- counters: A Field Test of Exchange Theory." SOCIAL PROBLEMS, 22 (1): 119-126, 1974.

This research focuses on a specific aspect of police-citizen encounters, field interrogation. Subscribing to an exchange theory model, the authors view a field interrogation as a two-way exchange between a police officer and a citizen. Extent of cooperation given by the citizen is considered a reward to the police officer. It is hypothesized that the level of cooperation is dependent upon the value placed on the actions of the police. Data for the study were derived from 200 interviews conducted with persons having the same characteristics (i.e., black males between the ages of 15-65, who were on the streets between 6 p.m. and 2 a.m.). As predicted, citizens are more cooperative when a reason is provided by the police officer for the interrogation. In addition, citizen cooperation increases when the reason given is a police activity viewed as appropriate and valuable by members of the community.

CHAPTER 4

LAW ENFORCEMENT - ISSUES

182 Arcuri, A. F. "Police Pride and Self-Esteem: Indications of Future Occupational Changes." JOURNAL OF POLICE SCIENCE AND ADMINISTRATION, 4 (4): 436-444, 1976.

The findings of a 3-month study are presented in which police officers from southern New Jersey were used to determine how police officers perceive changes. The questionnaire focused on variables that may be determinants of occupational changes: recruitment, personal pride, and job satisfaction. Pride, self-esteem, and a high level of job satisfaction describe the responses of most police officers in the study. The least desirable aspects of a law enforcement career are duties that waste an officer's time and talents and "politics" within departments. Changes are expected to occur within police departments as younger, more professional officers grapple with their more traditional counterparts for more autonomy and fewer bureaucratic rules.

183 Barker, T. "Peer Group Support for Police Occupational Deviance." CRIMINOLOGY, 15 (3): 353-366, 1977.

Police corruption has interested police scientists for many years. Unfortunately, there exists a dearth of reliable literature. Barker generates a theoretical frame of reference to guide subsequent study. He proposes that police corruption be studied as a form of organizational deviance. Thus, Barker identifies the manner in which the social conditions existing within the occupational milieu contribute to corruption. Barker examines how the opportunity structure and socialization practices within the occupation combine with peer group support to create a social situation where corrupt acts are tolerated and accepted. The article concludes by stating that police corruption is not a peculiar form of deviant behavior. Rather, it is like other forms of occupational deviance in its origin.

184 Baxter, J. C., and R. M. Rozelle. "Spatial Dynamics and Police-Community Relations." POLICE CHIEF, 41 (6): 66-69, 1974.

Aspects of the distance between interacting people are interrelated functions of stress, culture, situation, perceptions, and expectations. The value of these interactional considerations to police are significant, since the stressful context of most encounters makes accurate prediction of the other participant's behavior

difficult. This is most obvious when police encounter
members of different racial or ethnic groups.

185 Blackmore, J. "Are Police Allowed to Have Problems
    of Their Own?" POLICE MAGAZINE, 1 (3): 47-55, 1978.

    There is a growing awareness that job stress and its
attendant problems are inherent conditions of police
work. Police officers are subjected to many job-related
demands and stresses. This article reviews and discusses
numerous studies focusing on job stress and concludes
that the police organization itself may be a major source
of stress.

186 Bopp, W., P. Chignell, and C. Maddox. "The San
    Francisco Police Strike of 1975: A Case Study."
    JOURNAL OF POLICE SCIENCE AND ADMINISTRATION, 5 (5):
    32-42, 1977.

    The authors discuss the consequences of a police
strike for both public officials and citizens. Bopp and
his colleagues piece together events which led to the
strike, the strike itself, and its aftermath. The
article is noteworthy for identifying the effects of the
strike as well as the political response to the decision
of police to strike.

187 Broadway, F. M. "Police Misconduct: Positive Altern-
    atives." JOURNAL OF POLICE SCIENCE AND ADMINISTRA-
    TION, 2 (2): 210-218, 1974.

    Broadway argues that the investigation of complaints
against police is an effective instrument for reducing
complaints if it is corrective rather than punitive in
nature. Internal investigations are conducted mostly
outside the regular chain of command and are adversarial.
This situation relieves the complained-against officer's
superior of responsibility, and stops investigation of a
complaint if the complainant withdraws. To ameliorate
these conditions, Broadway suggests using peer review
panels, field tape recordings, and civilian review
boards.

188 Buller, A. "Legal Remedies Against Corrupt Law En-
    forcement Officers." JOURNAL OF CRIMINAL LAW, CRIMI-
    NOLOGY & POLICE SCIENCE 48 (4): 414-430, 1957.

    Civil removal actions should be employed only where
criminal prosecution will be unsuccessful. Use of one of
the two forms of remedies against corrupt law enforcement
officials depends largely on the type of obligations

which may have been broken--discretionary or ministerial. The public prosecutors duties are largely discretionary. He can decide whether or not to prosecute, can make use of bargain and compromise, or can order a nolle prosequi, based entirely upon discretion. The police officer has more ministerial obligations. Some discretion is available in manpower allocation, but most of the duties consist of carrying out orders. Civil remedies against corrupt officials are more widely used than criminal indictments. They are more flexible and do not require proof of a crime for initiation. There are three relevant types of civil actions--personal removal actions (either executive or judicial removal), quo warranto proceedings, and proceedings to remove the prosecutor's name from the rolls of the courts. They are useful in cases of incompetency or when sufficient proof of corruption is not available. Criminal remedies involve indictment for misconduct in office based on nonfeasance, malfeasance, or misfeasance. Use of criminal prosecution is a more potent weapon against organized crime.

189 Chang, D. H., and C. H. Zastrow. "Police Evaluative
    Perceptions of Themselves, the General Public, and
    Selected Occupational Groups." JOURNAL OF CRIMINAL
    JUSTICE, 4 (1): 17-27, 1976.

    This article reports on a study of the effects of increased strain and role confusion on police. Questionnaires were administered to 442 police officers employed in rural, urban, and suburban settings in two mid-western states. The respondents evaluated themselves and their profession highly, implying they had a positive self-concept and were favorably disposed to their career. The four most negatively evaluated groups were lawyers, college students, politicians, and prisoners.

190 Coleman, C. A., and A. K. Bottomley. "Police Concep-
    tions of Crime and 'No Crime'." CRIMINAL LAW REVIEW,
    1976 (3): 344-360, 1976.

    Coleman and Bottomley examine the problems police may experience in deciding whether a configuration of events is to be recorded as a "crime" and describes the process and problems involved in classifying an offense. The police conception of "crime" and the definitions of "no crime" are discussed. It is noted that a significant number of incidents reported to police are classified as "no crime" in police records. Among the types of cases classified as "no crime" were cycle thefts; crimes which police believed lacked a necessary element for crime classification, such as criminal intent; incidents in which the victim did not press charges; incidents shown not to be crimes during subsequent investigations;

domestic incidents; and cases involving insufficient evidence. Factors that may affect the police classification decision are briefly examined. Lastly, Coleman and Bottomley discuss how operational categories used by the police cannot always be assumed to have a standard meaning that will correspond to the laymen's or criminologist's conception of the categories.

191 Cory, B. "Minority Police: Tramping Through A Racial Minefield." POLICE CHIEF, 2 (2): 4-14, 1979.

An overview of the status of minorities in policing includes profiles of the police departments in Detroit and Dallas. The numbers of minorities on police forces have increased, attitudes of and toward minority police have improved, and minority police organizations have become increasingly vocal. However, old attitudes linger and take their toll on minority officers, who at times experience both scorn from the community and lack of respect from their white counterparts. In Detroit, the city's policy of promoting equal numbers of white and black officers to vacancies at the rank of sergeant has brought law suits charging reverse discrimination. The suits are of national importance because they challenge a "voluntary" affirmative action plan. In 1972, the Dallas police chief set an ambitious minority-hiring goal as part of an ill-fated 5-year plan to reform the department; the goal was not reached. Dallas' problem in recruiting minorities is linked by some to the department's requirement of college training for recruits. But police and city administrators deny a link, and the department's black officers support the requirement.

192 Dash, J., and M. Reiser. "Suicide Among Police in Urban Law Enforcement Agencies." JOURNAL OF POLICE SCIENCE AND ADMINISTRATION, 6 (1): 18-21, 1978.

Occupational stress and its possible relationship to police suicide rates are discussed, and suicide rates for officers in the Los Angeles Police Department are examined to determine influential factors. A number of studies have found police work to involve exceptionally high levels of stress related to organizational and role pressures on officers. So far, five studies of suicide rates among police have been completed. Suicide rates are high for New York and Wyoming officers, exceptionally low for Denver and London, and intermediate for other police departments. Suicide rates for the Los Angeles police between the years 1970 and 1976 are examined and found to be relatively low. The remainder of the article explores the possible reasons for their lower rates of suicide.

193 Dunne, J. A. "Counseling Alcoholic Employees in a
    Municipal Police Department." QUARTERLY JOURNAL OF
    STUDIES ON ALCOHOL, 34 (2): 423-434, 1973.

A rehabilitation program for alcoholics in the New
York City Police force is described. The chronic sick
list, accident, and disciplinary records were searched to
detect police officers with drinking problems. In these
cases, a member of the counseling unit arranged an
interview to offer hospitalization, if necessary, and
Alcoholics Anonymous-oriented treatment for 4 to 6 weeks
at a halfway house. This was followed by 90 days of
limited duty--no firearms--with therapy sessions and
daily Alcoholics Anonymous meetings. Followup interviews
revealed that among those individuals returned to duty,
disciplinary actions were reduced to zero and alcohol-
related and other sickness absences were reduced by about
90 percent.

194 Esbeck, E. S., and G. Halverson. "Stress and Ten-
    sion: Teambuilding for the Professional Police Offi-
    cer." JOURNAL OF POLICE SCIENCE AND ADMINISTRATION,
    1 (2): 153-161, 1973.

This pilot seminar was designed as a 5-day training
program for dealing with confrontation situations created
by the changing social role of police officers. The
civil disturbance planning section of the Michigan
Department of State Police developed a program to prepare
officers for this aspect of their changing social role.
Grasping and interpreting the effects of stress and team-
building were the two areas emphasized. The impact and
transferability of the training to operational situations
was evaluated from taped interview. with participants 90
days after the seminar experience. Excerpts from these
interviews show that participants retained and used what
they had learned in daily work and living situations.

195 Fabricator, J. M., and J. Dash. "Suicide, Divorce,
    and Psychological Health Among Police Officers."
    ESSENCE, 1 (4): 225-231, 1977.

This paper examines the informal consensus that
psychological dysfunction, manifested by suicide and
divorce, is high among police officers. Data collected
from Los Angeles Police Department sworn personnel are
compared to available data from military officers and
enlisted personnel for suicide and to local and national
rates for suicide and divorce. It is suggested that the
Los Angeles officers may, in fact, have lower
psychological dysfunction rates than presumed. Three
factors are proposed to account for this nonconfirmation:
(1) preemployment psychological screening efforts; (2)

the availability of psychological services from within
the police agency; and (3) the personality attributes of
individuals who select police work as a profession.

196 Goldkamp, J. S. "Minorities as Victims of Police
    Shooting: Interpretations of Racial Disproportional-
    ity and Police Use of Deadly Force." JUSTICE SYSTEM
    JOURNAL, 2 (2): 169-183, 1976.

     Two perspectives are examined that are frequently
invoked when racial disproportionality is being
interpreted, either in the realm of police killings or in
the realm of arrest rates for crimes of violence. The
first perspective, characterized as a quasi-labeling
stance, linked the disproportionately high death rates of
minority suspects to the impact of some differential
policing mechanism which seemed to be operating in
American society. The second perspective linked
disproportionate minority death rates to disproportionate
minority arrest rates for crimes of violence. A look at
recent victimization (and census) data revealed that
disproportionate minority arrests did appear to reflect a
disproportionate actual participation by minorities in
crimes of violence to a moderate degree based on the
victim's perception of the race of the offender. An
additional finding showing that the lowest income groups
(regardless of race) were the most highly victimized
segments of society. It is also suggested that without a
comparative analysis of violent interactions between
police and suspects (white and black) to determine when,
how frequently, and for whom deadly force is invoked as a
response by police, it is difficult to feel confident
merely assuming that higher offense and arrest rates
automatically extrapolate into higher death rates.

197 Goldsmith, J. "Police and the Older Victim: Keys to
    a Changing Perspective." POLICE CHIEF, 43 (2): 19-20,
    22-23, 1976.

     It is important for police to realize that crime
impacts more seriously on older people, that old people
are a valuable resource and have a vested interest in
crime prevention programs, and that they are influential.
Six keys to the changing police perspective on the
elderly are discussed: the differential impact and
distinctive aspects of crime against the elderly; full-
service policing; general victim orientation in criminal
justice; the systems approach in criminal justice;
community-based crime control and "segmentalism"; and
political activism and the prioritization and
legitimation of older persons' needs.

198 Grant, M. G. "Relationship of Moonlighting to Job
    Dissatisfaction in Police Officers." JOURNAL OF
    POLICE SCIENCE AND ADMINISTRATION, 5 (2): 193-196,
    1977.

     One hundred sixty three New York City police
officers completed a 52-item questionnaire to determine
what role, if any, job dissatisfaction played in
motivating them to moonlight. The data reveal variations
in degrees of job satisfaction. Of these, moonlighters
displayed the most dissatisfaction.

199 Greenstein, M. "Fear and Nonreporting by Elders: An
    Invitation to Law Enforcement." POLICE CHIEF, 44
    (2): 46-47, 1977.

     Greenstein explores the link between fear of crime
and the high rate of nonreporting among the elderly. He
advocates a system of support for the victim as a way to
increase confidence in law enforcement. The support
system described includes crime prevention education and
victim services components.

200 Gross, S. "Bureaucracy and Decision-Making: Viewed
    From a Patrol Precinct Level." POLICE CHIEF, 42 (1):
    59-64, 1975.

     The characteristics of the police bureaucracy and
its effects on the police officer's role and attitudes
are reviewed, and recommendations for improving police
accountability and operations are given. Bureaucracy is
characterized by a hierarchical arrangement of offenses,
rules for uniformity, and impersonality of relationships.
In the police organization, bureaucracy takes the form of
military concepts of lines of authority, unity of
command, division of work, and specialization of
functions. Several recommendations for improvement of
police operations are made, including increased police
education, increased inservice training, use of police
legal advisors, use of the neighborhood team concept in
policing, and increased community input into police
operations.

201 Guyot, D. "Bending Granite: Attempts to Change the
    Rank Structure of American Police Departments."
    JOURNAL OF POLICE SCIENCE AND ADMINISTRATION, 7 (3):
    253-284, 1979.

     Guyot points to the problems the rank structure has
caused for police management. Five problems are
identified: (1) lack of management flexibility in
personnel decisions, (2) too few incentives for line

officers, (3) militarism, (4) communication blockage within the agency, and (5) insularity of police, both within and outside the department. Her focus is on describing and assessing efforts by police organizations to overcome problems generated from the rank structure. She concludes that by changing the rank structure, the police would be more flexible in meeting community expectations.

202 Harring, S. L., A. M. Platt, R. Speiglman, and P. T. Takagi. "Management of Police Killings." CRIME AND SOCIAL JUSTICE, 8: 34-43, 1977.

    A critical analysis of research on police killings of civilians is the focus of this research. Conclusions are drawn about the management of police violence. A 1974 study using national data noted the dramatic increase of civilian deaths, particularly among blacks, caused by the police between 1962 and 1969. The same study noted that the police-caused death rate for blacks from 1958 to 1968 was consistently nine times higher than that for whites. Subsequent studies, using essentially similar data sets, arrived at different interpretations and police implications. All of the studies minimize the significance of nonstatistical data and fail to investigate the concrete circumstances of police killings of civilians. It is suggested that management of police violence must be understood in the context of a police system that is often unreliable and disorganized. It is concluded that the interests of the state lie in exploiting and publicizing the impact of police deaths in the line of duty, thereby restricting the ability of citizens to resist the illegitimate use of police power. The willingness of the state to use force is viewed as part of a broader social control mechanism. Aggressive police patrol practices, particularly in working class, nonwhite neighborhoods, rely substantially on the public's fear of police violence.

203 Hepburn, J. R. "The Impact of Police Intervention Upon Juvenile Delinquency." CRIMINOLOGY, 15 (2): 235-262, 1977.

    The labeling perspective suggests that official reaction will have a negative impact upon the actor. This study evaluates the effect of police intervention on juvenile delinquents' perceptions of themselves. Data came from two samples of juveniles. One was 106 randomly selected white male adolescents, ages 14 to 17, with no prior record of police contact. A second sample consisted of a random selection of white male adolescents, ages 14 to 17, who had formal contact with police; 119 official delinquents were identified. Data indicated the degree to which the frequency and severity of official delinquency, as well as the severity of disposition, affect the juveniles' self-satisfaction, delinquent identification, commitment to delinquent others, commitment to future delinquency, and attitudes toward police. Moreover, police intervention had little impact when socioeconomic status was controlled. The main conclusion drawn was that the juvenile's perception of himself and attitudes toward others are grounded in the experience of his delinquency involvement and not in the experience of coming in contact with police.

204 Huff, C. R., and J. M. Stahura. "Police Employment and Suburban Crime." CRIMINOLOGY, 17 (4): 461-470, 1980.

Often we hear calls for more police. People believe that one way to reduce crime is by expanding the police force. Unfortunately, this received wisdom has seldom been empirically verified. This study uses variables that are causally related both to crime and police employment rates for 252 suburbs for which police employment and crime data are available. The authors conclude that the relationship between crime rates and police employment was reciprocal.

205 Inn, A., A. C. Wheeler, and C. L. Sparling. "Effects of Suspect Race and Situation Hazard on Police Officer Shooting Behavior." JOURNAL OF APPLIED SOCIAL PSYCHOLOGY, 7 (1): 27-37, 1977.

An examination of incidents involving firing of shots by police officers found degree of hazard of situation most closely related to number of shots while race of victim had little correlation. A metropolitan police department that requires a report every time a police officer's weapon is discharged was used for this study. Examination of records from 1970 to 1972 found that 166 shots were fired at black suspects, 96 at white suspects. When these figures are compared by population of beat in which the shootings took place, it was found that blacks are disproportionately involved in shooting incidents with police but that white suspects are hit more often. Also, more shots are actually fired at white suspects. Since greater citizen contact was correlated with higher shooting incidence, this study has implications for policing strategies. Larger police forces relative to citizen populations may provide greater opportunity for violent confrontations between police and the public.

206 Jacobs, D., and D. W. Britt. "Inequality and Police Use of Deadly Force: An Empirical Assessment of a Conflict Hypothesis." SOCIAL PROBLEMS, 26 (4): 403-412, 1979.

Violence in contemporary society is not well understood. Two competing hypotheses are conflict and functional ones. Conflict theory says that force is the ingredient that holds unequal groups together. Functional theory, on the other hand, minimizes the importance of violence and stresses interdependence and consensus as the basis for social order. Data are provided that test these competing models. It is argued that if conflict theorists are correct, then we would suspect the control agents of the state to use extreme force when economic inequality is most pronounced. Data were derived from the number of killings by police officers for the years 1961-70. The data show that the conflict hypothesis does predict the amount of police-caused homicides more fully than does the functional model.

207 Janeksela, G. M., R. R. Deming, and T. M. Nida. "Attitudes Toward Police." POLICE LAW QUARTERLY, 5 (4): 14-30, 1976.

The authors report on the results of a study that considers the relationship between community size and attitudes toward the police and the police role. It was hypothesized that as community size increases, attitudes toward the police would be more negative and the desire for a crime-control police role would increase. All communities in Minnesota's seven county northeastern planning region were broken down into three categories: large, medium, and small. Attitude questionnaires were mailed to a one percent random sampling of the total population of each category. Contrary to the hypothesis, attitudes toward the police were most negative in the rural community category and most positive in the large community category. When occupation was controlled, attitudes became more positive as community size increases in the unskilled, farming, and unemployed categories. There was no significant relationship between attitudes toward the police role and community size. When occupation was controlled, citizens expressed a desire for human relations oriented police as community size decreased, particularly in the professional and semi-professional category.

208 Johnson, T. A. "Police-Citizen Encounters and the
    Importance of Role Conceptualization for Police-
    Community Relations." ISSUES IN CRIMINOLOGY, 7 (1):
    102-119, 1972.

    An analysis is made of the conflicting perceptions
of the police role by citizens and police themselves. A
better definition of the police role is crucial to
improved police-community relations. Police perceive
their two most important functions to be protecting the
security of persons and property and the enforcement of
laws. Although police practices and personal review
procedures emphasize the law enforcement role, most
police officers spend their time keeping peace; not
apprehending criminals. Role conflict is further
aggravated by citizens' demands for noncriminal justice
services. The problems of role conflict manifested by
many police-citizen interactions suggest that structural
and organizational deficiences must be addressed before
police-community relations will improve.

209 Kania, R. R. E., and W. C. Mackey. "Police Violence
    as a Function of Community Characteristics." CRIMI-
    NOLOGY, 15 (1): 27-48, 1977.

    This paper tests competing models of police violence
and concludes that the available explanations are not
designed to explain variations among the states in the
rates of police use of deadly force. Therefore, the
authors propose that existing models be modified. They
found that where public violence is normative, police use
more violence. On the other hand, where public violence
is neither normative nor accepted, police are more self-
restrained. From the data, they conclude police violence
is a culturally determined characteristic and not a
police occupation or officer pathology.

210 Lewis, R. W. "Toward an Understanding of Police
    Anomie." JOURNAL OF POLICE SCIENCE AND ADMINISTRA-
    TION, 1 (4): 484-490, 1973.

    Lewis presents a discussion of professionalism and
occupational danger-stress, two factors which are
advanced as causes of apathy, anxiety, and frustration.
The research is based on the thesis from Niederhoffer
that the ills afflicting modern police officers are
anomie and cynicism. Lewis concludes that police
officers are caught between the disruptive effects of
professionalism and danger-stress.

211 Lynch, G. W. "Contributions of Higher Education to
    Ethical Behavior in Law Enforcement." JOURNAL OF
    CRIMINAL JUSTICE, 4 (4): 285-290, 1976.

     The consequences of higher education for line-
officers has been the focus of considerable research.
Lynch studies the spoken and unspoken values of the
academic world and assesses their influence on police.
He concludes that college education is most beneficial in
increasing the ethical awareness of line-officers.

212 Marx, G. T. "The New Police Undercover Work." URBAN
    LIFE, 8 (4): 399-446, 1980.

     Marx explores an area of study not so well
developed--undercover work. He begins by arguing that
undercover work is becoming more and more dominant in
American policing, yet little is known about it.
Moreover, the nature of undercover work has changed in
recent years. Thus, the focus of Marx's article is to
explain changes in undercover activity, unintended
consequences, policy implications, and to identify
factors that account for the change and expansion. He
concludes by discussing the variation within undercover
activity.

213 Marx, G. T., and D. Archer. "Community Self-
    Defense." SOCIETY, 13 (3): 38-43, 1976.

     Marx and Archer provide a general discussion of
citizen patrols, their relationship with the police and
their communities, the recruiting and training of
personnel, their types of operation, the incentives for
group survival, and their effectiveness.

214 McNamara, J. "The Impact of Bureaucracy on Attempts
    to Prevent Police Corruption." Pp. 152-157 in A.
    Niederhoffer and A. Blumberg (eds.), THE AMBIVALENT
    FORCE: PERSPECTIVES ON THE POLICE, 2nd Ed. New York:
    Dryden Press, 1976.

     The elimination and prevention of police corruption
through the utilization of an organizational structure,
programs, or departmental procedures does not currently
exist. McNamara focuses on bringing about an
anticorruption climate to police departments by
identifying practices that may help reinforce the
determination to prevent corruption. He discusses the
need for an objective internal affairs unit, community
support of police programs to prevent corruption, dangers

of corruption, assignments in the department and the need
to emphasize pride, which provides an intolerance for
corrupt police practices.

215 Mills, R. B. "Simulated Stress in Police Recruit
    Selection." JOURNAL OF POLICE SCIENCE AND ADMINIS-
    TRATION, 4 (2): 179-186, 1976.

    Using simulated stress situations in the selection
of police recruits as a means of evaluating stress
handling, and recruits' psychological requirements for
certain police functions at a preemployment level is
examined. Mills describes situations utilized in the
Cincinnati Police Department's simulated stress group
method as well as phases of the program and reports on a
validation study of the method. Contributions made by
the simulated stress recruit selection method to the
development of a stress management model for police
systems are identified.

216 Murphy, P. V. "Police Accountability." Pp. 35-46 in
    J. Wolfie and J. Heaphy (eds.), READINGS ON PRODUC-
    TIVITY IN POLICING. Washington, D.C.: Police Founda-
    tion, 1975.

    Murphy examines the concept of police
accountability by elected officials and the public. He
notes that there is much resistance by the citizenry to
pay higher taxes for public services. Accountability is
a recent phenomenon for police executives, and they need
to become more accountable for their operations since
they receive a large portion of the total budget. Murphy
also argues that public officials reflect public opinion
concerning tax expenditures by local governments and
closely monitor police expenditures as they relate to
efficiency and effectiveness. Police departments must
develop methods for determining how well they provide
service and how they can improve their productivity
without increasing expenditures. Police executives must
adopt the managerial concepts of productivity measurement
and productivity improvement.

217 Pitcher, R. A. "Law Enforcement and the Battered
    Child." MILITARY POLICE LAW ENFORCEMENT JOURNAL, 1
    (4): 15-20, 1974.

    An investigation of the role police should play in
cases of child abuse, with emphasis on the cooperative
and complimentary relationship that should exist between
police and child protection and welfare agencies is
presented. The police role is outlined in the stages of
detecting and reporting child abuse, investigating and

evaluating child abuse cases, and disposing of child abuse cases. It is recognized that while police are best equipped for such areas as detecting cases, investigating serious criminal offenses, and cooperating with the public prosecutor in prosecution of child abuse cases, they may not be equipped to resolve cases, provide intervention or treatment, or fully investigate the social and psychological aspects of a child abuse case. These latter functions may best be achieved by the child welfare agency in cooperation with police.

218 Pogrebin, M. R., and B. Atkins. "Some Perspectives on Police Corruption." Pp. 55-69 in N. Kittrie and J. Susman (eds.), LEGALITY, MORALITY, AND ETHICS IN CRIMINAL JUSTICE. New York: Praeger, 1979.

The role of personal commitments, organizational constraints, and community standards are discussed. The authors note that the values of legislators and interest groups as embodied in legislation may differ from the values of police who are drawn from a different social class and who tend to isolate themselves from other occupational groups. Community attitudes toward the police are ambivalent; the community wants honest police officers but also wants to bribe them. Moreover, there is no community consensus on the enforcement of moralistic laws. This situation creates many opportunities for corruption; Pogrebin and Atkins discuss forms corruption may take.

219 Poister, T. H., and J. C. McDavid. "Victims' Evaluations of Police Performance." JOURNAL OF CRIMINAL JUSTICE, 6 (2): 133-149, 1978.

Police are concerned with citizen satisfaction with their services. Poister and McDavid assess attitudes toward police of a specific subset of citizens--victims. Data were derived from a community survey conducted in Harrisburg, PA. Personal interviews were completed with 423 persons, 127 who had been victimized during the preceding fifteen months. The findings were fourfold. First, satisfaction varies with type of crime and police response time. Second, follow-up investigations and arrests influence satisfaction. Third, satisfaction with police decreases as the process lingers. And fourth, for cases involving a follow-up investigation, satisfaction is affected by the follow-up.

220 Pope, C. E., and W. Feyerhern. "Review of Recent
    Trends: Effects of Crime on the Elderly." POLICE
    CHIEF, 43 (2): 48-51, 1976.

    A summary of several national surveys on the effects
of crime on the elderly is reported. Response statistics
of the elderly are given for the following topic areas:
fear of crime, victimization experiences, and attitudes
toward criminal justice issues. Fear of crime was
reported as the major social problem affecting those 65
and over, followed closely by poor health. Further, many
elderly citizens report their concerns with being robbed
or attacked when on the streets. Similarly, the elderly
do not report many of the personal victimizations which
they experience and also are likely to be differentially
affected by certain criminal acts like personal larceny
with contact.

221 President's Commission on Law Enforcement and Admin-
    istration of Justice. "Who Controls the Police?"
    Pp. 30-35 in the President's Commission on Law En-
    forcement and Administration of Justice, TASK FORCE
    REPORT: THE POLICE. Washington, D.C.: U. S. Govern-
    ment Printing Office, 1967.

    The President's Commission on Law Enforcement and
Administration of Justice addressed the issue of what
governmental agency should be responsible for reviewing
and controlling the police. An overview of the types of
controls implemented by various components of
governmental institutions is offered. The discussion
examines the roles of mayor, city council, district
attorney, and judges. Approaches for controlling police
are offered.

222 Price, B. R. "Police Corruption: An Analysis."
    CRIMINOLOGY, 10 (2): 161-176, 1972.

    Price presents an analysis of the group and
individual pressures leading to criminal behavior by
police. Structural and symbolic interactionist theories
are used to explain police corruption. The crux of the
structural argument is that legitimate means are not
available for police to fully secure goals. As a result,
police turn to non-legitimate sources of income. The
symbolic interactionists maintain that an individual's
group identification can be with either honest or
dishonest officers and that socialization into one group
or the other is predictive of behavior.

223 Rafky, D. M. "Racial Discrimination in Urban Police
    Departments." CRIME AND DELINQUENCY, 21 (3): 233-
    242, 1975.

    Rafky studies some of the problems associated with
discrimination against blacks in hiring practices. Rafky
adopts a conceptual model to describe the obstacles that
prevent blacks from being hired in predominantly white
police agencies. Rafky classifies the employment
obstacles for blacks according to organizational and
individual factors. The data show that white police do
not accept blacks to the degree that they are willing to
relinquish certain of their police roles.

224 Rafky, D. M. "Police Cynicism Reconsidered: An
    Application of Smallest Space Analysis." CRIMINOL-
    OGY, 13 (2): 168-192, 1975.

    Ever since Niederhoffer published BEHIND THE SHIELD,
police scientists have studied cynicism. Rafky offers
one of the first attempts at clarifying the concept. He
replicates Niederhoffer by testing the relationships
between cynicism and indices of frustration and anomia.
Rafky concludes that cynicism is not prevalent outside of
New York City.

225 Regoli, R. M. "An Empirical Assessment of
    Niederhoffer's Police Cynicism Scale." JOURNAL OF
    CRIMINAL JUSTICE, 4 (3): 231-242, 1976.

    Regoli adds to those studies that have evaluated
Niederhoffer's Police Cynicism Index. The difference
between Regoli's work and others is that Regoli used a
factor analysis approach. That aside, Regoli demonstrated that police cynicism is a multi-dimensional construct; not a unidimensional one. He concludes with a
discussion of this and related findings and presents
suggestions for subsequent studies. Regoli's data were
derived from questionnaire responses of 324 officers
representing nine police agencies in the Pacific Northwest. A modified police cynicism index is reproduced in
an appendix.

226 Regoli, R. M., and E. D. Poole. "Measurement of
    Police Cynicism: A Factor Scaling Approach." JOURNAL
    OF CRIMINAL JUSTICE, 7 (1): 37-52, 1979.

    Arthur Niederhoffer's police cynicism index is
assessed to identify and refine specific dimensions of
police cynicism. Using a principal component factor
analysis, a three-factor solution was identified. Three
factor scales were developed, and their internal

consistency, reliability, and predictive validity were
compared with those of the original index. Overall,
although less reliable, the factor scales were more
powerful predictors of salient criterion variables and
offer greater conceptual clarity in studying the effects
of police cynicism on other variables.

227 Reiser, M. "Mental Health in Police Work and Train-
    ing." POLICE CHIEF, 41 (8): 51-52, 1974.

    Reiser says that organizational roles and stresses
encountered in the police department and the situations
which an officer confronts have produced a need for more
police training in the behavioral sciences. Police work
is a high-stress occupation involving two types of
roles--punitive and helping. It is recommended that
discussion and counseling groups be held for police
officer's spouses to support and assist them in understanding and coping with the stresses stemming from the
police role.

228 Renshaw, B. H., R. Lehnen, L. Brown, H. Williams, T.
    A. Johnson, W. Drake, and J. E. Warren. "Blacks and
    Crime: Can America Break the Chain of Failure?"
    NATION'S CITIES, 16 (9): 11-18, 23-30, 1978.

    This article on blacks, crime, and the criminal
justice system is aimed at dispelling myths that have
evolved around blacks and their neighborhoods by citing
research data on victims, offenders, and criminal justice
personnel. It is a common belief that blacks are more
likely than whites to be victims and offenders and to
live in dangerous neighborhoods. Statistics reported in
LEAA's annual crime victimization surveys, however,
provide another picture: race is not a major factor in
victimization, but instead, factors such as residence,
age, and sex are more important. Young men residing in
central cities are most vulnerable to crime; blacks do
not suffer more from crime than whites. It is true,
however, that black communities experience a higher crime
rate, but the crime loss is not usually major. City
officials must begin to deal with this problem of blacks
and crime by clarifying their perspectives, analyzing
local conditions with precision and objectivity, and
educating the public in the socioeconomic and historical
background to black involvement in crime and reasons why
blacks perceive the criminal justice system as unfair.

229 Roebuck, J. B., and T. Barker. "A Typology of Police
    Corruption." SOCIAL PROBLEMS, 21 (3): 423-437, 1974.

        Corruption has plagued police departments for years.
This paper postulates an empirical typology of police
corruption derived from a content analysis of the
literature between 1960 and 1972. Police corruption is
assessed in terms of organizational deviance hinging
primarily on informal police peer group norms. Eight
types of police corruption were identified: (1)
corruption of authority, (2) kickback, (3) opportunistic
theft, (4) shakedowns, (5) protection of illegal
activities, (6) the "fix," (7) direct criminal
activities, and (8) internal payoffs. The types are
evaluated across several dimensions, including acts and
actors, norm violations, peer group support,
organizational degree of deviant practices, and police
agency's reaction.

230 Sandy, J. P., and D. A. Devine. "Four Stress Factors
    Unique to Rural Patrol." POLICE CHIEF, 45 (9): 42-
    44, 1978.

        Security, social factors, working conditions, and
inactivity are noted as stress factors influencing police
patrol in rural areas. Rural officers experience an
extreme sense of isolation in their attempts to confront
both domestic and criminal situations. One of the key
factors unique to rural police work is the absence of
anonymity that is usually more available to urban
officers. There is often no opportunity for rural
officers to deal with their community without being
perceived as officers. Due to the personnel selection
process, many officers hired by rural police departments
are "local boys" who have been born and reared in the
community they serve. As a result, they have developed
expectations and perceptual sets concerning members of
the community. Salary levels are often less for rural
officers than for officers in urban areas. The
possibility of training is severely limited due to lack
of funds and the inability of police departments to
provide replacements for officers participating in
training programs. Boredom resulting from long periods
of inactivity is often a factor contributing to job
dissatisfaction. Inactivity also influences officer
perceptions of themselves. Reevaluating the content of
police training curriculums to reflect on-the-job skills
needed by rural officers is recommended to reduce stress
caused by unrealistic attitudes.

231 Smith, D. C. "Dangers of Police Professionalism: An
    Empirical Anaylsis." JOURNAL OF CRIMINAL JUSTICE, 6
    (3): 199-216, 1978.

    Since August Vollmer, reformers have advanced
professionalism to remedy police ills. Smith examines
the consequences of professionalism and concludes that
professionalism does not have negative consequences; he
offers caveats for the interpretation of the data. Smith
argues for additional training both in the academy and
college classroom.

232 Spitzner, J. H., and D. H. McGee. "Family-Crisis
    Intervention Training, Diversion, and the Prevention
    of Crimes of Violence." POLICE CHIEF, 42 (10): 252-
    253, 1975.

    This article describes the results of a training
program on police officers and the families they dealt
with as a part of a family crisis unit in Columbus, OH.
The techniques stressed in the training were mediation
and referral. Police officers, although skeptical of
this training prior to the program's inception, were
satisfied with it and felt that it was an aid to them.

233 Swanson, C. R., Jr.   "An Uneasy Look at College
    Education and the Police Organization." JOURNAL OF
    CRIMINAL JUSTICE, 5 (4): 311-320, 1977.

    Many police scholars view a college education as
being necessary for police work. In this essay, Swanson
offers several observations about previous research and
concludes that it is neither rigorous nor critical. As
such, we do not know the answer to the questions posed
here. Swanson concludes by identifying research needs in
light of the fact that police departments will not
abandon their hierarchial structure.

234 Symonds, M. "Emotional Hazards of Police Work."
    AMERICAN JOURNAL OF PSYCHOANALYSIS, 30 (2): 155-160,
    1969.

    An examination is presented of common psychological
and personality traits of police officers and of the
relationship of those traits to the stresses of police
work. Stressors are considered in two categories: stress
due to the nature of police work and stress as a result
of the nature of the quasi-military police organization.
The type of police applicant often sought by police
departments is also discussed. Observations are drawn
largely from Symonds' experience as a police officer and
police psychiatric consultant.

235 Teahan, J. E. "Role Playing and Group Experience to
    Facilitate Attitude and Value Changes Among Black and
    White Police Officers." JOURNAL OF SOCIAL ISSUES, 31
    (1): 35-45, 1975.

    A description of the methodology and results of this
academy training program designed to improve
communication and understanding on community issues,
values, and attitudes between black and white officers.
Numerous studies have noted disparities between attitudes
held by black and white officers on community and
departmental issues. This training program sought to
increase understanding between officers by means of
weekly sessions involving role-playing and interpersonal
feedback. The study sample consisted of 149 white and 31
black police cadets; this sample was divided between
control and experimental groups. Contrary to
expectations, white officers became both more sensitized
to the presence of black-white problems and more
prejudiced toward blacks, whereas black officers became
more positive toward whites.

236 Terry, R. M. "Discrimination in the Handling of
    Juvenile Offenders by Social Control Agencies."
    JOURNAL OF RESEARCH IN CRIME AND DELINQUENCY, 4 (2):
    218-230, 1967.

    In this analysis of dispositions for 9,023 juvenile
offenses Terry found that the seriousness of offense
exhibited the strongest impact on of police disposition.
It is instructive to note that of all offenses appearing
in the police arrest records, the three most serious
offenses comprised only 6 percent of the total, while the
three least serious offenses accounted for 65 percent.
Conversely, the three least serious offenses represented
a mere 9 percent of the offenses that appear in juvenile
court, but the three most serious offenses comprised over
66 percent of the total offenses appearing in juvenile
court.

237 Terry, W. C. "Police Stress: The Empirical Evi-
    dence." JOURNAL OF POLICE SCIENCE AND ADMINISTRA-
    TION, 9 (1): 61-65, 1981.

    Research has examined the problem of police stress.
Terry brings the existing literature together and draws
some preliminary conclusions. While the article may be
termed "state of the art," Terry does present and analyze
data. He concludes by offering recommendations for
future research. According to Terry, research examining
the effects and consequences of police stress is needed.

238 Tifft, L. L. "Cop Personality Reconsidered." JOUR-
    NAL OF POLICE SCIENCE AND ADMINISTRATION, 2 (3): 266-
    278, 1974.

    Tifft examines specific task environments, task
demands, and organizational structures in five different
units in a major urban police department and how they
affect the attitudes and working personality of the
police. The research employed a variety of methods,
including general observation, interviews with command-
level personnel and with supervisors, controlled
observation of individual officers, and a small number of
interviews with the citizens involved in the observed
encounters. Police attitudes on topics such as the
police mission and the citizens they serve also were
found to differ between units. The data suggest that the
observed officers, regardless of their units, developed
an attitude of friendliness. Tifft concludes that
specific police tasks do give rise to differing police
attitudes, concerns, and behaviors.

239 Webb, S. D., and D. L. Smith. "Police Stress: A
    Conceptual Overview." JOURNAL OF CRIMINAL JUSTICE, 8
    (4): 251-258, 1980.

    Many writers have studied police ills. The ill
considered here is stress. The authors develop a model
to assess the interrelationships between stress and other
factors. The contribution of this paper is its
examination of the nature of stress, its sources and
consequences, and an identification of the gaps in the
traditional conceptualization of the problem area.

240 White, M. F., and B. A. Menke. "On Assessing the
    Mood of the Public Toward the Police: Some Conceptual
    Issues." JOURNAL OF CRIMINAL JUSTICE, 10 (3): 211-
    230, 1982.

    Translating public opinion surveys into public
policy is problematic. White and Menke examine some
methodological and theoretical aspects of public opinion
surveys with an eye to assessing the mood of the public
toward police. Their findings indicate that the public's
mood varies depending upon the level of specificity of
the items used to tap that mood.

241 Wilson, J. V. "Alternatives to Military Rank Titles
    in Law Enforcement." POLICE CHIEF, 41 (4): 16-17,
    1974.

    Wilson discusses the advantages/disadvantages of
abolishing the military rank system for police. He

indicates that the military rank system is often
rationalized as necessary to establish a visible chain of
command during emergency police operations. The
fundamental problem is that police promotion procedures
do not follow those of the military. This results in
public misunderstanding and status-motivated promotion
desires for police officers. Wilson argues that
discipline and efficiency in emergencies has been
maintained by numerous agencies without a visible rank
structure and suggests that this lead could easily be
followed by uniformed police forces.

CHAPTER 5

COURTS - HISTORY

242 Alschuler, A. W. "Plea Bargaining and Its History."
LAW AND SOCIETY REVIEW, 13 (2): 211-245, 1979.

Alschuler notes that for most of the history of common law, the encouragement of guilty pleas in Anglo-American courts was not supported. Plea bargaining has emerged as a frequent practice only after the American Civil War. By the end of the nineteenth century, reform groups actively questioned the practice and appellate courts seemed to frown upon the practice. However, since the period of the 1920's, plea bargaining has gained widespread acceptance. This article examines the changes in guilty plea practices and attitudes toward plea bargaining from their early Anglo-American origins to the present.

243 Blume, W. W., and E. G. Brown. "Territorial Courts and Law: Unifying Factors in the Development of American Legal Institutions. Part I, Establishment of a Standardized Judicial System." MICHIGAN LAW REVIEW, 61 (1): 39-106, 1962.

The authors trace the development of American legal institutions from the first plan of government for the western area developed by Thomas Jefferson in 1784. This plan provided for the establishment of a standardized judicial system. Major changes in judicial systems for the territories are examined in terms of pre- and post-1836, the period after which a systematic system appeared. Specific areas of law and the judicial system are examined and the influence of the judicial system on the frontier is considered.

244 Blume, W. W., and E. G. Brown. "Territorial Courts and Law: Unifying Factors in the Development of American Legal Institutions. Part II, Influences Tending to Unify Territorial Law." MICHIGAN LAW REVIEW, 61 (2): 467-538, 1962.

This is the second article in a two-part series regarding the early development of American legal institutions in the territorial areas. The authors focus on the sources of territorial law and the extent of legislative power. The authors closely examine the statutes and structural organization of the jurisdictions under consideration.

245 Feeley, M. M. "Perspectives on Plea Bargaining."
    LAW AND SOCIETY REVIEW, 13 (2): 199-210, 1979.

    This article is a review of the existing knowledge
on plea bargaining, the causes of plea bargaining, the
consequences of and legitimacy of plea bargaining, and
the directions of reform of the institution of plea
bargaining.

246 Flanigan, D. J. "Criminal Procedure in Slave Trials
    in the Antebellum South." JOURNAL OF SOUTHERN
    HISTORY, 40 (4): 537-564, 1974.

Flanigan suggests that Southern legislatures and courts
were often considerate of slaves' procedural rights in
major criminal cases with the nature of the offense
determining just how "considerate" the courts would be.
In addition, Flanigan concludes that there was a movement
in the nineteenth-century South legal system toward
greater procedural fairness for slaves to reconcile
fairness and legal equality with the dynamic and
perpetual institution of slavery.

247 Friedman, L. M. "San Benito 1890: Legal Snapshot of
    a County." STANFORD LAW REVIEW, 27 (3): 687-702,
    1975.

    Friedman provides an interesting insight into the
judicial system and administration of justice in San
Benito County, CA, in 1890. Based on an examination of
criminal court records, Friedman describes a reasonably
small, but perhaps very typical, community in California
just outside the dominant urban center of San Francisco,
one in which the courts played a significant role,
central to the lives and careers of "insiders." Citizens
used the courts frequently, and yet the court did not
appear to become the "moral steward" it had in many other
communities. The main function of the system was to keep
order and allow the economy to grow.

248 Friedman, L. M. "Plea Bargaining in Historical Per-
    spective." LAW AND SOCIETY REVIEW, 13 (2): 247-259,
    1979.

    Drawing on data from the criminal court of Alameda
County (Oakland), CA, from 1880 and the present, Friedman
explores the practice of plea bargaining. There is
strong evidence of "implicit plea bargaining" as early as
the late 19th century. He concludes that the causes of
plea bargaining must be found somewhere other than in a
reaction to crowded court dockets. A more likely loca-

tion of the causes would be the structural and social
changes in the criminal justice system, especially the
rise of professional police and prosecutors.

249 Haller, M. H. "Plea Bargaining: The Nineteenth Cen-
     tury Context." LAW AND SOCIETY REVIEW, 13 (2): 273-
     279, 1979.

     Haller examines the forces in the 19th century that
might account for the creation and institutionalization
of plea bargaining in American courts. Haller suggests
that while a number of factors were probably involved,
five changes were most important. These were: (1) the
creation of urban police departments; (2) development of
the modern prison system; (3) the reduced role of the
victim; (4) the relative independence of criminal justice
from legal norms; and (5) the growing corruption and
political manipulation of the criminal justice system.

250 Hartog, H. "The Public Law of a County Court: Judi-
     cial Government in Eighteenth Century Massachusetts."
     AMERICAN JOURNAL OF LEGAL HISTORY, 20 (4): 282-329,
     1976.

     An examination and discussion of the role of county
courts (or courts of general session) is presented based
on the records of the Middlesex County Court of General
Sessions of the the Peace, over a 75-year period from
1728-1803. The article describes the work of one court
to develop an understanding of the "strangeness of
eighteenth century governmental practice and of the ways
this legal institution began to change into something
more familiar."

251 Hewitt, J. D., E. D. Poole, and R. M. Regoli.
     "Felony Case Disposition Patterns in Middletown,
     1932-1975." CRIMINAL JUSTICE REVIEW, 7 (2): 58-67,
     1982.

     Sentencing patterns in a middle-sized, midwestern
town are examined from 1932 to 1975. Data were gathered
from the criminal court dockets and only included cases
originally filed as a felony and resulting in a conviction. The analyses indicate that: (1) prosecution of
felonies and subsequent convictions did not keep pace
with the increase in reported crime; (2) plea bargaining
became an extremely common practice in later years; (3)
the role of court-appointed defense counsel changed
dramatically; (4) time delays between filing of
information and sentencing increased greatly after the
mid-1960's; and (5) sentences to state penal institutions

declined over the period of study. Explanations for these changes and related developments are offered.

252 Hindus, M. S. "Black Justice Under White Law: Criminal Prosecutions of Blacks in Antebellum South Carolina." JOURNAL OF AMERICAN HISTORY, 63 (3): 575-599, 1976.

Hindus examines the relationship of the slave and free black to the criminal law. Were blacks protected by it, was plantation justice the dominant mode of dealing with slave criminality, and what was the fate of black defendants prosecuted in the criminal courts? Hindus examines closely the South Carolina legal structure and actual case files from various county courts and presents a quantitative analysis of black and white prosecutions. He concludes that "black justice may have served some bureaucratic need for certification, while at the same time soothing some slaveholders' consciences, but it was never intended to be just. And just it rarely was."

253 Hyman, H. M., and C. M. Tarrant. "Aspects of American Trial Jury History." Pp. 23-44 in R. J. Simon (ed.), THE JURY SYSTEM IN AMERICA. Beverly Hills, CA: Sage, 1975.

Beginning with a brief analysis of English jury history, the authors examine the evolution of the trial jury in America. Noting the great diversity in jury systems in the early American colonies, they reinforce the idea that the colonial courts were very autonomous from British influence. The impact of the Bill of Rights on jury structure and composition is discussed and aspects of the continuing contemporary legal debates regarding juries is noted.

254 Kaplan, M. T. "Courts, Counselors and Cases: The Judiciary of Oregon's Provisional Government." OREGON HISTORICAL QUARTERLY, 62 (2): 117-163, 1961.

Kaplan presents a study of the initiation, jurisdiction, and operation of the courts based on the premise that the word "government" denotes the existence of laws and the observance of them by the "governed" community. Her paper, then, provides a unique examination of the Oregon Provisional Government through the development of its judiciary.

255 Kimball, E. L. "Criminal Cases in a State Appellate
    Court: Wisconsin 1839-1959." AMERICAN JOURNAL OF
    LEGAL HISTORY, 9 (2): 95-117, 1965.

    Based on an examination of more than 1,400 opinions
in criminal cases handed down by the Wisconsin Supreme
Court from 1839 to 1959, Kimball explores the following
subjects: (1) the relative place of criminal law business
in the flow of general court business; (2) the individual
and social interests involved in these 1,400 criminal
appeals; and (3) continuities and changes in criminal
justice administration reflected in these appealed cases.

256 Kommers, D. P. "The Emergence of Law and Justice in
    Pre-Territorial Wisconsin." AMERICAN JOURNAL OF
    LEGAL HISTORY, 8 (1): 20-33, 1964.

    Kommers discusses the nature of law and justice in
Wisconsin before it became a territory. He indicates
that the structure of law and justice played a
significant role in disciplining the society and in
influencing the future course of institutional
development, in large part by the opportunity it provided
for men to become increasingly accustomed to the idea of
litigation in courts of law. As Kommers states: "The
evolution of the early judiciary partially represented
man's insatiable longing to be let alone and to get on
with his work."

257 Langbein, J. H. "The Criminal Trial Before the
    Lawyers." UNIVERSITY OF CHICAGO LAW REVIEW, 45 (2):
    263-316, 1978.

    Drawing upon "novel" sources, Langbein explores the
nature of the criminal trial just prior to the
introduction of lawyers in order to better understand the
relatively unique presence of lawyers in American
criminal prosecutions. The examination focuses on state
trials, jury composition, and laws of evidence in the
Continental system and then contrasts that with the
Anglo-American system. The author concludes that the
criminal lawyer and the adversarial system cannot be
defended as part of the American historic common law
bequest.

258 Langbein, J. H. "Understanding the Short History of
    Plea Bargaining." LAW AND SOCIETY REVIEW, 13 (2):
    261-272, 1979.

    Langbein examines the nature of plea bargaining as
it exists today and raises questions regarding its early

English and American origins. He notes that as late as the 18th century, the ordinary jury trial at common law as a judge-dominated, lawyer-free procedure which found plea bargaining to be unnecessary. He suggests that the major nonadversarial jury trials are preferential to adversarial trials.

259 Mather, L. M. "Comments on the History of Plea Bargaining." LAW AND SOCIETY REVIEW, 13 (2): 281-285, 1979.

Mather reviews a number of articles on the rise of plea bargaining in America. In addition, Mather suggests that the changing ideas of punishment and sentencing, and the expansion of the criminal law, provided an equally important contribution to the practice of plea bargaining in the U.S.

260 Mennel, R. M. "Origins of the Juvenile Court: Changing Perspectives on the Legal Rights of Juvenile Delinquents." CRIME AND DELINQUENCY, 18 (1): 68-78, 1972.

Mennel presents a lucid discussion of the origins of the juvenile court in America with special attention to the question of the legal rights of juveniles. He concludes that the origins of the juvenile court must be considered as both the culmination of distrust in custodial institutions and as an attempt to redefine the state's parental role in relation to juveniles.

261 Schultz, J. L. "The Cycle of Juvenile Court History." CRIME AND DELINQUENCY, 19 (4): 457-476, 1973.

Schultz presents an interesting discussion of the "cycle" of juvenile court history. By "cycle," Schultz means that at various periods the juvenile court has been viewed and interpreted differently. The most notable shift in interpretation of the juvenile court and its origins can be found in the works of Platt and Fox, each of whom has written "revisions" of earlier interpretations. Schultz questions this position for overstating claims, ignoring the role of private charities, and overlooking the importance of probation as the keystone of juvenile court reform.

262 Schwartz, H. E. "Demythologizing the Historic Role
    of the Grand Jury." AMERICAN CRIMINAL LAW REVIEW, 10
    (4): 701-770, 1972.

     Schwartz examines the role of the grand jury from a
historical perspective, tracing its development from its
creation under Henry II as part of the conflict between
the Crown and Church over ultimate political power. The
grand jury in its American form is reviewed and found to
have emerged out of equally conflict-ridden times shortly
prior to the Revolution. Citing cases, Schwartz notes
the numerous abuses of the grand jury system, especially
during times of political stress. She concludes by
cataloguing the ways the grand jury has worked as a
shield against political persecutions and how this shield
can be circumvented.

263 Serrill, M. S. "Determinate Sentencing: The History,
    The Theory, The Debate." CORRECTIONS MAGAZINE, 3 (3):
    3-13, 1977.

     Serrill discusses the abuses of discretion in the
criminal justice system and the movement to control its
practice. Proposals for reform and problems of
implementation are presented. The "determinate
sentencing" movement would tightly control discretion as
practiced by prosecutors in choosing charges or plea
bargaining, by judges in sentencing, by judges in
sentencing, by prison administrators in deciding prisoner
treatment methods, and by parole boards in releasing
prisoners. Clear, uniform penalties for all crimes,
prescribed either through legislation or guidelines,
would be adopted. A history of discretion in sentencing
and recent examples of sentencing disparity show that
discretion has often been abused. Sentencing reforms
cited advocate goals such as punishment of the offender
and humanization of correctional institutions, which
would be achieved through "presumptive" sentencing--a
particular sentence for a particular crime.

264 Spindel, D. J. "The Administration of Criminal Jus-
    tice in North Carolina, 1720-1740." AMERICAN JOURNAL
    OF LEGAL HISTORY, 25 (2): 141-162, 1981.

     Spindel explores the administration of justice in
colonial North Carolina from 1720 to 1740, a period
considered to be a transitional period from proprietary
to royal colony. It is a significant starting point for
the study of the criminal justice system. Questions
asked were: Who were the law enforcement personnel?
What crimes were most often and effectively prosecuted?
Who were the defendants? Was there a connection between

sex and social status and the nature of the crimes or
outcome of the trials?   Data were gathered on a total of
525 criminal indictments.   The author concludes that men
of property administered and directed the criminal
justice system and that the class structure of the colony
provided that the criminal justice system should work to
their advantage.

265 Surrency, E. C.   "The Courts in the American Colon-
    ies." AMERICAN JOURNAL OF LEGAL HISTORY, 11 (3-4):
    253-276, 347-376, 1967.

    Patterned after the existing court system in
England, the American colonial courts were initially
established by executive action, although later the
system was formalized by legislation.   Some courts were
created by virtue of rights arising from a large land
grant in which the authority was carried to hold a court
baron.   Surrency notes that a variety of factors led to
the development of courts that exercised similar
jurisdiction in different colonies under different
titles.   This article traces the evolution of the various
colonial courts and their similarities and
dissimilarities.

266 Surrency, E. C.   "Evolution of an Urban Judicial
    System: The Philadelphia Story, 1683-1968." AMERICAN
    JOURNAL OF LEGAL HISTORY, 18 (2):   95-123, 1974.

    This article traces the evolution of the judicial
system in Philadelphia from 1683 to 1968, at which time
constitutional amendments approved in Pennsylvania
significantly changed the structure of the courts in
Philadelphia County, a structure that had remained
largely unchanged for nearly 250 years.   Lessons to be
drawn from the development of this one court system
include first, that changes are difficult to effectuate,
with many reforms easily defeated, and second, that the
importance of the individuals appointed to the bench
should not be neglected.

267 Towne, S. C.   "The Historical Origins of Bench Trial
    for Serious Crime." AMERICAN JOURNAL OF LEGAL HISTO-
    RY, 26 (2): 123-159, 1982.

    Towne points out that little research has been
conducted on the practice of allowing the defendant the
opportunity to demand a bench trial.   Towne also says
that this is very much an American legal invention,
inasmuch as the British legal system has not provided for
bench trials.   She concludes that the history of the

bench trial in America is discontinuous, with the
practice emerging prior to the Revolution, declining, and
then reemerging in the late 19th and early 20th
centuries. She also suggests that the reforms that
brought the bench trial into greater use in the 19th
century also were responsible for the decline of the jury
trial.

268 Wishingrad, J. "The Plea Bargain in Historical Perspective." BUFFALO LAW REVIEW, 23 (Winter): 499-527,
1974.

Through an attempt to isolate the salient forces and
conditions within the criminal law that instigate plea
bargaining, as well as the directly opposed forces that
operate as obstacles to bargaining, Wishingrad describes
the historical development of plea bargaining from early
tribal society, through Anglo-Saxon England, up to the
19th century and the present. He also examines significant American legal decisions between 1804 and 1927.

CHAPTER 6

COURTS - ORGANIZATION

269 Alers, M. S. "Transfer of Jurisdiction from Juvenile to Criminal Court." CRIME AND DELINQUENCY, 19 (4): 519-527, 1973.

Alers' article deals with the standards for transferal of juveniles from juvenile to adult criminal court. She argues that the hearing for transfer should be considered, and treated as, a criminal stage in the juvenile's case. This means that the right to counsel for juveniles must be abided by in any case where a juvenile might be transfered to adult criminal court.

270 Alker, H. R., C. Hosticka, and M. Mitchell. "Jury Selection as a Biased Social Process." LAW AND SOCIETY REVIEW, 11 (1): 9-42, 1976.

The research that provides the basis for this article is an ongoing study of potential biases in the jury selection process in the Eastern Division of the United States District Court, District of Massachusetts. The authors model each stage of the jury selection process in order to identify any biases that may be operating. The findings support claims that jury selection procedures effectively discriminate against the poor, the young, racial minorities, women, and persons with both low and high educational levels. Sources of these biases were found in the use of outdated voter registration lists, unreturned jury questionnaires, and the excuse process. Recommendations for reform are provided.

271 Allenstein, M. B. "The Attorney-Probation Officer Relationship." CRIME AND DELINQUENCY, 16 (2): 181-184, 1970.

Given that lawyers are now much more involved in the juvenile court process, Allenstein explores areas of mutual concern between the attorney and the probation officer, suggesting that these participants have many opportunities to come together to work on common ground.

272 Allison, J. L. "The Lawyer and His Juvenile Court Client." CRIME AND DELINQUENCY, 12 (2): 165-169, 1966.

This article focuses on the role of the lawyer in the juvenile court and his relationship to the juvenile court client. Unlike his criminal court counterpart, the juvenile court lawyer should assume more responsibility for the advocacy of his client. While the role of lawyers in juvenile court proceedings remains ambiguous due to recent court decisions, Allison stresses that the advantages of a lawyer being present outweigh the possible disadvantages.

273 Alpert, L. "Learning About Trial Judging: The Socialization of State Trial Judges." Pp. 105-147, in J. A. Cramer (ed.), COURTS AND JUDGES. Beverly Hills, CA: Sage, 1981.

While the existing literature on the socialization of state trial judges is limited, Alpert draws upon organization behavior theory to conceptualize judicial socialization as involving "the social and psychological adjustment of men to their work settings." Based upon interviews with a number of Florida trial judges, five stages of socialization are identified: pre-bench, initiation, resolution, establishment, and commitment. These stages were then examined against data gathered from questionnaires sent to all Florida circuit judges in 1979. Among the more interesting findings were the observations that the local legal culture and the judge's background experience strongly influence the substance of the learning process. In addition, in spite of the seeming uniformity of socialization, judges are generally on their own in adjusting to the actual trial judging experience.

274 Arens, R., D. D. Granfield, and J. Susman. "Jurors, Jury Charges and Insanity." CATHOLIC UNIVERSITY OF AMERICA LAW REVIEW, 14 (1): 1-28, 1965.

This article expresses concern over the ability of jurors to comprehend instructions made to them regarding insanity, guilt, and burden of proof. Using data drawn from a jury experiment in the District of Columbia (229 students selected from sociology and psychology courses), the authors report that the level of comprehension of charged materials presented to the subjects was low. In the context of the insanity defense, jurors fall back to a jurisprudence all their own when clear-cut guidelines are not provided. They note that the comprehension of instructions seems to vary and depend on the nature of the instructions and their source and that the attitude of the judge toward the rights of the accused and the insanity defense may be instrumental in affecting the jurors' comprehension of instructions.

275 Ares, C. E., A. Rankin, and H. Sturz. "The Manhattan
    Bail Project: An Interim Report on the Use of Pre-
    Trial Parole." NEW YORK UNIVERSITY LAW REVIEW, 38
    (1): 67-92, 1963.

    This paper describes the Manhattan Bail Project
experiment that has become a classic work in the
evaluation of administrative changes within the court
system. The project, sponsored by the Vera Foundation,
was developed to test the premise that many more persons
may be successfully released on bail if selected verified
information concerning their character and ties to the
local community were available during bail determination.
In comparing data collected in 1960 with similar data
collected in the New York City Bail Study in 1956, the
authors conclude that, while little positive change had
occurred between 1956 and 1960, the evidence from the
recent study support the argument for pre-trial release
on the basis of careful screening of defendants.

276 Austin, K. M., and F. R. Speidel. "Thunder: An Alter-
    native to Juvenile Court Appearance." CALIFORNIA
    YOUTH AUTHORITY QUARTERLY, 24 (4): 13-16, 1971.

    The results of this California project suggest that
delinquents can be as effectively treated through group
techniques as with the individual casework approach.
Participants in this program, which utilized short-term
family group counseling, were compared with a group of
juveniles who were handled through court appearances.
Members of the comparison group were placed outside of
their homes more often, required more court petitions to
be filed, and spent a longer average period of time on
probation.

277 Benjamin, R. W., and T. B. Pedeliski. "The Minnesota
    Public Defender System and the Criminal Law Process:
    A Comparative Study of Behavior at the Judicial Dis-
    trict Level." LAW AND SOCIETY REVIEW, 4 (2): 279-
    320, 1969.

    The authors present a discussion of the expansion of
the public defender system between 1966 and 1967 in
Minnesota. This expansion was from the original two
districts to a total of six judicial districts. The
article discusses the effects of this expansion on the
criminal law process in terms of selected criminal
process variables, financial measures, and attitudes of
judicial personnel.

278 Berkson, L. C., S. J. Carbon, and S. W. Hays. MANAG-
ING THE STATE COURTS: TEXT AND READINGS. St. Paul,
MN: West, 1977.

This collection of 41 essays focuses on the routine
nature of day-to-day management of State trial courts and
includes pragmatic and concrete suggestions on how to
update judicial management machinery. The volume begins
with an appraisal of court reform in terms of its
historical and contemporary components. It then focuses
on potential impediments to systemic reform and the
various methods that have been utilized to overcome these
obstacles. Traditional topics of court reform
emphasizing unification and methods of selecting,
disciplining, and training judges are presented in the
ensuing chapters. Personnel who manage State judicial
systems--judges, court administrators, and court clerks--
are analyzed according to their administrative
characteristics, utilization, and methods of operation.
Additional chapters include an extensive discussion of
the means by which individual courts can improve their
managerial techniques, present alternative methods of
juror utilization, analyze budgetary problems, and
suggest various unique methods for their resolution.
Also examined are the uses of technology by the judiciary
and suggestions on ways to improve records, space, and
courthouse management. The final chapter explores two
rapidly developing areas of court management: planning
and evaluation. This book is designed as a principle for
introductory courses, or as a supplemental reader in
advanced classes exploring judicial administration.

279 Brennan, W. C., and J. H. Ware. "The Probation
Officer's Perception of the Attorney's Role in Juvenile Court." CRIME AND DELINQUENCY, 16 (2): 172-180,
1970.

The most significant outcome of the Gault decision
has been the increased use of lawyers in the juvenile
court. This paper evaluates the impact of this change on
the perceptions of thirty-two juvenile probation officers
in St. Louis. The four perception areas examined were:
(1) the nature of the lawyer's participation in the juvenile court; (2) the effects of the lawyer's involvement;
(3) conflict between probation officers and lawyers; and
(4) the resolution of such conflict.

280 Brown, D. W. "Eliminating Exceptions From Jury Duty:
    What Impact Will It Have?" JUDICATURE, 62 (9): 436-
    448, 1979.

    Brown explores the effects of eliminating exceptions
from jury duty in Riverside County, CA. Three questions
guided the research: (1) Did the occupational
composition of juries change with the removal of specific
occupational exemptions?; (2) Did the new composition of
the juries produce changes in jury decision?; and (3)
Were juries under the new system of no exceptions more
representative of the community? The findings indicate
that occupation makeup did change, that there were no
differences in jury acquittals, and that the age and sex
composition of juries did reflect the adult population.

281 Canon, B. C. "The Impact of Formal Selection Proces-
    ses on the Characteristics of Judges." LAW AND SOC-
    IETY REVIEW, 6 (4): 579-594, 1972.

    Canon explores the effects of the occupational
selection process on the characteristics of judges and
suggests that these background factors are indicative of
judges' decision-making behavior.   Selection or
recruitment patterns are divided into two main forms,
formal rule-structured processes and informal processes
shaped by less rigid norms or traditions. The author
concludes that institutional mechanisms in the
recruitment process have much less of an impact on
personal characteristics than anticipated.

282 Carp, R. A. "The Behavior of Grand Juries: Acquiesc-
    ence or Justice." SOCIAL SCIENCE QUARTERLY, 55 (4):
    853-870, 1975.

    Carp examines the behavior of grand juries utilizing
a participant observer methodology. The data were
derived from three sources: participant observation of
the 177th District Court Grand Jury (Houston) in-depth
interviews with former members of Harris County (Houston)
grand juries; and 156 questionnaires from persons who had
served on the Harris County grand juries from 1969 to
1972. The analysis focuses on two substantive questions:
(1) What are the distinguishing characteristics of grand
jury behavior? (2) How are the basic behavioral characteristics of the grand jury to be accounted for? Carp
concludes that the behavior leans toward a rapid
processing of cases with little deliberation. Such
dynamics seem to be accounted for by the type of people
who become grand jurors, their lack of training and
preparation, pressures of a heavy caseload, and legal

factors which allow for the prosecutor to dominate the grand jury proceedings.

283 Casper, J. D., D. Brereton, and D. Neal. "The Cali-
    fornia Determinate Sentence Law." CRIMINAL LAW
    BULLETIN, 19 (5): 405-433, 1983.

    Casper et al. examine the determinate sentencing law that went into effect in California in 1977. Focusing on the effects of the new law in three counties, the authors assess the effects of the law on prison commitment rates, rate and timing of guilty pleas, and its integration into the existing plea bargaining process. They conclude that, while short term effects are noticed, it is not clear if the law has caused substantial change in either sentencing patterns or the disposition process.

284 Casper, J. D. "Having Their Day in Court: Defendant
    Evaluations of the Fairness of Their Treatment." LAW
    AND SOCIETY REVIEW, 12 (2): 237-251, 1978.

    Little research has examined the defendant's view of court experiences. Casper's paper fills this gap. Casper analyzes the correlates of defendants' judgments about fairness. These correlates fall into two types: predispositions and case-specific variables. While both are related to perceptions of treatment, the latter type is the stronger of the two. Casper notes that a defendant's sense of equity is most strongly related to his sense of fair treatment. By limiting discretion and increasing consistency in sentencing, defendants convicted of similar offenses would be more satisfied in their sense of justice.

285 Champion, D. J. "The Organization of Trial Judges."
    Pp. 59-76 in J. A. Cramer (ed.), COURTS AND JUDGES.
    Beverly Hills, CA: Sage, 1981

    Champion examines the state trial court and its organization. His analysis focuses on a variety of court organization models: the "traditional model" (Texas); Pound's "simplified model"; two American Bar Association models based on the Pound structure; and a model designed for counties of more moderate size (Knox County, TN). The problems of the primary functions of trial court judges and their selection are discussed and suggestions made based on ABA judicial selection proposals.

286 Church, T. W., Jr. "Plea Bargains, Concessions and
    the Courts: Analysis of a Quasi-Experiment." LAW AND
    SOCIETY REVIEW, 10 (3): 377-402, 1976

    This paper is an examination of the impact of the
selective elimination of one form of plea bargaining on
the court system of a large suburban county in the
Midwest. With the election of a new prosecutor, a new
get-tough on drugs policy was implemented. This policy
initially involved no plea bargaining in any case where
the defendant was charged with the sale of a controlled
substance. Within the next two years, armed robbery and
carrying a concealed weapon were added to the "no-
reduction" policy. Data were analyzed on all drug sale
cases charged in the county in 1972. There was a clear
drop in the proportion of guilty pleas, but the potential
drop was mediated because judges began to take up the
role of "concession giver" abandoned by the prosecutor.
As a partial consequence, the pattern of "judge shopping"
increased.

287 Church, T. W., Jr. "Who Sets the Pace of Litigation
    in Urban Trial Courts?" JUDICATURE, 65 (2): 76-85,
    1981.

    Data for this study on the delay of criminal court
case processing were collected from the Wayne County
(Detroit) Prosecuting Attorney's Office case files and
questionnaires administered   to judges, assistant district attorneys and defense attorneys in four cities (New
York, Detroit, Miami, and Pittsburgh). The findings were
compared to the National Center for State Courts'
Pretrial Delay Project findings. The data suggest that
the local legal culture and its link to the speed of case
processing is the primary impediment to reducing delay in
the courts. To the extent that court participants find
the pace of case processing satisfactory, change is not
likely.

288 Cohen, M. "Lawyers and Political Careers." LAW AND
    SOCIETY REVIEW, 3 (4): 563-574, 1969.

    Cohen documents the importance of careers of public
office holding among lawyers and suggests that among
those that enter politics, the majority become
careerists. Cohen provides an explanation of this phenomenon by integrating propositions from two theoretical
approaches: visibility theory and availability theory.

289 Cox, S. "Lawyers in the Juvenile Court." CRIME AND
    DELINQUENCY, 13 (4): 488-493, 1967.

    Cox discusses the concept of the "right to counsel"
as it has been tied to the juvenile court. After
reviewing the background of the Gault decision, he
examines the effects of the intrusion of counsel into the
juvenile justice process. Among the more significant
consequences is the impact on prehearing custody policies
resulting in a great reduction in juveniles committed to
institutions. Finally, as the use of lawyers in juvenile
cases has increased, so has the backlog of cases in the
juvenile court. However, Cox argues that this backlog
should not detract from the important legal safeguards
that are available to juveniles.

290 Cramer, J. A. "Judicial Supervision of the Guilty
    Plea Hearing." Pp. 173-195 in J. A. Cramer (ed.),
    COURTS AND JUDGES, Beverly Hills, CA: Sage, 1981.

    A major criticism of the plea bargaining process is
that due process and the rights of the defendant are not
as clearly protected as in a trial situation. Critics
argue that it is the responsibility of the judge to
oversee the guilty plea hearing and to apply appropriate
standards, rules of criminal procedure, and case law in
this effort. To examine the extent to which such
supervision is provided in plea bargains, a two-phase,
three-year study was conducted. The data included
interviews, court simulations, and in-court observations
of guilty plea hearings. Four major questions are
addressed: (1) Did the court inquire about the factual
basis of the guilty plea? (2) Did the court determine
that the plea was entered with understanding and on a
voluntary basis? (3) Did the court inform the defendant
of the consequences of his plea? and (4) Was an in-court
record made of the specific plea agreement between the
prosecutor and defense? The findings showed that in
nearly one-half of the cases, the plea hearing took less
than three minutes; that a great deal of variation exists
among jurisdictions; and that a sizeable number of judges
operate in only a perfunctory manner.

291 Dawson, R. O. THE DECISION AS TO TYPE, LENGTH, AND
    CONDITIONS OF THE SENTENCE. THE REPORT OF THE AMERI-
    CAN BAR FOUNDATION'S SURVEY OF THE ADMINISTRATION OF
    CRIMINAL JUSTICE IN THE UNITED STATES. Boston:
    Little, Brown, 1969.

    This book presents procedural aspects of criminal
justice administration that occur after conviction of
crime, including the granting of probation and parole.

The process that begins with the sentence involves a number of interrelated decisions and a number of different decision-makers. Exercise of discretionary power and methods of control used to ensure against abuse, especially in the correctional process, are emphasized. Methods of obtaining presentence information and ensuring its accuracy are discussed. The judicial choice between probation and prison and the determination of the length of sentence are examined. An overview of the probation system is provided, and factors that influence the parole decision and probation and parole revocation are discussed. A discussion of the relation between the correctional process and the legal system and corrections of the future concludes the volume.

292 Dill, F. "Discretion, Exchange and Social Control: Bail Bondsmen in Criminal Courts." LAW AND SOCIETY REVIEW, 9 (4): 639-674, 1975.

After providing a general discussion of the history and functions of bail in the criminal court, Dill argues that the bail bondsman plays a primary and very functional role in the handling of pre-trial decisions. Court officials often turn to the bail bondsman for informal cooperation in managing the population of arrested persons.

293 Eisenstein, J., and H. Jacob. FELONY JUSTICE: AN ORGANIZATIONAL ANALYSIS OF CRIMINAL COURT. Boston: Little, Brown, 1977.

The theoretical framework of felony courts; felony dispositions in Baltimore, Chicago, and Detroit; and stages of the felony disposition process are discussed. Felony courts in Baltimore, Chicago, and Detroit were selected for study because their original interest was in plea bargaining. They determined that these cities had quite different procedures for negotiating pleas and used them to varying extents. The authors outline in detail the organizational model that provides the alternative perspective for their understanding of the felony disposition process. This perspective is supported by using observations and interviews for each of the three cities. Methods used for collecting and analyzing data are discussed. Preliminary hearing courtroom workgroups are examined, and an analysis of trial workgroups as they choose between plea negotiations and trials is offered. There is an analysis of the ways that punishment results from invocation of the felony disposition process. The authors note the differences in process and outcome of the trials of defendants accused of the same crime in the separate cities studied. Suggestions and general directions for reform are given.

294 Erlanger, H. S. "Jury Research in America." LAW AND
    SOCIETY REVIEW, 4 (3): 345-370, 1970.

    In this significant compilation of research on jury
behavior, Erlanger reviews the increasingly large body of
social science research over a 45 year period. The focus
of his analysis of the existing research is on the
issues of the competence of jury members and the
representiveness of persons selected to the jury.

295 Ferster, E. Z., and T. F. Courtless. "Intake Process
    in the Affluent County Juvenile Court." HASTINGS LAW
    JOURNAL, 22 (5): 1127-1153, 1971.

    Criteria and procedures for intake decisions are
discussed, as is evaluation of them in light of the
purposes of intake in the juvenile process. Communities
use different criteria to determine the cases subject to
informal disposition. The purpose of the intake
screening process is to determine whether the juvenile
court has jurisdiction, whether there is sufficient
evidence, and whether there is a sufficiently serious
offense involved. Another function performed by the
intake officer is the determination of whether referral
of the case for formal adjudication is in the best
interests of the child. The article discusses a court
decision in which the lack of specific intake criteria in
juvenile court laws was being challenged. The authors
examined the records of both formal and informal
dispositions. It was concluded that intake units, in
general, and in affluent counties, have no difficulty in
making appropriate decisions about the court's
jurisdiction and lack of evidence, but the decision-
making process is more complex when "seriousness" and
disposition are the problems.

296 Fishman, J. J. "The Social and Occupational Mobility
    of Prosecutors: New York City." Pp. 239-254 in W.
    F. McDonald (ed.), THE PROSECUTOR. Beverly Hills,
    CA: Sage, 1979.

    Fishman examines the screening process applied to
the legal profession. Data were gathered from New York
City prosecutors' offices in Kings and Bronx Counties in
1971 and 1978. Fishman concludes that the legal
profession is highly stratified and has limited mobility.
Assistant prosecutors in New York are found to be young,
white males of Catholic or Jewish background, second or
third generation Americans, have attended local law
schools, and come from lower socioeconomic origins. It
is noted that the emergence of a criminal justice/civil
service career line is likely to lock these prosecutors

into their positions for a longer time and they will
become, essentially, criminal justice civil servants.

297 Franklin, J., and D. C. Gibbons. "New Directions for
    Juvenile Courts: Probation Officers' Views." CRIME
    AND DELINQUENCY, 19 (4): 508-518, 1973.

     This article focuses on probation officers'
attitudes toward a variety of issues of due process for
juveniles and limitations on the scope and powers of
juvenile courts. The authors were interested in the
extent to which court workers were receptive to
alterations in court activities as a result of major
Supreme Court decisions (e.g., Gault and Winship). Data
for the study were collected from a probation office in a
large, metropolitan city in the Pacific Northwest.
Comparisons were made between the twenty-five non-
supervisory employees included in the study. In general,
very positive attitudes were expressed by the probation
officers and few differences were noted between social
workers and persons with other training or between
supervisors and other workers.

298 Fried, M., K. J. Kaplan, and K. W. Klein. "Juror
    Selection: An Analysis of Voir Dire." Pp. 49-66 in
    R. J. Simon (ed.), THE JURY SYSTEM IN AMERICA: A
    CRITICAL OVERVIEW. Beverly Hills, CA: Sage, 1975.

     This article examines the contradictory goals of
attorneys and prosecutors and how they affect the
selection and influence of prospective jurors. A
psychological model is developed to describe this process
based on the following: (1) juror's prior susceptibility
to conformity pressure; (2) juror predisposition to side
with authority; (3) juror openness of cognitive set; (4)
juror perception of the weight of evidence; and (5) juror
criteria for conviction.

299 Gallas, E. C., and E. C. Friesen. MANAGING THE COURTS.
    New York: Bobbs-Merrill, 1972.

     This book examines managerial and administrative
aspects of court operation. The specialized profession
of management has developed to meet the needs of
business, and many of its principles can be applied
within the judicial context. The authors provide an
overview of court structure and functions, pointing out
the similarities and differences between courts and
businesses. In order to facilitate the operation of the
courts, it is necessary to apply the principles of modern
management. A recent development has been the appearance
of professional court executives; they are nonlawyers

especially trained as professional managers to function within the courts. The functions of these court executives are identified. Suggestions are made for further professionalization of their work, as well as that of other personnel involved in the judicial process. Constraints on management which arise from the limited financial powers of courts are explored, and ways for the court executive to deal with these situations are suggested. Automated information systems are analyzed and offered as a viable means for improving court efficiency.

300 Gillespie, R. "An Analysis of the Allocation of
    Judicial Resources: The Illinois Experience." JOUR-
    NAL OF CRIMINAL JUSTICE, 3 (3): 207-216, 1975.

    This article is a quantitative analysis of the allocation of judicial services in the 21 circuit courts of Illinois. Judicial services is defined in terms of the provision of judgeships. Questions are raised as to whether the overall allocations are adequate and whether the allocation among the 21 circuits is consistent with the demand within each circuit. Gillespie concludes that serious misallocations exist, with the most urbanized circuit having too few judges while the other circuits have an excess. The basis for this misallocation is examined.

301 Glen, J. E. "Bifurcated Hearings in the Juvenile
    Court." CRIME AND DELINQUENCY, 16 (3): 255-263,
    1970.

    Glen examines the nature and procedures of the juvenile court in terms of the adjudication and disposition processes. Noting the problems of permitting certain dispositional functions to occur before the end of the adjudicaiton process, Glen argues that these two processes should be separated as in adult proceedings.

302 Glick, H. R. "The Judicial 'Firm': A Useful Model
    for Understanding Decision-Making in a Juvenile
    Court." JUDICATURE, 63 (7): 328-337, 1980.

    The American criminal trial courts and their juvenile court counterparts do not operate according to their textbook and television image. Rather, they tend to be organized around a fairly stable set of working roles and relationships. This article focuses on the ways a juvenile court organization interacts in processing cases and then suggests how certain facets of organization theory may be applicable to the juvenile court process. The author explains that, as a consequence of (except for the judges) the same few personnel having worked together for a number of years, the juvenile court is best a "firm" where the main features are: high goal compatibility, high consistency of participants, limited resource allocation to individual decisions, and norms against redistribution that may upset future work relationships.

303 Goddard, J. M., and L. A. Budd. "Volunteer Services in a Juvenile Court." CRIME AND DELINQUENCY, 13 (2): 344-351, 1967.

Based on the experiences of Lane County (Eugene) Juvenile Court, the authors discussed procedures for the recruitment and training of juvenile court volunteers. A number of advantages from the utilizaiton of volunteers were noted. Among them were: complementing the limited numbers of qualified staff, expanding the professional repertoire, providing sustained relationships, and educating the community.

304 Goldkamp, J. S. "Philadelphia Revisited: An Examination of Bail and Detention Two Decades After Foote." CRIME AND DELINQUENCY, 26 (2): 179-192, 1980.

Goldkamp compares two studies of bail and detention in Philadelphia. The first study, Caleb Foote's 1954 examination of the purposes behind bail decisions and the abuses that tended to go with such decisions, not only outlined numerous problems but made recommendations for improving bail practices. The second study, in which Goldkamp analyzes bail practices in Philadelphia in 1977, concludes that, while many of the major reforms suggested by Foote have been implemented, three issues have been left unresolved. These three issues have to do with excessive discretion practiced by judges, disparities in bail decisions, and the negative effects on defendants produced by bail decisions. This last issue, in which defendants not released on bail receive more severe sentences, is cited as of utmost concern for future research.

305 Goldstein, H. "Trial Judges and the Police: Their Relationships in the Administration of Criminal Justice." CRIME AND DELINQUENCY, 14 (1): 14-26, 1968.

Goldstein argues that the overriding concern for protecting the neutrality of the courts has created a vacuum between the trial courts and the police, thus hampering their working relationship. Coordination between these two segments of the criminal justice

system must be achieved in areas such as the scheduling
of court business, station house bail, issuance of arrest
and search warrants, and review of police practices
involving evidence and due process. As a step in
facilitating the improvement of this working
relationship, Goldstein recommends that an intermediary--
the prosecutor--be used as the contact between trial
judges and police.

306 Henderson, T. A., R. Guynes, and C. Baar. "Organiza-
    tional Design For Courts." Pp. 19-58 in J. A. Cramer
    (ed.), COURTS AND JUDGES. Beverly Hills, CA: Sage,
    1981.

    The authors examine the judiciary from an
organizational theory perspective and evaluate efforts to
improve court performance through changes in management
structures. Two technologies were identified as basic to
the core operation of the courts: mediating, essential
for the adjudication process; and intensive, characteristic of the sentencing process, juvenile courts, and
family courts. The authors conclude that no single
organizational design is most appropriate for all
circumstances, nor all parts of the court as a complex
organization. The organizational design must be
evaluated in terms of its utility in reducing uncertainty
in a way that reinforces the purposes of the court.

307 Hoffman, P. B., and L. K. DeGostin. "An Argument for
    Self-Imposed Explicit Judicial Sentencing Standards."
    JOURNAL OF CRIMINAL JUSTICE, 3 (3): 195-206, 1975.

    Hoffman and DeGostin argue for the development of
judicial sentencing guidelines along the lines of those
previously created for the United States Board of
Parole. The model that they propose would structure and
control judicial discretion at the district or circuit
level without completly removing individual case
consideration.

308 Houlden, P. "Impact of Procedural Modifications on
    Evaluations of Plea Bargaining." LAW AND SOCIETY
    REVIEW, 15 (2): 267-292, 1980-81.

    This discussion of plea bargaining is based on an
experiment conducted to assess the preferences of
undergraduates and inmates on two possible modifications
of plea bargaining. The two modifications were: allowing
the defendant to participate in the bargaining and the
inclusion of a paid or volunteer mediator in the
negotiations. Using a role-playing technique, Houlden
found that "defendants" preferred plea bargaining

procedures that included the defendant. Specific interactions between the two defendant categories and two modifications are then discussed.

309 Jacob, H. "Keeping Pace: Court Resources and Crime in Ten U.S. Cities." JUDICATURE, 66 (2): 73-83, 1982.

Rising crime rates, increased caseloads, and increased plea-bargaining in the criminal courts have all been tied in some manner to the inadequate allocation of resources to the courts. Jacob questions the assumption that court resources have not kept up with caseloads and examines the relationships between arrest rate, case backlog, police expenditures, and court resources in ten American cities. He notes that, while crime rates rose sharply over the last three decades, allocation of court resources increased more rapidly than did the inflow of new cases. Despite the increase in resources, case processing appeared to have lagged behind the inflow of cases. Various political and social explanations for this situation are explored.

310 Jacoby, J.E. "The Charging Policies of Prosecutors." Pp. 75-97 in F. McDonald (ed.), THE PROSECUTOR. Beverly Hills, CA: Sage, 1979.

Jacoby believes that the best way to understand the nature of prosecutorial policy is to understand the nature of the prosecutor. All prosecutorial policy is made within the boundaries of the three distinct roles of the prosecutor: the legal, the bureaucratic, and the political. This article examines the connection between prosecutorial policy and the disposition of individual decisions that represent that policy. Assuming that policy implies the existence of a value system, Jacoby looks at the outcomes of different policies as products of discretionary choice.

311 Kasunic, D. E. "One Day/One Trial: A Major Improvement in the Jury System." JUDICATURE, 67 (2): 78-86, 1983.

As a response to numerous problems associated with lengthy jury panel service, the concept of the One Day/One Trial Jury System was developed. Now, instead of being summoned to serve up to 30 days or more, jurors not selected to hear a case on the day they are summoned will be excused. This system is being used widely throughout the country and has met with positive changes in juror attitudes about the court, a more representative cross-section of the community, and money saved as a result of greater productivity.

312 Keiter, R.B.   "Criminal or Delinquent?:   A Study of
     Juvenile Cases Transferred to the Criminal Court."
     CRIME AND DELINQUENCY, 19 (4): 528-538, 1973.

     In Illinois statutory powers authorize the state's attorney extensive discretion in decisions about the transferring of juvenile offenders to adult criminal court.   The present study examines 67 juvenile cases transferred from the Cook County Juvenile Court to the Criminal Court in 1970 to detect variations in decisions. Variables examined in this all male sample included age, ethnic group, type of charge, past record, and gang involvement.   Keiter   concluded that while the state's attorney uses his discretion within the context of the criteria, there are occasions in which the goals of public policy intrude and override such criteria.

313 Kelley, T. M., J.L. Schulman and K. Lynch. "Decentra-
     lized Intake and Diversion: The Juvenile Court's Link
     to the Youth Service Bureau." JUVENILE JUSTICE,   27
     (1): 3-11, 1976.

     The effectiveness of a Wayne County program is measured according to its success in preventing recidivism and minimizing system penetration for project youth through placement in individually tailored multi-modal treatment plans.   Existing community services, youth service center resources, as well as direct individual and family counseling services were combined in action agreements designed to meet the special needs of each client type.   Compared to a control group of similar cases, the treatment group had significantly fewer official court contacts, fewer officially adjudicated delinquents, more case dismissed dispositions, and fewer institutional commitments.

314 Kessler, J.B.   "The Social Psychology of Jury Deliber-
     ations."   Pp.   69-93 in J. Simon (ed.), THE JURY
     SYSTEM IN AMERICA. Beverly Hills, CA: Sage, 1975.

     Kessler summarizes general small group research on jury deliberations and critiques the various methodologies involved.   Such research has included an examination of the types of stimuli as well as types of juror subjects, analysis of videotaped jury trials and mock jury experiments. In addition, many studies have examined the process of deliberations while other studies have focused on the products of such deliberations.   The lack of a consistent body of research literature leads

Kessler to conclude that a formalized theory of jury or even small group behavior is difficult to develop.

315 Kratcoski, P.C., and F. Hernandez. "The Application of Management Principles to the Juvenile Court System." JUVENILE JUSTICE, 25 (3): 39-44, 1974.

The juvenile court process in Summit County, Ohio is described. The management principles in use include resource utilization and planning for the needs of client and community. This court's philosophy is that juveniles should be diverted from the juvenile justice system. If that is not possible, the court strives to minimize penetration into the system through the widespread use of diversion projects. These diversion projects include referrals to private and public agencies, shelter homes, and volunteer counseling. In the case of recidivists, the intake screening process is intensified, but every effort is made to minimize involvement in the system.

316 Langley, M. H. "The Juvenile Court: The Making of a Delinquent." LAW AND SOCIETY REVIEW, 7 (2): 273-298, 1972.

Historically, the juvenile court has been viewed from two basic perspectives. The first sees the juvenile court as a model for youth rehabilitation and development. The second presents the juvenile court as a model for social control of youths. Langley examines data to see to what extent one juvenile court was able to implement the concept of individualized treatment in the processing of juveniles. He concludes that, while the individualized treatment function is clearly being achieved, there are still problems in the juvenile court with regard to equal provision of juvenile court services along race and class lines.

317 Langley, M. H., H. R. Graves, and B. Norris. "The Juvenile Court and Individualized Treatment." CRIME AND DELINQUENCY, 18 (1): 79-92, 1972.

One of the major functions of the juvenile court is to provide individualized treatment for the juvenile offender. However, the achievement of this goal is frequently questioned. This article examines 229 juveniles committed to a state training school in Tennessee. The time frame for the study covered a four year period to enable the researchers to assess the impact of the Gault decision on juvenile court operations. Their findings suggested that high rates of prehearing detention occurred regardless of the seriousness of the offense, that there was no evidence of racial bias, and that nearly half of the youths were committed to institutions without the services of a lawyer or a recommendation by a probation officer. The authors conclude on a critical note by suggesting radical alterations in the basic juvenile court organization.

318 Lagoy, S. P., F. A. Hussey, and J. H. Kramer. "The Prosecutorial Function and Its Relation to Determinate Sentencing Structures." Pp. 209-237 in W. F. McDonald (ed.), THE PROSECUTOR. Beverly Hills, CA: Sage, 1979.

While the prosecutor's role in the sentencing process has been examined in some limited research, that role within different sentencing structures has been ignored. The authors contend that under traditional sentencing structures, the primary concern of the prosecutor is to maintain efficiency in processing. With the extensive sentencing reform efforts of the past decade has come an increase in the power of the prosecutor, especially in relationship to the sentencing process. The statutory framework of the "new" determinate sentencing structures and the consequent impact on prosecutor role are examined for Maine, Illinois, Indiana, and California.

319 Levine, A. G., and C. Schweber-Koren. "Jury Selection in Erie County: Changing a Sexist System." LAW AND SOCIETY REVIEW, 11 (1): 43-56, 1976.

The authors discuss the sexual bias found in the Erie County, New York, jury selection process and attempt to eliminate this bias from the system. It was not until after the Attica Prison riot and subsequent attempts to ensure fair trials for prison inmates indicted for participation in the prison riot that systematic "woman's exemptions" were discovered in the jury selection process. By working with lawyers and social scientists to reform the local procedures, a new process that would more closely resemble the composition of the local community was achieved.

320 Long, L. "Innovation in Urban Criminal Misdemeanor Courts."Pp.173-206 In Herbert Jacob (ed.), THE POTENTIAL FOR REFORM OF CRIMINAL JUSTICE. Beverly Hills, CA: Sage, 1974.

Long focuses on the criminal misdemeanor courts in all American cities with populations of 100,000 or more. Questionnaires were sent in 1971 to the chief judge of each court requesting data about court operations.

Questions also were asked about a variety of court innovations and whether any of those listed had been attempted in their court. Based on a second questionnaire sent to 80 criminal justice experts, 36 specific court innovations were evaluated in terms of the degree of innovation for introduction into a criminal misdemeanor court. Findings suggest that most courts are similar in operations, that innovations in professionalizing court personnel have not progressed very far, and that the best predictors of innovativeness were the amount and quality of court interaction with LEAA-related agencies, city size, and level of police personnel organization.

321 Mather, L. M. "The Outsider in the Courtroom: An Alternative Role for Defense." Pp. 263-289 in H. Jacob (ed.), THE POTENTIAL FOR REFORM OF CRIMINAL JUSTICE, Beverly Hills, CA: 1974.

Mather suggests that the frequently described role of the defense attorney is one who is a passive cooperator who must operate within organizational parameters informally set by the court. However, an alternative role based on the adversary model, Mather contends, may be more accurate. Data were derived from extensive observations and interviews during a two year period (1970-71) in the Los Angeles Superior Court. Discussion focuses on the decision-making process of the defense attorney on the matter of a trial versus a plea of guilty. It was concluded that the cooperative role for defense did indeed dominate the court studied, but that such a role did not prescribe plea bargaining in every case. Defense attorneys would, on occasion, utilize the adversarial role when it was the only way to protect the clients' interests. Finally, Mather discusses the "maverick" public defender role occupied by those few attorneys who consistently engaged in the adversarial relationship.

322 McCune, S. D., and D. L. Skoler. "Juvenile Court Judges in the United States--Part I: A National Profile." CRIME AND DELINQUENCY, 11 (2): 121-131, 1965.

This article offers an in-depth profile of juvenile court judges across the United States. Based on over 1,560 responses, the authors found that among the more salient characteristics of this segment of the judiciary were that juvenile court judges are generally part-time; have "inadequate" professional training for the juvenile court; operate under difficult caseloads; are inadequately compensated; and are predominately older males.

323 McDonald, W. F. "The Prosecutor's Domain." Pp. 15-
     51 in W. F. McDonald (ed.), THE PROSECUTOR. Beverly
     Hills, CA: Sage, 1979.

     McDonald provides a framework for understanding the
role of the prosecutor in the criminal justice system.
However, instead of focusing on the "role" of the
prosecutor, McDonald suggests that it is more appropriate
to utilize the concept of "domain" which is not as fixed
and final. The domain of the prosecutor, then, is
analyzed in terms of the historical influences on it,
regional variations, and the relationship of changes in
the prosecutor's domain to changes in the wider criminal
justice system and the conflicts involved in such
changes.

324 McDonald, W. F., H. H. Rossman, and J. A. Cramer.
     "The Prosecutor's Plea Bargaining Decisions." Pp.
     151-208 in W. F. McDonald (ed.), THE PROSECUTOR.
     Beverly Hills, CA: Sage, 1979.

     Using a plea bargaining simulation experiment,
observations, and interviews with court personnel, the
authors examine the following questions: (1) Are certain
factors relevant to all plea bargains?; (2) How much of
an impact do specific factors have?; (3) Do their
respective impacts vary under different conditions?; (4)
Do prosecutors evaluate cases differently from defense
counsel?; and (5) How consistent is plea bargaining? The
strength of the case and the seriousness of the crime are
given special attention. Findings support earlier
studies that suggest the adversarial nature of plea
bargaining; however the authors note that their results
do not answer the question of whether plea bargaining
should be abolished.

325 Mileski, M. "Courtroom Encounters: An Observation
     Study of Lower Criminal Courts." LAW AND SOCIETY
     REVIEW, 5 (4): 473- 538, 1971.

     Mileski examines the lower criminal trial court as
a formal organization. She suggests that the processing
of defendants through court may be seen as a simple task
for court personnel in which the defendant is viewed as a
deviant if he or she does not conform to routine
expectations of the court. A defendant who disrupts the
court routine is subject to the moral exigencies of the
court itself. The article focuses on the court as a
business or an industry dealing with goods supplied by
the police. A number of features of the police-court
relationship also are examined.

326 Miller, F. W. PROSECUTION--THE DECISION TO CHARGE A
    SUSPECT WITH A CRIME. Chicago: American Bar Founda-
    tion, 1970.

    This text discusses the involvement of the
prosecutor in relation to the following: the decision to
charge; evidence required to charge; judicial involvement
in and review of the decision to charge; and discretion
and the charging decision. The decision to charge
requires the resolution of three related, but
independently important, issues. First, there must be a
determination of whether there is sufficient probability
of guilt to justify subjecting the suspect to a trial. A
judgment must be made about whether a jury will be likely
to acquit, either because they are unlikely to be
convinced of the guilt of the suspect, or for other
reasons unrelated to the likelihood of guilt. Second,
the prosecutor may conclude that prosecution is not in
the community interest. In that event, he must choose
between release and pursuing some alternative other than
criminal prosecution. Third, if a decision is made to
prosecute, the specific crime(s) with which the person is
to be charged must be selected. This may be influenced
by considerations of sentencing probabilities, ability to
secure guilty pleas, and the prosecutor's conclusion
about both the individual's and the community's
interests.

327 Nagel, S. S. "Judicial Backgrounds and Criminal
    Cases." JOURNAL OF CRIMINAL LAW, CRIMINOLOGY &
    POLICE SCIENCE, 53 (3): 333-339, 1962.

    Nagel studies the relationship between background
characteristics of judges and their decision making in
criminal cases. The data for the analysis were drawn
from 313 state and federal supreme court judges listed in
the 1955 Directory of American Judges and all of the
full-court criminal cases heard by these judges during
1955. Background characteristics included variables such
as political party affiliation, membership in "pressure"
groups, prior occupation, education, age, religion,
nationality, and liberal attitude score. Analysis of the
effects of each on case decision-making were provided
with a discussion of the implications.

328 Neubauer, D. W. "After the Arrest: The Charging
    Decision in Prairie City." LAW AND SOCIETY REVIEW, 8
    (3): 495-518, 1974.

    Neubauer examines the participants in the charging
decision (police, victim, and judge), the standards used
in evaluating cases for possible prosecution, and the
impact of these arrangements in Prairie City in 1970.

The State's Attorney dominated the charging decision but
operated more from a position of judgment rather than
from one of discretion.

329 Newman, D. J. CONVICTION--THE DETERMINATION OF GUILT
     OR INNOCENCE WITHOUT TRIAL. Chicago: American Bar
     Foundation, 1966.

     Newman describes the nontrial adjudication
practices--the guilty plea and the acquittal of the
guilty--in Kansas, Michigan, and Wisconsin. The
following are discussed: the guilty plea process,
including plea bargaining; trial judge discretion in
acquitting or reducing charges against defendants; trial
judge discretion in acquitting or reducing charges
against defendants; trial judge use of his acquittal
power to control other parts of the criminal justice
system; and the role of the defense counsel, particularly
in plea bargaining. Newman argues that all these
processes are characterized by informality and wide
variation in practices. He suggests that more attention
be given to these informal processes because of their
significant use in the criminal justice system.

330 Nietzel, M. T., and R. C. Dillehay. "The Effects of
     Variations in Voir Dire Procedures in Capital Murder
     Trials." LAW AND HUMAN BEHAVIOR, 6 (1): 1-13, 1982.

     The authors note that the use of psychologists and
social scientists in the courtroom is rapidly increasing.
One particular area of this increase is in jury
selection. However, they also note that there is
relatively little empirical data that would demonstrate
that expert assistance in jury selection has had desired
effects on jury verdicts. Nietzel and Dillehay suggest
three problems with existing research. First, there is
little "outcome data" on the effects of jury selection.
Second, most of the data have been derived from "mock" or
simulated jury experiments. And third, there is a gap
between psychologist's recommendations on the best
technique and the empirical data supportive of such a
recommendation. The authors examine transcripts and
notes from thirteen capital cases in Kentucky between
1975 and 1980. Techniques of jury selection were
classified as follows: questioning by judge and
attorneys of individual jurors sequestered from one
another; questioning by judge and attorneys of the panel
en masse, followed by questions to sequestered individual
jurors; questioning by judge and attorneys of the panel
en masse, supplemented with individual questions to
nonsequestered jurors; and questioning by judge and
attorneys of the panel en masse in open court. The
authors conclude that bias of potential jurors is best

identified when venire persons are questioned while
individually sequestered.

331 Nimmer, R. T. "Judicial Reform: Informal Processes
    and Competing Effects." Pp. 207-234 in H. Jacob (ed.),
    THE POTENTIAL FOR REFORM OF CRIMINAL JUSTICE.
    Beverly Hills, CA: Sage, 1974.

    Nimmer argues that judicial reform attempts are
often defeated or minimized because they assume as
relevant the adversary-adjudicatory model of criminal
justice, the failure to produce change in practice, and
their frequent creation of unexpected and objectionable
results. A specific examination of a single reform
effort--the omnibus hearing--as implemented in the
Federal District Court in San Diego is presented.

332 Noyes, A. D. "Has Gault Changed the Juvenile Court
    Concept?" CRIME AND DELINQUENCY, 16 (2): 158-162,
    1970.

    Noyes says that the 1967 Gault decision has resulted
in a transformation of the juvenile court in which due
process of law has come to mean a criminal proceeding for
juveniles. He argues that juveniles need more than the
bare minimum of legal rights accorded to adults. Rather,
the juvenile court should act as an advocate and
protector of juveniles based on the concept of parens
patriae. Noyes believes that the Gault decision has
significantly weakened the juvenile court process.

333 O'Donnell, H., D. E. Curtin, and M. J. Churgin.
    TOWARD A JUST AND EFFECTIVE SENTENCING SYSTEM--
    AGENDA FOR LEGISLATIVE REFORM. New York: Praeger,
    1977.

    Topics of discussion include Federal sentencing,
parole, probation, and related correctional problems. A
sentencing strategy is proposed to ensure effectiveness
and fairness. Against the backdrop of legislative
indifference, judicial neglect, and administrative
uncertainty, the authors develop a sentencing scheme to
address the following three documented flaws in the
Federal sentencing process: lack of legislatively
prescribed sentencing criteria; inadequate trial and
appellate court procedures to ensure rationality and
fairness and to lessen sentencing disparities; and a
dearth of information about all aspects of the
sentencing, parole, and corrections processes. The
authors propose a procedural framework that ensures a
just and effective sentencing system by requiring judges
to explain and justify each sentence; by supplanting the

parole system with a determinate sentencing scheme; by
providing for appellate review of sentences; and by
establishing a national commission on sentencing and
corrections that will devise guidelines for Federal
sentencing policy.

334 Platt, A. M. and R. Pollock. "Channeling Lawyers:
    The Careers of Public Defenders." Pp. 235-262 in H.
    Jacob (ed.), THE POTENTIAL FOR REFORM OF CRIMINAL
    JUSTICE. Beverly Hills, CA: Sage, 1974.

    This article examines the careers and ideology of
lawyers who have worked in the Public Defender's Office
in Alameda County, California. Drawing upon radical
theories of the state and the "new" working class, the
authors locate the concept of "career" within a larger
social and political context by an analysis of
recruitment patterns into public defender offices, the
basis for staying in such offices, and reasons for
leaving the public defender office for other careers.
Data were gathered from interviews with a total of 48
former public defenders and 37 lawyers who were working
in the public defender's office. Comparative references
also are drawn from data derived from Cook County,
Illinois.

335 Polow, B. "Reducing Juvenile and Domestic Relations
    Caseloads." JUVENILE JUSTICE, 24 (2): 55-59, 1973

    The Morris County, New Jersey, plan for a more
effective system for initial handling of juvenile and
family-oriented complaints has resulted in significant
diversion from the juvenile justice system. A reduction
in juvenile and domestic relations caseload was
accomplished through prevention of inappropriate
complaints in matters which should have been referred to
social, medical, welfare, educational, mental health, or
family counseling agencies. The project also proposed
establishment of better understanding and communications
between law enforcement and probation and court services.
Other services were referrals to juvenile conference
committees in appropriate situations and procedures to
ensure proper complaint forms and languages in cases
where complaints must be taken. Protection for the
juvenile was ensured by providing counsel where
appropriate, including advice on the right to counsel and
prohibition of lock-up of juveniles at any time without
prior permission of the juvenile court intake service.
Other aspects of this project involve greater
coordination with local police and frequent visits by
juvenile court intake personnel to all resource agencies
to which referrals are made.

336 Reasons, C. E.   "Gault: Procedural Change and Sub-
     stantive Effect." CRIME AND DELINQUENCY, 16 (2):
     163-171, 1970.

     This article is the second in a series on the Gault
decision and its impact on the juvenile court. Reasons
examines the court records of 3,225 juvenile cases from
Franklin County (Columbus, OH) during two periods in
1967. Both qualitative and quantitative changes were
noted in the number and nature of cases. While there
were fewer cases after the Gault decision, the number of
cases with counsel more than doubled. Reasons suggests
that this is a result of an increased emphasis on legal
fact-finding.

337 Rhodes, W. M., and C. Conly. "Federal Sentencing
     Guidelines: Will They Shift Sentencing Discretion
     From Judges to Prosecutors?" Pp.197-224 in J. A.
     Cramer (ed.), COURTS AND JUDGES. Beverly Hills, CA:
     Sage, 1981.

     Reacting to the criticism that sentencing guidelines
will significantly increase the discretionary power of
prosecutors while decreasing that of judges, the authors
look at five federal offenses and corresponding offender
types and examine the influence of both prosecutor and
judge on sentence outcome. Survey results indicated that
judges remained the dominant figure at the time of
sentencing, even in plea bargaining situations. The
authors note that sentence concessions were largely
derived from judicial initiatives and both charge and
count bargaining were less influential in the
determination of sentence. It is concluded that concerns
about the shift in discretion as a result of sentencing
guidelines is not warranted.

338 Robertson, J. A. ROUGH JUSTICE--PERSPECTIVES ON
     LOWER CRIMINAL COURTS. Boston: Little, Brown, 1974.

     This is an anthology of essays describing long-
tolerated conditions of assembly-line justice in lower
criminal courts. Except for the police department, no
formal legal institution has as much direct contact with
people as lower criminal trial courts. For a majority of
the population, these courts embody the law and judicial
process of our government. Except for encounters with
the municipal, misdemeanor, traffic, and magistrates'
courts of their communities, most citizens have no
experience with judges, trials, or courts. The
selections explore a wide range of problems facing the
lower courts. In Part 1, the historical development of
the lower court problem is discussed, and an overview of
issues currently facing the courts is provided. Part 2

includes several essays on the social organization of the lower courts. The authors take a functional system or exchange approach to show the influence of coordination with local police and frequent visits by juvenile court intake personnel to all resource agencies to which referrals are made.

339 Robin, G. D.   "Judicial Resistance to Sentencing
     Accountability." CRIME AND DELINQUENCY, 21 (3):
     210-212, 1975.

     Robin presents a social-psychological interpretation to judicial resistance to accountability in sentencing. He combines organizational theory and institutional change theory. Robin argues that the reaction of judges to attempts to impose limitations on their sentencing function is totally rational. The discretionary power involved in sentencing is seen as too great to give up; and judges, reacting much as police facing the imposition of civilian review boards, are indicating their desire to engage in territorial conflict to maintain power.

340 Rosenheim, M. K., and D. L. Skoler. "The Lawyer's
     Role at Intake and Detention Stages of Juvenile Court
     Proceedings." CRIME AND DELINQUENCY, 11 (2): 167-
     174, 1965.

     Rosenheim and Skoler present a discussion of the role of lawyers at both the intake and detention hearing stages of the juvenile process. In these stages lawyers can be of special assistance to a juvenile by playing either the traditional or special "defense counsel" role. They also support the idea of a lawyer always being present at the "trial" stage of the juvenile process, and that privately retained lawyers should be involved at every stage.

341 Rowland, C. K., W. A. MaCauley, and R. A. Carp. "The
     Effects of Selection System on Jury Composition."
     LAW AND POLICY QUARTERLY, 4 (2): 235-251, 1982.

     Following the line of reasoning that the demographic composition of juries is an important element in achieving justice, the authors compare federal and state grand juries in Harris County (Houston) and Dallas County, Texas, in terms of the representation of blacks, Mexican-Americans, and women. They conclude that only female representation is consistently higher under a random selection process.

342 Rubin, H. T. "The Juvenile Court's Search for Iden-
      tity and Responsibility." CRIME AND DELINQUENCY, 23
      (1): 1-13, 1977.

      Rubin takes to task the failure of the juvenile
court to come to terms with its proper role and what it
needs to do for its achievement. He argues that between
inadequate legal representation, overconcern with
protecting status offenders from themselves, paternalism,
and a lagging court administration, the juvenile court
cannot accomplish its goal of achieving justice within a
rehabilitative context. To achieve positive change,
Rubin calls for a strict adherence to legal procedures,
mandatory defense counsel, abolishment of the use of
referees as hearing officers, and repeal of the court's
jurisdiction over status offenders.

343 Ryan, J. P. "Adjudication and Sentencing in a Misde-
      meanor Court: The Outcome Is the Punishment." LAW AND
      SOCIETY REVIEW, 15 (1): 79-108, 1981.

      Ryan compares his findings from the Columbus, Ohio,
Municipal Court with Malcolm Feeley's study of New
Haven's lower court. While Feeley found that the dominant
punishment in misdemeanor cases comes during the
processing of the case, Ryan finds that the Columbus
Court is much more severe in final sanctions imposed on
defendants. Ryan attributes these differences largely to
contrasting local political cultures, police-prosecutor
relationships, and methods of judicial assignment.

344 Ryan, J. P., M. J. Lipetz, M. L. Luskin, and D. W.
      Neubauer. "Analyzing Court Delay-Reduction Programs:
      Why Do Some Succeed?" JUDICATURE, 65 (2): 58-75,
      1981.

      This study examines the attempts by four courts
(Providence, RI; Detroit, MI; Las Vegas, NV; and Dayton,
OH) to implement a delay-reduction program aimed at
reducing case processing time in criminal cases. The
authors suggest that the most significant finding from
their analysis is that, as case processing time was
reduced, case dispositions became similar. The trial
courts became more routinized in their handling of cases.
Probable explanations for the success of the delay-
reduction programs are presented.

345 Sherman, E. S. "The Role of a Juvenile Court Citi-
     zens' Advisory Committee." CRIME AND DELINQUENCY,
     14 (2): 151-154, 1968.

     Sherman argues for the establishment of Citizens'
Advisory Committees for Juvenile Courts. Drawing upon
the experiences of the Summit County (Akron), Ohio
Juvenile Court, she traces the problems faced in getting
citizens involved in their local court, how these
problems were resolved, and the major functions of the
Advisory Committee. She suggests that such an advisory
committee can be invaluable in establishing community
support to both the juvenile court and its programs.

346 Sheskin, A. "Trial Courts on Trial: Examining Domi-
     nant Assumptions." Pp. 77-102 in J. A. Cramer (ed.),
     COURTS AND JUDGES. Beverly Hills, CA: Sage, 1981.

     Research on trial courts must be evaluated in large
part in terms of the underlying assumptions that guide
the research. Assumptions that value social stability,
or value the competition of the "conflict" inherent in
the social structure, or operate from a position of
consensus of values in society, will affect the research
questions posed and the direction one looks for answers.
Sheskin criticizes the dominant functionalist approach to
the study of trial courts which fails to question the
basic assumptions of the perspective that leads to an
acceptance of institutions as given. When research
accepts such conservative values, both problems and their
solutions become tautological, thus thwarting progress in
court reform.

347 Sigler, J. A. "The Prosecutor: A Comparative Func-
     tional Analysis." Pp. 53-74 in W. F. McDonald
     (ed.), THE PROSECUTOR. Beverly Hills, CA: Sage,
     1979.

     Sigler compares the prosecutor in the American
criminal justice system with prosecutors in other countries from a structural-functionalist perspective. He
focuses on the following considerations and categories:
(1) private/public or mixed prosecution; (2) centralization or decentralization of organization; (3) detection
of offense; (4) investigative functions; (5) quasi-
legislative functions; (6) charging and plea negotiations; (7) trying cases; and (8) role at sentencing.

348 Siler, E. E. "The Need for Defense Counsel in the
    Juvenile Court." CRIME AND DELINQUENCY, 11 (1): 45-
    58, 1965.

        Should a juvenile have a right to defense counsel in
juvenile court proceedings? What are the advantages to
be accrued to the juvenile? Siler deals with the
questions of Constitutional right to counsel for
juveniles by examining earlier Supreme Court decisions as
well as a variety of state court rulings. Siler argues
that the unique needs of a juvenile at the court stage of
the process requires the involvement of a lawyer.

349 Snyder, E. C. "The Impact of the Juvenile Court
    Hearing on the Child." CRIME AND DELINQUENCY, 17
    (2): 180-190, 1971.

        Recent literature on juvenile delinquency has
focused on discovering the causal variables involved.
However, one area for consideration appears to have been
systematically overlooked: the juvenile court process
itself. Snyder interviewed three boys recently placed on
probation by the juvenile court to evaluate the effects
of the juvenile court hearing on the child. She observed
that fear was the dominant emotion experienced by the
juveniles, but that the children felt more hostile toward
the police and least hostile toward the judge. Snyder
concluded that the emotional experiences of juveniles
during the hearing process is important to consider in
attempting to initiate change.

350 Stephan, C. "Selective Characteristics of Jurors and
    Litigants: Their Influences on Juries' Verdicts."
    Pp. 97-121 in R. J. Simon (ed.), THE JURY SYSTEM
    IN AMERICA. Beverly Hills, CA: Sage, 1975.

        Based on experimental data from simulated juries and
actual jury trials, Stephan identifies those
characteristics of litigants and jurors that have the
greatest effect of final decision in the trial. He
concludes that socioeconomic status has the greatest
prejudicial effect while evidence on variables such as
race and sex is "contradictory and anecdotal" and thus
requires further research. Other factors that were not
significant predictors of jury decision-making were age,
military record, family history, and prior service on
juries.

351 Sudnow, D. "Normal Crimes: Sociological Features of
    the Penal Code in a Public Defender Office." SOCIAL
    PROBLEMS, 12 (3): 255-276, 1965.

    Certain prominent organizational features of the
public defenders office and the penal code's place in the
routine operation of that office are examined through an
analysis of the use of the guilty plea, the representation of defendants, and the role of the penal code and
guilty pleas in that representation. Sudnow concludes
that public defenders establish a preconceived notion
about "normal crimes" and that this guides the operation
of their office. He notes that: (1) the focus on "normal
crimes" is not on individuals but on offense types; (2)
the features attributed to offenders and offenses are
often not important for the statutory conception; (3)
features attributed to offenders and offenses are
specific to the community in which the public defender
works; (4) offenses whose normal features are readily
dealt with are those which are routinely encountered in
the courtroom; (5) offenses are ecologically specific and
attended to as normal or not according to the locales
within which they are committed; and (6) the achievement
of competence as a public defender is indicated by the
acquisition of professional standards as well as relevant
features of the social structure and criminological
wisdom.

352 Suffet, F. "Bail Setting: A Study of Courtroom
    Interaction." CRIME AND DELINQUENCY, 12 (4): 318-
    331, 1966.

    This article is an analysis of the process by which
bail is set in a criminal court in New York County. A
total of 1,473 bail settings were observed during a
three-month period in 1964. Issues guiding the research
focused on the typical patterns of interaction between
the judge, prosecutor, and defense attorney at bail
setting, the degree of disagreement over bail between
these parties, and who wields the greatest influence at
bail setting. Suffet says that bail setting has a significant latent function: the diffusing of the responsibility for the release of the accused and the creation of
a buffer between the potentially outraged public and the
court for "controversial" release decisions.

353 Utz, P. J. "Two Models of Prosecutorial Profession-
    alism." Pp. 99-124 in W. F. McDonald (ed.), THE
    PROSECUTOR. Beverly Hills, CA: Sage, 1979.

    Two California court systems (San Diego and Alameda
Counties) are compared in this examination of

prosecutorial discretion and negotiation. Observations
of felony proceedings, as well as interviews with judges,
probation officers, and defense attorneys, were combined
with statistical data from the California Bureau of
Criminal Statistics. Differences observed in the two
court systems were attributed to different conceptions of
the institutional role and professional ethics of the
prosecutor, and are exemplified in the two models
discussed: adversarial and magisterial.

354 Weimer, D. L. "Prosecution Management: Evaluating an
    Innovation." Pp. 47-62 in P. L. Brantingham and T. G.
    Blomberg (eds.), COURTS AND DIVERSION: POLICY AND
    OPERATIONS STUDIES. Beverly Hills, CA: Sage, 1979.

    A demonstration of how consideration of the
organization of an innovating agency facilitates an
indirect test of the impact of the innovation is
presented. One of the major claims is that formal
evaluation techniques such as those based on experimental
and quasi-experimental designs are very difficult to
apply to criminal justice agency innovations. This
particular study of an innnovation in the Alameda County,
California, District Attorney's Office focused on the
introduction of a process that more tightly monitored the
prosecution of cases, especially those that were to be
plea bargained. Using indirect measures subject to
multivariate analysis (offense charged, prior record,
case strength, resource saving, and other case and
defendant characteristics) various models are tested. It
was concluded that, while none of the models provided
clear results, such indirect evaluations of innovations
are valid approaches.

355 Wessel, W. "From Cracker Barrel to Supermarket:
    Taking the County Out of Prosecution Management."
    Pp. 137-150 in W. F. McDonald (ed.), THE PROSECUTOR.
    Beverly Hills, CA: Sage, 1979.

    Wessel compares the effects of growth in a
prosecutor's office to a country general store: when the
office reaches a certain size, the prosecutor must
establish controls and accountability in his or her
agency. Wessel goes on to discuss the differences
between the smaller rural or suburban prosecutor's office
and the larger urban office. The impact on discretion,
initial screening of cases, plea bargaining, and related
courtroom tactics are discussed.

356 Wice, P. B. "Judicial Socialization: The Philadel-
    phia Experience." Pp. 149-172 in J. A. Cramer (ed.),
    COURTS AND JUDGES. Beverly Hills, CA: Sage, 1981.

    Drawing upon interviews with 35 judges sitting in
the Philadelphia court of Common Pleas in 1980, Wice
examines the process of trial court judicial socialization, testing his findings against theories of judicial socialization. The major premise of such theories
is that all new judges know very little about being a
trial judge and are in need of proper "educating." The
most surprising finding is that the criminal court judges
did not see themselves being inadequate in any prior
sitting on the bench and, therefore, reported almost no
reliance upon socializing agents or training programs.
Wice considers the possibility that the Philadelphia data
may be unusual.

CHAPTER 7

COURTS - PROCESS

357 Abel, R. L. "Plea Bargaining." LAW AND SOCIETY RE-
VIEW, 13 (2):197-687, 1979.

Papers presented at a 1978 symposium discuss issues
in plea bargaining: its nature; its causes, consequences,
and legitimacy; and proposals to eliminate, reform, or
restructure it. This symposium, designed to overcome
some of the research difficulties, included papers which
moved beyond the confines of specific disciplines and
perspectives. Plea bargaining is placed in a historical
perspective to identify the factors that have contributed
to its growing use. A sense of the diversity of plea
bargaining procedures is evident in discussions of
English, German, and specific U.S. systems. Reviews of
nine recent books dealing with the plea bargaining
process also are presented, along with responses by four
of the authors.

358 Adams, K. "The Effect of Evidentiary Factors on
Charge Reduction." JOURNAL OF CRIMINAL JUSTICE, 11
(6): 525-538, 1983.

Based on an analysis of 1,790 felony prosecutions in
1974 drawn from the PROMIS data system for the District
of Columbia, Adams tests the hypothesis that the nature
of plea concessions by the prosecutor will be related to
the strength of the evidence in the case. The findings
indicate some support for the hypothesis and suggest that
such a process has become a routine adjudicatory
procedure, especially for property crimes.

359 Adler, F. "Empathy as a Factor in Determining Jury
Verdicts." CRIMINOLOGY, 12 (1): 127-128, 1974.

Adler claims that prior research on the determinants
of jury verdicts show nationality, race, and religion of
jurors to have an influence on the verdict rendered. In
her own study, however, she suggests that the
socioeconomic discrepancy between jurors and the
defendant is the most important extralegal factor. Using
fifty convicted defendants and fifty not guilty
defendants--matched on age, sex, race, and offense--Adler
examines the socioeconomic distance between jurors and
defendants. Statistically significant support for her
hypothesis was found.

360 Alschuler, A. W.   "The Defense Attorney's Role in
    Plea Bargaining. YALE LAW JOURNAL, 84 (6): 1179-
    1314, 1975.

    This article explores the extent to which the
presence of counsel provides a significant safeguard of
fairness in guilty plea negotiation and finds that
current conceptions of the defense attorney's role are
often more romanticized than real. The thesis of the
article is that the plea bargaining system is an
inherently irrational method of administering justice and
necessarily destructive of sound attorney-client
relationships. The author contends that this system
subjects defense attorneys to serious temptations to
disregard their clients' interests.

361 Alschuler, A. W.   "Prosecutor's Role in Plea Bargain-
    ing." UNIVERSITY OF CHICAGO LAW REVIEW, 36 (4): 50-
    112, 1968.

    Plea bargaining is discussed in relation to factors
guiding the prosecutor's decision, the flexibility of the
practice, and the practice of overcharging. In
bargaining and making concessions for pleas, the
prosecutor becomes to some degree an administrator, an
advocate, a judge, and a legislator. Other factors
influence the prosecutor in bargaining to a lesser
extent--personal relationships between the prosecutor and
defense attorney, attitudes of the police personnel
involved, the race and personal characteristics of the
defendant, and the desires of the victim.

362 Arcuri, A. F.   "Police Perceptions of Plea Bargain-
    ing: A Preliminary Inquiry." JOURNAL OF POLICE
    SCIENCE AND ADMINISTRATION, 1 (1): 93-101, 1973.

    This is a report of the demoralizing effect
negotiated pleas have on police attitudes without
affecting actual police performance. The author randomly
distributed questionnaires to police officers in Rhode
Island and analyzed their responses to 14 questions
concerning their attitudes toward plea bargaining. He
concluded that the high frequency of plea bargaining,
with their frequently more lenient sentences, has a
demoralizing effect on police. These attitudes, however,
do not appear to affect actual job performance. A
majority of those surveyed felt that plea bargaining
should continue.

363 Baab, G. W., and W. R. Furgeson, Jr. "Texas Sentencing Practices: A Statistical Study." TEXAS LAW REVIEW, 45 (3): 471-503, 1967.

This study used a multiple regression analysis of felony cases in a single jurisdiction in 1962. The sentence decision appeared to be affected by a number of factors, including sex, race, marital status, education, age, prior record, and plea of the defendant. In addition, the authors found that the judge was a significant variable in terms of its impact on the severity of sentence. Differences observed were attributed to conflicting penal philosophies, social backgrounds, personalities, and temperaments.

364 Bartell, T., and L. T. Winfree, Jr. "Recidivist Impacts of Differential Sentencing Practices for Burglary Offenders." CRIMINOLOGY, 15 (3): 387-396, 1977.

Bartell and Winfree report on judicial sentencing variations. Their unique study is of a probability sample of 100 offenders sentenced for burglaries in 1971 and then followed-up for those that were subsequently arrested, convicted, and sentenced. The results indicate that probationed offenders were somewhat less likely to be reconvicted than were offenders initially given non-probationary sentences. Length of sentence, type of release, and number of prior arrests appeared unrelated to later rates of recidivism.

365 Bayley, C. T. "Plea Bargaining: An Offer a Prosecutor Can Refuse." JUDICATURE, 60 (5): 1976.

This article is a discussion of the changes in the plea bargaining process in the Prosecutor's Office of King County (Seattle), Washington, in which the prosecutor has stopped reducing charges and recommending reduced sentences for defendants charged with certain "high impact" crimes. Rape, robbery, and residential burglary were given highest priority, and case filing standards developed for these crimes: all provable multiple counts would be filed; any weapons allegations would be filed; and when applicable, habitual criminal status would be charged. In addition, a scale of standard sentence recommendations was developed which would vary only in accordance with specified aggravating or mitigating factors relating to the crime committed and the seriousness of the defendant's criminal record.

366 Bedau, H. A. "Felony-Murder-Rape and the Mandatory
    Death Penalty: A Study in Discretionary Justice."
    SUFFOLK UNIVERSITY LAW REVIEW, 10 (3): 493-520, 1976.

    A study providing an examination of mandatory
capital sentencing for felony-murder-rape in Middlesex
and Suffolk Counties, Massachusetts, from 1946 to 1970
is presented. The research reported is part of a larger
study to determine the significance of the shift from
mandatory to discretionary capital sentencing. Data for
the study were obtained from special docket and superior
court records, Department of Correction files, the Bureau
of Vital Statistics, and the newspaper files of the
Boston Globe. Of the 17 cases during that time period in
which prosecution for felony-murder-rape with its
mandatory death penalty was plausible, no defendant was
indicted on that charge. The author concludes that
switching discretionary powers from the sentencing to the
charging phase of the trial in accordance with the
Supreme Court's ruling in <u>Furman</u> without standards to
guide the prosecutor is unconstitutional.

367 Bermant, G., M. McGuire, W. McKinley, and C. Salo.
    "The Logic of Simulation in Jury Research." CRIMINAL
    JUSTICE AND BEHAVIOR, 1 (3): 224-233, 1974.

    The authors question both the substantive and
methodological foundations of mock jury research. Based
on their own research, they conclude that the modal
verdict in the most realistic simulation was not the
verdict in the actual trial. Suggestions for further
research are offered.

368 Bishop, A. N. "Guilty Pleas in Texas." BAYLOR LAW
    REVIEW, 24 (3): 301-341, 1972.

    The author reviews procedures in Texas for accepting
guilty pleas and discusses the applicable case law.
Factual stipulation, rather than actual evidence, may now
be used in pleas directed toward the court. Bishop found
that the Texas courts adhere strictly to the statutory
procedural requirements to assure that pleas of guilty
are entered by persons who are sane and who understand
the consequences.

369 Blankenship, R. L., and B. K. Singh. "Differential
    Labeling of Juveniles: A Multivariate Analysis."
    CRIMINOLOGY, 13 (4): 471-490, 1976.

    This paper presents an analysis of the labeling
process in the juvenile court. Using data from case
records, the authors examine the discretionary process in

which differential labeling leads juvenile offenders to be placed into one of two categories of deviant: juvenile delinquent and mentally disturbed offender. The treatment recommended followed the type of label imposed. Prior delinquent record of the offender was the most important independent variable in determining the label.

370 Bond, J. E. "Plea Bargaining in North Carolina." NORTH CAROLINA LAW REVIEW, 54 (5): 823-843, 1976.

Bond reports the findings of a survey of several of the district attorney's offices in North Carolina regarding plea bargaining practices. The results of the survey of 20 of the 30 district attorneys' offices in the State revealed that plea bargaining practices vary widely and indicated two broad areas. The first group, process problems, encompasses topics such as judicial participation in plea bargaining and imposition of different sentences. Some problems from the second group, internal management problems, include informal substantive bargaining policies and unstructured office negotiating procedures. Bond concludes that plea bargaining must be structured to facilitate rather than frustrate the purposes of the criminal justice system.

371 Brigham, J. C., and R. K. Bothwell. "The Ability of Prospective Jurors to Estimate the Accuracy of Eyewitness Identifications." LAW AND HUMAN BEHAVIOR, 7 (1): 19-30, 1983.

Brigham and Bothwell's study tests the ability of prospective jurors to assess the accuracy of eyewitness identifications. Based on the assumption that "common knowledge" of a prospective jury member is sufficient to assess the reliability of eyewitnesses, the authors set up a study in which persons are presented with various scenarios involving "target present" lineup identifications. The results indicate that jury members overestimate the accuracy of eyewitness identifications. Therefore, expert testimony on the accuracy of eyewitness identifications should aid juror deliberations.

372 Broach, G. T., P. D. Jackson, and V. H. Ascolillo. "State Political Culture and Sentence Severity in Federal District Courts." CRIMINOLOGY, 16 (3): 373-382, 1978.

This paper explores the relationship between state politics and judicial sentencing policies in cases involving violations of the Selective Service Act. The authors find that a large portion of sentence variation is explained by the political, policy, and socioeconomic

environments of the states in which the case is heard.
Of these variables, the most important is the
socioeconomic environment. This finding is consistent
with other research on this subject.

373 Bullock, H. "Significance of the Racial Factor in
    the Length of Prison Sentences." JOURNAL OF CRIMINAL
    LAW, CRIMINOLOGY & POLICE SCIENCE, 52 (4): 411-417,
    1961.

     Bullock examines 3,644 cases drawn from the Texas
State Prison in 1958 to determine the nature of the
relationship between race of defendant and length of
prison sentence. While the plea of the defendant and
size of community from which the defendant was committed
appeared significant, control of these factors failed to
reduce the association between race and length of
sentence. Bullock concludes that racial discrimination
appears to be motivated more by the desire to protect the
order of the white community than to effect the
reformation of the offender.

374 Burke, P. J., and A. T. Turk. "Factors Affecting
    Postarrest Dispositions: A Model for Analysis."
    SOCIAL PROBLEMS, 22 (3): 313-332, 1975.

     The authors examined a 20 percent random sample of
adults arrested in Indianapolis in 1964 utilizing
Goodman's log-linear analysis. They found that there
were greater than average tendencies for persons under
the age of 25 to be sent to prison and less than average
tendencies for persons between 25 and 35 to receive
prison sentences. In addition, the race of the defendant
and immediate offense charged affected the sentence
outcome. However, when the immediate offense was
controlled for, the effect of race on disposition was
reduced.

375 Cargan, L., and M. A. Coates. "Indeterminate Sen-
    tence and Judicial Bias." CRIME AND DELINQUENCY, 20
    (2): 144-156, 1974.

     This study tested the hypothesis that, because of
individual judicial biases, the indeterminate sentence
does not reduce sentence disparity. The records of
felony cases handled by the common pleas court of
Montgomery County, Ohio, were examined for a 2-year
period. Emphasis was placed on the sentencing procedures
of the six regular judges in eight offense categories,
including robbery, forgery, breaking and entering, and
narcotics violations. Although the court system used the
indeterminate sentence, the study found differences among

judges in overall sentencing disparity, among different offenses handled by the same judge, and in the relative severity of the sentence according to the defendant's race. The authors conclude that the use of the indeterminate sentence alters, but does not eliminate, the expression of judicial bias as reflected in unjustified sentencing disparities.

376 Carter, R. M., and L. T. Wilkins. "Some Factors in Sentencing Policy." JOURNAL OF CRIMINAL LAW, CRIMINOLOGY & POLICE SCIENCE, 58 (4): 503-514, 1967.

An examination of the presentence probation report recommendation and its relation to the court dispositions, based primarily on data from the U.S. District Court for Northern California, 1964-1965, is presented. This report indicates that the relatonship between recommendations for and dispositions of probation are high, and that the relationship diminishes when viewed from the recommendations against and the subsequent grant of probation perspective. The overall relationship between recommendation and disposition does not vary from district court to district court, but rather remains relatively constant, regardless of the percentage use of probation. It is suggested that disparities in sentencing are supported by the probation officer and it appears that these differences, in part, are a reflection of the officer's academic training and experience.

377 Cei, L. B. "Indeterminate Sentence at the Crossroads." NEW ENGLAND JOURNAL ON PRISON LAW, 3 (1): 85-96, 1976.

Cei reviews the development of the indeterminate sentence and critically analyzes arguments for and against its effectiveness in inmate rehabilitation. It is suggested that, despite criticisms of arbitrary administration, the questionable constitutionality of using such terms as "mentally ill" and "dangerous" offender, and problems of behavior prediction, the indeterminate sentence should be employed--but only under strict control. Proposed safeguards include written sentencing guidelines that allow for appellate review, statutory definitions of the terms "dangerous" and "mentally ill," voluntary participation by first offenders, and elimination of a minimum time for parole eligibility.

144   CRIMINAL JUSTICE IN AMERICA

378 Chiricos, T. G., and G. P. Waldo. "Socioeconomic
    Status and Criminal Sentencing: An Empirical Assess-
    ment of a Conflict Proposition." AMERICAN SOCIOLOGI-
    CAL REVIEW, 40 (6): 753-772, 1975.

    In response to a growing body of literature from the
conflict perspective suggesting that judicial sentencing
patterns will display systematic bias against persons of
lower socioeconomic status, Chiricos and Waldo examine
prison sentences of 10,488 inmates in three southeastern
states. They found no support for the conflict
proposition, even when controlling for prior record and
demographic characteristics of the defendant.

379 Church, T. W., Jr. "Plea Bargains, Concessions and
    the Courts: Analysis of a Quasi-Experiment." LAW AND
    SOCIETY REVIEW, 10 (3): 377-401, 1976.

    Church assesses the impact of selective elimination
of one form of plea bargaining on the court system of a
large suburban county in the Midwest. Dispositional
information was obtained on drug cases for 1972 and 1973.
By the end of 1973, reduced-charge guilty pleas--the
predominant mode of disposition in 1972--were almost
totally eliminated. The trial rate increased greatly,
and the total proportion of cases decided through guilty
pleas fell considerably. The emphasis shifted from
reduction in charge, which the prosecutor could effect,
to reduction in sentence for a guilty plea, which only
the judge could decide. It was found that plea
bargaining is difficult to eliminate because it reduces
the uncertainties and risks inherent in a trial for all
court participants, including the defendant.

380 Clear, T. R., J. D. Hewitt, and R. M. Regoli. "Dis-
    cretion and the Determinate Sentence: Its Distribu-
    tion, Control, and Effect on Time Served." CRIME AND
    DELINQUENCY, 24 (4): 428-445, 1978.

    This article notes that sentencing reformers have
often criticized current sentencing practices as abusive
and rooted in untenable assumptions. An analysis of
Indiana's sentencing code suggests that the intent of
most sentencing reformers may not have been met by the
code's revisions. The potential for discretion has not
been reduced; substantial control over the sentence has
been placed in the hands of correctional staff through
credit time provisions; and the projection of the impact
of the code indicates that sentences may be almost 50
percent longer for some first-time felony offenders. The
authors conclude that many of the code's problems could
be eliminated by reducing the length of prison sentence.

381 Cleary, J. J. "Plea Negotiation and Its Effects on Sentencing." FEDERAL BAR JOURNAL, 37 (1): 61-75, 1978.

The impact of plea negotiation on the Federal criminal justice system is assessed, with attention given to the constitutional basis, procedures, and mechanics of plea bargaining and to existing sentencing alternatives. Following an overview of the roles played by the defense, prosecution, and judiciary in plea negotiations, Supreme Court decisions and Federal rules are cited to highlight the constitutional basis and the applicable Federal procedures regarding plea negotiations. After a discussion of the actual mechanics of plea bargaining, it is concluded that plea bargaining is an evil process which must be tolerated to avoid a breakdown in a criminal justice system incapable of handling the caseflow that would result if more than 15 percent of all Federal cases went to trial.

382 Cohen, L. E., and J. R. Kluegel. "The Detention Decision: A Study of the Impact of Social Characteristics and Legal Factors in Two Metropolitan Juvenile Courts." SOCIAL FORCES, 58 (1): 146-161, 1979.

Cohen and Kluegel examine the effects of social characteristics and legal factors in the preadjudication detention decision for juveniles. Utilizing a log-linear analysis, they observe that the nature of the juvenile's activity (conventionally active or idle), prior record, and orientation to juvenile justice held by the court determine the preadjudication detention decision. Second, there was no evidence of a direct racial or class bias held by the juvenile court in the detention decision, although some evidence of sexual bias was noted.

383 Cole, G. F. "The Decision to Prosecute." LAW AND SOCIETY REVIEW, 4 (3): 331-343, 1970.

Cole explores the prosecutors decision to prosecute using data from King County (Seattle), Washington, for the period 1955-1965. The analysis proceeds from two assumptions. First, the criminal justice process should be understood as a subsystem of the larger political system. Second, broadly conceived political considerations explain a large portion of the actual outcomes of the local system (who gets or does not get what and the quality of local justice). Cole concludes that the best way to view the process is in terms of an exchange in which market-like relationships operate and influence the various actors in the system. The prosecutor, then, is only able to exercise discretionary powers within this exchange network.

384 Cook, W. J. "'Bitch' Threatens, But Seldom Bites: A Study of Habitual Criminal Sentencing in Douglas County, Nebraska." CREIGHTON LAW REVIEW, 8 (July): 893-922, 1975.

Cook presents a study of the application of the habitual criminal sanction in 82 eligible Nebraska cases to examine patterns of application, reasons for its application, and sentence lengths for habitual criminals. Cook provides a review of past studies, articles, and inquires into the sentencing of habitual offenders in the United States. In the present study, eligible cases from 1971 and 1972 were examined. Of the 82 cases found eligible for habitual criminal sanctions, only 3 received sanctions. Possible reasons for this outcome are discussed.

385 Dean, J. M. "Deferred Prosecution and Due Process in the Southern District of New York." FEDERAL PROBA-TION, 39 (3): 23-26, 1975.

The deferred prosecution juvenile diversion program is explained and particular emphasis is accorded to the procedural safeguards that are built into the program, which is administered by the U.S. Probation Office. Young first offenders or mentally disturbed individuals are usually prime candidates for program intake although each case is judged on its merits. The final choice of whether to participate in the program is made by the defendant. Procedural protection built into this program includes the provision of counsel to all defendants and the evaluation of defendants for the program by an agency independent of the prosecutor.

386 Diamond, S. S., and H. Zeisel. "Sentencing Councils: A Study of Sentencing Disparity and Its Reduction." UNIVERSITY OF CHICAGO LAW REVIEW, 43 (1): 109-149, 1975.

The problems caused by sentencing disparity are reviewed, and a method of measuring disparity is developed and tested. The article reviews the problems created by sentencing disparity and recounts earlier efforts to study the phenomenon. It then develops a measure of disparity and uses it to assess the magnitude of the problem in two Federal district courts. Finally, it describes the operation of the sentencing councils in these two courts and tries to assess their ability to reduce disparity.

387 Ellenbogen, J., and E. Ellenbogen. "Perspectives on
    Plea Bargaining." CRIME AND CORRECTIONS, 1 (1): 5-
    10, 1973.

   The authors contend that plea bargaining
discriminates against the lower classes who, unable to
make bail, may be weakened by a jail experience to such
an extent that a "deal" will seem attractive. They add
that the process may deprive an accused of his right to
plead not guilty and his right to a jury trial. Finally,
the blind acceptance of the bargain as presented to the
court by the judge may appear to the defendant as the
ultimate failure of the criminal justice system. The
authors conclude that the purpose of plea bargaining, to
alleviate crowded court dockets, might be better served
by reform of the criminal codes.

388 Erickson, W. H. "Finality of a Guilty Plea." NOTRE
    DAME LAWYER, 48 (4): 835-849, 1973.

   Erickson examines the 17 American Bar Association
standards for criminal justice that relate to the acceptance of guilty pleas. Included in this article are
discussions of plea bargaining, voluntariness of the
guilty plea, and pretrial discovery. The possible
grounds for post-conviction review of a guilty plea also
are described.

389 Fenster, C. L. "The Adjudication of Male Codefen-
    dants: An Application of Societal Reaction Theory."
    Pp. 79-91 in P. L. Brantingham and T. G. Blomberg
    (eds.), COURTS AND DIVERSION: POLICY AND OPERATIONS
    STUDIES. Beverly Hills, CA: Sage, 1979.

   Drawing upon societal reaction theory, three
hypotheses regarding the adjudication process, and consequent official labeling, are generated for testing: (1)
characteristics of the criminal offense do not account
for all the explained variance; (2) characteristics of
the offender explain some of the variance; and (3) organizational variables will explain some of the variance. A
sample of 108 randomly selected pairs of male
codefendants charged with robbery, burglary, assault,
larceny-theft, or drugs were examined. While the first
two hypotheses were supported by the data, the third
hypothesis focusing on organizational variables was not.

390 Fenwick, C. R. "Juvenile Court Intake Decision-
    Making: The Importance of Family Affiliation."
    JOURNAL OF CRIMINAL JUSTICE, 10 (6): 443-454, 1982.

    Fenwick's article deals with the importance of
family affiliation-disaffiliation in the juvenile court
intake decisions about a formal hearing and whether or
not the juvenile should be held in preadjudicatory
detention. In his analysis of 350 cases randomly sampled
from the juvenile court records for 1976, Fenwick
concludes that the further a juvenile goes in the intake
decision-making process, the greater the impact of family
disaffiliation as an independent variable.

391 Ferster, E. Z., and T. F. Courtless. "Pre-Disposi-
    tional Data, Role of Counsel, and Decisions in a
    Juvenile Court." LAW AND SOCIETY REVIEW, 7 (2): 195-
    222, 1972.

    Based upon a three-year study of the juvenile
justice system in a single "affluent" county, the authors
examine the nature of the influence of clinical reports
and presence of counsel in case dispositions. The
authors indicate that while the quality of the clinical
reports vary, the reports themselves do not systematically determine outcomes. In addition, the role of
counsel was determined to be crucial but not actually
informative. In other words, their presence did reduce
the probability of a commitment to an institution, and
yet there was little informative substance derived from
their presence.

392 Finkelstein, M. O. "Statistical Analysis of Guilty
    Plea Practices in the Federal Courts." HARVARD LAW
    REVIEW, 89 (2): 293-315, 1975.

    Finkelstein analyzes guilty plea statistics from
various Federal district courts and concludes that the
fundamental assumption underlying the Supreme Court's
approval of plea bargaining is incorrect. The U.S.
Supreme Court has explicitly approved the practice of
plea bargaining but only on the assumption that
defendants who were convicted on the basis of negotiated
pleas of guilt would have been convicted had they elected
to stand trial. The author argues that prosecutors may
be using threats of lengthy sentences and other plea-
inducing practices to obtain convictions in cases in
which the government's evidence is insubstantial. The
author concludes that more than two-thirds of the
marginal plea bargain defendants would be acquitted or
dismissed were they to contest their cases.

393 Folberg, H. J. "Bargained for Guilty Plea: An Eval-
    uation." CRIMINAL LAW BULLETIN, 4 (4): 201-212,
    1968.

Folberg evaluates the desirability of the policy of
negotiated pleas in terms of the due process features of
accuracy, fairness, and insulation against corruption and
abuse. The major arguments in favor of plea negotiation
are examined as well as the statutory and practical
variations in the system, as practiced in some
jurisdictions, which appear to be a reasonable
alternative to the need for guilty plea negotiations.
Folberg concludes that the need for plea bargaining has
been assumed rather than empirically verified.

394 Foley, L. A., and R. S. Powell. "The Discretion of
    Prosecutors, Judges, and Juries in Capital Cases."
    CRIMINAL JUSTICE REVIEW, 7 (2): 16-22, 1982.

Foley and Powell study the effects of legal and
extralegal factors on the decisions of prosecutors,
judges, and juries in first degree murder cases in 21
counties in Florida between 1972 and 1978. They indicate
that legal and extralegal factors differentially affect
the three different decision-makers. Prosecutors were
influenced by the sex of the defendant, type of attorney,
and existence of accomplices. Judges were influenced by
race of victim and sex of the offender, while juries were
influenced only by the sex of the offender.

395 Gallagher, K. "Judicial Participation in Plea Bar-
    gaining: A Search for New Standards." HARVARD CIVIL
    RIGHTS/CIVIL LIBERTIES LAW REVIEW, 9 (1): 29-51,
    1974.

This article suggests standards to maximize the
benefits and fairness of conviction without trial through
exclusion of the judge in the plea negotiations and an
open and contractual approach to such negotiations.
Gallagher supports the belief that the trial judge should
be excluded from pre-plea negotiations. Gallagher then
considers the issues in terms of the constitutional
questions and the validity and application of recent
contractual approaches to plea bargaining.

396 Gaylin, W. PARTIAL JUSTICE--A STUDY OF BIAS IN SEN-
    TENCING. New York: Random House, 1974.

Through the examination of trial transcripts, taping
of judge sentencing seminars, and direct interviews with
judges, the author demonstrates factors which influence
sentencing and lead to sentencing disparity. The text

opens with a discussion of the various types of
sentencing disparity and its possible sources. Principles
of the sentencing process are next outlined. Four long
interviews with four very different judges are presented,
as well as shorter excerpts of interviews with other
judges. From the conclusions drawn from these
interviews, the author offers his own suggestions for
change in our legal system.

397 Gibson, J. L. "Race as a Determinant of Criminal
    Sentences: A Methodological Critique and a Case
    Study." LAW AND SOCIETY REVIEW, 12 (3): 455-478,
    1978.

    Previous research on racial discrimination in
judicial sentencing is taken to task in this article.
Findings of no discrimination in aggregate court data can
be misleading and may preclude the possibility that
individual judges may discriminate. Therefore, the unit
of analysis can have serious impact on substantive
conclusions. Using data drawn from the Fulton County,
Georgia, Superior Court, Gibson finds three patterns of
sentencing among judges: pro-black, anti-black, and
nondiscriminatory. Factors related to these three
patterns are then discussed.

398 Green, E. JUDICIAL ATTITUDES IN SENTENCING. London:
    Macmillan, 1961.

    Green presents the findings of a study of non-jury
court decisions in Philadelphia between 1956 and 1957.
While there was a high degree of consistency between
judges in cases involving serious offenses and minor
offenses, those cases that fell in between, in the intermediate range, experienced greater inconsistency in
sentencing by judges. The sex, age, and race of the
defendant played a minor role in disposition; guilty
pleas seemed to have no impact; prior arrests that did
not result in a conviction were insignificant; but the
degree to which the crime involved danger to the person
did appear significant.

399 Green, E. "Inter- and Intra-Racial Crime Relative to
    Sentencing." JOURNAL OF CRIMINAL LAW, CRIMINOLOGY &
    POLICE SCIENCE, 55 (3): 348-358, 1964.

    This is an analysis of 1,437 cases of convictions in
Philadelphia. Of the total number of cases, only the 409
cases of robbery and burglary in which the race of the
victim was available were used. Green found that the
evidence does not support the hypothesis that the court
differentiates the seriousness of crimes according to the

race of the offender relative to the race of the victim. There were slightly less severe sentences accorded black intra-racial offenders.

400 Greenwood, P. W., S. Wildhorn, E. C. Poggie, M. J. Strumwasser, and Peter De Leon. PROSECUTION OF ADULT FELONY DEFENDANTS IN LOS ANGELES COUNTY: A POLICY PERSPECTIVE. Santa Monica, CA: Rand Corporation, 1973.

Greenwood et al. studied over 70,000 felony defendants in Los Angeles county in 1970 and 1971. They found that defendants with more extensive prior records get more severe sentences; that across all categories of offense and prior record, defendants who plead guilty are sentenced more leniently; that the evidence on the effects of race are inconclusive; and that wide variation in sentencing among different courts and among judges within courts exists.

401 Hagan, J. "Extralegal Attributes and Criminal Sentencing: An Assessment of a Sociological Viewpoint." LAW AND SOCIETY REVIEW, 8 (3): 357-383, 1974.

Hagan presents a reanalysis of 17 studies dealing with extralegal attributes. He found rather inconsistent results concerning race. There was evidence of differential sentencing in inter-racial capital cases in the southern United States. But in samples of non-capital cases, with offense held constant, among persons with no prior record, the relationship between race and disposition was not significant. Socioeconomic status, age, and sex also were examined, but inconsistent findings were observed.

402 Hagan, J., J. D. Hewitt, and D. F. Alwin. "Ceremonial Justice: Crime and Punishment in a Loosely Coupled System." SOCIAL FORCES, 58 (2): 506-527, 1979.

This paper provides an alternative perspective to the dominant Durkheimian and Marxian models of criminal justice. The authors focus on the historical shift from a classical to a positivist philosophy of sentencing and the emerging profession of probation as a symbol of this transition. The analysis of sentencing decisions in felony cases in Seattle, Washington, suggests that the influence of probation officers in the presentencing process is subordinate to that of prosecutors. They suggest that the involvement of probation officers in sentencing decisions is often more ceremonial than real.

403 Hagan, J., I. H. Nagel, and C. Albonetti. "The
    Differential Sentencing of White-Collar Offenders in
    Ten Federal District Courts." AMERICAN SOCIOLOGICAL
    REVIEW, 45 (5): 802-820, 1980.

     The authors note that previous research on the
criminal sanctioning of white-collar offenders has taken
place within the context of state courts where
prosecutorial resources become focused largely on lower
status defendants. Analyzing data drawn from ten federal
district courts (where prosecutorial resources are
greater and more likely to be directed at higher status
offenders), they examine between and within court
variations in the prosecution and sentencing of white-
collar offenders. They conclude that there may be an
inverse relationship between the volume of white collar
prosecutions and the severity of sentences received.

404 Heumann, M. "A Note on Plea Bargaining and Case
    Pressure." LAW AND SOCIETY REVIEW, 9 (3): 515-528,
    1975.

     Heumann examines the relationship between case
pressure and plea bargaining. Data gathered from
Connecticut between 1966 and 1973 are presented. The
data show that case pressure has not been causally
related to the increased use of plea bargaining. Plea
bargaining appears to be an integral and inevitable feature of the lower criminal courts. Guilty pleas are
offered for reasons other than case pressure.

405 Heumann, M. PLEA BARGAINING: THE EXPERIENCES OF
    PROSECUTORS, JUDGES, AND DEFENSE ATTORNEYS.
    Chicago: University of Chicago Press, 1978.

     A study of the process by which newly recruited
defense attorneys, prosecutors, and judges adapt to the
use of plea bargaining is presented. The experiences of
both defense attorneys and prosecutors are traced from
their recruitment through the final stages of their adaptation to the plea bargaining process. A summary of the
adaptation process includes a recommendation that the
training of attorneys include some preparation for the
practice of plea bargaining. Suggestions for a plea
bargaining reform policy are presented, and recommendations are made for further research.

406 Hewitt, J. D. "Individual Resources, Societal Reac-
     tion, and Sentencing Disparity." WESTERN SOCIOLOGI-
     CAL REVIEW, 7: 31-56, 1976.

     Hewitt develops a conceptual framework from which to
explain and predict judicial sentencing disparities. It
draws upon the interactionist school by suggesting the
role of societal reaction in the creation of images about
an actor in a sentencing situation. Three propositions
specifying the relationship between an actor's individual
resources and the sentence received are presented. A
statistical analysis of 504 convicted adult felony cases
from Seattle, Washington, is presented.

407 Hewitt, J. D. "The Effects of Individual Resources
     in Judicial Sentencing." REVIEW OF PUBLIC DATA USE,
     5 (1): 30-51, 1977.

     This paper is an analysis of the effects of
"individual resources" on judicial sentencing. Using a
causal modeling approach and path analysis, the total
effects of the defendants individual resource variables
are decomposed into their respective direct and indirect
effects on sentencing. The analysis indicated that while
five of eight individual resource variables had statistically significant total effects, only the sex of the
defendant had any significant direct effects on any of
the sentence variables. The remaining variables had
their total effects largely mediated by the various
intervening variables in the model (present offense,
prior record, weapon or violence, bail, and prosecutor
and probation officer pre-sentence recommendations).

408 Hewitt, J. D., and B. Little. "Examining the Research
     Underlying the Sentencing Guidelines Concept in Den-
     ver, Colorado: A Partial Replication of a Reform
     Effort." JOURNAL OF CRIMINAL JUSTICE, 9: 51-62,
     1981.

     Hewitt and Little examine the criminal sentencing
guidelines developed in Denver, Colorado. Questions are
raised regarding the implications of extensive missing
observations across cases and the resulting shrinkage of
cases available for multivariate analysis. The original
data are reanalyzed in both their original form and in a
more complete form by estimating the missing data.
Implications of the weaknesses in the original data used
for constructing the sentence guidelines are discussed.

409 Hewitt, J. D., R. M. Regoli, and T. R. Clear. "Eval-
    uating the Cook County Sentencing Guidelines." LAW
    AND POLICY QUARTERLY, 4 (2): 252-262, 1982.

   This article examines the empirical basis for
current criminal sentencing guidelines being used in Cook
County, Illinois. The authors argue that, unlike in many
other sentencing reforms, guidelines have generally been
developed out of an empirical analysis of past sentencing
decisions through the identification of variables most
predictive of sentence. However, when the statistical
analysis is inadequate or faulty, the resultant
sentencing guidelines must be questioned. A reanalysis
of the original data used to develop the guidelines in
Cook County is presented. The authors conclude that the
current sentencing guidelines used in Cook County are not
predictive of sentence. Implications of this finding are
discussed.

410 Hewitt, J. D., and T. R. Clear. THE IMPACT OF SEN-
    TENCING REFORM: FROM INDETERMINATE TO DETERMINATE
    SENTENCING. New York: University Press of America,
    1983.

   This book examines the emerging philosophical debate
between the advocates for maintaining the traditional
indeterminate sentencing model with those who support the
determinate sentence. This debate was successfully won
in Indiana by the proponents of determinate sentences.
The process of that legal reform effort and the subsequent impact of radical changes in the state's sentencing
code are examined.

411 Hickey, W. L., and S. Rubin. "Suspended Sentences
    and Fines." CRIME AND DELINQUENCY LITERATURE, 3 (3):
    413-429, 1971.

   A review of domestic and foreign thinking and
legislation on suspended sentences and fines, outlining
the benefits and applicability of these sentencing
alternatives, is presented. The authors state that the
suspended sentence and the fine should be used more
often. Differences between probation and the suspended
sentence are indicated. The authors state that an
expanded use of the suspended sentence would free
probation staff for more serious cases while still
providing an appropriate disposition for those not
requiring supervision. Fines are seen as a valid
disposition not only when the motive for the offense is
economic gain, but in nonpecuniary offenses as well. The
authors maintain that imprisonment of indigents for

nonpayment of fines should be abolished, but those who
are able to pay but willfully refuse should be charged
with contempt.

412 Holt, I. L. "The Judge's Attitude and Manner at
    Sentencing." CRIME AND DELINQUENCY, 10 (3): 231-234,
    1964.

    This article deals with the impact of the judge's
attitude and manner during sentencing on both the
defendant's and public's perception of justice. After
noting the negative consequences of a judge's sentencing
in a routine, humorous, or harsh manner, Holt identifies
four "essentials" of attitude and manner for fair and
impartial sentencing: confidence,   dignity,   understanding, and impartiality. Failing to abide by these
essentials leaves the judge open to criticism.

413 Houlden, P. "A Critical Review of the Research Into
    the Effects of Defendant Attractiveness, Inadmissible
    Evidence, and Restriction of Verdict Alternatives on
    Jury Decisions." CRIMINAL JUSTICE REVIEW, 5 (1): 67-
    79, 1980.

    This article is a review of current social science
research on the effects of three variables on jury
decision-making: the defendant's attractiveness, inad-
missibility of evidence, and the restriction of verdict
alternatives.   Houlden draws the research findings
together to assess their usefulness. She concludes by
noting that the existing research is limited, and that
while some evidence of jury effects is found, the process
by which juries decide is unclear. Suggestions for future
research are offered.

414 Jones, J. B. "Prosecutors and the Disposition of
    Criminal Cases: An Analysis of Plea Bargaining
    Rates." JOURNAL OF CRIMINAL LAW AND CRIMINOLOGY, 69
    (3): 402-412, 1978.

    The effect of prosecutors' values and social back-
ground on their rate of plea bargaining was examined
based on data collected through a mail survey of
prosecuting attorneys and their assistants in Illinois.
The statistical analysis demonstrated that knowledge of
the prosecutor's religion, national origin, or family
status was not useful in predicting the plea bargaining
rate; that reality often overrides law school values and
perceptions, causing a prosecutor's legal training to
have little effect on the plea bargaining rate; that
depth of legal experience has almost no influence on a
prosecutor's willingness to negotiate; and that support

or nonsupport for efficiency has no effect on plea bargaining rate, although support for cooperation has a somewhat greater effect on the frequency of prosecutorial bargaining.

415 Kaplan, K. J., and R. J. Simon. "Latitude and Severity of Sentencing Options, Race of the Victim, and Decisions of Simulated Jurors: Some Issues Arising from the 'Algiers Motel' Trial." LAW AND SOCIETY REVIEW, 7 (1), 1972.

As an outcome of the controversy surrounding the "Algiers Motel" trial in Detroit, Kaplan and Simon utilize a jury simulation technique to explore the issues of the impact of the race of victim, strength of evidence, and latitude and severity of choice structure provided in jury instructions. The data were obtained from 307 white male and female undergraduate students. Based on their analysis, they conclude that race of victim has little effect, strength of evidence is important only when it is either "high" or "mixed," and choice structure had mixed results.

416 Kelly, H. E. "A Comparison of Defense Strategy and Race as Influences in Differential Sentencing." CRIMINOLOGY, 14 (2): 241-250, 1976.

This article is another study of sentencing disparities. While Kelly implies that he is attempting to study the impact of defense strategies on sentence, this variable is no more than a combination of plea of defendent and type of defense attorney (two variables often included in other research). In addition to defense strategy, Kelly looks at the effects of age, record, and present offense. A total of 2,090 convicted felons in a penal institution in Oklahoma were examined with comparisons made for both burglary and homicide. While plea and type of defense attorney were both statistically significant (based on a stepwise multiple regression analysis), the effects were greater for burglary cases than for the murder cases. Neither variable, however, contributed greatly to the overall explanation of sentence variation.

417 Kerr, N. L., D. R. Nerenz, and D. Herrick. "Role Playing and the Study of Jury Behavior." SOCIOLOGICAL METHODS & RESEARCH, 7 (3): 337-355, 1979.

The authors discuss the external validity of simulated trials and mock juries in research on jury behavior. They examined the role-playing nature of mock jury deliberations by randomly assigning students to

either a known role-playing mock jury or to a situation
in which the students were led to believe that they were
participants in an actual student discipline case. There
were no significant differences in their group or
individual verdicts, sentence recommendations, or
deliberation time.

418 La Free, G. D. "Variables Affecting Guilty Pleas and
    Convictions in Rape Cases: Toward a Social Theory of
    Rape Processing." SOCIAL FORCES, 58 (3): 833-850,
    1980.

      La Free argues that research on reactions to rape
have ignored the effects of important variables. Based
on a multiple regression analysis of 124 rape cases, he
tests his hypothesis that the likelihood of convictions
in rape cases will be affected by the extent to which
characteristics of cases approximate the stereotypes of
rape held by criminal justice personnel. His findings
support this hypothesis. Black women, women who allegedly
engaged in misconduct, women acquainted with the
defendant, and women who did not report the rape promptly
were significantly less likely to have their cases come
to trial or result in convictions.

419 Levine, J. P. "Using Jury Verdict Forecasts in Crim-
    inal Defense Strategy." JUDICATURE, 66 (10): 448-
    461, 1983.

      For decades lawyers have engaged in the criminal
jury selection process on the basis of long-standing
myths about jury preferences. Levine says the time has
come to reject this approach in favor of a more
systematic, technologically assisted style of "playing
the odds." With the expanding use of computers to store,
retrieve, and tabulate data, jury forecasting is greatly
enhanced.   However, Levine notes that there are
limitations to any statistical predictions, expecially
when making generalizations from one jurisdiction to
another.

420 Mather, L. M. "Some Determinants of the Method of
    Case Disposition: Decision-Making by Public Defenders
    in Los Angeles." LAW AND SOCIETY REVIEW, 8 (2): 187-
    216, 1973.

      Mather examines the factors involved in case
disposition decisions by the Public Defenders office
through an examination of data derived by interviews with
attorneys, judges, and court staff; analysis of case
files; and direct observations in court. Two factors
were found to be most crucial for choosing the method of

disposition--the strength of the prosecution's case and the seriousness of the the case in terms of the probable punishment on conviction.

421 McLeod, M. "Victim Noncooperation in the Prosecution of Domestic Assault." CRIMINOLOGY, 21 (3): 395-416, 1983.

   McLeod examines the problem of victim noncooperation in domestic assault prosecutions. After noting the related problems of noncooperation by police, proseuctors, and judges, she presents findings from an analysis of 6,201 cases of spousal assault filed in Detroit in 1979. Specific patterns of noncooperation emerge from each category (sex, marital status) at different decision points in the prosecutorial process.

422 Miller, W. B. "Indeterminate Sentence Paradigm: Resocialization or Social Control." ISSUES IN CRIMI-NOLOGY, 7 (2):101-124, 1972.

   A historical development of the indeterminate sentence concept and an analysis of California's system for administering such sentences is described. The expectations of proponents of the indeterminate sentence are outlined, as well as the flaws which critics predicted. The procedures that the California Adult Authority employs in reviewing indeterminate sentences are examined from the prehearing stage through parole review. It is concluded that the indeterminate sentence has not resulted in better prisons, better attitudes, or shorter terms, but that such sentences have protected society from dangerous offenders.

423 Myers, M. A. "Rule Departures and Making Law: Juries and Their Verdicts." LAW AND SOCIETY REVIEW, 13 (3): 781-797, 1979.

   Myers focuses on the issue of rule departure by juries when they engage in law-making activity in felony cases. The data for the study were 201 felony jury trials held in Marion County (Indianapolis), Indiana between 1974 and 1976. The analysis asked the following questions. To what extent do juries consider the evidence presented? What kinds of evidence have the strongest effect on the verdict of the jury? To what extent do verdicts reflect the jury members' own values in the fact-finding process? To what extent do jury findings reflect personal sentiments about the defendant and the law? Myers concludes that jury verdicts depended upon the evidence. However, not all evidence was weighted equally. Evidence given by the defendant was

seen as more persuasive than that of the victim. Juries
did not rely heavily on eyewitness identification or
expert testimony. Finally, juries appeared to use their
right to depart from the instructions provided by the
judge only in a limited number of circumstances. This
was more likely to occur in cases involving a serious
offense, a young victim, and an employed defendant.

424 Myers, M. A., and J. Hagan. "Private and Public
    Trouble: Prosecutors and the Allocation of Court
    Resources." SOCIAL PROBLEMS, 26 (4): 439-451, 1979.

    In this article, the decision-making process in
which private problems become elevated to public concern
through criminal prosecution is examined. Myers and
Hagan analyze 980 criminal cases filed in the Marion
(Indianapolis) County criminal courts between 1974 and
1976. The sample did not include victimless offenses.
The authors conclude that problems of older, white, male,
and employed victims are more likely to be considered
worthy of prosecution. They note, however, that the
influence of race is significant only when the strength
of the evidence is controlled.

425 Myers, M. A., "Judges, Juries, and the Decision to
    Convict." JOURNAL OF CRIMINAL JUSTICE, 9 (4): 289-
    304, 1981.

    Myers examines the dual functions of efficiency and
due process in the criminal prosecution process. She
compares the bench trial to the more traditional trial by
jury and finds striking differences in decision-making.
Judges used different criteria than jurors in determining guilt, although this varied between felony and misdemeanor cases. Myers concludes that while bench trials
are more efficient than jury trials, they are no more
"fair" in terms of their reliance on rules of evidence.

426 Nagel, S. S. "Plea Bargaining, Decision Theory, and
    Equilibrium Models, Part 1." INDIANA LAW JOURNAL, 51
    (4): 987-1024, 1976.

    A descriptive mathematical model of plea bargaining
is developed based on assumptions that defendants want to
minimize sentences and their likelihood of conviction
while prosecutors normally want to maximize them.
Decision theory and equilibrium modeling are used to
create matrices showing how a defendant and a prosecutor
in a hypothetical case each views the most likely
sentence with different probabilities of conviction. A
discussion of optimum strategies or bargaining limits
considers the role of benefits and costs other than

sentence years, such as the saving of time, money and reputation.

427 Nagel, S. "Bringing the Attitudes of Jurors in Line With the Law." JUDICATURE, 63 (4): 189-197, 1979.

Nagel explores one of the key aspects of jury decision-making: the juror's propensity to convict. He examines this concept in three ways: (1) by developing a method for determining the values of jurors regarding their propensity to convict or acquit; (2) to use that method to determine how those propensities vary across types of jurors and cases; and (3) by discussing how such propensities can be brought more into line with legal rules regarding "reasonable doubt." The most interesting conclusion from Nagel's study is that jurors in criminal cases apply a standard of guilt substantially below what "beyond a reasonable doubt" is usually interpreted by judges. Nagel suggests that more clear and specific instructions to jurors are needed.

428 Nagel, S. S., and M. Neef. "Plea Bargaining, Decision Theory, and Equilibrium Models, Part 2." INDIANA LAW JOURNAL, 52 (1): 1-61, 1976.

This is the second of two articles developing models to predict the likelihood of plea bargains under varying circumstances. This approach conceptualizes the prosecutor as the "seller" and the defendant as the "buyer" in the plea negotiating situations. Knowledge of contingent probabilities and defendant strategies both influence the decision to go to trial or to negotiate a plea.

429 Nardulli, P. F. "Plea Bargaining: An Organizational Perspective." JOURNAL OF CRIMINAL JUSTICE, 6 (3): 217-231, 1978.

A microlevel analysis of factors affecting the decision to plead guilty in felony trial courts of Chicago, Illinois, during 1972 and 1973 is presented. Chicago's felony court system is viewed from an organizational perspective, and guilty pleas are analyzed in light of the role they play in the court organization's overall design for handling its workload. While internal factors, interests of the elite, are important, environmental considerations are also significant. The notion of coalignment between internal and external factors is crucial to an organizational perspective on criminal court operations. Two situational indicators were employed concerning the number of other indictments pending against the defendant and the defendant's arrest record. Socioeconomic status

was employed as the economic indicator. Judge,
prosecutor, and defense counsel responsiveness to plea
bargaining and defendant perceptions of the chance for
ultimate conviction were assessed.

430 Nelson, S. H. "Mock Rape Trials: Sexual Behavior,
    Sex-Role Attitudes, and Verdicts." Pp. 93-104 in P.
    L. Brantingham and T. G. Blomberg (eds.), COURTS AND
    DIVERSION: POLICY AND OPERATIONS STUDIES. Beverly
    Hills, CA: Sage, 1979.

    A mock jury experiment was conducted to examine the
effects of differential social learning experiences on
decision-making in rape trials. The subjects in the
study included 51 women and 44 men ranging in age from 17
to 68 with a median age of 32. To avoid problems of
previous research which used college students, this
experiment drew its sample from lists of citizens
provided by the local courthouse. Among the findings
were: the sex of juror was associated with verdict (a
higher percentage of men voted to acquit); interaction
effects were found between age and sex and between sex
and education (younger women and college educated women
were less likely to acquit). The author concludes that
learning less traditional views of female roles may be
related to changes in perceptions of rape, rape victims,
and rape situations among women but not among men.

431 Newman, D. J. CONVICTION--THE DETERMINATION OF
    GUILT OR INNOCENCE WITHOUT TRIAL. Boston: Little,
    Brown, 1966.

    This book contains a description of the non-trial
adjudication practices--the guilty plea and the acquittal
of the guilty--in Kansas, Michigan, and Wisconsin.
Newman discusses the guilty plea process, including plea
bargaining, trial judge use of his acquittal power to
control other parts of the criminal justice system, and
the role of the defense counsel.

432 Nimmer, R. T., and P. A. Krauthaus. "Plea Bargain-
    ing: Reform in Two Cities." JUSTICE SYSTEM JOURNAL,
    3(1): 6-21, 1977.

    The impact of plea bargaining reforms implemented in
Detroit and Denver is assessed. In both cities, plea
conferences were created by the adoption of policies
requiring that all negotiations take place in semiformal
conferences involving all relevant parties, and that
failure to reach agreement during the conference
terminate further negotiation. The reforms were
considered successful in Detroit, but not in Denver. In

Detroit, substantial efforts were made to accommodate the interest of the local bar and judiciary in the reform. In Denver, no such efforts were made. The Detroit reforms represented only a small change, whereas in Denver the reforms marked a radical departure from prior practices. The significance of these differences in accounting for the differential impact of the reforms is discussed.

433 Pruitt, C. R., and J. Q. Wilson. "A Longitudinal Study of the Effect of Race on Sentencing." LAW AND SOCIETY REVIEW, 17 (4): 613-635, 1983.

Pruitt and Wilson examine the effects of race on sentencing outcome over a ten-year period in Milwaukee. Limiting their study to cases involving only charges of armed robbery or burglary (N=1,512), they found that race had a significant effect on both length of sentence and probability of imprisonment. However, these effects were not consistent over the ten-year period. During the later period of the study the authors found a reduction in racial bias and conclude that this was due to changes in the nature of the judiciary, increased bureaucratization of both prosecutor and defense, and the rise of decision rules reducing the effects of judicial bias on sentencing decisions.

434 Purves, R. F. "That Plea-Bargaining Business: Some Conclusions from Research." CRIMINAL LAW REVIEW, 1971 (8): 470-475, 1971.

Purves examines 112 British cases in which the defendants changed their pleas from not guilty to guilty in a plea bargaining situation. He states that there was no evidence that the police behaved aggressively in order to induce a defendant to change his plea. It is also asserted that there is no evidence that the English plea bargaining system operates to deny the defendant his right to "put the prosecution to its proof." Some justification was found for the objection that the defendant is not allowed enough time for due consideration of all aspects of of the negotiation. Finally, Purves stresses that the United States plea bargaining process differs significantly from the British process and argues that the British process eases the administration of justice without prejudicing the rights of the innocent or causing injustice to the guilty.

435 Rosett, A. "The Negotiated Guilty Plea." ANNALS OF
THE AMERICAN ACADEMY OF POLITICAL AND SOCIAL
SCIENCE, 374 (November): 71-81, 1967.

Rosett presents a well-reasoned discussion of the
advantages and disadvantages of the American plea bargaining process. After identifying the major problems
associated with negotiated pleas, Rosett lays out the
virtues of bargaining, drawing heavily on both the
National Crime Commission's recommendations and the American Bar Association's draft on plea bargaining. While
noting that reforms of current practices are necessary,
Rosett emphasizes that the modest reforms recommended by
the ABA leave the substance of the negotiations
unchanged. To really reform the substance may well require reform of the entire criminal justice system.

436 Ryan, J.P., and J. J. Alfini. "Trial Judges' Participation in Plea Bargaining: An Empirical Perspective." LAW AND SOCIETY REVIEW, 13 (2): 479-507,
1979.

Using national survey data, the role of the trial
judge in plea bargaining is examined. The authors
analyze the frequency with which judges participate in
plea bargaining and the organizational, social, and legal
contexts that affect the judicial role. They conclude
that trial judges perform a crucial role in plea
negotiations. Factors such as self-perceived skill at
negotiating and whether the state has a court rule or
case law prohibiting judicial participation are found to
influence the role that a judge adopts.

437 Scarpitti, F. R., and R. M. Stephenson. "Juvenile
Court Dispositions: Factors in the Decision-Making
Process." CRIME AND DELINQUENCY, 17 (2): 142-151,
1971.

The authors discuss findings from their three-year
study of influences on juvenile court decision-making.
Based on a sample of 1,210 adjudicated delinquents, they
suggest that a pattern emerges which shows that the
probability of a boy being sent to a reformatory is much
greater for juveniles who are more disadvantaged, more
delinquent, and psychologically atypical. Scarpitti and
Stephenson argue that, to the extent that juvenile
programs are organized progressively, juveniles with more
severe problems are placed in more controlled contexts.
This, they suggest, indicates that juvenile court judges
sort out cases according to "delinquency risk," rather
than caprice or chance.

438 Severance, L. J., and E. F. Loftus. "Improving the
    Ability of Jurors to Comprehend and Apply Criminal
    Jury Instructions." LAW AND SOCIETY REVIEW, 17 (1):
    153-197, 1982.

    This article examines the problems of providing
clear, understandable instructions to jurors in criminal
cases. The authors claim that current methods of
instructing the jury lead to confusion about the law and
a lessened ability to appropriately apply the
instructions. Based upon a three-stage study of jury
instruction techniques, the authors conclude that the use
of prewritten instructions significantly improve the
juror's ability to accurately and effectively apply the
law.

439 Shinn, H. J., "Do Lesser Pleas Pay: Accommodations
    in the Sentencing and Parole Processes." JOURNAL OF
    CRIMINAL JUSTICE, 1 (1): 27-42, 1973.

    This article contains an analysis of differences in
sentence lengths or actual incarceration according to
original charge, type of plea, conviction charge, and
magnitude of charge reductions. The study shows that
charge reduction may result in directly reducing the
maximum sentence possible and indirectly reducing the
actual amount of time served. There are indications,
however, that the parole process neutralizes the sentence
differentials associated with charge reduction. The
ratio between the time served and the sentence imposed
gets higher as the magnitude of charge reduction
increases.

440 Spohn, C., J. Gruhl, and S. Welch. "The Effects of
    Race on Sentencing: A Re-Examination of an Unsettled
    Question." LAW AND SOCIETY REVIEW, 16 (1): 71-88,
    1981.

    Spohn et al. present arguments suggesting that most
previous research on the effects of race on sentence
outcome are flawed by methodological problems. They cite
six problem areas: (1) the use of small numbers of
cases; (2) the use of small numbers of offenses; (3) the
use of inadequate controls of "legal" and "extra-legal"
var-iables; (4) the use of one sentence decision rather
than two; (5) the use of poor measures of sentence
severity; (6) the use of inadequate statistical techniques. Using data on 50,000 felony cases drawn from a
single large jurisdiction between 1968 and 1979, they
selected cases that had resulted in convictions for any
of the 14 most common offenses appearing in the sample.
After deleting cases for several reasons, they were left
with 2,366 cases. The sentence decision was separated to

reflect both its length and type. They first measured sentence on a 93-point scale that ranged from suspended to life in prison. The second measure dichotomized "incarceration" into prison or no prison categories. Besides sentence measures, eight independent variables were created. Path analysis was used to estimate the total, direct, and indirect effects. The authors found no direct racial discrimination in sentence severity. Although black males received harsher sentences, this was explained by their being charged with more serious offenses. Still, black males were more likely to receive prison sentences, even after controlling for offense.

441 Stanko, E. A. "The Impact of Victim Assessment on Prosecutors' Screening Decisions: The Case of the New York County District Attorney's Office." LAW AND SOCIETY REVIEW, 16 (2): 225-239, 1981.

Stanko explores the impact of the prosecutor's stereotype of the victim during the case screening process in serious felony cases. Based upon 13 months of observation in the prosecutor's office, she noted that the prosecutor frequently focused on the victim for a prediction of an assured conviction. Whether the victim is viewed as sufficiently "credible" becomes an over-riding concern. Stanko argues that prosecutors believe that both judges and juries will accept certain kinds of victim claims as credible depending upon the personal characteristics of the victim and the congruence between the situation and the individual.

442 Thomas, C. W., and C. M. Sieverdes. "Juvenile Court Intake: An Analysis of Discretionary Decision-Making." CRIMINOLOGY, 12 (4): 413-432, 1975.

This article studies the effects of extralegal variables on court decision-making. The authors examine the factors affecting the probability of a juvenile being referred for a formal hearing. Data were derived from a juvenile court in a small southeastern city from 1966 to 1969. Three hundred and forty-six cases were examined. The authors conclude that both legal and extralegal factors are taken into consideration in the formal hearing decision. While the effects of race, social class, age, and family stability appear to influence the decision, their relative and crime statistics show that only one-fourth of willful homicides are prosecuted for capital murder, with the likelihood of a death sentence being very small and that of execution even smaller. Moreover, the death penalty is applied selectively. The second major argument for the death penalty is deterrence. Executions in recent decades have become so rare that they could not possibly influence the

murder rate. Comparisons of homicide rates from states
where the death penalty has been abolished with
retentionist states yield   no evidence of the deterrent
power of the death penalty.

443 Von Hirsch, A. DOING JUSTICE--THE CHOICE OF PUNISH-
    MENTS. New York: Farrar, Strauss, and Giroux, 1976.

     This report proposes a new model of corrections in
which discretionary sentencing and the rehabilitative
ideal are replaced by a system characterized by
sentencing based on crime seriousness and alternatives to
incarceration. Theories about sentencing have long been
dominated by traditional assumptions--that prisons
rehabilitate the criminal or restrain him if he is
dangerous, and that to accomplish these aims, judges and
other officials should be given the widest discretion in
their decisions. This text points out the flaws in such
reasoning by documenting the failures of rehabilitation
and the futility of predicting recidivism, and then
presents an alternative. It argues that under a just
system the length of a sentence would be based primarily
on the offender's deserts--that the seriousness of the
crime dictates the punishment within defined limits.

444 Wechsler, H. "Codification of Criminal Law in the
    United States: The Model Penal Code." COLUMBIA LAW
    REVIEW, 68 (8): 1450-1456, 1968.

     Wechsler discusses the Model Penal Code's sentencing
provisions and how they depart from past patterns. The
Code prescribes criteria for courts to follow in
sentencing while stressing the utilization of probation.
Wechsler also discusses the Code's position on the nature
and duration of prison sentences, special and extended
sentences, first release on parole and the parole term,
and criteria for parole release. Wechsler encourages a
more "enlightened" use of parole and probation and an
avoidance of mandatory prison terms.

445 Wheeler, S., D. Weisburd, and N. Bode. "Sentencing
    the White-Collar Offender: Rhetoric and Reality."
    AMERICAN SOCIOLOGICAL REVIEW, 47 (5): 641-659, 1982.

     This article focuses on the relationship of social
class background to the sentencing of white-collar
offenders in federal district courts for the years 1976
through 1978. The authors suggest that among the most
important factors in the sentencing decision are:
seriousness of the criminal act; character of the
defendant; statutory category of the offense; district of
conviction; and extralegal variables such as sex and age

of the defendant. They also note that the probability of
imprisonment increases with the occupational status of
the defendant.

CHAPTER 8

COURTS - ISSUES

446 Ares, C. E., and H. Sturz. "Bail and the Indigent
    Accused." CRIME AND DELINQUENCY, 8 (1): 12-20, 1962.

    This is one of the early studies on the bail system
in the United States. Data were collected as part of the
Vera Foundation New York City bail project in 1961. The
major questions guiding the research were: (1) In
practice is bail required only to insure the defendant's
appearance?; (2) Is bail being set in an amount that will
allow the defendant a reasonable opportunity to gain
freedom yet insure appearance?; (3) how does the bail
setting judge arrive at his decision?; (4) Would the
process be improved if there were a systematic process
for providing the judge with accurate information for
evaluating risk? (5) Who ultimately determines who
makes bail?; and (6) For how many defendants does bail in
any amount mean a denial of release, and can greater use
of release on the defendant's own recognizance be made?
Discussion of each of these questions follows.

447 Ball, H. V., and L. M. Friedman. "The Use of Crimi-
    nal Sanctions in the Enforcement of Economic Legisla-
    tion: A Sociological View." STANFORD LAW REVIEW, 17:
    197-223, 1965.

    Ball and Friedman explore the relationship between
notions of popular morality and the use of criminal
sanctions in the regulation of business practices. They
identify a number of areas of concern and disagreement.
For example, when referring to the use of criminal
sanctions, does one mean simple authorization or actual
implementation? What is meant by the term "criminal
sanctions"? In what way should the criminal law be
utilized in economic regulation? The authors conclude
that any discussion of the use of criminal sanctions in
economic regulation should begin by listing exactly what
sanctions and types of economic regulations are under
debate.

448 Banfield L., and C. D. Anderson. "Continuances in
    the Cook County Criminal Courts." UNIVERSITY OF
    CHICAGO LAW REVIEW, 35 (2): 259-316, 1968.

    This article examines the impact of continuances on
the system of criminal justice in Cook County (Chicago)
using a sample of felony court records obtained during
the summer of 1966. Data were gathered on the
circumstances of the case and court appearance history.
The authors conclude that the race and economic status of

defendants have a significant effect on how they are
processed through the criminal justice system. These
disparities include differences in legal representation,
release on bail, change of pleas, the granting of
continuances, and findings of guilt. After an in-depth
analysis of the data, the authors suggest a variety of
reforms that may help to reduce the inequities.

449 Barbara, J., J. Morrison, and H. Cunningham. "Plea
    Bargaining: Bargain Justice?" CRIMINOLOGY, 14 (1):
    55-64, 1976.

    The authors present a discussion of the history of
plea bargaining as it has been practiced in America as
well as its current pattern of use. After noting the
general advantages and disadvantages of this legal
procedure, they present the findings from a study they
conducted in Pima County (Tucson), Arizona. Based on 500
cases of criminal convictions involving plea bargains,
the authors conclude that the recipients of the plea
agreements (defendants) not only willingly accepted the
bargain, but supported the continued use of bargaining
for justice. Recommendations for an independent,
external review of all plea bargains prior to their
finalization are suggested.

450 Blumberg, A. S. "The Practice of Law as Confidence
    Game: Organizational Cooptation of a Profession."
    LAW AND SOCIETY REVIEW, 2: 15-39, 1967.

    Blumberg questions the connection between the
Supreme Court's conception of the role of counsel with
social reality. For Blumberg, the organizational goals
and roles of the court impose realities on the court
participants well beyond those which are defined by the
legal statutes. The defense attorney, as well as other
participants, becomes coopted by the organization and in
turn perceives the primary goal as being the need to
reach a guilty plea. While the Supreme Court would
desire that defense attorneys function entirely on behalf
of the client, the organizational demands require that
the attorney work within the "system" in cooperation with
other regulars of the court. As a consequence, the
attorney must serve the court first, the client, second.

451 Brereton, D., and J. D. Casper. "Does It Pay To
    Plead Guilty? Differential Sentencing and the Func-
    tioning of Criminal Courts." LAW AND SOCIETY REVIEW,
    16 (1): 45-70, 1981.

    The authors examined sentencing patterns in three
California jurisdictions for a five-year period between

1974 and 1978. Limiting themselves to offenses that were originally charged as either burglaries or robberies, they use simple contingency table analysis to determine if high rates of guilty pleas result in reduced sentences. The dependent variable was whether the defendant was sentenced to the state prison. They could not determine the effects of guilty pleas on sentence length given the nature of the data. While not finding conclusive evidence that guilty pleas led to a reduced sentence, they did conclude that jurisdictions characterized by higher levels of induced guilty pleas were more likely to have greater sentence differentials.

452 Carter, T., and D. Clelland. "A Neo-Marxian Critique, Formulation, and Test of Juvenile Dispositions as a Function of Social Class." SOCIAL PROBLEMS, 27 (1): 96-108, 1979.

Carter and Clelland develop a neo-Marxian theory of juvenile court dispositions where they challenge the conceptualization and measurement of social class utilized in earlier studies. They distinguish between two offense patterns: traditional crimes against the person or property and crimes against the moral order. Using a multivariate analysis, they conclude that the influence of social class is significantly greater in juvenile dispositions for moral order than for traditional offenses.

453 Clarke, S. H., and G. G. Koch. "The Influence of Income and Other Factors on Whether Criminal Defendants Go to Prison." LAW AND SOCIETY REVIEW, 11 (1): 57-92, 1976.

Legal and extralegal variables that affect the sentencing outcome of defendants are explored. A sample of 798 burglary and larceny defendants charged in the Mecklenburg County (North Carolina) criminal courts is examined. Four variables were found to have the most significant effects on likelihood of a prison sentence: (1) severity of offense; (2) defendant's income; (3) prior arrest record; and (4) strength of case against the defendant. Sex, race, age, and employment had little or no effect.

454 Clayton, O. Jr. "A Reconstruction of the Effects of Race in Criminal Sentencing." CRIMINAL JUSTICE REVIEW, 8 (2): 15-20, 1983.

Clayton reviews past research on the effects of race on sentencing and concludes that much is wanting. Using data from the Georgia Correctional Department, he matched

743 individuals with similar adult and juvenile records.
Clayton finds that blacks with a prior juvenile record
tended to receive much harsher sentences than did whites
with similar records and background characteristics.

455 Cloyd, J. W. "Prosecution's Power, Procedural Rights,
    and Pleading Guilty: The Problem of Coercion in Plea
    Bargaining Drug Cases." SOCIAL PROBLEMS, 26 (4):
    452-466, 1979.

    Cloyd looks at the relationship between legal
coercion and a defendant's voluntary cooperation in the
plea bargaining process. Based on an examination of a
"representative" transcript, the author points out the
interaction between the defendant, defense attorney,
federal prosecutor, and drug enforcement officer. Cloyd
concludes that, at least in this case, legal tactics,
pursued within constitutional constraints,   were
successful in gaining the defendant's cooperation.

456 Cobden, L. "The Grand Jury: Its Use and Misuse."
    CRIME AND DELINQUENCY, 22 (2): 149-165, 1976.

    This article is a concise history, critique of
present operation, and call for reform of the grand
jury. Evidence is provided that shows the extensive
abuses of the grand jury system, especially the
interjection of politics. Specific criticisms include:
isolation of interrogation procedure from the public,
impact of secret testimony, exclusion of witness's
attorney from the jury room, and the discretionary use of
the subpoena power by the prosecutor. The suggestions
for reform focused on: witness protection; subpoena
issuance, immunity, and contempt; rules of evidence; jury
selection and quality; and issuance of reports.

457 Connick, E., and R. C. Davis. "Examining the Problem
    of Witness Intimidation." JUDICATURE, 66 (10): 38-
    447, 1983.

    Citing recent studies, the authors claim that
witness intimidation is a common problem which occurs in
all types of cases. Their own research, conducted in
1981 in the Brooklyn Criminal Court, focused on
interviews with 109 intimidated witnesses and 11 criminal
justice officials. They found that intimidation was
frequent and serious: 23 percent were vandalized,
burglarized, threatened with a weapon, or attacked by
either the defendant or defendants' associate.
Recommendations to begin dealing with this problem are
then offered.

458 Constantini, E., and J. King. "The Partial Juror:
    Correlates and Causes of Prejudgment." LAW AND
    SOCIETY   REVIEW, 15 (1): 9-40, 1981.

    Using a multivariate discriminant function analysis
of data from two 1979 potential juror surveys concerning
three criminal cases in Yolo County, California, the
authors conclude that a very strong relationship is shown
to exist between knowledge about a specific case, general
attitudes about crime, gender, and education level, on
the one hand, and propensity to prejudge guilt is the
single most significant predictor of prejudgment.

459 Costantini, E., M. Mallery, and D. Yapundich. "Gen-
    der and Juror Partiality: Are Women More Likely to
    Prejudge Guilt?" JUDICATURE, 67 (3): 120-133, 1983.

    Constantini et al. examine the issue of sex
differences in prejudging the guilt of criminal
defendants. Based on telephone survey data from three
independently drawn samples, the authors conclude that,
while women were significantly more likely to prejudge
guilt, the explanation for this finding was not easily
found. Neither level of information, attitude, nor
educational background was found to explain the greater
propensity of women to prejudge guilt.

460 Curran, D. A. "Judicial Discretion and Defendant's
    Sex." CRIMINOLOGY, 21 (1): 41-58, 1983.

    The legal model of the criminal justice system
assumes that all defendants will receive equal treatment
under the law. On the other hand, an increasing body of
research shows that there are very significant
differences in judicial treatment on the basis of the sex
of the defendant. Curran tests two competing theories
of gender disparities: labeling theory and the chivalry
hypothesis. After analyzing 543 adult felony cases from
Dade County, Florida, she concludes that there were
inconsistent differences in treatment by sex at each of
the levels of negotiation, prosecution, conviction, and
sentencing. Neither of the competing theories was
supported.

461 Daudistel, H. C., and M. D. Holmes. "Abandoning Plea
    Bargaining: A Case Study of Nonnegotiated Justice."
    Pp. 63-77 in P. L. Brantingham and T. G. Blomberg
    (eds.), COURTS AND DIVERSION: POLICY AND OPERATIONS
    STUDIES. Beverly Hills, CA: Sage, 1979.

    This study presents an analysis of one
jurisdiction's effort to eliminate plea bargaining and

the negotiation of cases. Two consequences of the reform are hypothesized: (1) that the elimination of plea bargaining would not substantially increase the number of trials; and (2) that elimination of the negotiated plea would increase the rationality and fairness of the system of justice. A total of 172 cases of robbery and burglary prosecuted between December 1975 and August 1977 were analyzed. The results indicated that while the number of trials did increase significantly, the issue of fairness was partially supported. Defense attorneys believed that case dispositions were more evenhanded now; however, statistical evidence suggests that racial and ethnic bias in sentencing actually increased with the elimination of plea bargains.

462 Davis, W. J. "No Place for the Judge." TRIAL, 9
    (3): 22, 43, 1973.

    Davis, a United States District Court Judge, argues against the use of plea bargaining and judicial participation in the process. The main objection to plea bargaining is that it enhances the possibility that an innocent person might plead guilty to avoid the death penalty or to avoid a lengthy incarceration. The opposition to judicial participation in the plea bargaining system is based on a belief that sentencing is within the judge's discretion and should not be subject to outside controls.

463 Dean, J. M. "Illegitimacy of Plea Bargaining."
    FEDERAL PROBATION, 38 (3): 18-23, 1974.

    Dean discusses the legitimacy of plea bargaining, its operation, and legal status as reflected in recent Supreme Court decisions. The author notes the dependence of the court system on plea bargaining and traces the gradual development of this procedure. Supreme Court decisions that have basically served to legitimize plea bargaining are also reviewed. Several approaches to diminishing the need to rely upon plea bargaining also are presented.

464 D'Esposito, J. C. "Sentencing Disparity: Causes and
    Cures." JOURNAL OF CRIMINAL LAW, CRIMINOLOGY &
    POLICE SCIENCE, 60 (2): 182-194, 1969.

    After examining the nature and extent of sentencing disparity, the author identifies its various causes. The primary cause is the trend toward greater individualization of sentences. While legislatures have attempted to provide sentencing alternatives that fit the offender, they have given little attention to the proper

use of such sentences. Noting that the Model Penal Code
and the Model Sentencing Act move in the right direction,
but not far enough, the author calls for greater
objectification of the process and a reduction in
judicial discretion.

465 Gazell, J. A. "State Trial Courts: The Increasing
    Visibility of a Quagmire in Criminal Justice."
    CRIMINOLOGY, 9 (4): 397-400, 1972.

    Gazell questions the assertion that the American
criminal justice system is a "system." He takes a close
look at one segment of the "system" or process--the
courts--and examines their many failures, providing a
brief series of suggested solutions for the difficulties
in the courts. The primary problems of the courts have
to do with management, case loads, and qualitative and
quantitative flaws such as discriminatory dispositions.
Gazell's suggestions for reform reflect the collective
recommendations of a number of judicial scholars.

466 Gelber, S. "Who Defends the Prosecutor?" CRIME AND
    DELINQUENCY, 14 (4): 315-321, 1968.

    Reacting to growing criticisms of the prosecutor,
Gelber argues that the prosecutor is actually hampered by
organizational, social, economic, and legal contraints.
Claiming that they are underpaid, understaffed, faced
with role conflict, and often enticed into more lucrative
positions, it is not surprising that prosecutors would
face problems in dealing with the growing demands of the
office. In the end, Gelber compares the role and
organization of the prosecutor's office in the United
States with that found in England and Europe. The
relative strengths and weaknesses of each are discussed.

467 Gertz, M. G. "The Impact of Prosecutor/Public Defen-
    der Interaction on Sentencing: An Exploratory
    Typology." CRIMINAL JUSTICE REVIEW, 5 (1): 43-54,
    1980.

    Gertz explores the relationship between the
prosecutor and public defender and the impact of this
relationship on sentencing outcome. The data for the
analysis were drawn from 197 felony cases in three
criminal courts in Connecticut in 1975. After
characterizing each of the three courts in terms of the
nature of the prosecutor-public defender relationship
("friendly, team-oriented," "middle-of-the-road," and
"uncooperative"), Gertz concluded that such

relationships did, indeed, have some effects on sentence outcome. More extreme sentences tend to be found in the uncooperative courts, while frequent charge dropping was found in the friendly courts. However, convictions on reduced charges were less frequent in the cooperative courts and willingness to go to trial more common in uncooperative courts.

468 Hagan, J., and I. N. Bernstein. "Conflict in Context: The Sanctioning of Draft Resisters, 1963-76." SOCIAL PROBLEMS, 27 (1): 109-122, 1979.

Hagan and Bernstein examine the criminal sentencing of draft resisters over a fourteen year period. Data were drawn from a content analysis of newspaper articles and editorials as well as from the federal district court records of a large American city. After dividing the fourteen year time frame into two distinct social and political periods, they isolate the effects of race and type of resistance on sentencing outcome.

469 Hagan, J., and I. N. Bernstein. "Sentence Bargaining of Upperworld Crime in Ten Federal District Courts." LAW AND SOCIETY REVIEW, 13 (2): 467-478, 1979.

Using both qualitative and quantitative data gathered from ten Federal District Courts, the authors explore the use of different types of sentence bargaining tactics. They distinguish between proactive and reactive prosecutorial orientations and hypothesize that the prosecution of upperworld crime is more likely to be proactive and associated with more explicit sentence bargaining, while the prosecution of underworld crime is likely to be reactive. Evidence in support of the hypotheses is offered.

470 Hall, E. L., and A. A. Simkus. "Inequality in the Types of Sentences Received by Native Americans and Whites." CRIMINOLOGY, 13 (2): 199-222, 1975.

While the traditional literature of American criminal justice stresses the notion of equal treatment under law, the "law in action" often seems to depart from the ideal. Hall and Simkus examine the patterns of sentences received by native American and white offenders in a district court of a western state. Their data strongly suggest systematic discrimination against native Americans, even when controlling for present offense, prior record, and other individual background characteristics.

471 Heininger, B. L. "Incompetency to Stand Trial: As Status, As Label, and As Potential Source of Sentencing Disparity." JOURNAL OF CRIMINAL JUSTICE, 10 (3): 191-198, 1982.

Heininger raises a question about the effects of a defendant's claim of incompetence to stand trial. By comparing the sentences received by a group of defendants who had raised the incompetency issue with a group of defendants who had not. The author finds that the simple raising of the issue is significant in the court's decision to dismiss the case but not in the type or length of sentence.

472 Heumann, M., and C. Loftin. "Mandatory Sentencing and the Abolition of Plea Bargaining: The Michigan Felony Firearm Statute." LAW AND SOCIETY REVIEW, 13 (2): 393-430, 1979.

The authors assess the consequences of a simultaneous attempt to abolish plea bargaining and introduce mandatory sentencing in Michigan. Using qualititative data drawn from interviews with judges, prosecutors, and defense attorneys, and quantitative data from criminal court files, the authors examine the attempt to impose mandatory prison sentences for firearms violations within a court that also was attempting to abolish plea bargaining. They conclude that, while some minor changes in patterns of prosecution were noted, disposition patterns did not seem to be altered dramatically. In many cases, sentences seemed to be "adjusted" to take the new mandatory two-year add-on into consideration.

473 Hindelang, M. J. "Equality Under the Law." JOURNAL OF CRIMINAL LAW, CRIMINOLOGY & POLICE SCIENCE, 60 (3):Pp. 306-313, 1969.

Hindelang examines a number of studies of sentencing outcomes to evaluate the claims of racial discrimination. He suggests that, while the historical evidence supports the claim that blacks have received harsher treatment at the hands of the courts, more recent evidence indicates greater equality of treatment. Based upon his examination of nearly a dozen studies of sentencing outcomes, Hindelang draws these conclusions. First, studies finding racial discrimination have used data collected from the South, while those finding no discrimination utilize data from northern states. Secondly, studies finding no discrimination control for relevant non-racial variables more closely. Thirdly, studies finding racial bias use data about ten years older than those studies finding no bias. Finally, Hindelang indicates that those studies finding bias examined mainly homicide offenses, while those finding no bias looked primarily at property offenses.

474 Hoey, J. P. "The Prosecuting Attorney and Organized Crime." CRIME AND DELINQUENCY, 8 (4): 379-384, 1962.

Inasmuch as organized crime is as pervasive and influential as it is, Hoey (a United States Attorney, Eastern District of New York) sees the best defense against it being the "honest, forthright, competent, intelligent prosecutor who has the proper perspective of the duties and responsibilities of office, a selective and realistic discretion, an awareness of the handicaps in his path and a will to overcome these obstacles." These points are discussed within the context of his examination of the prosecutor's role, criminal investigations, and the need for public relations and education on the subject.

475 Inbau, F. E. "The Social and Ethical Requirements of Criminal Prosecution." JOURNAL OF CRIMINAL LAW, CRIMINOLOGY & POLICE SCIENCE, 52 (2): 209-212, 1961.

Inbau's article is an indictment of the liberal direction which the courts had begun to take in the late 1950's. He characterizes the courts as having a "turn 'em loose" philosophy, motivated by judges attempting to be "fashionable in judicial circles" and claims that there has been a failure to communicate to the courts the police-prosecution side of the issues. He concludes that "the courts have no right to police the police" because it is not their proper function, and that they could better spend their time "getting their own house in order."

476 Jankovic, I. "Social Class and Criminal Sentencing." CRIME AND SOCIAL JUSTICE, 10 (Fall/Winter): 9-16, 1978.

Responding to recent studies critical of the conflict perspective in judicial sentencing research, Jankovic presents a more adequate test of the Chambliss-Seidman hypothesis that "when sanctions are imposed, the most severe sanctions will be imposed on persons in the

lowest social class." Based on his analysis of 2,250
persons sentenced in a California county court between
1969 and 1974, Jankovic finds that legal variables are
wholly irrelevant for explaining sentencing disparities.
Legal factors are, themselves, instruments of biased
control. It is noted that no study to date has found
that white and middle class persons were treated by the
courts more harshly than non white and lower class
persons. The reverse cannot be claimed.

477 Katz, J. "Legality and Equality: Plea Bargaining in
    the Prosecution of White-Collar and Common Crimes."
    LAW AND SOCIETY REVIEW, 13 (2): 431-459, 1979.

    Based on a study of a U.S. Attorney's Office, Katz
examines the differences in the prosecution of white-
collar and common crimes, specifically in the context of
their impact on plea bargaining. It is noted that the
social distance between the prosecutor and defendant is
greater in the enforcement of laws against common crimes
than for white-collar crimes. Because the social
distance is slight in the prosecution of white-collar
crimes, Katz believes that the formal record greatly
underrepresents the exercise of the prosecutor's
discretion not to prosecute. Reforms to correct the
imbalance in the use of plea bargains and to make them
more consistent are discussed.

478 Katz, L. R., L. B. Litwin and R. H. Bamberger. JUS-
    TICE IS THE CRIME--PRETRIAL DELAY IN FELONY CASES.
    Cleveland: Case Western Reserve University Press,
    1972.

    Excessive delay inherent in the present criminal
justice system is shown by presenting the time lapses
that exist between specific pretrial criminal procedures.
The maze of pretrial procedures has made the defendant's
journey between arrest and ultimate disposition in felony
cases a long and involved process. Paying particular
attention to due process goals of various criminal
procedures, the authors analyze specific pretrial
procedures such as arrest, preliminary hearing,
indictment, and plea bargaining in light of the delay
each procedure contributes to the process. The authors
note that while the initial decision to charge a person

with a crime is made by the police and the prosecutor,
charges against him may also be reviewed in a preliminary
hearing or by the grand jury. The authors recommend that
all jurisdictions enact strict time limitations requiring
ultimate disposition of felony cases within 60 days if
the defendant is in jail, and 120 days if he is free on
bail. In addition to various tables, appendixes include
a State-by-State review of basic pretrial criminal
procedures.

479 Krasnow, E. G. "Social Investigation Reports in the
    Juvenile Court: Their Uses and Abuses." CRIME AND
    DELINQUENCY, 12 (2): 151-164, 1966.

    Social investigation reports and their creation are
considered to be among the most important products of
the juvenile court. They are important to juvenile court
officials, to the client, and to researchers. This
article discusses issues surrounding the timing of the
social investigation and the proper uses of the social
investigation report by court officials: i.e., who may
see it, under what circumstances, to what ends. Suggestions for court guidelines regulating the disclosure of
the social investigation report are provided.

480 Kruttschnitt, C. "Social Status and Sentences of
    Female Offenders." LAW AND SOCIETY REVIEW, 15 (2):
    247-266, 1981.

    The effect of social status on sentence for female
defendants is examined. The analysis of a sample of
1,034 female defendants focuses on the effects of
economic rank, prior criminal record, age, and employment
status while controlling for seriousness of the
conviction offense. The findings indicate that these
indicators of social status are good predictors of both
the nature and severity of sentence.

481 Lefstein, N., V. Stapelton, and L.E. Teitelbaum. "In
    Search of Juvenile Justice: Gault and Its Implemen-
    tation." LAW AND SOCIETY REVIEW, 3 (4): 491-562,
    1969.

    This article is an examination of the response to
the Gault decision by three urban courts representing
slightly different styles and structure of operation.
The data were collected by field investigators who had
been observing the courts since early 1966 (conducting a

study on the impact of counsel). After the Gault decision the observers placed special emphasis on observing the compliance with the Gault requirements. The authors conclude that compliance with each of the basic requirements was only gradually being achieved. However, they note that, like the Miranda decision, overall compliance was slow but eventually obtained.

482 Lizotte, A. J. "Extra-Legal Factors in Chicago's Criminal Courts: Testing the Conflict Model of Criminal Justice." SOCIAL PROBLEMS, 25 (5): 564-580, 1978.

Lizotte challenges the claims by Chiricos and Waldo in their test of the conflict hypothesis regarding bias in criminal sentencing. The data were drawn from the Chicago trial courts for 1971. A total of 816 cases were selected and analyzed with path analysis. The findings suggest that there is great inequality in sentencing based on occupational status and race. This held true for both incarceration decision and length of sentence.

483 Martin, L. H., and P. R. Snyder. "Jurisdiction Over Status Offenses Should Not Be Removed From the Juvenile Court." CRIME AND DELINQUENCY, 22 (1): 44-47, 1976.

Martin and Snyder are responding to recent calls for the removal of status offenses from juvenile court jurisdiction. Rejecting the notion that the "incarceration" of status offenders involves an "injustice," they point out that data have shown that it is status offenders who are incarcerated longer and have higher rates of parole revocations. This, they claim, suggests that these juveniles are more difficult to aid than juveniles charged with delinquent acts. The authors stress the need for more facilities and programs to assist the court with providing alternative dispositions for status offenders while maintaining legal jurisdiction.

484 Miller, F. W. PROSECUTION--THE DECISION TO CHARGE A SUSPECT WITH A CRIME. Chicago: American Bar Foundation, 1970.

This text discusses the involvement of the prosecutor in relation to the following: the decision to charge; evidence required to charge; judicial involvement in and review of the decision to charge; and discretion and charging decision. The decision to charge requires

the resolution of three related, but independently
important, issues. First, there must be a determination
of whether there is sufficient probability of guilt to
justify subjecting the suspect to a trial. A judgment
must be made about whether a jury will be likely to
acquit, either because they are unlikely to be convinced
of the guilt of the suspect, or for other reasons
unrelated to the likelihood of guilt. Second, the
prosecutor may conclude that prosecution is not in the
community interest. In that event, he must choose
between release and pursuing some alternative other than
criminal prosecution. Third, if a decision is made to
prosecute, the specific crime or crimes with which the
person is to be charged must be selected. This may be
influenced by considerations of sentencing probabilities,
ability to secure guilty pleas, and the prosecutor's
conclusion about both the individual's and the
community's interests.

485 Nagel, I. H. "The Legal/Extra-legal Controversy:
    Judicial Decisions in Pretrial Release." LAW AND
    SOCIETY REVIEW, 17 (3): 481-515, 1983.

     This article examines the relative impact of legal
and extra-legal factors on pretrial release decisions.
This study was based upon 5,594 criminal defendants
processed through a borough criminal court in New York
during 1974 and 1975. Statutory law was the indicator of
legal variables and was found to have an effect on bail
outcome. However, extra-legal factors such as bench bias
and status characteristics of the defendant did influence
the nature of the bail decision.

486 Nagel, S. S. "The Tipped Scales of American Jus-
    tice." TRANSACTION, 13 (4): (May/June): 3-9, 1966.

     Nagel's article is a brief analysis of data gathered
by the American Bar Foundation from state trial court
dockets in 1962 sampled from 194 counties across the
country. A total of 11,258 cases were generated. Nagel
contends that, despite the Bill of Rights guarantees to
the right to a lawyer, a grand jury indictment, a speedy
trial, and a trial by jury, there continue to be
widespread inequities. The "least equal" in America,
those for whom the Bill of Rights was primarily designed
(blacks, poor, and the ignorant), benefit little from its
protections. Nagel examines the relationships of social
class, sex, race, age, and geographic jurisdiction to
basic safeguards (preliminary hearings, bail, defense
counsel, grand jury, delay, trial by jury, and conviction
and sentencing).

487 Oaks, D. H. "Studying the Exclusionary Rule in Search
    and Seizure." UNIVERSITY OF CHICAGO LAW REVIEW, 37
    (4): 665-757, 1970.

    This article focuses on the effects of the
exclusionary rule on the criminal justice system.
Specifically, it looks at the impact on law enforcement
personnel. The article reviews the state of existing
knowledge on the exclusionary rule in the following
areas: (1) history and justifications of the exclusionary
rule; (2) positions by the Supreme Court and prominent
scholars regarding the rule; (3) empirical evidence of
the effect of the rule on police search and seizure; (4)
the relationship of deterrence to the rule; (5)
limitations of deterrent effectiveness of the
exclusionary rule; and (6) negative effects of the rule.

488 Padawer-Singer, A. M., and A. H. Barton. "The Impact
    of Pretrial Publicity on Juror's Verdicts." Pp. 125
    -139 in R. J. Simon (ed.), THE JURY SYSTEM IN AMERICA.
    Beverly Hills, CA: Sage, 1975.

    Data for this study come from a jury experiment run
in courts in two counties in New York to determine the
extent to which jurors are prejudiced by (1) exposure to
specific media information, (2) the characteristics of
media-susceptible and influenced jurors, and (3) possible
solutions for countering prejudice in the minds of
jurors. The authors found that, in addition to exposure
to case-specific publicity, national and even
international events may have a biasing effect. They
conclude that jurors exposed to unfavorable publicity are
more likely to find the defendant guilty than are jurors
not so exposed. A careful use of the voir dire is
recommended to minimize pretrial prejudice.

489 Parnas, R. L., and R. J. Atkins. "Abolishing Plea
    Bargaining: A Proposal." CRIMINAL LAW BULLETIN, 14
    (2): 101-122, 1978.

    Forces behind the movement to abolish plea
bargaining are examined, attempts to restrict plea
bargaining in four jurisdictions are reviewed, and a plan
to replace plea bargaining with charge setting hearings
is proposed. Serious constitutional questions surround
the practice of plea bargaining. The article discusses
the implications from the following question: How can a
democratic system of government condone a process whereby
people who choose to exercise their constitutional right
remain charged with criminal conduct bearing greater
potential punishment than the lesser charges they would
be offered were they to forego the exercise of their
constitutional rights?

490 Pollack, H., and A. B. Smith. "White-Collar v. Street
    Crime Sentencing Disparity: How Judges See the Prob-
    lem." JUDICATURE, 67 (4): 174-182, 1983.

    Pollack and Smith deal with the issue of sentencing
disparities between   white-collar and street crimes.
While many critics suggest that it is simply indicative
of the racial and class bias of the larger criminal
justice system, more subtle factors may actually be more
directly involved. Pollack and Smith note that the very
definition of "white-collar crime" is ambiguously understood by both judges and attorneys. In addition, they
indicate that any assessment of this problem is
confounded by the fact that white-collar crime is
ultimately a sociological concept while sentencing is a
legal process.

491 Pettigrew, H. W. "The University, the Arrested
    Student, and Bail." LAW AND SOCIETY REVIEW, 5 (4):
    563-570, 1971.

    Pettigrew argues that in situations in which a
transient college student is arrested, cash bail is
usually not necessary to assure the defendant's appearance in court. However, the problem with such cases is
that the court almost always requires cash bail for any
transient, and thus students should not be exempt on
principle. Pettigrew suggest an alternative to cash bail
for arrested transient college students: Release on
Recognizance based on the student's academic commitment
as an indicator of a community tie.

492 Poythress, N. G. "Psychological Issues in Criminal
    Proceedings: Judicial Preference Regarding Expert
    Testimony." CRIMINAL JUSTICE AND BEHAVIOR, 10 (2):
    175-194, 1983.

    This paper examines the attitudes of a sample of
circuit court judges in Michigan on mental health and
behavioral sciences expert testimony on criminal justice
issues.   The focus of the study was to test the
assumption that judges preferred expert testimony from
medically trained expert witnesses. The conclusions
suggest that while psychiatrists and medical groups received the highest ratings among six professional groups,
there were some moderating effects due to the judges
perception of the expert witnesses' ability to demonstrate either training or experience in psychopathology,
regardless of other medical training.

493 Reid, S. T. "Rebuttal to the Attack on the Indeterm-
    inate Sentence." WASHINGTON LAW REVIEW, 51 (3): 565-
    606, 1976.

        Reid discusses the history and treatment philosophy
underlying the indeterminate sentence, focusing on the
philosophical and practical problems of implementing the
treatment philosophy. It is concluded that the system
itself should not be viewed as solely responsible for its
shortcomings because abuses of the system, as well as
practical implementation problems, are responsible for
the current dissatisfaction with the indeterminate
sentence.

494 Roesch, R., and S. L. Golding. "Legal and Judicial
    Interpretation of Competency to Stand Trial Statutes
    and Procedures." CRIMINOLOGY, 16 (3): 420-429, 1978.

        Roesch and Golding discuss the conflicting interpre-
tations of the competency statutes in North Carolina.
Views of trial judges and defense attorneys are compared
and their explanations for existing procedures are noted.
The authors point out that competency hearings were often
not held, and in a number of cases where the defendant
was found to be incompetent, that judges often believed
that involuntary commitment to a mental institution
should be automatic regardless of perceived dangerousness. These issues demand more attention and research to
provide resolution according to the authors.

495 Ruffra, P. S. "Hypnotically Induced Testimony:
    Should It Be Admitted?" CRIMINAL LAW BULLETIN, 19
    (4): 293-324, 1983.

        Should hypnotically induced testimony be admitted as
evidence in criminal trials? An increasing number of
courts are allowing such testimony to be presented
because they view the issue to be one of credibility, not
of admissibility. Other courts only allow such testimony
to be admitted under very restricted circumstances. On
the other hand, Ruffra points out that still other courts
exclude hypnotically induced testimony altogether. The
author examines the views in each of these three
situations as they currently exist in California.

496 Sigler, R. T., and W. A. Formby. "The Necessity of
    Bail Reform." CRIMINAL JUSTICE REVIEW, 3 (1): 1-7,
    1978.

        Sigler and Formby argue that the original formal and
informal objectives of bail (to insure that the accused
will appear for trial and to protect society from

dangerous offenders) are not being met in our present
system. As a consequence, bail simply becomes a factor
for detaining the indigent and relatively inexperienced
offender. They suggest a variety of reforms to the
present system.

497 Smith, A. B., and A. S. Blumberg. "Objectivity in
    Judicial Decision-Making." SOCIAL FORCES, 46 (1):
    96-105, 1967.

    Smith and Blumberg present an interesting analysis
of the problems attendant to objectivity in judicial
decision-making. They suggest that the particular
judicial role set of the judge plays an overriding part
in the judge's perception of cases and the consequent
outcomes.   Six major judicial role patterns are
identified and discussed: (1) the Intellectual-Scholar;
(2) the Routineer-Hack; (3) the Political Adventurer-
Careerist; (4) the Judicial Pensioner; (5) the Hatchet
Man; and (6) the Tyrant-Showboat-Benevolent Despot. The
authors conclude that the specific role performance of a
judge will be largely determined by that judge's role
set.

498 Sperlich, P. W. "...And Then There Were Six: The
    Decline of the American Jury." JUDICATURE, 63 (6):
    262-279, 1980.

    Sperlich expresses strong concern over what he
perceives to be a decline in the American jury system as
a consequence of the introduction of two significant
changes: the reduction in size from twelve to six jurors
and the elimination of the unanimous verdict. Citing
Supreme Court decisions over the past decade, Sperlich
argues that a revolution in jury law has occurred and
that such change suggests the possible existence of four
hidden agendas: jury cost, court delay, judicial power,
and law and order. After examining these hidden agendas,
Sperlich makes a final call for the prevention of any
further decline in the trial by jury concept and the
historical role of the ordinary citizen in the criminal
jury.

499 Sperlich, P. W. "Social Science Evidence in the
    Courts: Reaching Beyond the Adversary Process."
    JUDICATURE, 63 (6): 280-289, 1980.

    What is the proper role of findings from social
science research in court decision and policy-making?
Sperlich explores this question and argues that: (1) the
courts should not isolate themselves from the work and

findings of the scientific community; (2) the courts
must take the initiative to go beyond the reliance on
briefs and records to obtain relevant social facts; (3)
better procedures must be developed to facilitate the
court in dealing with technical fact materials; and (4)
the testing mechanisms of the adversary process cannot be
relied upon exclusively to establish the validity of
social fact assertions. Suggestions for modification of
court procedural rules are offered.

500 Starrs, J. E. "Southern Juvenile Courts: A Study of
    Irony, Civil Rights, and Judicial Practice." CRIME
    AND DELINQUENCY, 13 (2): 289-306, 1967.

    This paper discusses the problems confronted in the
juvenile court in Hinds County (Jackson), Mississippi
during 1965. The author focuses on the reaction of the
juvenile court to nearly 400 juveniles arrested for
public demonstrations. It was noted that when the
constitutional protections are minimal (as they are in
juvenile court), the latitude of the court can become an
instrument for repression. Specific problems of
detention, bail, hearings, and appeals are examined.

501 Sternberg, D. "The New Radical-Criminal Trials: A
    Step Toward a Class-For-Itself in the American Prole-
    tariat?" SCIENCE AND SOCIETY, 36 (3): 274-301, 1972.

    Sternberg examines the emergence of a new challenge
to the traditional operations of the criminal justice
system: the radical-criminal trial. Sternberg's article
is broken down into three sections. The first deals with
the major distinctions between the more traditional
criminal trials in the United States and those which he
designates as radical-criminal trials. The author also
attempts to tie the emergence of trials of radicals to
the nature of political protest in the United States.
The second section of the article deals specifically with
an "anatomy" of a radical-criminal trial. The final
section is devoted to evaluating the potential impact of
such trials on the immediate future of the administration
of criminal justice in the United States. Sternberg
takes an admitted Marxist approach in his orientation to
the subject.

502 Suffet, F. "Bail Setting: A Study of Courtroom
    Interaction." CRIME AND DELINQUENCY, 12 (4): 318-
    331, 1966.

    This study examines the interactions in a courtroom
among the principal participants in the bail-setting
decision. Observing the existence of a judge-prosecutor

coalition, and the minimal influence of the defense
attorney, Suffet concludes that conflict over bail amount
is suppressed. Bail-setting serves the latent function
of diffusing the responsibility for the defendant's
release. Suffet also notes that the three general types
of bail disposition--release on recognizance, bail in a
dollar amount, and remand--are seen as progressively
decreasing the judge's responsibility in releasing the
accused.

503 Susman, J. "Juvenile Justice: Even-Handed or Many-
    Handed? An Empirical Investigation of Decision Pro-
    cesses in Disposition Hearings." CRIME AND DEL-
    INQUENCY, 19 (4): 493-507, 1973.

    Susman assesses the impact of court reorganization
on juvenile justice. The independent variables
considered were the occupational background and
experience of the judge, and the dependent variable was
the disposition hearing decision process. This variable
included the length of time of the hearing, interaction
of the participants, and roles and role conflicts. A
total of 169 nonrandom cases (with a total of eight
judges hearing the cases) were observed in the Juvenile
Branch of the Superior Court of the District of Columbia
during a four month period in 1971. Among the findings
were: probation officers were more succesful than defense
attorneys in getting judges to accept their recommendations; and experienced judges were more likely to
impose harsher sentences on juveniles than were less
experienced judges.

504 Wald, P. M. "Poverty and Criminal Justice." Pp.
    139-151 in the President's Commission on Law Enforce-
    ment and Administration of Justice, TASK FORCE RE-
    PORT: THE COURTS. Washington, D.C.: U.S. Government
    Printing Office, 1967.

    This stinging indictment of the American criminal
justice system examines the impact of poverty on the
processing of criminal defendants. Utilizing empirical
data and participant observations, Wald notes that at
each stage of the criminal processing of defendants, the
poor are at a severe disadvantage and face outright
discrimination. She concludes that, until the conditions
that produce poverty are dealt with, no reforms in the
criminal justice process can reduce the burdens of
poverty in the processing of defendants. However, the
immediate need is to ease such burdens by assuring the
poor those basic rights granted to all citizens.

---

505 Walker, T. G. "A Note Concerning Partisan Influences on Trial Judge Decision-Making." LAW AND SOCIETY REVIEW, 6 (4): 645-650, 1972.

Walker asserts that prior research into the influence of political party affiliation on judicial decision-making has remained unclear and inadequate to the task. Based on 1,177 decisions during the years 1963-1968 for which the identity of political party affiliation of the judge was available, Walker concludes that political party of judge was not related to outcomes.

506 Wheeler, G. R. "The Benefits of Legal Representation in Misdemeanor Court." CRIMINAL LAW BULLETIN, 19 (3): 221-233, 1983.

This article presents the findings from a study of 871 first-time offenders in a misdemeanor court during August 1981. Offenses were limited to driving while intoxicated, theft, or possession of marijuana. The author's analysis is consistent with previous research regarding pretrial punishment (the absence of an attorney seems to have no impact on bail decisions), but goes against studies claiming that legal representation has no effect on disposition. Indeed, he points out that defendants represented by counsel fared better than those without counsel, regardless of charge or bail status. In conclusion, Wheeler calls for improving legal services for the poor, removing barriers to bail, and an increased use of nonincarcerative sentencing options for misdemeanor cases.

507 White, W. S. "A Proposal for Reform of the Plea Bargaining Process." UNIVERSITY OF PENNSYLVANIA LAW REVIEW, 119 (3): 439-465, 1971.

The nature of plea bargaining in Philadelphia and New York, the practices utilized to induce guilty pleas, salient problems with these practices and suggestions for improvement are presented. While noting that the plea bargaining practices found in the two cities are "detrimental to society's interests", the author maintains that plea bargaining will remain as an integral part of the administration of justice. The development of "fair" plea bargaining policies must be jointly developed by prosecutors, defense attorneys, and judges.

508 Wice, P., and R. J. Simon. "Pretrial Release: A
    Survey of Alternative Practices." FEDERAL PROBATION,
    34 (4): 60-63, 1970.

    Wice and Simon compare findings from the Vera
Foundation Bail Project Study in New York with data
collected in a survey focusing on the Illinois plan for
pretrial release. Questionnaires were sent to three
officials in 15 cities. Two major conclusions were
presented. First, bail reform can work for the benefit
of the defendant without causing undue harm to society.
Second, the Illinois Plan was found to be most successful
in releasing the largest number of defendants as well as
in eliminating the bondsman from the judicial scene. It
was also viewed as best suited for cities with
populations between 25,000 and 100,000.

509 Williams, K. M. "Few Convictions in Rape Cases:
    Empirical Evidence Concerning Some Alternative Expla-
    nations." JOURNAL OF CRIMINAL JUSTICE, 9 (1): 29-39,
    1981.

    Traditionally, rape cases have low rates of convic-
tion. Among recent explanations for this phenomenon is
the unwillingness of rape victims to continue the prosecution and the possibility of outright discrimination
against females. The primary basis for a dismissal
decision appeared to be the weakness of the victim's
credibility. Williams used a multivariate approach to
analyze types of rape cases that did result in conviction
and was able to identify eight statistically significant
independent variables.

510 Willick. D. H., G. Gehlker, and A. M. Watts. "Social
    Class as a Factor Affecting Judicial Disposition:
    Defendants Charged with Criminal Homosexual Acts."
    CRIMINOLOGY, 13 (1): 57-77, 1975.

    The authors test the proposition that social class
of the defendant influences judicial disposition with
lower class defendants receiving more severe sanctions.
Based on data from cases involving felonious homosexual
acts, they conclude that there is no support for the
hypothesis.

511 Zeisel, H. "Methodological Problems in Studies of
    Sentencing." LAW AND SOCIETY REVIEW, 3 (4): 621-
    632, 1969.

    Zeisel discusses the variety of methodological
approaches taken in the study of judicial sentencing.

Breaking the past research into two categories (those that aim at finding out the whole range of determining causes and those that were designed to test a particular variable), Zeisel evaluates the relative strengths and weaknesses of selected studies.

CHAPTER 9

CORRECTIONS - HISTORY

512 Bittner, E., and A. M. Platt. "The Meaning of Pun-
    ishment." ISSUES IN CRIMINOLOGY, 2 (1): 79-99, 1966.

Evidence from pre-literate societies indicates that
legal punishment is a recent development. Modern defense
of punishment is based on the principles of retribution
and deterrence. The deterrence argument has supplied the
official punishment justification for the past 150 years.
Also, during this period the severity of punishment has
progressively declined, while modern psychology has grown
in influence. Today a schism exists within penology
between the treatment approach and the punitive approach.
The acceptance of psychological remedies will depend to a
great extent on the formulation of legal regulations of
the right and duty to treat, in a manner akin to the ways
in which the right and duty to punish has been legally
regulated in the past.

513 Empey, L. T. "Correctional History." Pp.267-273 in
    P. Lerman (ed.), DELINQUENCY AND SOCIAL POLICY. New
    York: Praeger, 1970.

A historical view of society's approach to criminals
is summarized as a succession of three R's: revenge,
restraint, and reformation. Revenge was the primary
response prior to the first revolution in the eighteenth
and nineteenth centuries. It was replaced during that
revolution by an emphasis on restraint. When the second
revolution occurred in the late nineteenth and early
twentieth centuries, reformation became an important
objective. Attention was focused upon the mental and
emotional make up of the offender and efforts were made
to alter these as the primary sources of difficulty. It
is suggested that another revolution may be in the
making--one in which the effects of society, social
group, and culture or subculture are seen as dominant
forces in criminality. The conflicts between the various
philosophies and their implications for the success of
various treatment procedures are discussed.

513a Foucault, M. DISCIPLINE AND PUNISHMENT: THE BIRTH OF
     THE PRISON. New York: Pantheon, 1977.

Arguments about the failures of penal institutions
are as old as prison itself. These failures are an
inherent part of an institution which never functioned to
eliminate criminals but only to define, refine, and
perpetuate crime. This study explores the transition
from the medieval customs of public torture and execution

to today's system of correctional institutionalization. The concept of corrective incarceration has brought about a revolution in the treatment and understanding of crime and punishment. This philosophy of rehabilitation created and expanded sophisticated methods of repression and behavior transformation. Prisons cannot be separated from the societies they serve; they are the concentrated expression of a discipline that has spread throughout schools, armies, factories, and hospitals since the 17th century. With regularized routines and rigidly organized labor, prisons epitomize the ways people are controlled and repressed today.

514 Grupp, S. E., (ed.). THEORIES OF PUNISHMENT. Bloomington: Indiana University Press, 1971.

This collection of readings discusses the following classical punishment theories: retributive, deterrent, rehabilitative, and integrative. There exists today a high degree of public and individual ambivalence toward punishment. Sustained controversy over the death penalty and erratic enforcement of vice laws are two cases in point. The editor contends that differing approaches to corrections cannot be argued to an ultimate conclusion because our administration of justice is based on an amalgam of conflicting punishment ideologies. Other factors which he sees contributing to the confused state of affairs are public indifference and insensitivity to many phases of the crime problem. The editor concludes that progress toward unifying our penal policy cannot be made without informed and comprehensive consideration of the issues and objectives of sentencing, corrections, and punishment theory in general.

515 Hawkins, G. "Punishment and Deterrence: The Educative, Moralizing, and Habituative Effects." WISCONSIN LAW REVIEW, 1969 (2): 550-565, 1969.

The classic theorists have defined deterrence as a responsive, systematic intimidation by threat of punishment designed to outweigh any pleasure to be derived from crime. This definition is somewhat misleading in that it neglects the more subtle points which are fundamental. What is variously called educative moralizing function of the law, the moral or socio-pedagogical influence of punishment, or the educative, and habituative effects of our penal sanctions, have been disregarded. It is reasonable to suppose that the deterrent force of capital punishment operates not only by affecting the conscious thoughts of individuals tempted to commit murder but also by building up in the community, over a long period of time, a deep feeling of peculiar abhorrence of the crime of murder.

It has been argued that the death penalty cannot be useful, since inflicting such punishment becomes an act of barbarity. The article draws attention to important aspects of punishment which have long been obscured by adherence to an inadequate theoretical model.

516 Hibbert, C. THE ROOTS OF EVIL: A SOCIAL HISTORY OF CRIME AND PUNISHMENT. Boston: Little, Brown, 1963.

Public attitudes toward criminals, methods of detection, and punishment have changed enormously since the eighth century but the view that punishment for its own sake is evil does not yet prevail throughout the United States. Medieval methods of judgment such as trial by ordeal gave way to more scientific methods of determining guilt, and the severity of punishments has been slowly reduced. The questions of capital punishment and corporal punishment, still very much alive, were raised in the eighteenth century by European thinkers such as Beccaria and Montesquieu. In England Sir Samuel Romilly worked diligently for the limitation of capital sentences, while in Italy thinkers such as Lombroso and Ferri initiated studies of criminal psychology that became the foundation for later advances.

517 Irwin, J. PRISONS IN TURMOIL. Boston: Little, Brown, 1980.

This analysis of the social organization of the prison examines how inmates cope with prison, inmate systems of social order, and the influence of administrators and policymakers on these systems. It also traces historical developments in penology from the early 1900's. Prisons are separated into three types according to their social organization: the "Big House"; the Correctional Institution; and the Contemporary Prison.

518 Jacobs, J. B. STATEVILLE: THE PENITENTIARY IN MASS SOCIETY. Chicago: University of Chicago Press, 1977.

A historical examination of the total organization of the Stateville maximum security penitentiary in Illinois is presented. The author presents an overview of various phases of the institutional life of the prison during a half-century, along with an account of its administrators, guards, prisoners, and special interest groups that were involved with the prison. The history of the prison is traced from a period of instability following its construction in 1925 to the emergence of a professional administration between 1970 and 1975.

519 Jenkins, P. "The Radicals and the Rehabilitative
    Ideal, 1890-1930." CRIMINOLOGY, 20 (3-4): 347-372,
    1982.

    An examination of the development of a radical
critique of positivist penology emphasizes the
contradictory elements of rehabilitation and determinism.
The socialist left in the U.S. and Great Britain in the
early twentieth century strongly embraced the cult of
science and technology as a method for social reform and
progress. Yet the popular tenets of Social Darwinism and
scientific determinism were inherently inconsistent with
interventionist ideals of rehabilitation. Thus, the
radical left failed to formulate an intellectual assault
upon positivist penology until the assumptions of
scientific determinism were challenged.

520 MacNamara, D. E., and E. Sagarin, (eds.) PERSPECTIVES
    ON CORRECTION. New York: Thomas Y. Crowell, 1977.

    A variety of perspectives on punishment is presented
in a collection of essays and excerpts from the writings
of law professors, a sociologist, a criminologist, a
psychiatrist, a philosopher, a historian, a novelist and
playwright, and of Eldridge Cleaver as a prison inmate
and of Timothy Leary. The underlying thesis rejects
retributive punishment and questions the efficacy of
threatened penalties in reducing crime and delinquency.

521 McGee, R. "What's Past Is Prologue." ANNALS OF THE
    AMERICAN ACADEMY OF POLITICAL AND SOCIAL SCIENCE,
    381 January: 1-10, 1969.

    The primitive forms of criminal sanctions were based
primarily on ideas of revenge and retribution.
Execution, physical torture, and public degradation were
the most common methods in use until near the close of
the eighteenth century. Imprisonment as the principal
method did not come into general use until the beginning
of the nineteenth century. Concepts of retributive
punishment have persisted, but superimposed upon them
were other purposes, such as deterrence, public
protection, and rehabilitation. The trend in Western
civilization for the past 150 years has been steadily in
the direction of more commitment of rehabilitation and
resocialization of offenders. However, implementation of
these ideas has been extremely slow and hampered by lack
of financial support and the excessive fragmentation of
the public agencies responsible.

522 Menninger, K.   THE   CRIME   OF   PUNISHMENT.   New
    York: Viking Press, 1969.

    The continuing problem of criminality indicates that
society secretly wants, needs, and gains definite
satisfaction from criminality.   Violence and crime
intrigues and excites us.   The experience of observing or
even   participating in   it gives   us acute pleasure.
Because violence no longer has legitimate purposes as it
did in primitive times, its control involves the
symbolic, vicarious expression of violence.   Our penal
system   illustrates   an   incorporation   of   violence
vicariously.   It is this psychological need which
prevents the public from accepting a therapeutic approach
to correction rather than a punitive one.   Until a
comprehensive, constructive social attitude--therapeutic
in some instances, restraining in others, but preventive
in its total social impact--replaces the philosophy of
punishment, we cannot expect to begin to eliminate
criminality.

523 Meyer, J.   "Reflections on Some Theories of   Punish-
    ment." JOURNAL OF CRIMINAL LAW, CRIMINOLOGY, AND
    POLICE SCIENCE, 59 (4): 595-599, 1968.

    Society can protect itself from crime in three ways.
It can protect itself by permanently isolating the
offender. Secondly, society can attempt to return the
criminal to the community   with respect for and
appreciation of the conventional values. Thirdly, society
can deal with causations of crime and attempt to prevent
crimes from occurring. Retribution, deterrence, or
rehabilitation will not accomplish these goals in all
cases. No one type of punishment fits all criminals.
Some criminals are sensitive to pain, others to
humiliation, others to confinement, and others may
require guidance for the results of the punishment to be
successful.

524 Miller, M. B. "At Hard Labor: Rediscovering the 19th
    Century Prison." ISSUES IN CRIMINOLOGY, 9 (1): 91-
    114, 1974.

    This article argues that life for the prisoner has
changed relatively little in a hundred years. Although
we now have different names for prisoners, prisons, and
guards and improved physical circumstances and security,
the essence of the prison is unchanged. The same
attitudes toward prisoners prevail, and many of the
dilemmas of the nineteenth century penal scene are still
present. The myth that the evolution of   social work,
probation, the reformatory, the mental hospital, and the
"correctional community" was all made possible by

humanitarianism and democratic progress is criticized as having been constructed ex post facto by liberal historians.

525 Moberly, W. THE ETHICS OF PUNISHMENT. Hamden, CT: Archon Books, 1968.

This book is a comprehensive treatment of the ethics of punishment. The first part is an analysis and comparison of the following traditional theories of punishment: deterrence, reformation, and retribution. In Part II these ideas are examined more closely and the symbolic conception of punishment is analyzed. In Part III the conclusions reached in the earlier sections are tested by applying them to specific questions of prison reform, capital punishment, the Nuremberg Trials, and sin and eternal punishment.

526 Morgan, D. I. "Treatment or Retribution?" AUSTRAL-IAN AND NEW ZEALAND JOURNAL OF CRIMINOLOGY, 12 (2): 19-29, 1979.

A philosophical discussion of rehabilitation versus retribution in the American criminal justice system emphasizes that social justice can occur only in a just society. The integrity of the justice concept becomes highly questionable when criminal law is employed as a means of treatment rather than punishment. Punishment is justifiable and necessary even though it neither prevents crimes nor results in the offender receiving help.

527 Mueller, O. W. "Punishment, Corrections, and the Law." NEBRASKA LAW REVIEW, 45 (1): 58-98, 1966.

Of the punishment known to contemporary law, that of imprisonment has come to be regarded as a synonym of punishment. Three alleged non-utilitarian ingredients of the correction system are vindication, retribution, and penitence; three utilitarian ingredients are neutralization, deterrence, and resocialization. The aims of correction are not static, and at any given time there should be a dynamic interplay between them. The law should take a firm stand as to the goals to be pursued by corrections.

528 Newman, G. THE PUNISHMENT RESPONSE. Philadelphia: J.B. Lippincott, 1978.

Modern literature on punishment has severed the concept of punishment from its historical and cultural roots. Punishment is first a cultural process and second a mechanism of particular institutions, of which criminal law is but one. Reforms should affirm history rather than try to usurp it, and they should try to reaffirm the symbolic aspects of punishment rather than its actual aspects. In criminal sentencing reform, changes should be based soundly on the historical precedents of criminal law and not on grand schemes that will eliminate all of what we now have.

529 Powers, E. CRIME AND PUNISHMENT IN EARLY MASSACHU-
    SETTS, 1620-1692: A DOCUMENTARY HISTORY. Boston:
    Beacon Press, 1966.

This work is a history of the administration of criminal justice and criminal law in Massachusetts from 1620 to 1692. Described in detail are the various laws of the period, ranging from individual rights and liberties to the church and governmental administrations. The types of punishments, capital and corporal, as well as the crimes to which they were applied are also documented. The book also contains statistical data on the incidence and prevalence of crimes. Special sections are devoted to the lawmaking process, lawmakers, and the administrators themselves.

530 Rothman, D. J. THE DISCOVERY OF THE ASYLUM: SOCIAL
    ORDER AND DISORDER IN THE NEW REPUBLIC. Boston:
    Little, Brown, 1971.

The implementation of public institutions for the care of the deviant and dependent population in the United States is discussed from their early development in the era of Jacksonian democracy. The purpose of the examination is to determine the political factors and social conditions which led to the construction of penal institutions, almshouses, reformatories, and insane asylums. Early attitudes toward deviancy are described, as well as the administration, routine, and objectives of the institutions themselves. Further emphasis is on the problems of social control and welfare that have confronted public officials in varying forms throughout the nineteenth century and the changes in attitude toward the proper treatment and rehabilitation of the inmate.

531 Rothman, D. J. "Social Control: The Uses and Abuses
    of the Concept in the History of Incarceration."
    RICE UNIVERSITY STUDIES, 67 (1): 9-20, 1981.

This article reviews the evolution and transformation of the concept of "social control." Historically a conservative notion, social control was

premised on stability, collective order, and cohesion.
Early scholarly interest focused on the sources of
stability, ignoring the role of change. By the 1940's,
interest in social control waned among sociologists. But
during the 1950's and 1960's a new conception of social
control emerged, with a focus on coercion and conflict
rather than cooperation and harmony. Social control was
now interpreted in terms of the mechanisms by which the
ruling class kept the lower class subordinate.
Oppressive social control may be seen connected to the
growth of capitalism. Thus, the emergence of prison as a
mode of social control for those members of society who
threaten the interests of the capitalist represents an
economic innovation.

532 Spitzer, S. "Punishment and Social Organization: A
    Study of Durkheim's Theory of Penal Evolution." LAW
    AND SOCIETY REVIEW, 9 (4): 613-637, 1975.

    Forty-eight societies were analyzed to examine the
relationship between punishment and social structure, and
the societies were categorized into four types based on
decreasing severity of punishment. In addition to the
analysis of punishment, data were gathered on crime in
the societies. The evidence challenges the contention
that collective definitions of deviance disappear as
societies become more complex. More complex societies
are generally characterized by harsher penalities coupled
with a larger number of collective crimes. Controls
involving social and geographic segregation are not
represented by incarceration alone and are not peculiar
to advanced societies.

533 Stastny, C., and G. Tyrnauer. WHO RULES THE JOINT?
    THE CHANGING POLITICAL CULTURE OF MAXIMUM SECURITY
    PRISONS IN AMERICA. Lexington, MA: D.C. Heath,
    1982.

    The evolution of American penology following the
remodeling of Philadelphia's Walnut Street Jail in 1790
is represented as five distinct eras, lasting
approximately forty years each. The early American
prison system (1790-1830) featured mediation and moral
instruction of offenders. The Pennsylvania and Auburn
systems (1830-1870) stressed discipline and religion,
coupled with judicial reprieve. The reformatory era
(1870-1900) introduced vocational training, education,
parole, and age segregation of offenders. The industrial
era (1900-1940) focused primarily on keeping inmates busy
and productive in prison industries. The case work era
(1940-1980) developed diagnostic and classification
procedures and featured treatment and rehabilitation
programs. The present era (post-1980) has attempted to

assess the past ideologies and practices, to evaluate the
successes and failures, and to integrate this information
in developing new approaches. The authors assess these
evolutionary stages through a conflict perspective
focusing on competing interests an power struggles.

534 Toby, J. "Is Punishment Necessary?" JOURNAL OF
    CRIMINAL LAW, CRIMINOLOGY, AND POLICE SCIENCE, 55
    (3): 332-337, 1964.

The question of whether punishment is necessary is
discussed in regard to the three social control functions
of punishment-- crime prevention, sustaining the morale
of conformists, and the rehabilitation of offenders.
Whether punishment is or is not necessary rests
ultimately on empirical questions: (1) the extent to
which identification with the victim occurs, (2) the
extent to which nonconformity is prevented by the
anticipation of punishment, (3) what the consequences are
for the morale of conformists of punishing the deviant or
of treating his imputed pathology, and (4) the
compatibility between punishment and rehabilitation.

535 van den Haag, E. PUNISHING CRIMINALS: CONCERNING A
    VERY OLD AND PAINFUL QUESTION. New York: Basic
    Books, 1975.

If laws are needed to restrict conduct for the sake
of social welfare; if threats of punishment are needed to
control violations by those tempted to break the law; and
if threats remain credible only if carried out when
violations do occur--then retribution must be inflicted
as threatened on those guilty of crime. Retribution will
be useful by making the laws effective, and it will be
just if inflicted only on the guilty according to what is
deserved by their guilt. When laws are made and
punishments prescribed, the requirements of order
(utility) must prevail; when laws are applied, justice
according to law should prevail, tempered by charity.
All three principles--utility, justice, and charity--must
ultimately coalesce in the criminal justice system.
Imprisonment is the proper sanction for three groups of
offenders: those whose crime is considered so odious by
the public that imprisonment is required, convicts who
willfully fail to pay fines, and offenders who must be
incapacitated because they are dangerous to the
community.

536 Wilkins, L. T. "Equity and Republican Justice."
    ANNALS OF THE AMERICAN ACADEMY OF POLITICAL AND
    SOCIAL SCIENCE, 423 (January): 152-161, 1976.

     The imprisonment of offenders with a view to their
reformation was a social invention of the early
Americans--the Quakers of Pennsylvania--some two hundred
years ago. The view that the goal of rehabilitation of
offenders is either impossible or undesirable or both is
now gaining ground rapidly. It has also become widely
accepted that the simplification of the problem of crime
to the problem of the offender leads nowhere. The
concept of equity has come to be preferred over the
concept of justice. Parole determinations, for example,
may be "arbitrary" but they must not be "capricious."
Justification of punishment for socially damaging
behavior relies on the idea of commensurateness
("deserts"). This raises to a new level of urgency the
issue of doing justice in an unjust society--a difficulty
which the prior philosophy of the treatment of offenders
was able to avoid.

537 Wright, E. O. POLITICS OF PUNISHMENT: CRITICAL
    ANALYSIS OF PRISONS IN AMERICA. New York: Harper and
    Row, 1973.

     Observations, interviews, and inmate narratives
centering on two broad issues--the internal operation of
prisons and the relationship of prisons to society at
large--are discussed. Three interrelated themes are
explored in the discussion of prison internal operations.
Rehabilitation is seen as a device used by prison
administrators to manipulate and control prison
populations. The author examines the discretionary power
held by prison officials and how its misuse leads to
conditions of lawlessness and totalitarianism. The
author stresses the ultimate need to restructure
fundamental aspects of society before prisons can be
significantly humanized.

CHAPTER 10

CORRECTIONS - ORGANIZATION

538 Akers, R. L., N. S. Hayner, and W. Gruninger. "Homosexual and Drug Behavior in Prison: A Test of the
Functional and Importation Models of the Inmate System." SOCIAL PROBLEMS, 21 (3): 410-422, 1974.

   Which of the two major models of the inmate system--
the importation or the functional--better accounts for
inmates' drug use and homosexual behavior was tested in a
sample of inmates from seven U.S. prisons classified into
three types along a custody-treatment continuum. The
reported levels of these two kinds of behavior in the
different types of prisons were examined against their
relationship to seven inmate background characteristics.
The analysis revealed that the amount of drug and
homosexual behavior among inmates is more a function of
the type of prison which holds them than of the social
characteristics which they bring with them from the
outside.

539 Albanese, J. S., B. A. Fiore, J. H. Powell, and J. R.
Storti. IS PROBATION WORKING? A GUIDE FOR MANAGERS
AND METHODOLOGISTS. Lanham, MD: University Press of
America, 1981.

   Based on a review of over 130 studies on adult and
juvenile probation, this book assesses the effectiveness
of probation and emphasizes the methodological
shortcomings of previous research. Problems in the use
of probation revocation and recidivism as criteria for
failure and in causal interpretations of findings are
examined. The report also assesses the results of
attempts to manipulate the size and type of probation
caseloads to improve success rates. Efforts to use
probation as an alternative to institutionalization are
reviewed, and settings where this has been tested are
examined. The report assesses various counseling
techniques, job placement, vocational training, and the
use of volunteers, in improving the effectiveness of
probation as a correctional alternative. Treatment in
its relation to probation is viewed from the perspectives
of both the law enforcement and therapeutic communities.
In addition, the report describes attempts to apply
prediction methods in probation settings.

540 Atkinson, D., A. C. Fenster, and A. S. Blumberg.
    "Employer Attitudes Toward Work Release Programs and
    the Hiring of Ex-Offenders." CRIMINAL JUSTICE AND
    BEHAVIOR 3 (4): 335-344, 1976.

    This survey assessed the attitudes of potential
employers toward various aspects of work release programs
in order to identify the most likely participants and the
viability of expanding such programs. Since the
attitudes of potential employers are critical to the
successful continuation and expansion of these programs,
this study investigated the attitudes of a cross section
of potential employers toward the hiring of offenders in
work release programs. Analysis of the results of a
group administered questionnaire--given to a group of
potential employers who were members of service
organizations, the Lions Club and the Rotary Club--
revealed that a clear majority of this group of potential
employers were sympathetic, though there were some
reservations noted. While employers of ex-offenders and
victims of crime expressed fewer positive responses,
about 40 percent of these groups were also willing to
hire work releasees.

541 Austin, W. T., and F. L. Bates. "Ethnological Indica-
    tors of Dominance and Territory in a Human Captive
    Population." SOCIAL FORCES, 52 (4): 447-455, 1974.

    The relationship between social rank and spatial
territory possessed by 45 inmates confined to a Georgia
work camp is discussed. Observed was a barracks-style
dormitory (bullpen) in which the inmates were housed for
a major part of the day. One of the findings validated
from an earlier study was that the higher the inmate's
rank, the greater was his possession of valued bullpen
territory. Of the 45 inmates examined, those who were
incarcerated on violent offenses were not necessarily
more dominant than other inmates, but did appear to
possess more valued objects or bullpen space than inmates
confined on nonviolent offenses. Findings indicated that
those inmates located toward the top of the dominance
hierarchy were in possession of single bunks, were in
less congested areas, and had a clear view of the
television set. In no case was a violent offender devoid
of special territorial recognition.

542 Beha, J. A. "Halfway Houses in Adult Corrections:
    The Law, Practice, and Results." CRIMINAL LAW
    BULLETIN, 11 (4): 434-477, 1975.

    An evaluation of the overall effectiveness and value
of halfway houses is presented. This article begins by
placing the halfway house for adult offenders in the

context of the larger community corrections movement.
It then traces the history of the adult house through a
series of overlapping phases that have culminated in its
integration into the correctional process. Next, the
article reports on the present and potential applications
of the halfway house model at stages other than
postincarceration. Three separate rationales for the
halfway house--humanitarian motives, cost-effectiveness,
and reduction of recidivism--are then explored. The last
section focuses on the available evaluation research
measuring the ability of halfway house programs to reduce
recidivism.

543 Brookhart, D. E., J. B. Ruark, and D. E. Scoven. "A
    Strategy for the Prediction of Work Release Suc-
    cess." CRIMINAL JUSTICE AND BEHAVIOR, 3 (4): 321-
    334, 1976.

    In an attempt to identify factors that distinguish
successful from unsuccessful work release program
participants, twenty-one pre-program characteristics were
examined on each of 250 randomly chosen adult male felons
who had participated in the Work Release Program of the
Virginia Department of Corrections between 1973 and 1975.
Linear discriminant analysis indicated that successful
participants could be significantly distinguished from
unsuccessful participants by a linear predictive strategy
utilizing eight of the pre-program characteristics:
emotional maturity, relationship to parole eligibility,
number of adjustment reports, time to discharge, total
number of convictions, number of felony convictions, type
of offense, and occupation. The discriminant function
derived from these characteristics demonstrated a high
degree of accuracy in the identification of successful
work releasees.

544 Brown, B. S. "Training Program as a Correctional
    Change Agent." CRIME AND DELINQUENCY, 17 (3): 302-
    309, 1971.

    Because correctional change moves toward greater
emphasis on rehabilitation, the guard role of correctional officers has become less acceptable. Officers would
be encouraged to view control as a means to an end rather
than as an end in itself and the conflict which often
characterizes officer-inmate relations would be reduced
by increasing the officers' interpersonal understanding
and skills. Training programs that would help achieve
these goals, however, are often resisted by correctional
officers who view the instigators, generally treatment
staff, as insufficiently concerned about security needs,
lacking real understanding of inmates, and sometimes
conveying the threat of innovation and organizational

change. An alternative model is to recruit from within
the institution training staff who represent both
treatment and security, accept institutional change,
enjoy both formal and informal status within their
respective communities, and can work together.

545 Burkhart, K. W. WOMEN IN PRISON. Garden City, NY:
    Doubleday, 1973.

     Articles on the prison experience of the female
offender, with discussion of the legal and psychological
aspects of institutionalization, are presented. The
information for this work was gathered from interviews
with 400 female inmates and prison officials in both
state and federal institutions. Considerable attention
is given to the psychological effects of prison on a
woman incarcerated or employed by the penal system. Many
female inmates express feelings of self-defeat and
loneliness resulting primarily from separation from their
children. The correctional officers and prison officials
express both pride and frustration about the way the
system operates. The author discusses the dehumanizing
aspects of prisons--gynecological examinations, body
searches, loss of personal belongings, and monitoring of
incoming and outgoing mail and visitors. The author also
points out that some of the vocational programs offered
to inmates, such as cosmetology, are of limited use to
the prisoners because, in most states, felony convictions
prevent state licensing.

546 Carroll, L. HACKS, BLACKS, AND CONS: RACE RELATIONS
    IN A MAXIMUM SECURITY PRISON. Lexington, MA: D.C.
    Heath, 1974.

     This research was undertaken as an exploratory case
study of how race relations are organized in prison. The
data were gathered by means of participant observation
over a fifteen-month period from October 1970 through
December 1971 at the Rhode Island State Prison. The book
focuses on race relations in the prison as a result of
both prison reform and black nationalism. In addition,
the prison power structure and informal collective
adaptations to the prison structure made by both the
staff and the inmates are examined. The final chapter
analyzes the disruption of the structure of race
relations by one external event, the riot at Attica.

547 Cheek, F. E., and M. D. Miller. "The Experience of
    Stress for Correction Officers: A Double-Bind Theory
    of Correctional Stress." JOURNAL OF CRIMINAL JUS-
    TICE, 11 (2): 105-120, 1983.

    This study focuses on the perceptions of the nature
and causes of job stress among correctional officers.
Data were obtained from 204 corrections personnel participating in sessions at the New Jersey Correction Officer
Training Academy over a six-month period. The major
sources of job stress identified by the officers
included: a lack of clear guidelines for job performance,
faulty communication of institutional policies, crisis
situations, conflicting orders from superiors, etc.
While noting stressful aspects of their working environment, most officers did not report themselves as particularly stressed. Officers seem to adopt or present a
"macho" working personality which serves to deny or
minimize the impact of stress personally. Still, the
bind is that vague job guidelines, contradictory directives, and lack of support from superiors place officers
in a problematic position between administration and
prisoner expectations and demands.

548 Clarke, S. H. "What is the Purpose of Probation and
    Why Do We Revoke It?" CRIME AND DELINQUENCY, 25 (4):
    409-424, 1979.

    Courts give little attention to purposes of
probation, impose numerous unnecessary and vague
conditions, and tend to use probation solely as a token
punishment. Consequently, the probation officer is
compelled to decide which conditions to emphasize, with
the result that administrative convenience has too much
influence on supervision and the decision to seek
revocation proceedings. In particular, using probation
as a token punishment may lead to unjust revocation and
imprisonment for noncriminal probation violations of an
offender whom the court originally found no retributive
need to imprison. In plea bargaining and sentencing,
prosecutors, defense attorneys, and judges should
concentrate on setting specific goals of probation in
individual cases and articulating the conditions to
achieve these goals. Restraint is another important goal
of probation and can be realized by (1) setting specific,
enforceable probation conditions to limit probationers'
opportunities for further crime and to make their
activities more visible; and (2) revoking probation only
if probationers cannot abide by reasonable restraints.

549 Cohen, J. "Correction Academy." CRIME AND DELIN-
QUENCY, 25 (2): 177-199, 1979.

Although the 1967 President's Commission on Law
Enforcement and Administration of Justice found that
most states lacked organized training programs for
correctional officers, subsequent federal support enabled
state corrections departments to develop such training
programs. By 1973, there were 20 correction academies,
with the most advanced facilities located in New York and
Illinois. Both of these representative academies altered
their initial academic or "West Point Model" programs and
developed vocational or "basic training" methods. The
training tasks of an academy are examined, along with the
rehabilitative function of prisons.

550 Conrad, J. P. "Who Needs a Door-Bell Pusher? The
Case for Abolishing Parole." PRISON JOURNAL, 59 (2):
17-26, 1979.

The institution of parole should be abolished and
the relocation of ex-offenders into the community should
be given increased attention. As rehabilitative programs
appear to have no consistent or detectable influence on
prisoners, there is no apparent basis for differentiating
sentences in accordance with change in the social and
psychological status of offenders. Sentencing could be
reduced to the considerations of punishment, incapacitation, and deterrence. The parole board, administering
indeterminate sentences, would have no evident function
if flat-term sentencing were to be imposed by the courts
with remission for good time to be administered by the
prison warden on strict conditions laid out in the law
and audited by functionaries independent of the correctional system. Although good behavior in prison is no
guarantee of early release, the provision of credits for
good time is an essential control strategy. Thus, a
referral service should be made to prisoners needing and
wanting help in preparation for release, and more volunteers should be working in prisoner assistance.

551 Cormier, B. M., and D. J. Williams. "The Watcher and
the Watched: A Study on Deprivation of Liberty."
ANNALES INTERNATIONALES DE CRIMINOLOGIE, 9 (2): 447-
452, 1970.

The most common reaction to loss of liberty is a
feeling of being persecuted by society. In a prison
setting, the guards are a symbol of society. Society, an
abstraction, cannot be attacked but the symbols can be
hated and persecuted. Thus, the persecuted become
persecutors. Emotive and real transactions exist between

the supervised and supervisors and, ultimately, it becomes difficult to differentiate between them. Before therapeutic relations can be established between custodians and prisoners, the paranoid association which unites and separates them must be broken.

552 Crouch, B. M., (ed.). THE KEEPERS: PRISON GUARDS AND
     CONTEMPORARY CORRECTIONS. Springfield, IL: Charles
     C. Thomas, 1980.

     This anthology focuses on the job of prison guards in modern corrections. An introductory analysis discusses why individuals become guards, how they meet the daily demands of a complex job, and how they respond to changing conditions. Narratives on inmate relations in maximum-security prisons show that guards have limited power over inmates and, for a number of reasons, are reluctant to use the power their positions signify. The problem of uncertainty in guard work is described by examining four sources of unpredictability: malfunctions of plant and equipment, problems among employees, problems created by inmates, and difficulties produced by the free community. Finally, the book discusses several ways in which guards react to changing prison conditions such as retirement, violence, and unionization.

553 Crozat, P., and J. D. Kloss. "Intensive Community
     Treatment: An Approach to Facilitating the Employment
     of Offenders." CRIMINAL JUSTICE AND BEHAVIOR, 6 (2):
     133-143, 1979.

     The Complex Offender Project (COP) was designed to educate ex-offenders with multiple employment handicaps on how to search for and secure desirable competitive employment. As part of a comprehensive community treatment program, COP services include counseling, independent living skills training, crisis intervention, social skills training, job-seeking skills training, and referral to and coordination of other agencies. To evaluate the effectiveness of COP, researchers gathered data on 119 clients 4 months prior to their referral and for 28 months after referral. The combination of job-seeking skills and personalized job services has immediate effects on job placement. The average number of jobs held increased to 1.5 jobs per client during the first 4 months, and the amount of time unemployed decreased more than 20 percent. The results clearly indicate that offenders with multiple employment handicaps can be assisted in programs like COP, but that such programs should also help clients to learn social and other skills necessary to hold jobs.

554 Davidson, R. T. CHICANO PRISONERS: THE KEY TO SAN
    QUENTIN. New York: Holt, Rinehart, and Winston,
    1974.

    Results of an anthropological study of the prisoner
subculture of San Quentin prison in which the author, as
a participant observer, examined factors responsible for
the violence and program nonparticipation of Chicanos.
The research period extended from June 1966 to February
1968. The author first describes the prison setting and
facilities, the process of entering and adapting to
prison life, and the prison routine. A discussion of the
types of prisoners found in San Quentin is then provided.
The author describes how the Chicano prisoners are able
to present a strong, unified front to the staff and other
prisoner groups through the creation of a "baby mafia"; a
secret group has been renamed "family." The prisoner
economy, sociopolitical prisoner leadership, and methods
of social control are also examined in detail.

555 Denfield, D., and A. Hopkins. "Right On From the
    Inside: Racial-Ethnic Identification in Prisons."
    CRIME AND DELINQUENCY, 2 (1): 8-17, 1974.

    Status in prison is decreasingly a function of one's
criminal exploits and increasingly a function of one's
courage and eloquence in representing the collective
interests of one's ethnic-racial group. Associated with
the rise of racial-ethnic awareness has been the desire
of black, Puerto Rican, and Chicano inmates to organize
self-help and self-awareness groups. These groups exhibit
all the features characterizing effective anticriminal
groups. While giving rise to anticriminal identities,
increased racial-ethnic awareness also increases the
possibility of conflict between racial-ethnic groups.
Guards play an important part in fomenting racial
conflict, and racial violence in prisons cannot be
attributed solely to the racial-ethnic solidarity of
inmates. Instead of resisting the introduction of
cultural and social activities designed to promote
racial-ethnic solidarity, prison officials should
encourage them.

556 Dietrich, S. G. "Probation Officer as Therapist:
    Examination of Three Major Problem Areas." FEDERAL
    PROBATION, 43 (2): 14-19, 1979.

    Probation officers' professional qualifications to
serve as change agents or therapists are examined.
Three major problem areas are identified which involve
widening the expectations of the probation officer's
supervisory function to include clinical or therapeutic

interventions. First, probation officers may not have
adequate educational backgrounds to qualify them for
effective counseling. Second, simplistic, short-term
advice is offered to probation officers; it is frequently
suggested that an officer should covertly coerce the
probationer into change by giving proper humanistic
interpersonal contact. Such advice tends to be vague,
contradictory, and difficult to apply to specific situations. Finally, the realistic legal requirements of the
officer's job prohibit full confidentialty. In a real
sense, the probation officer represents both the
probationer and the state. The responsibilities of the
officer should be reevaluated in recognition of
professional skills, limitations, and role expectations.

557 Duffee, D. "Correction Officer Subculture and Organ-
    ization Change." JOURNAL OF RESEARCH IN CRIME AND
    DELINQUENCY, 11 (2): 155-172, 1974.

        The correctional officer subculture is founded on
the frustrating belief that inmates on the whole deserve
better treatment than officers are capable of giving
under present circumstances. Training and manpower
development in corrections has become an increasingly
important issue. Most such training on the correctional
officer level is based upon an academic model of
education. This kind of training approach is likely to
be ineffective because of a hypothesized officer
subculture, the values of which are antagonistic to the
policy and values implicit in the training. Three
scales, measuring correctional policy, supervisory
behavior, and social climate of institutions, were
administered in the correction department of a
northeastern state. It was found that officers differed
considerably from managers on both policy and social
climate. Suggestions are made for changing the officer
subculture values based upon small group dynamics
techniques that affect the way in which officers perceive
themselves to be managed and alter the perceived rewards
for behaving in ways compatible with managerial policy.

558 Esselstyn, T. C. "The Social System of Correction
    Workers." CRIME AND DELINQUENCY, 12 (2): 117-124,
    1966.

        A sample of 31 California correction workers
returned questionnaires exploring their off-duty social
relationships and the influence of this social system on
their behavior. Findings confirmed the view that the
occupational group has become highly important. It
provides the basis for correction workers' relationships
both on and off the job. The social system exerts a
powerful influence on job behavior itself, on the forms

and content of knowledge with which correctional workers
deal, and quite probably on recidivism. The study has
implications for the analysis of organizations, for
formulation of correctional theory, and for review of
administrative practice.

559 Fairchild, E. S. "Politicalization of the Criminal
    Offender: Prisoner Perceptions of Crime and Poli-
    tics." CRIMINOLOGY, 15 (3): 287-318, 1977.

    In-depth interviews with Washington State inmates
were used to explore the dimensions of a political or
state-oriented model of crime and criminal justice. The
political model of crime focuses on the role of political
order as lawmaker and guardian of social values and
includes three major propositions: (1) crime is both
defined and controlled by those who control the state and
by their agents; (2) social pathology within the
political order fosters the situations that create crime
and therefore is implicated in, or is even a
justification for, criminal action; (3) the nature and
extent of crime can be influenced by the nature of the
offender's political perception and consciousness. The
average offender brings to prison political socialization
experiences which have resulted in alienation but not
ideological estrangement from the political order.
Politicizing processes in prison, coupled with the
failure of rehabilitative efforts, have made the
political model acceptable to many offenders. This model
is not acceptable to prison administrators, however, and
the result is that administrators and clients
increasingly operate from conflicting viewpoints.

560 Farmer, R. E. "Cynicism: A Factor in Corrections
    Work." JOURNAL OF CRIMINAL JUSTICE, 5 (3): 237-246,
    1977.

    Correctional officers' attitudes were surveyed to
examine cynicism as a role characteristic.
Questionnaires were completed by 50 randomly selected
correctional officers employed in three county houses of
correction in a northeastern state. Two of the
institutions are described as traditional and the other
as open or treatment oriented. Analysis of the responses
revealed a moderately high level of operating cynicism
among the correctional officers. There were almost twice
as many cynics in the group of officers from the
"treatment institution" as in the other two groups. The
cynical responses offered by the officers are seen as an
adaptation to a conflict situation.

561 Fisher, S. "Informal Organization in a Correctional
    Setting." SOCIAL PROBLEMS, 13 (2): 214-222, 1965.

    The official action patterns within a correctional
setting are frequently "messed up" by the processes of
"victimization" and "patronage" in social interaction
both among inmates and among staff and inmates. These
processes create two distict groups among the inmates:
the "disfranchised" who are frequently victimized by the
staff and the "licensed" who enjoy a certain degree of
immunity and are frequently sought out as patrons by
other inmates. These two groups appear to be
distinguished by the level of esteem in the eyes of both
staff and peers, licensed inmates being over represented
in high evaluations by both groups, and the disfranchised
under represented; clique affiliations, clique members
being over represented among the licensed and under
represented among the disfranchised; and with regard to
physical size, the licensed are usually the larger boys.
The authoritarian system represents a social arrangement
which does not permit a mutual adjustment between rules
and those governed by them. Thus, the conditions are
present for the development of mechanisms subversive of
the formal order, like the license-disfranchisment
mechanism.

562 Frazier, C. E., W. E. Bock, and J. C. Henretta. "The
    Role of Probation Officers in Determining Gender
    Differences in Sentencing Severity." SOCIOLOGICAL
    QUARTERLY, 24 (2): 305-318, 1983.

    The effects of gender in processing offenders in the
criminal justice system are explored via data obtained
from presentence investigation reports filed in a six-
county judicial area in Florida. Gender is shown to have
little explanatory power for either the jail detention
decision or during charge reduction negotiation; however,
at the sentencing stage, males have a 23 percent greater
chance of being incarcerated than women after
statistically controlling for various sociodemographic,
legal (e.g., number of prior arrests and convictions),
and process (e.g., plea bargaining and pre-sentence
recommendation) variables. A content analysis of
information contained in presentence investigation
reports revealed that probation officers stressed prior
record, offense seriousness, and employment history in
cases involving males. In contrast, for female
offenders, the emphasis was placed almost exclusively on
pyschological factors.

563 Foster, T. W. "Make-Believe Families: A Response of
Women and Girls to the Deprivation of Imprisonment."
INTERNATIONAL JOURNAL OF CRIMINOLOGY AND PENOLOGY, 3
(1): 71-78, 1975.

Research on the informal inmate social structures of
correctional institutions for women and girls has
disclosed the existence of complex patterns of pseudo-
kinship.   Prison family members normally adopt roles
traditionally assigned to family members in a larger
society, and interactions between role players often
resemble those which occur in an actual extended family.
The major empirical dimensions of the prison family are
explored and a general explanation for its existence is
offered. Research data from five studies of the inmate
family are brought together for comparison and
evaluation. Researchers have tended to agree upon the
functional nature of make-believe families and upon their
use as important sources of need-satisfaction for many
incarcerated females.   The relationship between
homosexuality and the prison family has not been clearly
defined.   While membership in prison families may
contribute to anti-authority attitudes, it may also serve
to preserve noncriminal identities, to stabilize inmate
social relationships, to fulfill a variety of personal
and group needs, and to encourage participation in group-
oriented treatment programs. "Familying" has generally
been tolerated, if only because it seems so pervasive and
difficult to control.

564 Fox, J. G. ORGANIZATIONAL AND RACIAL CONFLICT IN
MAXIMUM SECURITY PRISONS. Lexington, MA: D.C. Heath,
1982.

A comparative organizational study of five state
maximum security prisons in New York, New Jersey,
Minnesota, Oregon, and California examined conflict among
management, guards, and inmates. Management staff
stressed uniformity and conformity in prison organization
and resisted change initiatives, particularly those
involving greater inmate participation in decision-
making. Guards were generally concerned with power,
control, and safety in organizational arrangements. They
were at odds with both management and inmates, perceiving
the latter as posing greater security threats and the
former as unwilling to back them up against the inmates.
The inmates were stratified along racial and ethnic
lines. Rather than adhering to some universal inmate
code, they have adopted a rather provincial normative
system geared to the needs of their particular clique.
As a result, inmates have failed to organize in any
collective effort at organizational change. The author
contends that the development of formal prisoner
organizations is the key to integrating inmates in

organizational decision-making. Through this collaborative management approach, conflict between administrators, guards, and inmates may be reduced.

565 Geis, G., and E. Cavanaugh. "Recruitment and Reten-
     tion of Correctional Personnel." CRIME AND DELIN-
     QUENCY, 12 (3): 232-239, 1966.

     In order to assess recruitment and retention in
corrections, questionnaire inquiries were sent to 30
state correctional agencies responsible for the largest
offender populations and to the 30 probation departments
serving the largest metropolitan areas in the United
States. About 40 percent of the questionnaires were
returned; the uninspired nature of the responses was
their most marked feature with an almost universal
emphasis on a need to increase wages and fringe benefits
of employees. Restricted by formal regulations and
hampered by the feelings of the political system and the
public, the agency heads appeared to add to this burden a
passive set of procedures and ideas for retaining manpower. In conclusion, it appeared that the definition of
corrections work in the larger society is the most important ingredient in policies concerning correctional manpower; as a job comes to be defined as important in terms
of those values regarded highly by the society, to that
extent will it be treated well by the society, and to
that same extent will its personnel situation be
enhanced.

566 Genego, W. J., P. D. Goldberger, and V. C. Jackson.
     "Parole Release Decision-Making and the Sentencing
     Process." YALE LAW JOURNAL, 84 (4): 810-902, 1975.

     Until recently, parole boards have been left free to
operate with unstructured discretion. The U.S. Parole
Board has implemented major changes in response to prior
criticism of their unstructured and unreviewable exercise
of discretionary power. Among these innovations are
improvements in the parole release hearing and the
introduction of an explicit, detailed Guideline Table
that determines in most cases how long an inmate must
serve before release. The Guideline Table consists of
two basic indices on which inmates are scored: an
"Offense Severity" index and a risk prediction of
"Salient Factor" index. Part I of this analysis details
the basic features of the federal parole system and
criticisms of past procedures. Part II considers the
minimum constitutional and statutory procedural
requirements applicable to parole release hearings and
then suggests those procedures that are best designed to
insure fairness and accuracy in the parole decision.

Part III examines the legality of the parole Guidelines' substantive criteria for decision-making. Part IV discusses the implications of present parole release decision-making for the sentencing process and for the larger criminal justice system.

567 Glaser, D. "The New Correctional Era: Implications for Manpower and Training." CRIME AND DELINQUENCY, 12 (3): 209-216, 1966.

Changes in the treatment of criminals usually have required increases in size and changes in training of treatment staffs. The pattern currently emerging involves less exclusive reliance on highly trained treatment specialists and more infusion of treatment concerns and skills in line staff. Also, the boundary between institution and community treatment is becoming obscured because of new transitional procedures and facilities. Strains develop with these changes because of inmate and staff comfort in fixed statuses, defects in much new treatment, inadequate research to evaluate treatment, and failure to recognize that optimum treatment varies with the type of offender. The changes also create severe manpower problems. Shortages in research personnel can be met by new recruitment strategies and by procedures which combine operations and research records, thus improving both. The primary need, however, is in recruitment and training of line personnel who are committed to correctional careers and oriented to correctional change.

568 Goldmeier, J., R. H. Sauer, and E. V. White. "Half-Way House for Mentally Ill Offenders." AMERICAN JOURNAL OF PSYCHIATRY, 134 (1): 45-49, 1977.

This paper describes a program of community intervention for recovering mentally ill male offenders through Hamilton House, a halfway house in Baltimore to which they were released. It focuses on how this halfway house began and on aspects of its program, and also evaluates its outcome after three years. A number of guiding principles are discussed in connection with the care of this high-risk population. Evaluation of the program after three years showed a lower than average rate of recidivism and relatively low operating costs. In addition, it appeared that predictions regarding possible dangerousness can be made with greater confidence when halfway house residence is part of the treatment plan for this type of population.

569 Gottsfredson, G., and D. Lipstein. "Using Personal
    Characteristics to Predict Parolee and Probationer
    Employment Stability." JOURNAL OF APPLIED PSYCHOLO-
    GY, 60 (5): 644-648, 1975.

    Predictors of employment stability were investigated
for 341 male parolees and probationers under supervision
in the Maryland Division of Parole and Probation's Impact
Project. Significant correlations were found between
stability (inferred from job referral records) and
occupational consistency, job skill, socialization, prior
job tenure, incarcerations, auto theft, and a base
expectancy measure, but not parole agent ratings.
Results suggest the importance of vocational skill and
consistency in promoting employment stability and provide
a tool using both personal history and current
occupational descriptors to identify men in need of
vocational assistance.

570 Grupp, S. E. "Work Release in the United States."
    JOURNAL OF CRIMINAL LAW, CRIMINOLOGY & POLICE
    SCIENCE, 54 (3): 267-272, 1963.

    The objectives of a work release program, the merits
of the various types of work release legislation, major
difficulties encountered in work release, and work
release as an effective penal sanction are discussed. It
is recommended that officials administering work release
programs should not be swayed by jail conditions, appeals
of businessmen for cheap labor, or political pressures.
Administration record keeping, checking prisoners in and
out, job finding, and other routine details are called
the biggest problem and the major reason why work release
is not used more often. Work release seems more
satisfactory than probation because the offender is
removed from the community at night and on week-ends. It
also meets the public's demand that the criminal not be
"coddled." Restitution is also facilitated by work
release programs.

571 Grupp, S. E. "Work Furlough and Punishment Theory."
    CRIMINOLOGY, 8 (1): 63-79, 1970.

    The philosophy of punishment refers to the rationale
behind the system of dealing with the adjudicated
criminal. It refers primarily to the objectives of the
correctional system which are basically retribution,
deterrence, and rehabilitation. During the course of
this century, there has been an ascendancy of the
rehabilitative theory of punishment. The keynote of this
approach is the individualization of the treatment,
working with the individual in such a way that he will
make a satisfactory, or at least noncriminal, adjustment

to society when he is released from custody. In this respect, work furlough or work release, has enjoyed increasing interest in the United States and other countries. It involves community based extramural procedures, usually for the purpose of private employment, but occasionally for some type of educational program. Since a correctional device succeeds to the extent to which it makes sense within the framework of punishment philosophy, the contribution of work furlough to the integrative theory of punishment is unique.

572 Hazelrigg, L. E. "An Examination of the Accuracy and Relevance of Staff Perceptions of the Inmate in the Correctional Institution." JOURNAL OF CRIMINAL LAW, CRIMINOLOGY & POLICE SCIENCE, 58 (2): 204-210, 1967.

A study was made of staff perceptions of three traits: "inmate loyalty," "criminality," and "criminal identification" as compared with profiles obtained by direct testing of the inmate. It appears that staff perceptions may be largely governed by an unfavorable stereotyped image of inmates: both custody and treatment personnel overestimated inmates on all three traits as compared with inmate self-reporting data.

573 Hodgetts, D. F. "Selecting Inmates for Work Release: Assessing Risk to the Community and the Institution." JOURNAL OF OFFENDER COUNSELING, SERVICES, AND REHA-BILITATION, 5 (2): 39-46, 1981.

A study of the association between commitment offense, legal category (misdemeanant or felon), and nature of rule violations for residents committed to the Southern Illinois Community-Based Corrections Center during 1978 revealed (1) that misdemeanants and property offenders were more likely to violate institutional rules than were felons who had committed crimes against persons, but (2) that neither commitment offense nor legal category was related to rule violations detrimental to community safety. It is argued that the traditional policy of keeping "high risk" violent offenders out of work release programs may have the latent consequence of selecting those types of offenders (misdemeanants and property offenders) who pose a greater risk to institutional security.

574 Huff, C. R. "Unionization Behind the Walls." CRIM-INOLOGY, 12 (2): 175-194, 1974.

The militancy which has developed among prison inmates has increasingly been channeled into organized protests, strikes, riots, and political oratory. The most recent development is the emergence of prisoners' unions. This study analyzes the development and impact of the Ohio Prisoners' Labor Union and compares it with similar movements in the United States and abroad. The OPLU, once formed, rapidly signed up 3,210 of the state's over 8,000 inmates and attempted to establish a bona fide union of prisoners, with outsiders serving only in advisory capacities. Inmate support was strongest in maximum and medium security institutions and weakest at reformatories and facilities housing older inmates. The activities of the union were directed chiefly toward legal issues and the conditions of confinement. Inmate leaders were self-appointed and charismatic. Institutional sanctions and retaliatory tactics employed by the correction departments were effective in destroying such unions.

575 Hussey, F. A. "Parole: Villain or Victim in the Determinate Sentencing Debate." CRIME AND DELIN-QUENCY, 24 (1): 81-88, 1978.

The argument that the alleged failure of parole justifies abandoning the indeterminate sentencing system in favor of determinate sentencing is countered. Implementation of the rehabilitative ideal demanded an indeterminate sentence. Because the length of time it would take to correct or rehabilitate an offender was not known at the time of sentencing, a mechanism for release upon completion of rehabilitation was needed, and parole fulfilled this decision-making role. In addition, parole provided community supervision, theoretically to aid the offender in his transition to the community. Several studies have questioned the ability of prisons to rehabilitate offenders and have concluded generally that rehabilitative programs within the correctional system do not reduce recidivism. To expect parole to rehabilitate inmates who have been debilitated by the correctional process is asking too much. It is the rehabilitative ideal itself that is at issue. As faith in that ideal diminishes, justification for the indeterminate sentence and for the decision-function of the parole system becomes less tenable.

576 Hussey, F. A., and S. P. Lagoy. "Determinate Sentence and Its Impact on Parole." CRIMINAL LAW BULLE-TIN, 19 (2): 101-130, 1983.

New determinate sentencing laws have virtually eliminated the parole boards' role in making release decisions. Parole is closely allied with the inde-terminate sentence and the rehabilitative ideal. If states adopt a strict "just deserts" philosophy, there is

no place for a parole system. The movement toward
determinate sentencing in the seven states examined
resulted in the almost total abolition of parole board
release decision-making. Legislatures seemed uncomfort-
able with just deserts and prescribed lengthier
sentences, perhaps in response to a perceived public
demand to "get tough" on crime. This rejection of just
deserts tenets has resulted in large time-reduction
decisions by correctional staff. If parole boards are to
make time-reduction decisions, it may be possible for
them to coexist with determinate sentencing. Parole
boards' use of guidelines could achieve the ends of
determinacy by eliminating accusations of "tyranny."

577 Hylton, J. H. "Rhetoric and Reality: A Critical
    Appraisal of Community Correctional Programs." CRIME
    AND DELINQUENCY, 28 (3): 341-373, 1982.

An assessment of the assumptions and effects of
community-based programs raises questions of
effectiveness, humaneness, and economy relative to
institutional options. It is argued that while community
corrections is viewed as less interventionist than
incarceration, the former programs actually "widen the
net" to include offenders who, if such programs were not
available, would have been released outright from the
criminal justice system. Thus, community programs
actually extend state control over an increasing
proportion of the population. An alternative theoretical
framework is proposed to account for social control
efforts in an advanced capitalist state.

578 Irwin, J., and D. R. Cressey. "Thieves, Convicts,
    and the Inmate Culture." SOCIAL PROBLEMS, 10 (2):
    142-155, 1962.

A discussion of the behavior patterns among prison
inmates is presented, and the influence of the external
situation on such behavior is emphasized. It is
suggested that much of the inmate behavior classified as
part of the prison culture is not peculiar to the
institution itself but is part of an existing culture
that criminals bring with them upon entering. The notion
that internal conditions stimulate inmate behavior of
various kinds appears to be overemphasized as a result of
the use of a form of structural functional analysis in
research and observation. Noting that the origins of the
thief subculture and the convict subculture are both
external to a prison should change expectations regarding
the possible reformative effect of that prison. It has
been shown that it is not correct to conclude, as
reformers have so often done, that prisons are the
breeding grounds of crime. It probably is not true

either that any particular prison is the breeding ground
of an inmate culture that significantly increases
recidivism rates.

579 Jacobs, J. B. "Street Gangs Behind Bars." SOCIAL
    PROBLEMS, 21 (3): 395-409, 1974.

    A participant observation study was carried out at
Stateville Penitentiary, a maximum security prison in
Illinois during the summer of 1972. Contrary to the
traditional structural-functional explanation for inmate
organization, which focuses upon situational variables,
this analysis supports the Irwin-Cressey position that
much of what has been termed inmate culture is actually
imported from outside the prison. The most significant
reality behind Stateville's walls is the existence of
four lower class Chicago street gangs that have brought
into the prison their street activities, hierarchies,
rivalries, and ideologies. The purpose here is to
describe the social organization which has emerged as a
result of this phenomenon and to relate this development
to the traditional literature.

580 Jacobs, J. B. "What Prison Guards Think: A Profile
    of the Illinois Force." CRIME AND DELINQUENCY, 24
    (2): 185-196, 1978.

    A survey of the backgrounds and attitudes of 929
guards in Illinois prisons is documented. The survey
questionnaire was administered at Illinois' Correctional
Training Academy between July 1974 and October 1975.
Findings are presented with regard to the demographic
characteristics of the guards, their attitudes toward
their jobs, and their feelings about imprisonment and
inmates. The demographic profile shows that guards
continue to be recruited from the lower levels of the
workforce, with very few having been exposed to higher
education. The guards' attitudes toward inmates and
imprisonment do not support the stereotype of guards as
stern or brutal disciplinarians. Most of the guards
expressed opinions about the causes of crime that
parallel the liberal sociopolitical position. Responses
to several questions indicate that minority guards have a
more punitive attitude toward inmates than do white
guards. The findings indicate widespread dissatisfaction
with promotion policies, as well as strains in the
relationship between line officers and their superiors.

581 Jensen, G. F. "Age and Rule-Breaking in Prison: A
    Test of Sociocultural Interpretations." CRIMINOLOGY,
    14 (4): 555-568, 1977.

This study examined whether age differences in rule
violations within prisons can be attributed to differences in values, norms, and commitments rather than to
age itself or nonsociological correlates. A questionnaire dealing with issues in recent prisonization
research was administered to a random sample of 175
female inmates in a minimum security institution in North
Carolina. Older inmates were less prone to rule violations. Younger inmates were twice as likely to report
that they had been punished for rule violations, which
may indicate a more punitive official reaction to rule
infractions by younger inmates. The relationship between
age and rule violations seems to be specific to a particular category of inmates--those who have spent most of
their lives in an urban setting. Among urban inmates,
age differences are caused by related normative orientations and commitments rather than age itself or related
losses of "energy," "daring," or "vigor." Results lend
support to the position that prison experiences are
affected by characteristics imported into the system as
well as by intrasystem characteristics.

582 Jensen, G. F., and D. Jones. "Perspectives on Inmate
    Culture: A Study of Women in Prison." SOCIAL FORCES,
    54 (3): 590-603, 1976.

This study explores issues bearing on prisonization
research using questionnaire data gathered from 172
incarcerated female felons and misdemeanants. The study
population came from a prison for women in Raleigh, North
Carolina. The analysis addresses three major issues: (1)
the relation of traditional situational variables (career
phase and group contact) to inmate perspectives, (2) the
relative impact of situational and noninstitutional
characteristics on inmate perspectives, and (3) variation
in traditional patterns among different categories of
inmates. In general, it was found that the patterns
involving career phase and group contact were similar to
those found in early research among males. On the other
hand, the relationship between career phase and
subscription to the inmate code was quite variable among
different categories of inmates. The variation noted
appears relevant for reconciling divergent findings in
prisonization research among female inmates.

583 Johnson, E. H. "Work Release: A Study in Correc-
    tional Reform." CRIME AND DELINQUENCY, 13 (4): 521-
    530, 1967.

    Data on work release prisoners are used to
illustrate a conception of correctional reform as a
process of accommodations and new relationships among
groups. Reform stimulated by the correctional agency is
viewed as preferable to reform externally induced. In
North Carolina, changes in the economic base of the
prison department motivated other agencies to support
work release as a new strategy. The introduction of
work release initiated a series of accommodations
resulting in changes that promise to be genuine reform.
New relationships have emerged among the prisons, the
parole board, the courts, and private employers. Within
the prison, new relationships between staff and inmates
support the growth of a motivational system conducive to
rehabilitation. Although the North Carolina program is
successful when measured against its original goals,
current limitations include the restricted place of work
release within the labor force structure of the state.

584 Johnson, R. CONDEMNED TO DIE: LIFE UNDER SENTENCE OF
    DEATH. New York: Elsevier, 1981.

    This book examines the personal impact of
confinement to death row, using in-depth interviews
conducted during September 1978 with 35 of the 37 death
row inmates in Alabama. The interviews elicited the
prisoners' perceptions of the human experience of death
row confinement and explored the dominant problems and
pressures. The discussions revealed three broad themes
in the death row experience: powerlessness, fear, and
emotional emptiness. "Living death" was the term many
condemned prisoners used to capture the essential or
cumulative death row experience. With emphasis on
implications both for correctional reform and for the
larger moral issues of capital punishment, the text
examines the human costs of confinement and the death
penalty.

585 Johnson, R. "Informal Helping Networks in Prison:
    The Shape of Grass-Roots Correctional Interven-
    tion." JOURNAL OF CRIMINAL JUSTICE, 7 (1): 53-70,
    1979.

    Data from interviews with 48 custodial and treatment
workers in two New York State prisons are analyzed in a
study of informal helping networks for inmates. The
interview data are used to reconstruct the parameters of
informal helping networks, to identify factors that
encourage or inhibit their development, and to assess

their utility in the helping process. The findings show that few treatment workers had established systematic working links with custodial personnel. Guards made relatively few referrals to treatment staff, and in turn were rarely called upon to act as resources for problem management and crisis intervention. The interview data point to conditions that inhibit the emergence of such mechanisms (i.e., conflict and antagonism between custodial and treatment staff). Given the likelihood that resources with which to pursue the goal of rehabilitation will be reduced, corrections managers would do well to look to informal staff networks as a means of reducing the debilitating effects of imprisonment.

586 Kalinich, D. B.   INMATE ECONOMY.   Lexington, MA: D.C. Heath, 1980.

The structural, organizational, and social factors supporting the development and maintenance of a sub rosa inmate economy are examined at the State Prison of Southern Michigan. Data were derived from interviews with 49 guards and staff and 207 inmates who had been transferred to the institution's parole camp; moreover, questionnaires were administered to 27 former inmates of the prison. While guards feel the control of contraband goods and services is essential in maintaining order and stability in the prison, inmates view the sub rosa economy as essential in meeting their needs in a highly deprived environment. Ironically, the inmate economy contributes to prison stability by supporting an informal power structure that satisfies inmates needs and thus provides incentives to adhere to the norms of the inmate subculture.

587 Kassebaum, G. G., D. A. Ward, and D. M. Wilner. "Some Correlates of Staff Ideology in the Prison." JOURNAL OF RESEARCH IN CRIME AND DELINQUENCY, 1 (2): 96-109, 1964.

A survey of staff members of the California Department of Corrections was conducted to gather data on attitudes toward inmates across institutional settings. Eight prisons were ranked on selected characteristics of their inmate populations according to age, criminal history, and institutional infractions. Staffs from institutions housing a relatively large proportion of inmates involved in serious prison incidents were more authoritarian and maintained higher levels of social distance toward inmates than staff at institutions with less disruptive inmates. Pessimism was highest among staff in prisons housing younger inmates with little prior confinement and few institutional infractions.

Readiness to withhold treatment was highest among staff
in prisons housing younger inmates with high infraction
rates.

588 Katsampes, P. "Changing Correction Officers: A
    Demonstration Study." INTERNATIONAL JOURNAL OF
    CRIMINOLOGY AND PENOLOGY, 3 (2): 123-144, 1975.

    An examination of the effectiveness of training
program participation in changing correction officers'
attitudes and role concepts. Three hundred and fifty
corrections officers participating in a training program
were asked to indicate how they would respond to a series
of hypothetical situations. After several discussion
sessions, they were again asked to indicate their
response. In the original test, a majority of officers
chose "non-constructive" responses in four of nine
situations. In the retest, a majority chose non-
constructive responses in only one situation of
evaluation forms. The officers classified group
discussion as the most influential category of learning
and lecture classes as the least.

589 Katz, J. F., and S. H. Decker. "An Analysis of Work
    Release: The Institutionalization of Unsubstantiated
    Reforms." CRIMINAL JUSTICE AND BEHAVIOR, 9 (2): 229-
    250, 1982.

    This work critically assesses over forty evaluations
of work release programs in terms of their economic
advantages, effectiveness in reducing recidivism,
enhancement of job opportunities and family support, and
personality and social benefits. Generally, the authors
found that the methodological adequacy of the studies was
negatively related to the positive effects reported for
the work release programs. It is argued that work
release programs have been perceived as major reform
efforts and alternatives to coercive control. Thus,
their proliferation and continued support, in spite of
their negligible results, have instead expanded state
control by satisfying current trends in correctional
ideology.

590 Liechenstein, M. I. "Community-Based Corrections:
    Perspectives and Prognosis." INTERNATIONAL JOURNAL
    OF CRIMINOLOGY AND PENOLOGY, 6 (2): 179-184, 1978.

    The concurrent mandates to protect the public and to
rehabilitate and reintegrate the offender pose a central
dilemma in correctional policy. The contradictory nature
of these directives is mirrored in public attitudes
towards criminal justice which espouse rehabilitation on

an intellectual level and retribution through legitimized punishments on the emotional level. Community-based correctional alternatives are particularly prone to vagueness because of their potentially broad compass, and the abundance of unsystematic variation in programs, goals, philosophies, and operations. Community acceptance and cooperation are essential to program implementation. Fragmentation and maldistribution of resources within the criminal justice system and in the community will have to be overcome.

591 Lombardo, L. X. GUARDS IMPRISONED: CORRECTIONAL OFFICERS AT WORK. New York: Elsevier, 1981.

Based on systematic interviews with prison guards and six years of participant observation at Auburn Correctional Facility (New York), this book explores the work experiences of prison guards. The study portrays guards as people who show diverse responses to the various work environments of the prison community, including the cell block, the yard, and prison industries. Guards are portrayed as actively engaged in and influencing the life of the prison as they informally handle inmate rule violations, cope with the demands of inmates, manipulate the prison's informal communications network, and sabotage administrative demands. The study found that job security was a main factor in recruitment for one-half of the interviewees. The degree of sympathetic understanding guards felt for inmates was much greater than expected. Officers responded as individuals to inmates whom they judged as individuals. The book recommends that administrators alleviate job dissatisfaction and alienation by designing training sessions to encourage officers to share information concerning successful methods of dealing with inmate problems. Such training sessions are seen as helping to break down the isolation experienced by many officers and to increase their participation in decisions affecting their work situation.

592 Martinson, R. "Solidarity Under Close Confinement: A Study of the Freedom Riders in Parchman Peniten-tiary." PSYCHIATRY, 30 (2): 132-148, 1967.

A group of about 300 freedom riders, who had been recruited from all over the United States during the summer of 1961, were arrested in Jackson, Mississippi, for attempting to integrate bus and train terminals, convicted of "breach of the peace," and subsequently imprisoned in the Mississippi State Penitentiary in the maximum security unit. It was observed that under close confinement a social bond or solidarity developed, which minimized the strain of social interaction. These

special group processes disappeared suddenly when the
inmates were transferred from maximum security to a more
open type of prison unit.   It was concluded that the
social solidarity of the closely confined is unlike its
counterpart on the outside and is an indigenous solution
to life in such a unit.

593 McSparron, J. "Community Correction and Diversion:
     Costs and Benefits, Subsidy Modes, and Start-Up Re-
     commendations." CRIME AND DELINQUENCY, 26 (2): 226-
     247, 1980.

     A uniform basis for discussion of community
corrections requires an understanding of common
structures and objectives of community corrections
programs, of some pitfalls, and of subsidizing
mechanisms. Basic conditions of community corrections
are (1) placement of responsibility for corrections
within a political subdivision other than the state and
(2) less segregation of offenders from the free world.
Advantages of community corrections are purported to be a
greater harmony with other facets of criminal justice,
almost all of which are now operated by local government,
cost effectiveness, and humanitarianism.   However,
arguments espousing these benefits can be misleading.
The lower costs of community corrections must be weighed
against rehabilitative quality, the uncanceled fixed
costs of remaining prisons, the likelihood of saving or
merely postponing expenditures, and the effectiveness of
incapacitation. Furthermore, community corrections is
used by many dispositional decision-makers as an alternative to probation rather than to institutionalization,
thus reducing social control.

594 McWhorter, W. L. "Inmate Identification in an Insti-
     tutional Setting." CRIMINAL JUSTICE REVIEW, 1 (2):
     81-92, 1976.

     An organizational analysis of various inmate groups
within the Mississippi State Penitentiary calls into
question the "cohesion" model of inmate groups which
remain firmly united against the prison administration.
The organizational structure of the Mississippi prison
presents a highly stratified version of inmate society.
Not only were inmates utilized in the management and
operation of the prison, as is traditional in most penal
institutions, but a highly select group of inmates, known
as trusties, were given the responsibility for the maintenance of social control over fellow inmates.   The
higher grade custody prisoners, the trustees, cooperated
with and trusted the staff more than the other inmates.
The lower grade custody prisoners, gunmen, were intensely
hostile toward the trustees.   Trusty involvement with

staff and progressive isolation from inmate society were related to the development of a positive identification with the staff. The trustee was cautioned to remain isolated from those over whom he had control. He was expected to align himself with the staff, to whom he was responsible, and to repudiate his former relationships with lower ranking inmates.

595 Minor, W. W., and M. Courlander. "Postrelease Trauma Thesis: A Reconsideration of the Risk of Early Parole Failure." JOURNAL OF RESEARCH IN CRIME AND DELIN- QUENCY, 16 (2): 273-293, 1979.

The postrelease trauma thesis, i.e., the time immediately after prison release that causes the offender particular stress, is examined. The postprison period is marked by trauma induced by extreme discontinuity in role expectations, degree of independence, and responsibility. However, much of the literature has stressed that inmates maintain a continued role throughout their careers. Further, there is little evidence that transition-easing programs significantly affect inmates leaving prison. Some researchers have suggested that the most common method of computing parole failure rates may exaggerate risk of failure during the first few months. Parole statistics may ignore the factors of the parole agent's discretionary power, his criteria in decision-making, and his application of different standards to different categories of offenders. Finally, belief in early parole failure may result in a self-fulfilling prophecy, since increased surveillance after release is then justified and increases the chances of parole revocation.

596 Moore, J. N., and S. E. Grupp. "Work Release Admin- istrators' Views of Work Release." OFFENDER REHABIL- ITATION, 3 (3): 193-206, 1979.

Views of 80 misdemeanant work release administrators are reported in terms of their perceptions of the ideal and actual objectives of work release as well as their views of the relative performance of their programs. Administrators operating programs at the local or county level were selected from a 1971-72 directory of work release programs and from a list of possible programs provided by the American Justice Institute. In all, 220 known programs throughout the country were located. The most frequently cited work program objective is refor- mation, especially in terms of enhancing inmates' con- structive behavior. The economic benefits of work release was the next most frequently mentioned objective followed by enhancement of family stability and strength- ening of the program. The most frequently mentioned ideal objective was reformation. The administrators felt that their programs were very effective in achieving program objectives.

597 Moseley, W. H. "Parole: How Is It Working?" JOURNAL OF CRIMINAL JUSTICE, 5 (3): 185-203, 1977.

Guidelines formulated by the U.S. Parole Commission demonstrate that release decisions can be structured to (1) enhance equity, (2) facilitate the explanation for decision variance, and (3) expose decision policy to public evaluation and debate. Parolees have a higher success rate or lower proportion of new convictions than those released in other ways. To what extent this is due to the ability of parole boards to select good risk cases as opposed to the effectiveness of supervision as a release method must await further research. The determinate sentencing proposals discussed in this paper appear to have displaced discretion to other areas where it is less visible and, hence, less subject to control.

598 Mouledous, J. C. "Organizational Goals and Structural Change: A Study of the Organization of a Prison Social System." SOCIAL FORCES, 41 (3): 283-290, 1963.

A study of the organization of the Louisiana State Penitentiary, with emphasis on the inmate and staff relationship and the basis of control, is summarized. The results support the generalization that if an egalitarian approach is held, administration relinquishes control of the total penal environment and allows for the development of an inmate social system which gradually dominates the environment and becomes the main reference for inmate standards and behavior. If administration maintains control of the penal environment by developing an authoritarian rather than an egalitarian approach, behavior and standards can be oriented to those of administration. If, on the other hand, an authoritarian administration maintains its power by also involving inmates in various activities, by distributing to them various material resources and freedoms of movement in exchange for their cooperation, administration then becomes the orientation of inmate behavior and standards. Furthermore, through such an approach administration fragments the penal population into numerous interest groups which not only help prevent the development of an inmate social system but also help minimize and solve conflicts when they arise.

599 Nardini, W. "The Impact of Institutionalization on
    Youth Correction Offenders." BRITISH JOURNAL OF
    CRIMINOLOGY, 6 (2): 193-202, 1966.

        In order to implement the U.S. Federal Youth
Corrections Act, an institution emphasizing intensive
treatment of youthful offenders was constructed at
Lorton, Virginia. To assess the impact of this type of
institution on youthful offenders sentenced under the
Act, the self-image and identification of 28 newly-
admitted inmates, 91 inmates in the middle of their
sentences, and 22 inmates about to be released, were
analyzed through the use of unstructured or essay-type
questions. Results show that the inmates identified very
positively with correctional officers but little with
professional treatment personnel; they identified most
positively with free community persons. The tests also
indicate that there is a general lack of motivation on
the part of inmates to improve themselves and that the
traditionally administered professional treatment
programs are far too formalistic and distant for the
great majority of inmates. Results strongly support the
contention that at no time is there strong attachment to
the so-called prison or criminal culture in this setting.

600 Neal, A. G., E. E. Snyder, and J. K. Balogh.
    "Changing Alienation as Consequences of Imprison-
    ment." CRIMINAL JUSTICE REVIEW, 1 (2): 93-105, 1976.

        To measure the effects of internal and external
variables on alienation, questionnaires were answered by
30 percent of the inmates at a medium security institution for males in a midwestern state. The social
characteristics of community size, educational level, and
occupational status were not significantly related to
degree and kind of alienation. The longer the amount of
time in prison, the lower the levels of powerlessness,
meaninglessness, normlessness, and social isolation. The
larger the number of previous convictions, the lower the
levels of normlessness and powerlessness. Blacks were
consistently higher on each of the alienation variables
than whites. Higher levels of alienation scores were
obtained from the single than from the married inmates.

601 Nelson, E. K. "Community-Based Correctional Treat-
    ment: Rationale and Problems." ANNALS OF THE AMERI-
    CAN ACADEMY OF POLITICAL AND SOCIAL SCIENCE, 374
    (November): 82-91, 1967.

        The nation's correctional services should place a
much greater emphasis upon community-based treatment of
offenders. Offenders should be released on work furloughs and educational leaves, and halfway facilities

should be developed which would allow for resumption of
community responsibilities in a gradual and closely
supervised fashion. Probation and parole should be
greatly increased and strengthened. In moving toward the
increased use of community treatment, many problems must
be overcome, including a lack of research information on
the effectiveness of particular techniques; resistance to
needed changes on the part of traditionalist staff and
organizational systems; the difficulty of creating new
and noncriminal identities for ex-offenders; and the need
to draw community institutions into the task.

602 Panton, J. H. "Characteristics Associated With Male
    Homosexuality Within a State Correctional Popula-
    tion." QUARTERLY JOURNAL OF CORRECTIONS, 2 (1): 26-
    31, 1978.

    Demographic, institutional, and psychodiagnostic
variables are compared for homosexual and other inmates
in North Carolina prisons. The homosexual sample
included 40 male inmates identified as practicing
homosexuals prior to their confinement. A random sample
drawn from the general prison population served as
controls. Homosexuals exhibited greater difficulties in
handling stress, frustration, and impulse control, were
more alienated from both staff and other inmates, and
were more likely to act out their frustrations through
rule infractions and escape attempts. The finding that
illicit sexual activity is more common among the
homosexual sample than among the general inmate
population suggests that homosexuals attempt to continue
their homosexual activity during confinement. The
finding that none of the proven incidences of homosexual
involvement by members of the homosexual sample were
assaultive suggests that homosexual inmates do not become
assaultive in their attempts to gain homosexual contact.

603 Parisi, N., (ed.). COPING WITH IMPRISONMENT.
    Beverly Hills, CA: Sage, 1982.

    Eight papers examine causes of and responses to
prison stress. Stresses upon entering confinement are
studied through interviews with prisoners and staff in a
large urban jail. The study describes the psychological
impact of environmental fluctuations on inmates
struggling with a new and confusing living situation,
inability to satisfy needs, and lack of status and
recognition. Sexual harassment by inmates usually
results in victims' becoming violent themselves, joining
protective cliques, or confining themselves to their
cells. The final papers concern stress related to
uncertainty about release and the trend toward
determinate sentencing. One study suggests that prison

conduct did not affect parole board decisions regarding release date, while another found that prisoners serving determinate sentences suffered less stress than those with indeterminate sentences. An assessment of disciplinary violations during the 20-month period when Indiana moved to a presumptive sentencing system showed that revisions in "good time" rules did not encourage prisoner misconduct.

604 Piliavin, I. "The Reduction of Custodian-Professional Conflict in Correctional Institutions." CRIME AND DELINQUENCY, 12 (2): 125-134, 1966.

The conflict between custodial and professional personnel in correctional institutions results from differences in aims, methods and functions, and personal attributes. The mechanisms used with some success to reduce conflicts in commercial and industrial organizations are valueless in correctional institutions, where goals are unspecified, correspondence between a worker's performance and his achievement is poor, and tasks are not clearly defined. An alternative means for reducing conflict lies in doing away with or greatly reducing the distinction between custodial and professional workers, so that their functions would overlap. No evidence is available to show that this move would vitiate the treatment potential of correctional institutions. On the contrary, by removing many of the current barriers to integrating staff efforts, the move would enable the treatment potential of correctional institutions to be more fully realized.

605 Poole, E. D., and R. M. Regoli. "Role Stress, Custody Orientation, and Disciplinary Actions: A Study of Prison Guards." CRIMINOLOGY, 18 (2): 215-226, 1980.

Major shifts in correctional ideologies and institutional policies concerning the control of inmates have contributed to experiences of role stress among prison guards. This study sought to evaluate a model specifying the processes by which role stress, custody orientation, and selected backgrond variables affected the disciplinary actions of prison guards. Data were derived from the questionnaire responses of 144 guards working in a maximum security prison in the midwest during 1978. Guards attempted to reduce role stress by increasing their commitment to the custody role. A major consequence of this is a higher rate of filing disciplinary reports. On the other hand, the longer the length of service, the fewer the reports filed. Since a high frequency of disciplinary actions was viewed by superiors as evidence of poor work performance and inability to handle inmates, guards learned to maintain control by relaxing rules and overlooking minor infractions. Selective nonenforcement of the rules served both to reward and ensure inmate compliance.

606 Potter, J. "Guards' Unions: The Search for Solidarity." CORRECTIONS MAGAZINE, 5 (3): 25-35, 1979.

Focusing on the problems of correctional officer unions, Potter examines the new militancy of prison guards. During the last 10 years, prison guards have been expressing their discontent through dozens of strikes, job actions, and work slowdowns. Analysts of the prison guard labor movement attribute the movement to the frustrations experienced by these lower-middle class citizens whose jobs are held in contempt by both the prisoners and the public. Guards are embittered by court decisions which improve prison conditions or add to inmates' rights but, as they perceive it, undermine prison discipline and guards' jobs of custody and security. Court decisions, such as those extending inmates' due process rights during disciplinary proceedings and administrative decisions establishing inmate grievance mechanisms, have particularly disturbed correctional officers. In contract negotiations and grievance procedures, the issues that cause the most concern, aside from money and safety, are "job bidding" based on seniority and the increase in programs for prisoners. Overall, the redistribution of organizational power brought about by collective bargaining has given the guards more job security, more control over their work assignments, and more participation in decision-making.

607 Ross, J. G., and E. Heffernan. "Women in a Coed Joint." QUARTERLY JOURNAL OF CORRECTIONS, 1 (4): 24-28, 1977.

Observations on the impact of coeducational correctional facilities on female inmates are presented. The observations were made during field work conducted in an evaluation of coeducational facilities. The major issues related to heterosexual relations in coed institutions--normalization to "street" behavior and extent of bisexual activity--require systematic investigation. There is little evidence that the "return to street behavior" syndrome is widespread in coed institutions. A pattern of "relating to the opposite sex by day and the same sex by night" has been observed among some women in integrated institutions, particularly where the level of integration is low or declining. The women

continue their homosexual relationships for support and
engage in heterosexual relations for financial purposes.
Other major relational effects of integration involve
power struggles, family patterns, and role structure.

608 Omitted

609 Scott, R. J. "Contract Programming in Probation:
    Philosophical and Experimental Bases for Building a
    Model." JUSTICE SYSTEM JOURNAL, 4 (1): 49-70, 1978.

    Correctional literature has reflected growing
disenchantment with rehabilitative/reformative objectives
and renewed interest in retributive or deterrent goals.
However, there has been increasing development in the use
of community-based alternatives to institutionalization.
The movement toward alternatives to incarceration is
based on a number of factors, among them the court's
perception that incarceration is too severe either for
some offenses or some offenders. However, sentences
involving alternatives have come to be unfairly perceived
as lenient. To avoid such a characterization, a policy
of primary reliance on probation-based sentences is
needed to provide a range of sentencing alternatives that
could meet retributive/deterrent objectives as well as
reformative/rehabilitative ones. A model for a contract
probation program is proposed, with emphasis on
minimizing the inherent disparities between the
probationer and the court or probation department
representatives in negotiations. Administrative
preparations, client selection, contract negotiation, and
modification, revocation, and termination procedures are
discussed, along with appeal and evaluation processes.

610 Smith, R. R., M. A. Milan, L. F. Wood, and J. M.
    McKee. "Correctional Officer as a Behavioral Techni-
    cian." CRIMINAL JUSTICE AND BEHAVIOR, 3 (4): 345-
    360, 1976.

    A correctional officer training program in the
principles and applications of the social learning model
is described. An assessment of the effects of the
training program indicated that correctional officers can
master the requisite skills of the behavioral technician
and can successfully apply these in a systematic behavior
change project. In addition, the trained officers, in
comparison to nontrained peers, increased both their
total number and proportion of positive interactions with
inmates. Finally, the trained officers indicated that
the techniques they learned assisted them in their work
with the inmates, and the inmates indicated that the
officers who had received training appeared to have
improved in general caliber as well as become less

punitive and more concerned with the welfare of inmates. Implications of these findings for comprehensive rehabilitation programming are discussed.

611 Stanley, D. T.   PRISONERS AMONG US: THE   PROBLEM
    OF PAROLE. Washington, D.C.: Brookings Institution, 1976.

    When parole boards decide upon releasing prisoners they are uncertain (of what the standards should be), hasty (in making decisions), and neglectful (of the rights of prisoners). Parole officers seldom succeed in either of their conflicting assignments: policing the parolee to keep him from crime and helping him to resume membership in ordinary society. When the parolee seems to be failing, the parole board must decide whether to send him back to prison. Such decisions are commonly influenced by bureaucratic considerations; they reflect inconsistently applied standards and are often inadequate in procedural protection. The analysis suggests that prisoners should serve definite terms and that the charade of parole release decision-making should be abolished, but only if more rational and humane sentences are provided by law--an uncertain legislative possibility. Parole surveillance should be abolished, and assistance should be available but only as parolees seek it voluntarily.

612 Stone-Meierhoefer, B., and P. B. Hoffman.   "The
    Effects of Presumptive Parole Dates on Institutional Behavior: A Preliminary Assessment." JOURNAL OF CRIMINAL JUSTICE, 10 (4): 283-297, 1982.

    The U.S. Parole Commission studied the effect of presumptive parole (the setting of a firm parole date) on prison misconduct and program participation. Using an experimental design, researchers assigned inmates from a pool of eligible cases to either the presumptive parole group or the traditional parole group. The groups exhibited no significant differences in terms of either frequency or severity of disciplinary infractions. The data did indicate, however, that those inmates given presumptive parole dates enrolled in fewer programs than did those in the traditional parole group.

613 Sullivan, D. C., T. R. Clear, and L. J. Siegel.
    "Halfway House, Ten Years Later: Reappraisal of Correctional Innovation." CANADIAN JOURNAL OF CRIMINOLOGY AND CORRECTIONS, 16 (2): 188-197, 1974.

    A critical evaluation of the research on prerelease centers and of the design and operations of the programs

themselves is described. The authors contend that
negative findings regarding the value of the halfway
house as an effective mode of correctional treatment
should be reexamined since researchers have avoided or
overlooked some important factors. These include program
design, population, program administration, and
organization. The authors suggest that study designs
which incorporate these variables could more accurately
measure halfway house effectiveness.

614 Takagi, P. T., and J. Robinson. "The Parole
    Violator: An Organizational Reject." JOURNAL OF
    RESEARCH IN CRIME AND DELINQUENCY, 6 (1):   78-86,
    1969.

    One important aspect of parole recidivism rates is
the parole agent's designation of the client as a
"success" or a "failure." This means that recidivism is
not totally an attribute of the client but that it
represents, in part, a judgment by the worker. Parole
agents' responses to 10 hypothetical case histories of
parolees and the factors that influence these responses
are examined. The study subjects were members of a
statewide parole agency responsible for the handling of
adult males. They included 258 caseload-carrying agents,
38 district supervisors and regional administrators, and
15 additional members from regional and headquarters
staff. Results suggest that parole agents vary in their
responses and judgments. Geographic area was related to
differences in definition of a given act as deviant, but
a more powerful influence appeared to be at the district
supervisor level, where there is a high degree of
correspondence between district supervisors and their
subordinates on the case recommendation task. This
finding suggests that the selective enforcement of some
rules is as much a characteristic of the officials as
selective adherence to rules is a characteristic of the
violator. Findings also indicate that agents, district
officers, and regions which tend to define acts as
return-to-prison violations have higher rates of parole
violations.

615 Thomas, C. W. "Toward a More Inclusive Model of the
    Inmate Contraculture." CRIMINOLOGY, 8 (3): 251-262,
    1970.

    Inmates approach their incarceration experience with
a fairly well developed set of attitudes and values
originating in the various dimensions of their preprison
socialization. Such socialization processes provide the
inmates with the basic tools to adapt to the
institutional setting. Correctional institutions are
resocialization, not socialization, agencies. Their

potential for success is not, therefore, contingent only on their specific programs and structures, but, in addition, on how effectively such programs and structures deal with the varieties of preprison experiences which the inmates bring to the institution, the types of contact the inmates maintain with the larger society while incarcerated, the inmates' evaluation of their postrelease life chances, and, finally, the number and potency of the problems which institutional structures present to the inmate population.

616 Thomas, C. W., and R. J. Cage. "Correlates of Prison Drug Use: An Evaluation of Two Conceptual Models." CRIMINOLOGY, 15 (2): 193-210, 1977.

This study represents an attempt to evaluate the utility of two theoretical paradigms in accounting for illicit drug use in a prison setting. Based on self-report data obtained from a sample of 273 adult felons who were confined in a medium security penitentiary in a southeastern state, the analysis demonstrates that virtually all inmates who reported drug use within the prison had also used drugs before their confinement. Thus, contrary to the implications of the "deprivation model," but fully consistent with the "importation model," this particular pattern of prison behavior is not a direct function of the conditions of confinement. Instead, while the structure of the prison may well influence the probability that those who have used drugs before confinement will continue to do so while in prison, drug use appears to be an example of a type of behavior within the prison which is best predicted by preprison socialization and experience.

617 Thomas, C. W., and E. D. Poole. "The Consequences of Incompatible Goal Structures in Correctional Settings." INTERNATIONAL JOURNAL OF CRIMINOLOGY AND PENOLOGY, 3 (1): 27-42, 1975.

Thomas and Poole undertook a study to examine the effect of alienation on the effectiveness of the prison in achieving change-oriented goals. Alienation was conceptualized as one of the several determinants of prisonization, an assimilative process which provides at least one means by which inmates can attempt to reduce the problems inherent in serving time. Data were collected in 1970 from a maximum security penitentiary located in the southeast United States. Questionnaire materials supplemented by matching questions with official institutional records were gathered for 276 inmates. An analysis of the data revealed the following. Alienation was associated with prisonization. Prisonization was linked with opposition to the legal, system opposition to the prison organization, and criminal identification. The adoption of a coercive prison structure appears to contribute directly to a process which will be counterproductive to the change goals of the organization. Levels of prisonization which are in part attributable to confinement in a coercively oriented setting elicit high levels of opposition to the legal system and significant degrees of self-identification as a criminal.

618 Tittle, C. R., and D. P. Tittle. "Social Organization of Prisoners: An Empirical Test." SOCIAL FORCES, 43 (2): 216-221, 1964.

     In a study of the social organization of prisoners, five hypotheses were derived from theories about the inmate social organization of prisons. Interview and institutional record data were gathered in a hospital serving imprisoned narcotic addicts. The results generally affirm that a prison code is an institutional product expressive of the norms of a prisoner social organization, which serves to help inmates overcome the deprivations of prison living. Evidence also indicates that individual ties to the outside community, as well as individual expectations of possible legitimate rehabilitation, affect the solidarity of that prison social group.

619 Toch, H. "Is a 'Correctional Officer' by Any Other Name a 'Screw'?" CRIMINAL JUSTICE REVIEW, 3 (2): 19-35, 1978.

     Interview excerpts are presented to illustrate ways in which correctional officers exercise discretion to provide support to vulnerable inmates, thereby extending their role beyond custodial care. Important functions officers can serve in prison, including critical contributions they can make to the survival and mental health of inmates, are currently exercised by a significant minority of officers, whose contributions are neither recognized nor rewarded. The correctioal officer interviews, from which these excerpts are drawn, were aimed at defining these functions. The excerpts should stimulate thinking about what is possible within the guard role in relation to mental health services and other noncustodial services. They point out that constructive exercise of discretion includes invoking noncustodial prison staff and circumventing resistance to changes. Officers also form personal relationships with inmates which deescalate conflict, ameliorate crises, and provide susceptible inmates with rehabilitative role models.

620 Toch, H. LIVING IN PRISON: THE ECOLOGY OF SURVIVIAL. New York: Free Press, 1977.

Toch offers a comprehensive view of prison life, from the inmate's perspective. Interviews with 1,000 inmates and guards were conducted in five of New York's seven maximum security prisons for male offenders in order to discover what factors the prisoners themselves regard as important in determining whether a given setting is a good or a bad place to "do time." Several salient inmate concerns emerged: privacy, safety, structure (stability of environment), support (prison programs), feedback (outside ties), activity, and freedom. The study develops a "prison preference inventory" to measure the relative importance of environmental concerns for individual prisoners. The inventory illustrates the variability of responses by individuals to the same setting and the differential impacts of settings on the same person. Organizations are more likely to achieve their objectives if an attempt is made to match persons, with their distinct patterns of preference, with relevant characteristics of particular surroundings.

621 Tyrnauer, G., and C. Stastny. "The Changing Political Culture of a Total Institution: The Case of Walla Walla." PRISON JOURNAL, 57 (2): 43-55, 1977.

In November 1970, the director of the Department of Institutions ordered a series of liberalizing measures to be implemented at the Washington State Penitentary. They included the abolition of censorship and hair and dress codes, the extension of phone and visiting privileges, the reduction of disciplinary regulations, and the easing of access to the outside through special furlough programs. The core of the reform experiment was the Resident Government Council, a representative body elected by the inmates for a six-month term and operating within the framework of a written constitution. This structure took effect in April 1971; it lasted nearly four years and involved eight different resident councils. The outcome of the Walla Walla reform experiment can be best described as a "restoration," so far as was feasible, of the structure of power and authority traditional in a maximum security prison. At the same time, the abolition of a self-government "superstructure" did not mean a retotalization of the political structure. The pluralistic character of the prison society had already taken root in the process of liberalization.

622 Van Wormer, K. S., and F. L. Bates. "A Study of Leadership Roles in an Alabama Prison for Women." HUMAN RELATIONS, 32 (9): 793-801, 1979.

A study of 33 inmates enrolled in educational programs at the State Penitentiary for Women in Wetumpka, Alabama, focused on the relationship between leadership patterns and inmate criminal history, education, and homosexual activity. Observational and interview data revealed that females incarcerated for crimes of violence, involved in homosexual relations while in prison, and with higher educational levels tended to assume leadership roles within the inmate subculture. Degree of inmate masculinity was found to be unrelated to leadership position.

623 Vetter, H. J., and R. Adams. "Effectiveness of Probation Caseload Sizes: A Review of the Empirical Literature." CRIMINOLOGY, 8 (4): 333-343, 1971.

A review is given of a number of reports which deal with the effect of relative size of probation officers' caseloads on rehabilitation efforts for parolees, largely narcotics offenders in this instance. Critical comments are made on the theoretical nature of past research efforts on the variable of caseload size, and attention is directed to the implications for corrections of the empirical studies. It is concluded that although the evidence suggests that correctional efficiency is contingent upon early detection, the influence of caseload size on early intervention has not yet been scientifically investigated.

624 Von Hirsch, A., and K. J. Hanrahan. QUESTION OF PAROLE: RETENTION, REFORM, OR ABOLITION? Cambridge, MA: Ballinger, 1979.

Recommendations for modifying traditional parole release and supervision practices and for restructuring the role of parole boards are presented. The discussion opens with an outline of the features of the traditional parole system and a statement of assumptions regarding the moral principles fundamental to penal systems. The parole system's processes for releasing offenders from prison and supervising them in the community are examined in light of these assumptions. Four basic changes are recommended: (1) specific standards governing duration of confinement, based primarily on a just deserts rationale, should replace discretionary release decisions based on considerations of rehabilitation or incapacitation; (2) release data decisions should be made early, at sentencing or shortly thereafter; (3) ex-prisoners suspected of crimes should be prosecuted as any other

suspect, rather than being subjected to a parole
revocation procedure with lower standards of proof; and
(4) the supervision of ex-prisoners should be eliminated
entirely (or at least reduced in scope and in severity of
sanctions for noncompliance, and scrutinized carefully
for effectiveness and cost).

625 Waldo, G. P., and T. G. Chiricos. "Work Release and
    Recidivism: An Empirical Evaluation of a Social
    Policy." EVALUATION QUARTERLY, 1 (1): 87-108, 1977.

    The work release program in the Florida Division of
Corrections was empirically assessed. A classical
experimental design was used in which 188 persons were
randomly assigned to a work release group and 93 to a
control group. Those selected for the control group
continued to participate in the correctional programs in
which they were then involved. Length of participation
in work release ranged from two to six months. Follow-up
interviews were conducted in the community, and
recidivism data were obtained from the Division of
Corrections files and from FBI records. The work release
and control groups showed no appreciable differences on
any of the recidivism measures, and length of time in
work release also failed to be consistently related to
recidivism. Controls were introduced for 16 demographic,
prior record, and job-related variables, which did not
alter the original findings.

626 Wallace, R. "Ecological Implications of a Custody
    Institution." ISSUES IN CRIMINOLOGY, 2 (1): 47-60,
    1966.

    The structure of a custodial prison, with various
cellblocks of different living standards to which inmates
are assigned on a basis of differential rewards and
punishments, has an effect on the behavior of the
inmates. Though intended to be a means of teaching
conformity to prison values in preparation for reintegration into the larger society, the system actually
teaches conformity to the cellblock subculture against
the rest of the prison. In the process, an ecological
pattern manifests itself wherein certain cellblocks
exhibit certain social and behavioral characteristics,
while others do not.

627 Ward, D. A., and G. G. Kassebaum. "Homosexuality: A
    Mode of Adaptation in a Prison for Women." SOCIAL
    PROBLEMS, 12   (2): 159-177, 1964.

    This study considers sex-role differences in the
free community and the features of male prisons as a way

of understanding the female prison and the prevalence of homosexual relationships. Demographic and background data were obtained through analysis of the record files of 832 inmates, not all of whom were confined at the same time, of the largest prison for women in the United States. Over a period of 16 months repeated interviews were conducted with 45 inmates. These individual interviews provided basic information necessary to conceptualize the process and varieties of adaptive behavior. An anonymous 69-item questionnaire was administered to 293 inmates representing a 45 percent random sample of the population. A questionnaire was also administered to all staff members who had sustained any direct contact with inmates. Results indicated that more inmates resort to homosexuality than to psychological withdrawal, rebellion, colonization, or any other type of adaptation.

628 Ward, D. A., and G. G. Kassebaum. WOMEN'S PRISON. Chicago: Aldine, 1965.

A study was made at a women's prison to determine whether there were female prison types consistent with reported characteristics of male prisoners. The greatest distinction among the female inmates was between those who were and those who were not engaged in homosexual behavior in prison, and then, between the masculine and feminine roles. When new prisoners are admitted they quickly become aware of the existence of the homosexual subculture. From the beginning they must fight to reconcile their own self-concept to prison life; they must adapt themselves to the loneliness, the complex value structure, and the pressures from homosexuals. Homosexual liaisons form the foundation of the social structure in a women's prison. Many women who have never before engaged in homosexual activities and who may have had satisfactory heterosexual relationships turn to homosexuality as a temporary substitute for male affection. It has been found that most of the staff are either antagonistic toward homosexuality or they try to ignore its existence.

629 Wellford, C. "Factors Associated With Adoption of the Inmate Code: A Study of Normative Socialization." JOURNAL OF CRIMINAL LAW, CRIMINOLOGY & POLICE SCIENCE, 58 (2): 197-203, 1967.

To determine the factors that most highly related to the degree of adoption of the inmate code, a study was made of 120 inmates of a correctional institution in the District of Columbia. It was found that length of time served was not significantly related; phase of stay and criminal social type were both related to prisonization

but were independent of each other. It appears likely
that the level of prisonization is largely determined by
the characteristics of the individual prior to his
commitment, especially his involvement with the criminal
subculture, and partially determined by the phase of his
institutional stay.

630 Wheeler, S. "Socialization in Correctional Communi-
     ties." AMERICAN SOCIOLOGICAL REVIEW, 26 (5): 697-
     712, 1961.

     An empirical test of Clemmer's propositions on
socialization in correctional institutions is provided
and the socialization process is related to other
features of such institutions. This theory is strongly
supported when inmates are classified according to the
length of time they have served; the theory is adequate
as a description of changes over time. It fails to
account for the U-shaped distribution of high conformity
responses.   Recent attempts to develop a theory
accounting for the content of the inmate culture provide
some understanding of the possible bases for these two
types of change. Two explanations have been offered to
account for the content of the inmate culture, one
focusing on the process of negative selection, the other
on problem solving processes. Based on these interpretations of the inmate culture, the conditions, both
personal and institutional, that affect prisoner's
response and the suggestion that inmate response is
basically adaptive are treated, including possible relationships to the impact of incarceration on future parole
conduct.

631 Wicks, R. J. "Indigenous Correctional Paraprofes-
     sionals: Bourgeois Nigger or Empathetic Worker?--A
     Brief Position Paper." JOURNAL OF SOCIOLOGY AND
     SOCIAL WELFARE, 3 (6): 672-678, 1976.

     The extensive use of paraprofessionals in probation
and prison programs is advocated as a means of
stimulating helping relationships between offenders and
paraprofessionals (often ex-offenders) who come from
similar backgrounds.   Rehabilitation efforts are
effectively extended at a lower cost than would otherwise
be required. A problem foreseen in this is the possible
evolving alienation between the paraprofessional who has
joined the system and the inmate of similar background
who harbors hostility and disillusionment about any
representative of the system. To remedy this problem, it
is suggested that recent ex-offenders with successful
reentry for as briefly as one year be employed for

temporary paraprofessional work to help with inmates not inclined to accept a relationship with career paraprofessionals.

632 Wilmer, H. A. "The Role of the 'Rat' in the Prison." FEDERAL PROBATION, 29 (1): 44-49, 1965.

In a prison there exists two antagonistic cultures: custody and prisoners. Each views the other with fear and suspicion. To survive and maintain solidarity each group keeps strict control of communication. Since the convict code forbids informing, the rat, fink, stool pigeon, or snitch represents a hated, feared and despised prisoner role. The emergence of the rat neurosis seen as an obsessive phobia stems from culturally determined fears. It employs the mechanism of identification with the aggressor, colored by paranoid features. The feelings of defenselessness, alienation, isolation, rejection, frustration, fear, and hopelessness are normal for the custody-oriented culture. Since it is necessary to suppress hostility in the prison, anxiety is generated. To deaden that anxiety the rat neurotic reaction represents a form of submissive compliance and offers an illusory promise of affection, protection, and reward. The taboo of the "normal" prisoners represents a counter-phobic defense. It is a pathetic attempt to regain self-respect, for informing creates a loss of respect from both custody and inmates, thus intensifying the factors which caused the anxiety.

633 Wilson, N. K. "Styles of Doing Time in a Coed Prison: Masculine and Feminine Alternatives."Pp. 150-171 in J. D. Smykla (ed.), COED PRISON. New York: Human Sciences Press, 1980.

This paper presents findings from a study of the first year of a minimum security facility which converted from an all-male to a coeducational facility. The author reviews literature on masculine and feminine alternatives for coping with imprisonment and describes the research site. Solidarity and homosexuality among the residents are discussed in terms of the author's own observations and information from interviews with the inmates. Styles of doing time and sex differences are analyzed using data on disciplinary actions taken in the facility during the study period. Disciplinary data and relevant research literature are also cited in considering differences in felonious identity. This paper supports the theory that the way in which felons do time is a function of their preprison identities.

634 Zalba, S. R.   "Work Release: A Two-Pronged Effort."
    CRIME AND DELINQUENCY, 13 (4): 506-512, 1967.

Most incarcerated persons face major discontinuities
in their resocialization into the "free" society. Seldom
are provisions made for them to learn or practice certain
crucial socioeconomic roles, such as wage-earner, self-
supporter, and worker in the free community.
Consequently, they are often unable to perform in ways
necessary to successful readjustment once they are
discharged.   The work release approach has demonstrated
that these roles can be provided in a correctional
program which also has custodial features.

CHAPTER 11

635 Ali, B. "A Comparative Study of Two Types of Parole
Violators." CRIMINOLOGICA, 4 (3): 32-38, 1966.

An attempt was made to determine differences in
social background and personality characteristics between
parole violators who technically violate the rules of
parole and those who violate parole by committing a new
crime. The source of data was a sample of 100 inmates
who were paroled from the Ohio Penitentiary and returned
as parole violators. Fifty of these men had violated the
technical rules of parole, and 50 had committed new
crimes. The technical violator was more likely to have a
better work record, to have spent less time in penal
institutions, to be a first rather than a habitual
offender, to have a good conduct record in the
penitentiary, and to have lasted longer on parole before
being returned.

636 Ayllon, T., M. A. Milan, M. D. Roberts, and J. M.
McKee. CORRECTION REHABILITATION AND MANAGEMENT:
A PSYCHOLOGICAL APPROACH. New York: John Wiley,
1979.

After studying current diagnostic procedures, this
volume reports that behavior modification can be an
effective and ethical approach to rehabilitation and
management. An examination of the principles and
techniques of behavior modification programs with adult
criminals develops into a detailed examination of the
ethical questions which have arisen concerning this
technique. A detailed study of two behavior modification
programs being conducted at state correctional facilities
in Alabama and Georgia is described. Results of these
two programs found that a token reward system was needed
to ensure participation, and a need existed to provide
continuing support to participants when they were
released into the community.

637 Babst, D. V., M. Koval, and M. G. Neithercutt. "Relationship of Time Served to Parole Outcome for Different Classifications of Burglars Based on Males
Paroled in Fifty Jurisdictions in 1968 and 1969."
JOURNAL OF RESEARCH IN CRIME AND DELINQUENCY, 9 (2):
99-116, 1972.

A key decision in the correctional process is
determining when to release an offender to parole.

Setting the optimum time to be served is difficult. One of the purposes of this study is to see if research based on past experience can provide some future guidelines for determining optimum time for different types of offenders. The study groups consisted of males convicted of burglary offenses who were paroled and reported to Uniform Parole Reports. These groups consisted of 7,200 parolees in 1968 and 7,600 parolees in 1969. An experience table with different offender classifications was developed to achieve the maximum logical differentiation as to parole outcome. The classifications developed for 1968 parolees fairly accurately predicted the 1969 parolees' experience. In the process of developing the offender classifications, supportive evidence was found for the maturation concept.

638 Babst, D. V., and J. W. Mannering. "Probation Versus Imprisonment for Similar Types of Offenders: A Comparison by Subsequent Violations." JOURNAL OF RESEARCH IN CRIME AND DELINQUENCY, 2 (2): 60-71, 1965.

Male offenders who were imprisoned were compared with similar types who were placed on probation to determine which program produces less subsequent criminal activity. In Wisconsin, 7,614 cases comparable in original disposition, county of commitment, type of offense, number of prior felonies, and marital status were examined. Of the first felony offenders, those on parole had lower violation rates than those imprisoned and then paroled. For probationers and parolees with one prior felony, rates were about the same. For those with two or more prior felonies, violation rates were higher for probationers than parolees. The frequency with which judges sentenced offenders to probation rather than incarceration varied directly with the extent to which the offenders were likely to violate. Judges tended to place those offenders with low violation rates on probation, the major exception being assault cases, where imprisonment was more frequently used.

639 Bailey, W. C. "Correctional Outcome: An Evaluation of 100 Reports." JOURNAL OF CRIMINAL LAW, CRIMINOLOGY & POLICE SCIENCE, 57 (2): 153-160, 1966.

A sample of 100 correctional outcome reports was subjected to a content analysis in an effort to evaluate the status of correctional treatment. Results of the analysis indicated that despite the fact that well over half the reports were concerned with some form of group treatment, only a few described treatment procedures conceptually based upon the group relations premise. On the basis of this sample of outcome reports, evidence supporting the efficacy of correctional treatment is slight, inconsistent, and of questionable reliability. The main problem still confronting correctional researchers is how to account for the fact that although the operational means and resources of correctional outcome research have substantially improved, there has been no apparent progress in the actual demonstration of the validity of various types of correctional treatment.

640 Beck, J. L. "The Effect of Representation at Parole Hearings." CRIMINOLOGY, 13 (1): 114-117, 1975.

In 1972, the U.S. Board of Parole initiated a pilot project, one facet of which allowed inmates to have representatives appear for them at parole grant hearings. This study examined the following questions: (1) Does the presence of representatives have an effect on the outcome of the parole decision? (2) If so, does this effect vary with types of representatives? Data were collected on all initial hearings in the pilot project from October 1972 through August 1973; 1,100 initial cases were examined and an analysis was run on 1,023 review cases. The results for review hearings showed that cases with representatives were paroled 80.6 percent of the time, while those without representatives were paroled 72.5 percent of the time.

641 Beck, J. L., and P. B. Hoffman. "Time Served and Release Performance: A Research Note." JOURNAL OF RESEARCH IN CRIME AND DELINQUENCY, 13 (2): 127-132, 1976.

The association between length of time served in prison and release outcome is examined for a sample of 1,546 adult male federal prisoners with control exercised for base expectancy (salient factor) score. All forms of release (parole, mandatory release, expiration of sentence) are included, with a two-year, follow-up period utilized for each case. No substantial association between time served and release outcome was observable from the data for this sample. However, the percentage of cases with favorable outcomes generally does appear to decrease slightly as one moves within risk categories from the groups serving shorter to longer periods of time.

642 Bennett, L. A., and L. Chatman. "What Works in Adult Corrections? New Careers Revisited." OFFENDER RE-HABILITATION, 3 (4): 325-339, 1979.

This report summarizes an 8- and 10-year follow-up of the New Careers Development Project. Project participants (offenders and parolees) spent 50 percent less time incarcerated, on the average, than a comparison group. Participants were compared in terms of favorable versus unfavorable outcome after two years against what might be expected from their intake characteristics. Outcome after ten years was evaluated using a comparison group of 150 inmates released from the same institution during the same time. In addition, an 8-year follow-up study based on interviews, questionnaires, and secondary source information was made. A discussion of the findings and suggestions for future research is provided.

643 Berecochea, J. E., and D. R. Jaman. TIME SERVED IN PRISON AND PAROLE OUTCOME: AN EXPERIMENTAL STUDY. Sacramento: California Department of Corrections, 1981.

This study examined the effects of time served in prison on recidivism by employing an experimental design. Inmates were randomly assigned to experimental and control groups, where the former served six months less in prison than their original sentences would have allowed and the latter served their original prison terms. Experimentals served an average of 31.3 months; controls served 37.9 months. Recidivisim was operationalized to include any return to prison, as well as any long jail sentences and absconding from parole. During the first and second years following their release from prison, the experimentals and controls did not differ in recidivism rates; moreover, there were no statistically significant differences between experimentals and controls among those not returned to prison. The authors conclude that prison terms could be reduced without increasing the risks of recidivism.

644 Bloom, H. S. "Evaluating Human Service and Correctional Programs by Modeling the Timing of Recidivism." SOCIOLOGICAL METHODS AND RESEARCH, 8 (2): 179-208, 1979.

This method for evaluating programs designed to reduce crime, drug abuse, and alcoholism is based on a model that assumes that the longer persons avoid recidivism, the more likely they will continue to do so. It provides evaluators with (1) a means of examining short-run program impacts on the postponement of recidivism through estimates of the average time at which recidivism occurs; (2) a way of measuring long-run program impact on the prevention of recidivism through estimates of the ultimate probability of recidivism; and (3) a way to determine if individuals have been successful long enough to be considered "safe" through using estimates of their probability of recidivism. A new model postulates that similar individuals have the same probability of failure upon release. By chance, some of these individuals fail almost immediately. Those who avoid recidivism have a smaller future probability of failure; the rate of failure continues to decline as their successful time at risk increases.

645 Bloom, H. S., and N. M. Singer. "Determining the Cost-Effectiveness of Correctional Programs." EVALUA-TION QUARTERLY, 3 (4): 609-628, 1979.

An evaluation of the Patuxent Institution in Jessup, MD., is presented in terms of cost-effectiveness and effect on recidivism; facility description, analytical framework, and results are highlighted. The study was designed to determine Patuxent's impact on postrelease criminal behavior. The treatment sample included 106 inmates paroled in 1971 to 1972. The comparison sample consisted of 54 offenders diagnosed at Patuxent as "defective delinquents" but not so adjudged by the courts and therefore sent to prison. Analysis showed that Patuxent offers both prevention and postponement benefits when compared to prison.

646 Blumstein, A., and J. Cohen. "Control of Selection Effects in the Evaluation of Social Problems." EVAL-UATION QUARTERLY, 3 (4): 583-608, 1979.

An evaluation of a college program in a maximum security prison applies the techniques of discriminant and base expectancy analysis to compensate for possible selection bias in nonrandom assignment to experimental groups. Used to demonstrate the usefulness of the two techniques, the study assessed the rehabilitative efficacy of the program as measured by reduced criminal activity. It permitted selection of a treatment, control, and nonexperimental group from the same base population. The college program had no general beneficial effects to counteract serious recidivism; however, within different risk levels, some benefits appeared for those inmates who were least likely to succeed without the treatment represented by the college program.

647 Brown, B. S. "The Casework Role in a Penal Set-ting." JOURNAL OF CRIMINAL LAW, CRIMINOLOGY & POLICE SCIENCE, 58 (2): 191-196, 1967.

Due to the ideological conflict between custody and treatment in corrections, the caseworker role in the penal setting has inherent conflicts which may significantly affect both his work role and his conception of himself. Two critical role demands which may create conflict and cause the caseworker to compromise with custodial goals are: (1) the secondary status of rehabilitation;and (2) the essentially non-masculine role of casework in an all-male environment. The caseworker may attempt to solve conflicts by increased acceptance of the custodial philosophy. Some modifications in the casework role could relieve some of the conflict: correctional and casework staff roles could be organized to provide more mutual interaction, cooperation, and sharing of duties; caseworkers could spend more time consulting with correctional staff; and the caseworker could work more with families and the community.

648 Burstein, J. Q. CONJUGAL VISITS IN PRISONS: PSYCHO-LOGICAL AND SOCIAL CONSEQUENCES. Lexington, MA: D.C. Heath, 1977.

A phenomenological approach was used to assess the effect of conjugal visits on prisoners at the Correctional Training Facility for men in Soledad, CA, in terms of both their marriage relationship and their successful reintegration into society. The general strategy of the research was to contrast the differential outcomes of an experimental group of 20 inmates who received conjugal visits with a comparative group of 20 inmates whose wives were permitted only regular visits. Analysis of the data confirms a positive relationship between conjugal visits and subsequent marital stability. It also revealed that conjugal visits in prison increase the likelihood of a positive parole outcome.

649 Callahan, T. J. "Potentialities and Limitations of the Ex-Offender Paraprofessional in a Correctional Setting." PROBATION AND PAROLE, 5 (1): 64-70, 1973.

The greatest value of the ex-offender as a paraprofessional correction worker is that he is able to act as a liaison between largely white middle class professionals and predominantly lower class minority clients. Success of self-help programs has been attributed to the fact that such programs require the ex-offender to perform the role of reformer and enable him to gain experience in a role that the group has identified as desirable. Another important factor discovered by those who have utilized ex-offenders in correctional work is that they help themselves in helping others. Problem areas that may limit the effectiveness of ex-offenders are also discussed.

650 Carney, F. J. "Predicting Recidivism in a Medium
    Security Correctional Insititution." JOURNAL OF
    CRIMINAL LAW, CRIMINOLOGY & POLICE SCIENCE, 58
    (3): 338-348, 1967.

    Base expectancy scores, which predict the likelihood
of recidivism, were derived for 363 inmates released from
a medium security correctional institution. For this
study, any subject who was returned to a federal or state
prison, a county house of correction or jail for 30 days
or more counted as a recidivist. Seven of the 14
variables analyzed discriminated between recidivists and
non-recidivists. These factors were, in order of their
significance: (1) age at present commitment, (2) prior
penal commitments, (3) age at first arrest, (4) number of
prior arrests, (5) institutional conduct, (6) type of
offense, (7) behavior disorders. The most crucial
variables in predicting recidivism were found to be the
combination of age at present commitment and prior penal
record.

651 Carney, F. J. "Correctional Research and Correc-
    tional Decision-Making: Some Problems and Prospects."
    JOURNAL OF RESEARCH IN CRIME AND DELINQUENCY, 6
    (2): 110-122, 1969.

    An examination of the relationship between research
and decision-making is presented which is based primarily
on experience in the Massachusetts correctional system.
Research findings have not been readily incorporated into
the decision-making context, particularly where findings
have implications for changes that are contrary to the
basic assumptions or orientations of correctional
administrators. What seems to be necessary is the
development of a research orientation within the
correctional setting wherein research would be considered
an essential ingredient of the overall correctional
enterprise.

652 Carroll, J. S. "Causal Theories of Crime and Their
    Effect Upon Expert Parole Decisions." LAW AND HUMAN
    BEHAVIOR, 2 (2): 377-388, 1978.

    Carroll offers a framework for analyzing judgments
about crime and criminals and argues that causal attributions are prevalent and important in the way lay people
and experts understand crime. To illustrate this
approach, the role of attribution in parole decisions is
extensively described. Specifically, research has demonstrated that expert parole decision-makers make causal
attributions in the process of deliberating about the
release of offenders, with the most typical attributions
regarding the causes of crime being substance abuse,

profit, victim precipitation, influence of associates, personality deficiencies, and domestic problems. Implications of attributional analysis for segments of the criminal justice system are indicated.

653 Carroll, L., and M. E. Mondrick. "Racial Bias in the Decision to Grant Parole." LAW AND SOCIETY REVIEW, 11 (1): 93-107, 1976.

The cases of 243 prisoners who appeared before the parole board of an eastern prison between October 1, 1970, and September 30, 1971, are examined for evidence of racial discrimination. Although black prisoners were paroled in approximately the same proportion as white prisoners, blacks were evaluated by different criteria. Most black prisoners had to meet an additional requirement not imposed upon white prisoners—particpation in institutional treatment programs. The result was that most black prisoners who were paroled had served significantly longer proportions of their sentences than had white parolees. There was an apparent tendency on the part of the parole board to favor older black prisoners and black prisoners with prior convictions and to penalize younger black prisoners and those with no prior convictions.

654 Cavior, H. E., and S. H. Cohen. "Evaluative Research: Perspectives from a Corrections Setting." CRIMINAL JUSTICE AND BEHAVIOR, 2 (3): 237-257, 1975.

This paper examines issues related to the process and product requirements of evaluative research in a corrections setting. Process requirements include the relationship of the evaluator to management and line staff, methods for encouraging accurate reporting of data, and the implications of the evaluator's position in the organizational structure. Product requirements include distinguishing between in-program and post-program outcome measures; defining adequate post-program measures; and the validity of measures, in particular recidivism. Various methodological problems that are discussed include evaluating dynamic programs with dynamic populations, the selection of comparison groups, and the effects of differential post-release experiences on outcome.

655 Coates, R. B., and A. D. Miller. "Evaluating Large
    Scale Social Service Systems in Changing Environ-
    ments: The Case of Correctional Agencies." JOURNAL
    OF RESEARCH IN CRIME AND DELINQUENCY, 12 (2): 92-106,
    1975.

     A correctional agency is used for an evaluation
design which permits evaluation to be done within the
changing environment of social service systems. The
authors distinguish among sets, strategies, and programs
and identify a time perspective in the use of evaluative
criteria that focuses on client relationships both within
and outside programs. The model described should permit
research teams to address system administration concerns
while at the same time taking advantage of the natural
changing setting for testing theoretical propositions.

656 Cobean, S. C., and P. W. Power. "Role of the Family
    in the Rehabilitation of the Offender." INTERNA-
    TIONAL JOURNAL OF OFFENDER THERAPY AND COMPARATIVE
    CRIMINOLOGY, 22 (1): 29-38, 1978.

     Objectives in counseling the family of an offender
at specific stages in the criminal justice process are
discussed, and the requisite helping skills are
described. In discussing work with the families of
offenders, intensive liaison work between the offender
and his family during the incarceration period is
stressed. It is indicated that the helping professional
should stimulate the expression of feelings and
communication within the family, develop outside support,
and facilitate any necessary alterations in family roles.
When family life was reasonably intact prior to
incarceration, it is believed intervention has proven
crucial in keeping families together during a critical
period.

657 Conley, J. A., and S. E. Zimmerman. "Decision-Making
    by a Part-Time Parole Board: An Observational and
    Empirical Study." CRIMINAL JUSTICE AND BEHAVIOR, 9
    (4): 396-431, 1982.

     This paper examines the decision-making process to
grant parole in Oklahoma. The five-member, part-time
Parole and Pardons Board was divided into two coalitions
mediated by the board chair: the "Yes Voter" coalition
consistently favored granting parole, expressing concerns
with inmate rehabilitation; the "No Voter" coalition was
less consistent in its voting patterns, expressing
concerns for punishment. The most dominant criterion in
decision-making for both groups was institutional order.

658 Cressey, D. R. "Social Psychological Foundations for Using Criminals in the Rehabilitation of Criminals." JOURNAL OF RESEARCH IN CRIME AND DELINQUENCY, 2 (2): 49-59, 1965.

The principle of differential association and the broader symbolic interactionist theory provide the foundations for the development of a set of theories for the rehabilitation of criminals. If social conduct is a function of attitudes embodied in words learned from membership in reference groups, then attempts to change that conduct should concentrate on processes for some verbalizations and acquiring others. In these processes, criminals themselves can be used effectively to introduce guilt and shame into the psychological makeup of those who would commit crime, as well as to avoid production of further criminality, or a different form of criminality, among the population whose change is sought.

659 Cressey, D. R. "Theoretical Foundations for Using Criminals in The Rehabilitation of Criminals." KEY ISSUES, 2: 87-101, 1965.

The "symbolic interaction" theory supports the idea that criminals can be used effectively to introduce "guilt" and "shame" into the psychological makeup of those who would commit crimes. The symbolic interactionist theory tells us that cultures and subcultures consist of collections of behavior contained in the use of words in prescribed ways. Words are necessarily learned from persons who have had prior experience with them. "Guilt" and "shame" are contained in verbalizations that makeup a culture. The problem of changing criminals is a problem of insuring that criminals become members of intimate groups whose verbalizations stress that criminal conduct is wrong. The criminals who have rejected procriminal verbalizations should be more effective in changing the criminals' self-conceptions than those unfamiliar with pro-criminal verbalizations. They should also be more efficient in avoiding verbalizations appropriate to a new kind of criminality or deviancy.

660 Dembo, R. "Recidivism: The 'Criminal's' Reaction to 'Treatment'." CRIMINOLOGY, 8 (4): 345-356, 1971.

The difficulties and frustrations facing a parolee attempting to lead a law abiding life are analyzed as factors influencing the decision to again reject conventional moral values. Three factors appear vital to this decision: a lack of community receptivity evidenced by inadequate educational facilities and limited opportunities for employment; restrictions preventing self-fulfillment and meaningful relationships with

others; and the extent of previous criminal socialization. Presuppositions by law enforcement representatives that the parolee is morally deficient make his
own attempts at rehabilitation particularly difficult.
It is concluded that, for the parolee to succeed, conventional alternatives must be attractive enough to initiate
and encourage conforming behavior in the face of over-
whelming adjustment problems.

661 Elion, V. H., and E. I. Megargee. "Racial Identity,
    Length of Incarceration, and Parole Decision-Making."
    JOURNAL OF RESEARCH IN CRIME AND DELINQUENCY, 16 (2):
    232-245, 1979.

    Entry sentence, rather than race, was shown to be
significantly associated with decisions to grant parole
in this study of black-white sentence patterns at a
federal correctional institution. Data from 1,345
inmates at the Federal Correctional Institution,
Tallahassee, FL, were collected over four years (1970-
74). Among the findings were (1) that although blacks
and whites did not differ in the actual time served,
blacks served a larger amount of their entry sentence;
(2) entry sentence was the primary determinant in the
decision to grant parole along with such factors as adult
maladjustment and deviance, violence of offense,
disciplinary report rate, and juvenile conviction record;
(3) adjustment played a more important role for black
inmates, while personal and social adjustment before
prison appeared more important factors in parole
decisions for white inmates.

662 England, R. W. "Ideologies and Corrections." PRISON
    JOURNAL, 45 (2): 17-22, 1965.

    The body of research evaluating the effectiveness of
correctional measures consistently concludes that they
have been much less successful than was assumed a priori.
The apparently high rates of disappointing outcome in
correctional programs are, in considerable degree,
manifestations of a cultural legacy inherited from
humanitarianism, utilitarianism, and the middle class
ethic which bind these programs to ideologies rather than
to scientific knowledge. Although abandonment of
ideological orientations is impracticable, the foregoing
would suggest the exercise of greater restraint in
automatically assuming the soundness of ideological
elements in preventive-correctional programs.

663 Fisher, S. "Therapeutic Community in a Correctional
    Establishment." BRITISH JOURNAL OF CRIMINOLOGY, 8
    (3): 275-284, 1968.

    An experimental program begun in California in 1962
was designed to assess the rehabilitative effectiveness
of a community treatment center based on a therapeutic
orientation for parolees with a history of narcotics use.
The program failed due to the absence of certain
ingredients traditionally viewed as generic to an
effective treatment process. For treatment to be
effective, the patient must overcome his initial
reluctance and ambivalence about its relevance for him--
he must voluntarily involve himself; and both patients
and staff must have freedom of expression. Under the
conditions imposed by the halfway house in the California
experiment, patient involvement and free expression were
not possible. The failure of residents to view the staff
and program as providing them with a useful social
experience indicates a failure to develop positive
identifications between staff and residents.

664 Fishman, R. CRIMINAL RECIDIVISM IN NEW YORK CITY: AN
    EVALUATION OF THE IMPACT OF REHABILITATION AND DIVER-
    SION SERVICES. New York: Praeger, 1977.

    An adaptation of an evaluation report on the impact
of rehabilitation and diversion programs on recidivism is
presented; intake forms from 18 New York City services
constituted the basis of the study. The unit of
measurement for determining rates of recidivism was
arrests. Standardized intake forms from the
rehabilitation and diversion services were analyzed: the
universe size was 2,860 men and boys. It was concluded
that the amount and type of criminal recidivism are so
high in their cost to the victims that the rehabilitation
services fail as approaches to the prevention and control
of crime, particularly violent crime. Further,
differences among the projects, such as the amounts and
types of rehabilitation services provided or
environmental factors such as unemployment, did not
appear to be related to the failure. Implications of the
findings for approaches to the problem of violent crime
are examined.

665 Galliher, J. F. "Training in Social Manipulation as
    a Rehabilitative Technique." CRIME AND DELINQUENCY,
    17 (4): 431-436, 1971.

    The traditional goal of prison rehabilitation
programs has been to bring about a major change in the
individual's personality. There is widespread opinion
that this cannot be accomplished in prisons.

Sociological anomie theory emphasizes blocked opportunity structures rather than individual personality problems in the etiology of deviant behavior. It appears that training in the techniques of social manipulation opens new avenues for achieving success, some legal, some illegal but nonviolent, and some neither strictly legal nor clearly illegal. Since more avenues for achieving success are available to those with this training, the motivation for deviance, especially physically aggressive deviance, may be lessened.

666 Gendreau, P., and R. R. Ross. "Effective Correctional Treatment: Bibliotherapy for Cynics." CRIME AND DELINQUENCY, 25 (4): 463-489, 1979.

A review of literature on correctional treatment published from 1973 to 1976 demonstrates that some successful correctional rehabilitation programs do exist. Studies meeting the requirements to be included in the literature review had to employ at least a quasi-experimental design, contain a statistical analysis of the data, and report on a follow-up period of at least 6 months. A total of 95 programs treating antisocial behaviors was evaluated. The literature was classified into the following groups: family and community intervention, contingency management, counseling, diversion, biomedical assistance, and miscellaneous treatment. Additionally, a summary of studies that deal with such related problems as alcoholism and drug abuse is included. Results point to several intervention programs that have proven successful with offenders.

667 Glaser, D. EFFECTIVENESS OF A PRISON AND PAROLE SYSTEM. Indianapolis: Bobbs-Merrill, 1964.

For many years it has been said that between sixty and seventy percent of the men released from prison today will be back again within five years. This myth, as well as other popular misconceptions about offenders and their treatment has been debunked by a five-year research project. This five-year study on federal releasees, sponsored under the financial auspices of the Ford Foundation, questions the feasibility of some of the present correctional methods and substantiates the effectiveness of others. Many separate conclusions are summarized in a single overall theory of recidivism which points to sources of differential anticipations of criminal and non-criminal success in the experience of prisoners, their crime and non-crime career cycles, their tendency to recapitulate at each release from prison, and struggles to shift from childhood to adult role relationships.

668 Glaser, D.   "Incentives Motivating Prisoner
    Behavior." PRISON JOURNAL, 47 (1): 12-20, 1967.

    Incentives which shape human behavior most
significantly are the responses of other persons and the
experience of success in performing challenging tasks.
The traditional prison provides such incentives to
prisoners primarily in order to maintain an orderly
institution. The collaborative model of prison
operation, the opposite of the traditional model, focuses
on community correctional services and can achieve an
equally orderly institution. Most important, however, it
motivates the offender and helps him to attain self-
sufficiency in a non-criminal post-release life.

669 Glaser, D. ROUTINIZING EVALUATION: GETTING FEEDBACK
    ON EFFECTIVENESS OF CRIME AND DELINQUENCY PROGRAMS.
    Washington, D.C.: National Institute of Mental
    Health, 1973.

    This manual of evaluation techniques includes
statistical and cost-benefit analysis, and discussion of
how to encourage routine application of evaluative
findings. The manual provides methods for evaluating the
policies, procedures, and organization of prisons,
probation officers, treatment centers, clinics, training
schools, and other agencies which attempt to alter their
clients' deviant behavior. It provides analyses of the
evaluation process of defining and measuring success,
choosing among alternative measures, assessing efficiency
in monetary terms, resisting spurious evaluations,
determining what subjects to compare when measuring
success, and processing data on subjects and programs.
The sections on processing data include methods of
consolidating statistics and extensive descriptions and
illustrations of procedures for replacing narrative
reports with precoded forms.

670 Glaser, D. "Remedies for the Key Deficiency in
    Criminal Justice Evaluation Research." JOURNAL OF
    RESEARCH IN CRIME AND DELINQUENCY, 11 (2): 144-154,
    1974.

    More useful criminal justice evaluation research
would differentiate offenses and offenders on the basis
of causal theory and would interrelate several levels of
abstraction. This is illustrated in correctional
practice evaluation by a linkage of behavior
modification, symbolic interactionist, and sociocultural
diffusion theory, from which three propositions on the
effectiveness of specific treatment methods for
particular types of offenders are derived. Research thus

far supports the validity of these propositions. Boards of autonomous criminologists and public representatives supervising criminal justice statistics and research agencies would foster more grounding of inquires in policy-relevant theory.

671 Gottfredson, D. M., M. R. Gottfredson, and J. Garofalo. "Time Served and Parole Outcomes Among Parole Risk Categories." JOURNAL OF CRIMINAL JUSTICE, 5 (1): 1-12, 1977.

This study examines whether time served in prison is related to success on parole. Subjects were 5,349 males and 238 females paroled in Ohio between 1965 and 1972, comprising a 10-percent sample of all parolees during this period. Among males, nine risk categories were defined with rates of success ranging from 65 to 99 percent. Generally, success rates decreased as time served increased up to fifty months, but increased somewhat thereafter. When the risk groups were studied separately, however, either no relation was found or no single pattern obtained.

672 Gottfredson, M. R. "Treatment Destruction Techniques." JOURNAL OF RESEARCH IN CRIME AND DELINQUENCY, 16 (1): 39-54, 1979.

In line with the conventional wisdom in criminology that treatment programs have been ineffective, several methods often used to challenge the philosophical and empirical underpinnings of rehabilitation efforts are outlined. Of methods for challenging rehabilitation approaches, contaminating the treatment is most universally applicable. Another approach, stressing criterion problems, focuses on measurement issues. Since many treatment strategies aim to reduce the probability of recidivism, they require as a criterion measure some indicator of illegal behavior. It is impossible to measure such conduct accurately, and every study is vulnerable to attack on the basis of the criterion problem. Still another approach involves showing that massive efforts have failed. Using time or money as units of analysis, critics appeal to common sense by arguing that no future experimentation is warranted because past massive investments in programs and personnel have failed to produce unambiguous demonstrations of effectiveness. A final and best known destructive technique involves seeking universals; that is, to raise serious doubts about a program it is necessary only to show that although the treatment method has been found to work with some offenders, it is ineffective with others.

673 Gottfredson, M. R. "Parole Guidelines and the Reduction of Sentencing Disparity: A Preliminary Study."
JOURNAL OF RESEARCH IN CRIME AND DELINQUENCY, 16 (2):
218-231, 1979.

This report examined whether parole boards,
operating under explicit decision guidelines, achieved a
substantial sentence equalization function. Data on
sentence length and time served were obtained for 4,471
adult cases appearing before the federal parole
commission for the initial setting of release dates
between October 1977 and May 1978. Only the most
frequently occurring offenses were analyzed. The most
striking result was that for every category of equally
situated offenders, the coefficient of variation was
markedly smaller for the decisions as to time served than
for the decisions regarding sentence length. Parole
commission decisions, therefore, were less disparate than
judicial decisions, regardless of the prior record or
offense severity of the category examined. The findings
also suggest that systems with concrete guidelines for
reducing inequities may have advantages over other
proposed systems that place the authority for sentence
review with the judiciary.

674 Gottfredson, M. R., and K. Adams. "Prison Behavior
and Release Performance: Empirical Reality and Public
Policy." LAW AND POLICY QUARTERLY, 4 (3): 373-391,
1982.

A review of the debate concerning whether or not an
inmate's behavior while in prison is related to his/her
behavior after release is provided. The study then
assesses the impact of prison misconduct and risk on
parole failure for individuals released from federal
correctional institutions during 1970 and 1972.
Controlling for risk, the authors report some association
beteen officially recorded institutional infractions and
postrelease violations. This finding is evaluated in
terms of policy issues concerning the propriety and
fairness of predictive judgments and the relative merits
of different loci of parole decision-making.

675 Halleck, S. L. "Violence: Treatment Versus Correction." Pp. 377-393 in I. L. Kutash, S. B. Kutash,
and L. B. Schlesinger (eds.), VIOLENCE: PERSPECTIVES
ON MURDER AND AGGRESSION. San Francisco: Jossey-
Bass, 1978.

Issues and problems surrounding the rehabilitation
of violent offenders are discussed, and arguments for
retaining rehabilitation as a criminal justice goal are
presented. Three views of rehabilitation are outlined:

the prevention of recidivism by any means; the prevention of recidivism while guarding the welfare of the offender; and the prevention of recidivism while attempting to make the offender a good citizen. The third view is said to be most difficult to advance when there is emphasis on deterrence and retribution. The case for retaining rehabilitation as a criminal justice goal is based on the following points: rehabilitation has not been proved ineffective; deterrence and rehabilitation can be compatible; length of incarceration should not be affected by length of rehabilitation; humane people naturally try to rehabilitate others.

676 Heilbrun, A. B. "Race, Criminal Violence, and Length of Parole." BRITISH JOURNAL OF CRIMINOLOGY, 18 (1): 53-61, 1978.

The relationship between race of the criminal, violence of the crime, and length of the parole period on the success or failure of the parole is studied from files of the Georgia Board of Pardons and Paroles. Records of 1509 male felons were drawn from the files. It was found that violent offenders had greater parole success for shorter periods of time, but as the tracking period extended they were no better risks than nonviolent offenders. The offender most subject to impulsive behavior which results in parole violation is the black violent offender. This becomes more of a factor as the tracking period lengthens.

677 Heilbrun, A. B., L. C. Heilbrun, and K. L. Heilbrun. "Impulsive and Premeditated Homicide: An Analysis of Subsequent Parole Risk of the Murderer." JOURNAL OF CRIMINAL LAW AND CRIMINOLOGY, 69 (1): 108-114, 1978.

The relationships among race, criminal impulsivity, violence, and parole behaviors and outcome were studied in a sample of 164 convicted male murderers in the Georgia prison system for whom there were final parole decisions in the period between 1973 and 1976. The impulsivity and premeditation variable was rated by investigators of data gathered by the arresting authorities at the time of the crime's commission. Analysis of data indicates the following: (1) unsuccessful parolees tend to have committed more impulsive murders than successful parolees; (2) the tendency for impulsive murderers to fail on parole is more evident than the tendency for premeditated murderers to succeed; (3) black and white murderers do not differ in degree of impulsivity characterizing the murder or in their rates of success/failure of parole; (4) violent crime recidivism is higher among black parole failures than among white parole failures; (5) both racial groups have relatively high violation rates for drinking-related problems, but blacks are significantly more often in violation of parole for possession of firearms.

678 Heinz, A. "Sentencing by Parole Board: An Evalua-
    tion." JOURNAL OF CRIMINAL LAW AND CRIMINOLOGY, 67
    (1): 1-31, 1976.

    The influence that various information contained in an inmate's file has on the Illinois Parole Board's decisions to grant or deny parole is examined. The sample consists of files on 294 inmates who had parole hearings from 1970 through 1972. The decisions of the Illinois Parole Board in the cases analyzed were found to be associated with the seriousness of the inmate's commitment offense, the number of prior offenses, participation in educational programs while in prison, the inmate's record of infractions of the prison's rules, his or her prospects for employment after release, seriousness of the prior offenses, the length of the sentence the inmate was serving, the number of previous hearings on this parole decision, and the inmate's prison work assignment or participation in vocational training programs. The most striking finding was the very strong association between the Parole Board's decisions and the official predictions or "prognoses" about an inmate's future behavior that are recorded by correctional sociologists within the institutions.

679 Hindelang, M. J. "A Learning Theory Analysis of the
    Correctional Process." ISSUES IN CRIMINOLOGY, 5 (1):
    43-58, 1970.

    Examples are given of some of the aspects of the prison environment in which the present practices are not only failing to contribute to rehabilitation of inmates, but are, from a learning theory point of view, undermining that rehabilitation. (1) The present system fails to motivate inmates adequately so that they use their time in a manner that will be beneficial to them when they are released. (2) The present system of rewards and punishments is self-defeating. (3) It was shown how the perception of consequences as not contingent on one's behavior tends to subvert the goals of motivation toward self-improvement and resistance to transgressions. It is concluded that a learning theory approach in the correctional setting seems promising because in the short run such a program should reduce recidivism considerably, and, in the long run, a behavior modification program would probably be more economical.

680 Hippchen, L. J., E. D. Flynn, C. D. Owens, and A. C. Schnur (eds.). HANDBOOK ON CORRECTIONAL CLASSIFICATION: PROGRAMMING FOR TREATMENT AND REINTEGRATION. Cincinnati: Anderson, 1978.

Prepared by members of the American Correctional Association's Committee on Classification and Treatment, these papers provide guidelines for the classification and treatment of offenders. The opening chapter presents the early history and philosophy of corrections and explains the trend and rationale behind the current use of classification. Then follows an overview of the total classification process and its purpose. The next two chapters introduce the idea and explain the need for new uses and applications of classification at the community level. Three chapters deal with classification at various points in the criminal justice and institutional processes. The need for adequate information systems for evaluating classification effectiveness and monitoring offenders in their rehabilitation progress is discussed in another chapter. The final discussion involves innovative ideas for community classification in the future.

681 Hoffman, P. B. "Mandatory Release: A Measure of Type II Error." CRIMINOLOGY, 11 (4): 541-554, 1974.

The outcome rates for parole and mandatory releases in New York State during 1968 are presented. The sample consisted of 1135 adult male indeterminate sentence offenders originally released by parole or mandatory release during 1968, who had been convicted of robbery, burglary, or manslaughter. The robbery and burglary cases were further subdivided on the attribute of history of narcotic usage. Results of a statistical analysis of the data revealed that parolees do substantially better than mandatory releasees, with more favorable outcomes and fewer new arrests for every group comparison, and fewer technical or absconding violations in every comparison but one. Discussion of the results focuses on the parole decision-making error of not paroling an inmate who would have completed parole without violation. This is referred to as Type II error.

682 Hopper, C. B. "Conjugal Visiting at the Mississippi State Penitentiary." FEDERAL PROBATION, 29 (2): 39-46, 1965.

The development of conjugal visiting in the Mississippi State Penitentiary has largely been due to the social and physical organization of the penitentiary itself. The features considered important in its development are: the rural environment in which the

penitentiary is located; the plantation life the
penitentiary follows; the small semi-isolated camp
organization of the institution; the economic motives of
the penitentiary; and the segregation of the races at the
penitentiary. A poll of the inmates receiving conjugal
visits revealed that over fifty percent of them felt that
such visits were influential in keeping their marriages
from breaking up. This fact helps the prisoners and the
citizens of Mississippi not only accept the practice, but
also take pride in it. The fact that such visits
developed in an unofficial, unplanned manner shows the
magnitude of the problem of sexual adjustment in penal
institutions.

683 Hopper, C. B. "Conjugal Visiting: A Controversial
    Practice in Mississippi." CRIMINAL LAW BULLETIN, 3
    (5): 289-299, 1967.

The conjugal visiting privilege at the Mississippi
State Penitentiary has developed informally and
unofficially and is believed to have been permitted since
the institution was first opened in 1900. Inquiries have
resulted in some of the following findings. (1) All 14
sergeants of camps having conjugal visits
enthusiastically supported the program as being of basic
importance. (2) Of 822 unmarried inmates to whom the
privilege does not apply, only 10.3 percent reported any
resentment whatever. (3) Of 462 inmates participating in
the program, only 9.1 percent said that they were in any
way embarrassed by taking part in the program. The most
consistent praise from inmates was that the visits helped
to keep existing marriages intact. (4) An investigation
of inmates indicates that the recidivism rate for
prisoners who receive the privelege will be quite low.

684 Johnson, E. H. "Administrative Techniques in Correc-
    tions as a Tool for Theoretical Research." PRISON
    JOURNAL, 45 (2): 34-43, 1965.

The practical problems of initiating theoretical
research within action agencies are symptomatic of
ideological conflicts inherent in the field of
corrections and in research as a professional activity.
In the field of corrections, ideological conflicts can be
summarized under the labels of innovation versus ritual-
ism, treatment versus punishment, treatment versus safekeeping, and standardization versus individualization of
treatment procedures. Issues in theoretical research
involve the question of pure versus applied research,
professional values versus administrative goals, and
scientific versus moral questions. Beyond these
problems, it can be stated that the future of theoretical
research rests on the development of skills in the

behavioral sciences among all correctional personnel
involved in the treatment programs.

685 Johnson, E. H. "Correctional Research as a Bridge
    Between Practice and Theory." CANADIAN JOURNAL OF
    CORRECTIONS, 10 (4): 545-552, 1968.

    The field of corrections is entering a period of
unprecedented change which demands that correctional
practice be based on conscious use of theories to direct
administration and afford a rational framework for daily
task performance. Major changes in attitude among
practitioners, university leaders, and the general public
support genuine convergence of theory and practice. If
research is to become a vehicle for intelligent
direction of correctional administration, it must be
integrated within the agency's programs rather than
function independently of administrative actions. The
administrators must make a greater financial and
psychological investment in research than is found in the
usual host-guest relationship between the prison
administrator and the university researcher.

686 Johnson, V. S. "Behavior Modification in the Correc-
    tional Setting." CRIMINAL JUSTICE AND BEHAVIOR, 4
    (4): 397-428, 1977.

    The literature on behavior modification in
correctional settings is reviewed. The first section
reviews published studies of behavior modification
according to the specific techniques applied. The second
provides brief descriptions and assessments of major
programs that have attempted intervention through large-
scale behavioral technology. Most of the studies were
designed to demonstrate the feasibility of a technique in
dealing with specific behavior in a correctional setting
rather than in accomplishing "rehabilitation" per se.
The studies provide reason for optimism concerning the
capacity of positive reinforcement to effect change in a
correctional setting. Unfortunately, researchers have
not addressed the issue of modification of illegal acts
following release.

687 Kassebaum, G. G., D. A. Ward, and D. M. Wilner.
    PRISON TREATMENT AND PAROLE SURVIVAL. New York: John
    Wiley, 1971.

    The results of an experimental study of the effects
of prison group counseling on inmate behavior and parolee
recidivism are discussed. The test population was the
inmates at California Men's Colony - East, in Los Padres.
Effectiveness was measured by parole survival over a 36-

month period. Training for group counselors, the program
itself, and the inmates reaction to it are all described.
Findings revealed that group counseling did not alter
inmates' existing anti-social attitudes. Additionally,
it was found that parole performance did not
significantly differ, irrespective of participation, type
of program, exposure, voluntariness, and stability of
group leadership. The implications of these results for
correctional administrators and treatment professionals
are discussed. This study provides empirical and
illustrative support for the notion that social control
is the primary goal in prisons and parole decisions.

688 Katrin, S. E. "Effects on Women Inmates of Facilita-
    tion Training Provided Correctional Officers." CRIM-
    INAL JUSTICE AND BEHAVIOR 1 (1): 5-12, 1974.

     Effectiveness of a forty-hour, thirteen-week human
relations training program for correctional officers is
measured in terms of inmate change. Selected behavior,
feelings, and perceptions of a randomly selected sample
of 105 female inmates at the Georgia Rehabilitation
Center for Women were investigated. The correctional
staff training program involved empathic understanding in
interpersonal processes and role-playing. Results
revealed that the inmate anxiety level was significantly
decreased, their interest in social relationships
increased, and the correctional officers' ability to
communicate and discriminate at a higher facilitative
level was significantly increased.

689 Kitchener, H., A. K. Schmidt, and D. Glaser. "How
    Persistent Is Post-Prison Success?" FEDERAL PROBA-
    TION, 41 (1): 9-15, 1977.

     An eighteen-year follow-up was performed for 1956
federal prison releasees (N=903) to analyze the extent of
post-release criminality. Failure after release was
defined to include either return to prison as a parole
violator or receiving any new sentence for a felony or
felony-like offense. The crucial period for failure was
between one and two years after release, with 20 percent
of all failures in eighteen years occurring between
twelve and sixteen months after release and the first two
years accounting for over half the total failures. After
five years, four-fifths of those who would fail during
eighteen years had already done so, and at ten years the
failure rate was 94 percent. It would appear that any
post-release assistance which reduces failure rates, as
economic aid demonstrably does for many who would
otherwise be poor risks, should be available when needed
for at least two years and preferably for five years.

690 Knox, G. W., and W. A. Stacey. "Determinants of
    Employment Success Among Ex-Offenders." OFFENDER
    REHABILITATION, 2 (3): 205-214, 1978.

    Seven Comprehensive Offender Manpower Program
projects providing job placements for ex-offenders were
compared using a form of cost-benefit analysis. Data
were derived from 1,660 client cases. The key effect
variables assessed included recidivism, job retention,
and projected earnings. Typical client populations
varied among the seven programs. The cost-benefit ratios
obtained for the seven programs were all greater than
unity, ranging from a low of 4.24 to a high of 16.88.
The overall cost-benefit ratio for one of the projects in
Illinois was 6.56, which may be interpreted as meaning
that for every program dollar spent, a savings of $6.56
is realized by the government and society in terms of
averted costs and direct gains.

691 Lillyquist, M. J. UNDERSTANDING AND CHANGING CRIMI-
    NAL BEHAVIOR. Englewood Cliffs, NJ: Prentice-Hall,
    1980.

    A broad spectrum of approaches to understanding and
changing criminal behavior is presented along with a
model of the approaches. Part I discusses person-
centered, situation-centered, and interactionist models
of criminal behavior, along with the role of penology,
corrections, and intervention as three modes of response
to crime. A second section outlines psychiatric and
medical approaches in individual treatment; counseling
and other nonmedical approaches; concepts of the self and
ego psychology, including transactional analysis;
concepts of reality and crime; and deviant value systems.
Also discussed are social psychological approaches in
treatment. Various behavioral learning theories are also
described as are the types and effectiveness of
deterrence and the role of community, environment, and
culture in crime prevention. The final chapters discuss
evaluation in the areas of offender classification,
correctional treatment programs, and community
corrections.

692 Lipton, D., R. Martinson, and J. Wilks. THE EFFEC-
    TIVENESS OF CORRECTIONAL TREATMENT: A SURVEY OF
    TREATMENT EVALUATION STUDIES. New York: Praeger,
    1975.

    This book presents a compilation and an analysis of
research studies conducted between 1945 and 1967 to
evaluate the treatment of criminal and juvenile
offenders. Each of the 231 studies included in this
survey has been annotated. The annotations have been

classified into various sections. In each section the studies are discussed, critically analyzed, and summarized. Study findings are classified according to 11 treatment methods (independent variables) and 7 desired areas of change (dependent variables). The independent variables considered include imprisonment, parole, casework and individual counseling, milieu therapy, and medical methods. The dependent variables discussed are recidivism, institutional adjustment, vocational adjustment, educational achievement, drug and alcohol readdiction, personality and attitude change, and community adjustment. The implications of the findings of the studies are discussed.

693 Lubenthal, J. S.   "Rehabilitation as Beating the Rap: The Structural Ambivalence of Correction."   CRIME AND DELINQUENCY, 17 (3): 256-265, 1971.

The rehabilitation worker who tries to reconcile what he does with what he thinks his work is supposed to accomplish can do so only by ignoring certain realities that constitute the penal setting defining his client's world. By contrast, the client's insight into this world and his perspective on rehabilitation are unencumbered by the worker's ideology: they are determined experientially. The price paid for subordinating this insight and perspective to agency needs is the continuing inability of rehabilitation to extract from the penal system the resources that would enable workers to pursue their professed goals more effectively and with less conflict. This subordination perpetuates a closed system whose main advantage is that it enables success to be defined and measured in terms of whatever official activities are occurring and in light of organizational needs. The assertion of client interests will occur as a result of realizing the extent to which continuation of the present system depends on client participation and cooperation. This assertion will produce new alignments, techniques consistent with goals, and ultimately revolutionary changes in the administration of criminal justice.

694 Martin, S. E., L. B. Sechrest, and R. Redner (eds.). NEW DIRECTIONS IN THE REHABILITATION OF CRIMINAL OFFENDERS. Washington, D.C.: National Academy Press, 1981.

This volume features a report by the Panel on Research on Rehabilitative Techniques of the National Research Council, plus 10 commissioned papers about sociological theories of crime, limitations on intervention, and restitution. The panel report explores the contributions that theory can make to program design and implementation, identifies areas suggested by various theoretical or conceptual frameworks as most likely to yield knowledge relevant to policy change, and proposes a research strategy for increasing knowledge about rehabilitative efforts. Furthermore, intervention programs and research should be developed jointly as a coordinated activity designed to test detailed theoretical propositions explicitly. Following the panel's report, the 10 commissioned papers provide background support, resource materials, and suggestions for further research related to the specific concerns of the panel.

695 Martinson, R. "What Works? -- Questions and Answers About Prison Reform." PUBLIC INTEREST, 35 (Spring): 22-54, 1974.

Analysis of 231 studies that evaluated correctional treatment methods between 1945 and 1967 to determine what works in correction supplied no evidence of success or effectiveness of educational programs for juvenile or adult inmates and of programs of individual or group counseling. Youths who participate in milieu therapy programs such as California's Marshall Program at least do no worse than their counterparts in regular institutions; special programs, moreover, may cost less. Strictly medical treatment to change behavior also had little effect on recidivism in general. Length of sentence had no clear relationship to recidivism. Studies of probation with intensive supervision indicate that specially treated youthful probationers were less recidivistic; some major studies--e.g., the Warren studies in California--present a much bleaker picture of the possibilities of intensive supervision with special treatment. The results are ambiguous with intensive supervision of adult offenders. No sure way of reducing recidivism through rehabilitation has been found.

696 Martinson, R. "California Research at the Crossroads." CRIME AND DELINQUENCY, 22 (2): 180-191, 1976.

The primary reason for the impact of "What Works?" is the extraordinary gap between the claims of success made by proponents of various treatments and the reality revealed by good research. The real conclusion of "What Works?" is that the addition of isolated treatment elements to a system in which a given flow of offenders has generated a gross rate of recidivism has very little effect in changing this rate of recidivism. To ask "which methods work best for which types of offenders and under what conditions or in what types of settings" is to impose the narrowest of questions on the search for knowledge. The essence of the new "social planning" epoch is a change in the dependent variable from recidivism to the crime rate. The public does not care whether a program will demonstrate that the experimental group shows a lower recidivism rate than a control group; rather, it wants to know whether the program reduced the overall crime rate.

697 Mathieson, T. "The Sociology of Prisons: Problems for Future Research." BRITISH JOURNAL OF SOCIOLOGY, 17 (4): 360-379, 1966.

Sociologists have had the tendency to simplify social relations in prisons by presenting them as if many complicating factors were constant or neutralized. Although this procedure is justifiable in the first stage of research, prison sociology should go beyond that stage and examine the prison as a dynamic institution. Future research on prisons could be profitably concentrated in five strategic areas which would make-up a fairly unified research program: (1) formal aspects of the prison social structure; (2) differences between prisons; (3) change of prisons; (4) the organizational environment; and (5) the effects of personality variables on social relations in prisons.

698 McCleary, R. "How Structural Variables Constrain the Parole Officer's Use of Discretionary Powers." SOCIAL PROBLEMS, 23 (2): 209-225, 1975.

To determine the extent to which discretion by the parole officer (PO) may be structurally constrained, participant observation and interviews were used to study 42 parole officers, five branch officer supervisors, and eleven officials employed by the Cook County Adult Field Services branch of the Illinois Department of Corrections. The degree of freedom a PO will have in making a case decision is determined by the situation, as defined by the organization, the PO's own perception of a client, and the PO's professional reputation. The PO's freedom is generally proportional to the strength of his reputation for fairness and competence. This relationship between freedom and reputation is based on three principles: the incompetent PO cannot "lie" successfully to outside agencies, he cannot depend on his supervisor for "protection," and he may be subjected to close scrutiny from his supervisor. PO's maximize their freedom within the organization by manipulating their reputations. Programs meant to rehabilitate the client or to protect society are used instead for reputation building. This finding raises questions about the construct validity of parole outcome studies. The agent of failure may lie in the parole supervision agency rather than in parolee characteristics, societal norms, or rehabilitative treatments.

699 Moos, R. H. "Differential Effects of the Social Climates of Correctional Institutions." JOURNAL OF RESEARCH IN CRIME AND DELINQUENCY, 7 (1): 71-82, 1970.

This study assesses the differential effects of the social climates of 16 correctional units. It was hypothesized and shown that units which were different in social climate were also different on variables related to general resident reaction to the unit and on the initiatives which residents perceived themselves as taking in the unit. For example, the results indicated that units with greater emphasis on spontaneity, affiliation, insight, variety, and autonomy had residents who were more likely to like the staff and to feel that they were able to test their abilities and to increase their self-confidence; and that units with greater emphasis on affiliation, insight, and autonomy had residents who perceived themselves as more likely to take both submissive and autonomous initiatives toward the staff, i.e., who generally interacted more with the staff. The results substantiate the idea that different unit social climates have different predictable effects on the residents who live within them.

700 Moseley, W. H., and M. H. Gerould. "Sex and Parole: A Comparison of Male and Female Parolees." JOURNAL OF CRIMINAL JUSTICE, 3 (1): 47-57, 1975.

Male and female parolees released in 1970 with a 2-year follow-up were compared in terms of personal attributes, time served, and parole outcome. The study showed that the two sexes were substantially different in five commitment offenses, prior prison sentences, age at admission to confinement from which paroled, and alcohol and drug involvement. They were relatively similar in the proportion of prior non-prison sentences. Women, on the average, serve less time in prison before parole than men. The proportion successfully continued on parole is the same for both sexes.

701 Moule, D. M., and J. K. Hanft. "Parole Decision-Making in Oregon." OREGON LAW REVIEW, 55 (3): 303-347, 1976.

Discussion of the results of an examination of the factors considered by parole board members to be influential in decision-making and of the relative weights given to each. Board members were asked to

indicate the importance of 52 named factors in helping
them decide whether to grant, deny, or reset parole.
Factors which correlated with earlier than average
release on parole include conviction of robbery or
fraudulent crimes (as opposed to violent crimes),
unemployment at time of arrest, participation in
educational or vocational programs, youthfulness, high
IQ, fair or poor physical health, poor mental health,
Oregon residency, multiple infractions of institutional
rules, and serious discipline for violation of
institutional rules. It is recommended that the board's
policy of not paroling inmates with lost good time be
rejected, that the board's guidelines be available to
prisoners and to the public, and that most prisoners be
informed, shortly after incarceration, of the approximate
date of their release.

702 Nietzel, M. T. CRIME AND ITS MODIFICAITON: A SOCIAL
    LEARNING PERSPECTIVE. Elmsford, NY: Pergamon Press,
    1979.

    This text evaluates effects of institutional
behavior modification, nonresidential behavior therapy,
and community-based modification founded on social
learning theory and makes recommendations for
improvements. Behavioral corrections are evaluated
against several criteria for effective community
psychology intervention, and basic issues pertaining to
the measurement and etiology of crime are reviewed.
Next, a more detailed attempt is made to integrate
various social learning factors that have been offered as
explanations for criminal behavior, including control
theories, symbolic interaction, classical conditioning,
and social labeling. Final chapters present principles
for improving correctional behavior modification. They
examine the ethical and legal status of behavior
modification. It is suggested that new procedures for
influencing human behavior can be developed which will be
compatible with emerging legal-ethical requirements in
corrections.

703 Owens, C. E. MENTAL HEALTH AND BLACK OFFENDERS.
    Lexington, MA: D. C. Heath, 1980.

    This book addresses the issues of racism and
racism's effect on black people's behavior, special
training programs, and service-delivery models. Research
on causal factors of black crime and the role that mental
health professionals have played in criminal justice are
discussed. An evaluation and discussion of black mental
health and mental illness precedes a description of
prison environments and prison relationships, including
the expectations of black inmates in relation to mental

health professionals. The book reviews relevant research on therapeutic models presently used in penal settings and some problems associated with using therapy with blacks. The focus then turns to the role of the black family, community, schools, and the mental health professional in crime prevention. Strategies which the mental health professional can use to alter the criminal justice system and reduce racial friction are highlighted.

704 Palmer, T. "Martinson Revisited." JOURNAL OF RE-
    SEARCH IN CRIME AND DELINQUENCY, 12 (2): 133-152,
    1975.

    A focus on the positive findings and optimistic observations and on their significance causes a re-assessment of Martinson's sweeping conclusion that "with few and isolated exceptions, the rehabilitative efforts that have been reported so far have had no appreciable effect on recidivism." An expansion of the data not generally covered by Martinson illustrates that a number of promising leads do exist in correctional intervention. The following are among the trends that have emerged so far: (1) various methods of intervention are more likely to be associated with positive behavioral outcome (less recidivism) in relation to some offenders compared with others, and (2) these "middle risk" offenders appear to be better suited than the remaining offenders for placement on probation or parole in lieu of institutionalization. Martinson emphasized the indisputable fact that no sure way of reducing recidivism had been found in connection with any of the treatment categories under consideration. Although "patterns" were considered to be relevant in the original context, they were omitted from the summary statement. Rather than asking what works for offenders as a whole, we must increasing ask which method works best for which offenders and under what conditions.

705 Palmer, T. CORRECTIONAL INTERVENTION AND RESEARCH:
    CURRENT ISSUES AND FUTURE PROSPECTS. Lexington, MA:
    D.C. Heath, 1978.

    This book is largely a response to the uproar over the Martinson and related observations about the effectiveness of correctional treatment. To assess the validity of this viewpoint, supportive research studies on correctional treatment and their conclusions are evaluated for research quality, differential weighting of variables, and insignificant changes. It is suggested that research has ignored offenders' individuality and the fact that treatment, to be useful, does not have to be effective in all or the majority of cases. Data from the Community Treatment Project in California is used to support the suggestion that a combination of modalities should be used with offender groups, either within or outside the framework of determinate sentencing. Correctional treatment programs should not be evaluated by their effects on recidivism and should have offender-centered roles. Attitudes of decision-makers and the public regarding treatment theories are discussed, and prospects and strategies for correctional treatment which would maximize the information yield of existing research are considered.

706 Palmer, T. "The 'Effectiveness' Issue Today: An Overview." FEDERAL PROBATION, 46 (2): 3-10, 1983.

Following the controversy began in the 1970's concerning the effectiveness of correctional rehabilitation, the author identifies two major views of the issues raised. The "skeptical" view recognizes that some rehabilitation programs may be working but that the paucity of sound evaluation of most efforts leaves the effectiveness debate unresolved. The "sanguine" view argues that while most treatment approaches have not demonstrated across the board success, many programs appear to work for specific types of offenders. This perspective focuses on two postions: (1) "differential intervention" -- matching specific programs with those offenders most likely to benefit; and (2) "basic treatment-amenability" -- dealing with those offenders (e.g., intelligent, motivated, etc.) who are likely to respond to many different treatment approaches, while recognizing that other offenders are likely to respond to few, if any, approaches. Both skeptics and sanguines agree that programs involving serious or multiple offenders must necessarily be broader based and more intensive. Finally, issues of rehabilitative effectiveness should not overshadow concerns with inmate rights and prison reform efforts.

707 Peters, J. M. "How an Inmate's Expectancies Affect His Performance." AMERICAN JOURNAL OF CORRECTION, 31 (3): 18-20, 1969.

The extent to which an inmate feels that he has control over his environment is an important determinant of his behavior. Research has found such feelings to be related to an inmate's ability to learn certain informa-tion and to his participation in occupational/educational programs. Implications of such findings include the need to identify and change the inmate's feelings of lack of control over his environment, and thereby increase his chances of responding positively to rehabilitative efforts. An understanding of the effects of differing expectancies of control and appropriate corrective action by prison officials should add to the effectiveness of rehabilitative efforts of our correctional institutions.

708 Petersen, D. M., and P. C. Friday. "Early Release From Incarceration: Race as a Factor in the Use of 'Shock Probation'." JOURNAL OF CRIMINAL LAW AND CRIMINOLOGY, 66 (1): 79-87, 1975.

Legal and nonlegal variables that differentiate between those prisoners who are released on probation by the courts after a period of short-term incarceration and those who remain imprisoned are examined. Data to determine the variables which differentiated between those felons who received early releases and those who remained in the institution were collected at a medium security prison for male offenders between the ages of sixteen and thirty. The sample design included all persons granted early release from prison. The following nonlegal variables were found to be associated with early release: race, education, father's education and legal residence. The legal variables were related to early release probation department recommendation, offense, prior record, number of bills of indictment, and plea.

709 Petersilia, J. "Which Inmates Participate in Prison Treatment Programs?" JOURNAL OF OFFENDER COUNSELING SERVICES AND REHABILITATION, 4 (2): 121-135, 1979.

Recent findings have shown that a substantial percentage of prison treatment programs can be differentially effective and that future prison treatment policy will center on resource allocation to certain inmates. Data were gathered from a 1974 survey of 10,400 inmates from 190 state correctional facilities. Results showed that 40 percent of inmates nationwide participated in some treatment program while incarcerated. Moreover, 22 percent of the inmates were found to require alcohol rehabilitation, 23 percent to need drug rehabilitation, 31 percent to require job training, and 68 percent to need further education. One in four or five inmates with identified needs participated in prison treatment programs related to these needs. Older inmates were more likely to receive alcohol treatment, whereas younger inmates more often received education and job training. Whites were more likely to receive alcohol rehabilitation and blacks to receive drug treatment. Inmates serving more than 5 years were preponderantly found in job training programs. Treatment programs appear to be used randomly with persons of all racial, age, and prior criminal histories.

710 Petersilia, J., P. Honig, and C. Hubay. PRISON EX-
    PERIENCE OF CAREER CRIMINALS. Santa Monica, CA: Rand
    Corporation, 1980.

     The treatment needs and custodial problems
associated with career criminals are explored, along with
the question of whether these inmates are treated
selectively. Data were obtained from samples of about
1,300 inmates from 11 prisons in California, Michigan,
and Texas. Education and vocational training programs
appeared to be vigorous, while alcohol and drug
rehabilitation programs, as well as counseling, seemed
minimal. Analysis of all program types shows that nearly
half of the inmates who had participated felt the program
would reduce their future criminality. There was little
evidence that career criminal inmates have greater
treatment needs than the general prison population or
that they participate less in relevant prison
rehabilitation programs. Neither do prison staffs
identify and selectively deal with career criminals.
Career criminals were not found to be the primary source
of prison violence. Younger inmates committed more
serious and frequent infractions of every type. Further,
it is suggested that no special rehabilitation programs
for career criminals be established at this time.

711 Pittman, J. T., and P. Gray. "Evaluation of Prison
    Systems." JOURNAL OF CRIMINAL JUSTICE, 2 (1): 37-54,
    1974.

     Models are developed for the flow of prisoners
through the Georgia prison system and are used to
evaluate the effectiveness of alternative correctional
programs. Markov models are used to model the various
states of an individual as he passes through the criminal
justice system. Markov models are based on the
assumption that the probabilities of transition from
state to state (e.g., from imprisonment to parole) depend
only on the current state and not on previous states.
Using Georgia prison data averaged for the years 1967-
1971, transition matrices were constructed for assault,
robbery, burglary, and larceny offenders with respect to
the states of: in prison for conviction, in prison for
parole violation, out of prison on parole, and out of
prison because sentence or parole completed. Several
cost matrices were also constructed. The applications of
this modeling technique to the evaluation of correctional
alternatives are discussed.

712 Prus, R. C., and J. R. Stratton. "Parole Revocation
    Decision-Making: Private Typings and Official Desig-
    nations." FEDERAL PROBATION, 40 (1): 48-53, 1976.

A study of a midwestern state parole department attempted to locate the underlying concerns affecting parole officers' definitions of the revocability of their parolees. The final parolee definition reflects a routing of revocation definitions through several negotiation points. The agent arrives at a private assessment of a parolee relative to revocation. If he decides the man should be revoked, he examines the realistic possibility of the revocation, given the nature of the parole situation and the system in which he works. When revocation is seen as a good possibility, he may decide to make his private assessment known to others. The first critical negotiation occurs when the agent seeks the approval of his supervisor. When, after this negotiation, the parolee is still considered a revocation candidate, the request will be forwarded to the parole board for further processing. If the revocation recommendation is not turned down, it becomes a final definition. Parole officers endeavor to create official parolee definitions consistent with those they consider most desired by the organization network to which they find themselves accountable.

713 Ray, E. T., and K. L. Kilburn. "Behavior Modification Techniques Applied to Community Behavior Problems." CRIMINOLOGY, 8 (2): 173-184, 1970.

A case is presented for the adoption of behavior modification techniques in probation. Such techniques are particularly well suited to professionals in probation because their use does not depend on extensive psychological or psychiatric training. Various kinds of behavior modification programs have been successful in institutions because it has been possible to control essential elements of the environment. A frequent criticism of extention of similar programs to community settings is that conditions which made programs feasible in institutions are not available in community settings. It is stated that some of the institutional conditions do exist in the community. Implications for parole officers are outlined.

714 Regens, J. L., and W. G. Hobson. "Inmate Self-Government and Attitude Change: An Assessment of Participation Effects." EVALUATION QUARTERLY, 2 (3): 455-479, 1978.

The effects of participation in an inmate self-government program on inmates' self-esteem, self-competence, acceptance of others, and acceptance of law and authority are examined. The study focuses on the attitudinal changes attributable to participation in an inmate self-government program initiated in 1971 at the

2

80 CRIMINAL JUSTICE IN AMERICA

Washington State Penitentiary. The program was designed to give inmates actual policy-making responsibilities through a system of collaborative management. The principal component of self-government was an inmate-elected 11-member council responsible for formulating policy objectives and for coordinating inmate participation. A pretest-posttest design was used to evaluate the program's effects on a stratified random sample of 173 male inmates. Evaluation data reveal that participation consistently fostered a more positive sense of social responsibility among inmates, whereas the attitudes associated with social responsibility deteriorated consistently among inmates who did not participate in self-government.

715 Ross, R. R., and P. Gendreau (eds.). EFFECTIVE COR-
    RECTIONAL TREATMENT. Scarborough, Ontario: Butter-
    worth, 1980.

This book discusses the principles, techniques, and results of 23 of the most effective correctional treatment programs conducted between 1973 and 1978. Introductory chapters review the correctional treatment literature, describe evidence of the effectiveness of correctional treatment, examine some of the fallacies inherent in the "nothing works" doctrine, and suggest reasons for the apparent failure of some programs. Chapters on diversion programs discuss the effect of these programs on rearrests, describe an exemplary program conducted by the Dallas Police Department, and present a multifaceted program which could serve as a model for replication in other jurisdictions. Three essays evaluate community treatment programs, assess a heroin addiction treatment program, and summarize a 3-year Canadian research project that examined the effectiveness of probation officers and volunteers in counseling adult probationers.

716 Rossi, P. H., R. A. Berk, and K. J. Lenihan. MONEY,
    WORK, AND CRIME: EXPERIMENTAL EVIDENCE. New York:
    Academic Press, 1980.

The Transitional Aid Research Project (TARP) was a large-scale field experiment designed to determine whether providing released prisoners with limited financial support would reduce their recidivism rates for property crimes. Beginning in early 1976, selected prisoners released from state institutions in Georgia and Texas were offered financial help for up to six months following release in the form of unemployment insurance benefits. Released prisoners were randomly assigned to experimental and control groups and followed for one year after release. Former prisoners who had received

financial aid had lower rearrest rates than their
counterparts who did not receive benefits and who had
worked comparable periods of time. Ex-prisoners in the
treatment group took longer to find jobs than did the
controls and generally worked less during the year
following release. Still, there was little difference in
the total annual earnings between the two groups.

717 Sacks, H. R., and C. H. Logan. DOES PAROLE MAKE A
    DIFFERENCE? West Hartford: University of Connecti-
    cut School of Law Press, 1979.

    In response to the 1974 Connecticut Supreme Court
decision holding that the Connecticut constitution was
violated by the sentencing of persons who had committed
minor felonies to excessive prison terms, over 400
offenders were quickly discharged from their sentences.
The 167 offenders in institutions were unconditionally
released to the community, and 115 were used as an
experimental group in a study of the effects of parole.
A control group of 57 parolees had been previously
discharged. A 1-year follow-up of both groups revealed
data related to criminal conduct and civil commitments
after release. The finding that only 37 percent of the
parolees returned to crime, while 63 percent of the
experimental nonparolees returned to crime, is considered
statistically significant. Parole had a definite, but
only modest effect on recidivism. Moreover, the
experimental group, while failing at a higher rate than
the parolees, did not commit more serious crimes, and
they were not less successful in terms of total time
spent back in the community. Alternative explanations
for the study's findings include the effect of parolee
status on gaining employment, and the psychological
phenomenon known as the "Hawthorne effect" which refers
to changes in subjects caused by the attention which they
receive during the study.

718 Scott, F. M. "Therapy With Female Offenders." IN-
    TERNATIONAL JOURNAL OF OFFENDER THERAPY AND COMPARA-
    TIVE CRIMINOLOGY, 21 (3): 208-220, 1977.

    A heuristic outline for working with female
offenders is presented, and some therapy suggestions are
offered. Using case histories, the author discusses the
general categories of female offender behavior patterns:
(1) interpersonal--having to do with the most common
patterns of relationships with significant men and with
their children; (2) intrapersonal--having to do with the
psychological patterns of the individual; (3) para-
social--having to do with patterns of behavior such as
prostitution and drug abuse; (4) impersonal--dealing with
crime patterns such as forgery, robbery, and theft; and

(5) the future diagnostic trend--considered to be paranoid behavior as women enter the business and professional world in greater number. It is advised that, for most female offenders, a male therapist is preferable to a female therapist since negative relationships with men are most central to deviant female behavior. The therapist's extension of empathy coupled with efforts to guide the client toward behavioral change to deal with her present life situation are considered difficult aspects of the therapeutic relationship which must be given primary attention for progress to occur.

719 Scott, J. E. "The Use of Discretion in Determining the Severity of Punishment for Incarcerated Offenders." JOURNAL OF CRIMINAL LAW AND CRIMINOLOGY, 65 (2): 214-224, 1974.

The locus of this study is the criteria utilized by parole boards in determining the proper amount of punishment a convicted adult felony offender should receive. Data were gathered at three adult penal institutions for felony offenders in a midwestern state. The research sample comprised the records of all female inmates released from the state's women's prison in 1968 (N=34) and a 25 percent random sample of the records of all male inmates released from the same state's adult felony penal institutions during 1968 (N=325). The seriousness of crime for which inmates were convicted was the best indicator of the severity of punishment. Those inmates receiving the most disciplinary reports were incarcerated the longest, even when the legal seriousness of the crime and all other independent variables were controlled. The parole board punishes older offenders more severly than younger offenders. Inmates who had completed more schooling were granted parole earlier than those with less education, and inmates with higher IQ's were granted parole sooner than those with lower IQ's. Blacks were punished more severely than whites, and women were punished less severely than men. Inmates with higher socioeconomic status received more lenient treatment than those with lower SES.

720 Sechrest, L. B., S. O. White, and E. D. Brown (eds.). REHABILITATION OF CRIMINAL OFFENDERS: PROBLEMS AND PROSPECTS. Washington, D.C.: National Academy of Sciences, 1979.

The report of a panel that examined the effectiveness of correctional rehabilitation programs and associated evaluative research is presented. After nearly two years of study, the panel concluded that the methodology used to evaluate offender rehabilitation programs is generally so inadequate that only a

relatively few studies warrant any unequivocal interpretations. It is recommended that research on offender
rehabilitation be pursued more vigorously,
systematically, imaginatively, and more rigorously.
Specifically, treatments should be based upon strong
theoretical rationales, perhaps involving total programs
rather than weak or piecemeal treatments. The five
commissioned papers consider (1) an evaluation model for
medical care based on information about patient outcomes
and its replicability for offender rehabilitation
programs; (2) methodological factors obstructing
effective evaluation of offender rehabilitation programs
and ways of improving correctional program evaluations;
(3) models of criminal recidivism designed to predict the
length of time from release to commission of another
offense, based upon offender characteristics; (4)
recommendations involving the measurement of recidivism;
and (5) areas of economic research with potential for
improving the efficiency of criminal justice
rehabilitation programs.

721 Smith, A. B., and L. Berlin. TREATING THE CRIMINAL
    OFFENDER, (2nd ed.) Englewood Cliffs, NJ: Prentice-
    Hall, 1981.

    The basic philosophy of this volume affirms the
validity of the rehabilitative goal of corrections and
the efficacy of casework and psychotherapy techniques in
the treatment of offenders. The programs selected for
description take into account the characteristics of
treater and treated as well as the setting in which the
treatment occurs. The wide program range reflects the
fact that many treatment modalities exist and that some
approaches are effective only with specific target
populations. Theoretical issues are discussed in
chapters devoted to the causes of crime and to punishment
versus treatment theories. Problems and issues in
corrections are also addressed, including those referring
to confidentiality, community versus custodial treatment,
and race relations. Remaining chapters deal with
treatment issues for particular types of offenders or
offenses. Attention is given to drug addiction, sexual
offenders, violent offenders, alcoholism, family crises,
gambling, white-collar crime, and female offenders.

722 Steadman, H. J. "New Look at Recidivism Among Pa-
    tuxent Inmates." BULLETIN OF THE AMERICAN ACADEMY
    OF PSYCHIATRY AND THE LAW, 5 (2): 200-209, 1977.

    Recidivism rates for inmates at a Maryland facility
for the confinement and treatment of dangerous offenders
are analyzed and compared with rates for other Maryland
inmates. All criminal activity during the first three

years after return to the community through parole,
sentence expiration, or court mandate was analyzed for
each of five research groups: (1) all Patuxent inmates
placed on parole status in 1971 and 1972; (2) all
Patuxent inmates released in 1971 and 1972 through
redetermination hearings or legal technicalities; (3) all
inmates from 1964 through 1972 who were evaluated at
Patuxent and found to be defectively delinquent but not
committed to the institution by the court; (4) all
inmates referred for evaluation by Patuxent staff in 1967
and found not to be defectively delinquent; and (5) a
sample of 100 inmates paroled in 1971 and 1972 from
Maryland correctional facilities. According to the
analysis, offenders who completed the Patuxent program
and were paroled came to the institution with longer and
more severe arrest records than any of the other groups
but after release were arrested approximately as often as
the other groups.

723 Sterne, R. S. "A Reevaluation of Parole Prediction."
    CRIMINOLOGICA, 3 (4): 3-7, 1966.

    At the present time, prediction efforts stress an
anatomical diagraming of the statistical relations
between static background factors and success or failure
on parole, a variable which itself remains undefined.
Yet, in the analysis of any type of behavior, parole
behavior included, one must have a thorough grasp of all
of the factors. Statistical methods could profitably be
used since they enable us, in a multivariate situation,
to pick out treatable factors with the highest relation
to behavior. The methods can then indicate what services
need strengthening, modification, or creation. But the
technical process known as parole prediction must, at all
times, be kept strictly in harness in order to advance
correctional goals. If important elements in behavior
are omitted in the study of deviants, correctional goals
are not advanced. Instead, the status quo is frozen,
and, ultimately, penological principles are defeated.

724 Studt, E., S. L. Messinger, and T. P. Wilson. C-
    UNIT: SEARCH FOR COMMUNITY IN PRISON. New York:
    Russell Sage Foundation, 1968.

    In order to experiment with a person-in-context
approach to corrections, a therapeutic community was
established in a California prison for young adult male
offenders. An administration that relies solely on its
own coercive resources can make little contribution to
the reconstruction of prison life or to the creation of
environments that encourage autonomy or self-respect. A
system that engages the full resources of its participants accepts the risk of occasional disorder. The most

effective treatment is that which does the most for the
inmate's sense of self-worth and responsibility. The
best way of achieving this is through a social
environment which is based on justice, participation, and
protection of personal dignity. The ultimate
effectiveness of behavior and value changes achieved in
resocialization depends on continuing support during the
parole period. This model for resocialization emphasizes
the offender and his community as crucial factors and
interpersonal relationships as the proper tools of
change.

725 Takagi, P. T., and R. M. Carter. "Persistent Prob-
    lems and Challenges in Correctional Supervision."
    CRIMINOLOGICA, 5 (3): 36-46, 1967.

    Correctional research has to overcome the customs of
the past and undue reliance upon traditional correctional
methods. The entire area of supervision of probationers
and parolees, particularly its administrative, research,
and operational components, needs reexamination. There
is a need to redefine the role of the probation and
parole officer and to develop discriminating criteria for
the classification of offenders. Persistent problems in
the structure of correctional organizations are: administrative versus professional conflicts, role orientations
in relations with the police, and worker disagreement
with supervisors as to the objectives of supervision.
Examination focused on such features of the social organization of corrections as: the worker operating with a
group of peers; the impact of top level decisions in
response to crisis situations; and the effect of
"accidental" factors such as high unemployment conditions
and limited bed space in prisons.

726 Van Dine, S., J. P. Conrad, and S. Dinitz. RESTRAIN-
    ING THE WICKED: THE INCAPACITATION OF THE DANGEROUS
    CRIMINAL. Lexington, MA: D.C. Heath, 1979.

    An empirical study of the practicality of
incapacitation as the primary objective of the criminal
justice system is reported. Drawing on the criminal
histories of 342 adults arrested for violent crimes in
Franklin County, OH, in 1973, the study explores the
preventive effects of various incapacitative sentencing
policies by calculating how many of the 1973 crimes would
have been avoided had the policies been in force at the
1973 arrestees' last previous conviction for felonies.
The most severe policy--a mandatory 5-year prison term
for any felony conviction--would have prevented 210
crimes for which arrests were made in 1973. If it is
assumed that recidivists commit the same proportion of
cleared and uncleared crimes, the 5-year/all felonies

policy might have prevented 26.7 percent of all reported
crimes of violence in 1973. If applied throughout the
state, the policy would increase the prison population
from 13,000 to at least 65,000 in 5 years. The less
restrictive policy of sentencing all violent offenders to
5-year prison terms would produce a 90 percent positive
rate; i.e., only 10 percent of those incarcerated would
have committed another violent crime had they not been
incarcerated.

727 Vasoli, R. H. "Some Reflections on Measuring Proba-
      tion Outcome." FEDERAL PROBATION, 31 (3): 24-32,
      1967.

      Probation performance is usually evaluated on the
basis of violation rates. But this measurement of the
adjustment of probationers has both drawbacks and merits,
as do such other measures of probation success as:
petitions for revocation; issuance of a warrant,
revocation, recidivism, adjustment, and a combination of
these measures. None of the existing measures of
probation is entirely satisfactory; at worst, they
exaggerate the rate of success and understate the rate of
failure; at best, they afford close approximations of the
information desired.

728 Waldron, J. A., and H. R. Angelino. "Shock Proba-
      tion: A Natural Experiment on the Effect of a Short
      Period of Incarceration." PRISON JOURNAL, 57 (1):
      45-52, 1977.

      This study was conducted to determine the
characteristics of shock probationers, to obtain
recidivism estimates, and to test the hypothesis that a
short incarceration is more effective in reducing
recidivism than a long incarceration. The subjects were
418 male inmates released from Ohio prisons during 1969.
An additional 136 female felons released between 1966 and
1970 were also studied. Data were collected from
institutional files, presentence reports, Ohio records,
and the FBI. Postrelease arrest and conviction data were
obtained for a minimum of four and one-half years after
the men were released and a minimum of three and one-half
years after the women were released. The black shock
probationers had been convicted of relatively more
serious crimes than the white subjects. Twenty-six
percent of the men and 18 percent of the women were
returned to prison during the time period covered. Thus,
shock probation is not especially effective in reducing
recidivism.

729 Williams, V. L., and M. Fish. "Rehabilitation and
    Economic Self-Interest." CRIME AND DELINQUENCY, 17
    (4): 406-413, 1971.

    Capitalism may be used as a model for the design of
a modern prison system in which the economic incentive of
self-interest is used to rehabilitate inmates. In the
prison model developed, the individual would be fined a
set sum of money as a penalty for his crime. He would be
required to pay the stated sum to obtain release from
prison. The inmate must earn, from activities within the
prison system, all the wealth needed for his release.
The prison authorities would control the means by which
inmates could acquire wealth. For example, a cooperative
payment would be earned for participation in
rehabilitation programs or for work in the prison
factory. Economic incentives can create a highly
motivated individual if he is earning to buy a product he
wants, such as release from prison. From the perspective
of society, the exploitation payment becomes the
mechanism that allows a compromise between those who
demand punishment and those who seek rehabilitation.

730 Wright, K. N. ORGANIZATIONAL APPROACH TO CORREC-
    TIONAL EFFECTIVENESS. Jonesboro, TN: Pilgrimage
    Press, 1979.

    This study involves two considerations: (1) Are
organizational differences important when assessing
outcome differences?; and (2) Is the environment related
to outcome? Procedures used in correctional outcome
evaluations are elaborated in order to produce more exact
analyses. One important finding resulted from these
analyses of past research efforts: correctional
organizations with high overall commitment rates are more
likely to have higher recidivism rates than organizations
that do not have high commitment because the
incarceration experience in the former institutions
reinforces criminal identity. Several recommendations
for future studies are offered. Theoretical concepts
should be refined and elaborated in order to provide a
more useful model for studying organizational processes.
A 3-year tracking period should be used in studies on
evaluation outcome. Outcome studies should incorporate
methods to adjust for time-at-risk, and data quality can
be improved by consulting personally with the parole
officer or subject. Finally, studies should consider the
post-correctional community environment and its effects
on recidivism.

731 Adams, W. L. "Inadequate Medical Treatment of State
Prisoners: Cruel and Unusual Punishment?" AMERICAN
UNIVERSITY LAW REVIEW, 27 (1): 92-126, 1977.

The Eighth Amendment right to freedom from cruel and
unusual punishment is explored as a jurisprudential basis
for inmate complaints about denial of needed medical
treatment. The origin and evolution of the prohibition
against cruel and unusual punishment are traced, and the
federal courts' interpretation of the prohibition as a
flexible concept that changes with society's evolving
correctional values is discussed. The expansion of the
prohibition to encompass the treatment of state prisoners
and, later, the adequacy of medical treatment is
considered. The standard developed by the courts to
detect denials of treatment that violate the
constitutional prohibition is evaluated. The standard
which focuses on the intent of those accused of denying
treatment is found wanting. A revised standard is
suggested, which emphasizes the adequacy of treatment and
requires the complainant to show only that medical
treatment was needed and that correctional personnel
failed to provide adequate treatment.

732 Austin, J., and B. Krisberg. "Unmet Promise of Alternatives to Incarceration." CRIME AND DELINQUENCY,
2 (3): 374-409, 1982.

A review of research on alternatives to
incarceration suggests that their promise of reducing the
prison population has remained unfulfilled. For each
reform strategy, the nonincarcerative options were
transformed, serving goals other than reducing
imprisonment. Sentencing alternatives such as
restitution and community service reinforced the
sanctions of probation and fines instead of replacing
incarceration. Similarly, post-incarceration release
programs such as work release and work furlough often
escalated the level of control over clients and served
primarily to control prison populations. Increasing the
availability of community corrections facilities has not
reduced prison populations; it has merely changed the
place of imprisonment from state institutions to county
jails. Progress in alternatives will be frustrated until
reforms are more carefully implemented and until
proponents of alternatives are willing to test theories
through rigorous research. A new political consensus
must emerge outside the criminal justice system in which

punishment and public safety are rationally balanced against fiscal constraints and competing claims for public revenue.

733 Bailey, W. C. "Deterrence and the Violent Sex Offender: Imprisonment vs. the Death Penalty." JOURNAL OF BEHAVIORAL ECONOMICS, 6 (1-2): 107-143, 1977.

The deterrent effects of imprisonment and capital punishment are assessed and compared in a statistical analysis of state data. Analysis of data for 1951 and 1969 reveals that severity and certainty of imprisonment, as well as execution, are inversely related to rape rates in both years. However, execution is less strongly associated with offense rates than either severity or certainty of imprisonment. Unemployment also is more strongly associated with rape rates than execution for each year and time-lag period studied. Further analysis suggests the possibility that the threshold of the deterrent effect of the certainty of punishment for rape is such that rape rates are not seriously affected when certainty levels drop from 50 to 20 percent.

734 Barzun, J. "In Favor of Capital Punishment." CRIME AND DELINQUENCY, 15 (1): 21-42, 1969.

Capital punishment should be retained, bearing in mind the possibility of devising a painless, sudden, and dignified death. The propaganda of abolition is inconsistent, narrow, or blind; the absolute sanctity of human life is, for the abolitionist, a slogan rather than a considered proposition. Yet, it deserves examination, for upon our acceptance or rejection of it depend such other highly civilized possibilities as euthanasia and seemly suicide. If a person has not been endowed with adequate controls against irrationally taking the life of another, that person must be judicially, painlessly, regretfully killed. Capital punishment is irrevocable, but so is imprisonment in its effect upon the personality and character of its victims.

735 Bedau, H. A. "The Death Penalty as a Deterrent: Argument and Evidence." ETHICS, 80 (3): 205-217, 1970.

Arguments and evidence are discussed concerning the death penalty as a deterrent, as presented by van den Haag. van den Haag's main contentions are reviewed, and argument revolves around the point of retaining or abolishing the death penalty as that issue turns on the question of deterrence. The argument is summarized, and the heart of the dispute is the contention that deterrence has not been demonstrated statistically, but that it is a mistake to think that nondeterrence has been. The argument is that the point is correct in what it affirms, but wrong and misleading in what it denies. Each of van den Haag's five major views are discussed and rebutted in detail.

736 Berkman, R. OPENING THE GATES: THE RISE OF THE PRISONERS' MOVEMENT. Lexington, MA: D.C. Heath, 1979.

Political activism of the 1960's pervaded prison life as politically aware inmates entered institutions. This study of two maximum security prisons examines this politicism in the context of the prisoners' movement. Three groups of inmates in a California prison were interviewed for the study, including a group of those who held leadership positions in recognized aboveground political groups, a randomly selected group, and a group who had been incarcerated at one of three other California prisons. Two groups of inmates from a New Jersey prison were also interviewed. Responses indicated a marked and lasting effect of the prisoners' movement on the life of prisoners. They generally regard the administration as a lawless body unwilling to follow legal rules set by courts and unprepared to yield any portion of power. The administration, in prisoner's eyes, forces compliance through use of threats, intimidation, and policies of social control which divide the prisoners. The prisoners have a better understanding of the use of racism inside and outside of prison, a growing class consciousness, and a perception of incarceration as a tool for maintaining the interests of the status quo. As a result of the prisoners' movement, specific political and organizational changes have come about at the two prisons. These include development of collective prisoner organizations revolving around social, religious, and ideological constituencies; incentive programs to reward prison labor forces and bolster productivity; and avenues of prisoner redress.

737 Berns, W. FOR CAPITAL PUNISHMENT: CRIME AND THE MORALITY OF THE DEATH PENALTY. New York: Basic Books, 1979.

Despite the predominance of abolitionists in the intellectual community, public support for the death penalty persists. People who support the death penalty feel that murderers should be paid back, not treated, even if treatment would mean rehabilitation. Punishment arises from this feeling--from the demands of angry people for justice. The function of law is to tame the public's anger both by satisfying (and thereby justifying) it, and by moderating it. Punishment satisfies the public's anger and promotes the law-abidingness which, it is presumed, accompanies it. Punishment is the means by which the criminal law is embued with sufficient awesomeness to remind people of the moral order that assures their survival. In modern times, the only penalty able to lend this necessary awesomeness to the law is the ultimate penalty. The second function of the law--moderating the public's anger--would be better served were executions carried out in public. In developing these lines of thought, the discussion reviews critically the arguments against capital punishment; assesses the impact of the rehabilitative ideal on crime and criminal justice; examines at length questions concerning deterrence and the morality of punishment; and considers problems in administering the death penalty.

738 Bidna, H.   "Effects of Increased Security on Prison Violence."   JOURNAL OF CRIMINAL JUSTICE, 3 (1): 33-45, 1975.

    This study examines the consequences of the stricter security measures inaugurated in California institutions by comparing violence rates in the institutions before and after tighter security was imposed.   The stricter security measures in California correctional facilities were instituted in an attempt to reduce prison violence. After imposition of the new security measures, a significant decline in the rate of total stabbings was noted, as well as significant changes in stabbing patterns within the institutions.   However, despite the tighter security measures, no significant decrease occurred in the rates of either fatal stabbings or assaults by inmates on staff.   Population increases, crowding, lack of exercise, changing characteristics of the inmate population, attachment of the violent label, the nature of security housing, and the ability of correctional officials to control inmates are discussed as possible influences on institutional violence.

739 Bowker, L. H.   PRISON VICTIMIZATION.   New York: Elsevier, 1980.

    The research literature on prison victimization is reviewed.   The author focuses on physical victimization (rape, assault, etc.), economic victimization (e.g., gambling, theft, loansharking, protection rackets), psychological victimization (fear, intimidation, threats, etc.), and social victimization (resulting from an inmate's group membership).   Special attention is given to these topics in institutions for male juveniles and those for women and girls.   Victim-offender encounters are explored for prisoner-prisoner, staff-prisoner, prisoner-staff, and staff-staff relationships. A preliminary taxonomy of the causes of prison victimization is then developed. Three major groups of solutions to prison victimizations are offered, ranging from minor (e.g., improved classification and conjugal visitation) and major (e.g., cocorrections and therapeutic communities) to radical (e.g., lowering incarceration rates and closing of institutions).

740 Bradley, H. B. "Designing for Change: Problems of Planned Innovation in Corrections." ANNALS OF THE AMERICAN ACADEMY OF POLITICAL AND SOCIAL SCIENCE, 381 (January): 89-98, 1969.

The major theme of the paper is the need to design correctional organizations that can respond to change. "Adaptive innovation" is defined as a reaction to a situation after the fact; it is the kind of innovation most commonly encountered in corrections. "Planned innovation" is defined as a response to a need in advance of the situation that actively demonstrates the need; it presupposes a system that is designed to respond to change. Several problems encountered in designed-for changes are discussed and the need for research and evaluation of correctional practices is stressed. Tasks, as contrasted with functions, are seen as highly amenable to measurement and evaluation; and correctional organizations that emphasize task-orientation over functional performance are advocated. Lastly, the need to view change as a process, rather than as isolated single events, is emphasized. Correctional organizations of the future must be designed on flexible forms that permit planned innovations in response to changing attitudes, values, technology, and laws.

741 Brody, S. A. "The Political Prisoner Syndrome." CRIME AND DELINQUENCY, 20 (2): 97-106, 1974.

The "sick" role that was offered in the past by prison psychiatrists was rejected by prisoners, who favored the "bad" role because it gave them peer group support and an acceptable outlet for their aggressions. The "bad" role has, in turn, been supplanted by the "political prisoner" role, which began among isolated groups of black prisoners and has now spread to all racial and ethnic groups. The political prisoner role is attractive because it permits the inmate to rationalize his predicament and to blame society at large for his imprisonment. In his mind, he is not a criminal but a victim of society's repression, racism, and warped system of justice. Support for this attitude comes not only from inside the prison--from his fellow inmates--but from outside, in press and television reporting that excuses or justifies crime and violence of blacks and "demonstrators." As the population of prisons has shifted to include greater numbers of young, black, and more violent inmates, in-prison activism has grown. The trend toward politicalization of prisoners may be reversed by employing more minority group members on prison staffs, by including prisoners on some decision-making committees, and by dispersing agitators throughout the prison system rather than collecting them in one facility.

742 Christianson, S. "Corrections Law Development: Legal Assistance for Prisoners." CRIMINAL LAW BULLETIN, 14 (4): 347-351, 1978.

The decision (Bounds v. Smith) by which the U.S. Supreme Court ordered states to ensure prisoners adequate access to the courts is summarized; problems encountered by New York in trying to comply with the decision are discussed. Before the Bounds case, New York had only a handful of local programs to meet prisoner needs. In 1975, the New York State Commission of Corrections was reorganized and empowered to act as the state's monitor of prisons and jails. The New York State Bar Association began a comprehensive, statewide legal aid program for inmates. The program was designed to offer free legal assistance to indigent prisoners in three major areas: (1) civil matters; (2) criminal convictions or sentences and parole issues; and (3) prison problems, including conditions of confinement, disciplinary procedures, and medical care.

743 Clark, L. D., and G. M. Parker. "Labor Law Problems of the Prisoner." RUTGERS LAW REVIEW, 28 (4): 840-860, 1975.

This article examines the history of prisoners as workers during incarceration, the goals their work has been seen to fulfill, and the legislative and judicial decisions which have shaped their legal status. The litigation discussed covers employment-related injury and disability, minimum wages, job seniority and security, pensions, and unions. The authors conclude that in every appropriate way prisoners should be accorded the same rights as other workers and integrated into the general work force. They advocate an end to the state-use system of prison labor so that prisoners can learn skills and work in jobs they can perform on release, the elimination of arbitrary disqualification of prisoners from certain employment on release, and legislation authorizing prisoner unions.

744 Clear, T. R. "Correctional Policy, Neo-Retribution-
    ism, and the Determinate Sentence." JUSTICE SYSTEM
    JOURNAL, 4 (1): 26-48, 1978.

    The neo-retributive movement, with its emphasis on
minimizing correctional treatment and restructuring
sentencing discretion, is criticized. Arguments against
rehabilitative treatment seem to flow from two differing
viewpoints: the pragmatic position, which sees nothing
inherently evil in treatment, but finds that the
implementation of treatment requires caution; and the
idealistic position, which finds treatment to be
inherently wrong. The central point of the idealistic
position is that punishment is the only proper purpose of
corrections. Neo-retributive thinking has resulted in
determinate sentencing reform in some states. A return
to the determinate sentence ideally will eliminate
sentence disparity, but virtually all authorities agree
that a system of total enforcement with identical
penalties for legally equivalent acts would be
impossible, intolerable, and unjust. Determinate
sentencing may also lead to prison overcrowding and may,
with "good time," replace parole, lead to administrative
manipulation of inmates by the correctional staff and the
loss of the due process safeguards applicable to parole
board hearings.

745 Clements, C. B. "Crowded Prisons: A Review of Psy-
    chological and Environmental Effects." LAW AND HUMAN
    BEHAVIOR, 3 (3): 217-225, 1979.

    Psychological and environmental effects of prison
crowding are examined, based on evaluation of the New
Mexico State Penitentiary action suits claiming
oppressive conditions. In prisons, crowding is an
interacting variable, sometimes causing, sometimes
resulting from, and often simply exacerbating the impact
of other conditions and practices. The inability of
inmates to control privacy and social space can induce
stress. Reactions to stress may include aggressiveness,
vigilance, guardedness, aloofness; physical and verbal
aggression will increase. Prison crowding both produces
exaggerated ways of coping and undermines treatment
efforts. Insufficient jobs or programs lower both self-
esteem and skills. Organizing into protective groups,
aggressive behavior, and attempts to be transferred to
single cells are additional responses to crowding.
Crowding directly heightens frequency of interpersonal
friction and resulting violence. Although systematic
offender classification would be a desirable management
tool, overcrowding both prevents its use and exposes its
deficiencies.

746 Cohen, S. "The Punitive City: Notes in the Dispersal
    of Social Control." CONTEMPORARY CRISES, 3 (4): 339-
    363, 1979.

        Trends embracing decarceration ideology have been
    promised on the desire to limit state intervention. This
    desire is founded on diverse assumptions: inadequacy of
    the treatment model, need to limit criminal sanctions,
    disenchantment with paternalistic control, benefits of
    noninterventionism, and pragmatic concerns with limited
    resources of an overburdened system of criminal justice.
    Ironically, such alternative programs as community-based
    corrections and   diversions have led to an increase in
    intervention strategies, supplementing the existing
    system of control by extending further into the community
    and reaching more types of deviants. As new programs
    develop, clients are found to fill them. The extention
    of social control within alternative programs in the
    community blurs the issue of expanded intervention.

747 Colvin, M. "The 1980 New Mexico Prison Riot."
    SOCIAL PROBLEMS, 29 (5): 449-463, 1982.

        A case study of the New Mexico State Penitentiary
    traces the conditions and events of the 1970's that led
    to the most brutal riot in United States penal history in
    1980. An assessment of the changes in inmate relations
    from solidary opposition to fragmentation and mutual
    antagonism provides insight into the predisposing factors
    of the riot.

748 Conrad, J. P. "Prisons and Prison Reform." CURRENT
    HISTORY, 53 (August): 88-93, 1967.

        Prison reform is no longer concerned with ending the
    barbarous abuses of the past. Former practices already
    have been replaced by bureaucratic processes of main-
    taining a routine. Prison reform now must require prison
    officials to manage correctional institutions dynamically
    and to use public funds to achieve public objectives.
    Through research and experimentation correctional admin-
    istrators will determine the proper role of incarceration
    in the continuity of correctional services. Although it
    is unlikely that society will discontinue the use of
    prisons, it is probable that incarceration need not be
    used as often as it is now.

749 Culbertson, R. G. "Corrections: The State of the
    Art." JOURNAL OF CRIMINAL JUSTICE, 5 (1): 39-46,
    1977.

    The failure of the correctional system to
rehabilitate the offender hinges upon external and
internal issues that have inhibited the establishment of
goals. External problems include the possibility that
crime and the criminal serve a useful purpose in society.
American people want, desire, lust for, and need crime
and criminality. A second external problem includes the
latent function of correction: prisons provide a supply
of criminals sufficient to maintain the criminal justice
system; reduce the level of unemployment; provide
subjects for scientific research; and provide a safety
valve for racial tensions in American society as America
incarcerates the minorities and the poor. The
correctional process is also limited by certain internal
constraints, including (1) the absence of a theoretical
framework; (2) the lack of negative feedback mechanisms
and the prevalence of "groupthink," in which a group's
actions are collectively rationalized and create an
illusion of unanimity when in fact they are the result of
conformity pressures; and (3) the inappropriate use of
the medical model in the correctional process.

750 Davis, A. J. "Sexual Assaults in the Philadelphia
    Prison System and Sheriff's Vans." TRANS-ACTION, 6
    (2): 8-16, 1968.

    This article is based on the results of an
investigation conducted jointly by the Philadelphia
District Attorney's Office and the police department. It
was found that during a 26-month period there had been
156 sexual assaults in the Philadelphia prison system
that could be documented and substantiated. There were
assaults on at least 97 different victims by at least 176
different aggressors. Taking various factors into
consideration it is estimated that about 2,000 sexual
assaults had occurred during the period under study and
that only 96 were reported to prison authorities. Of the
96 only 64 were mentioned in prison records; of the 64
only 40 resulted in disciplinary actions against the
aggressors; and only 26 incidents were reported to the
police for prosecution.

751 Desroches, F. J. "Patterns in Prison Riots." CANA-
    DIAN JOURNAL OF CRIMINOLOGY AND CORRECTIONS, 16 (4):
    332-351, 1974.

    A comparison of common trends in prison riots since
1950, with special attention given to inmate cooperation,
the taking and treatment of hostages, inmate demands, and

the brutalization of less favored inmates, riots at San Quentin, Attica, Ohio Penitentiary, Jackson Prison, Trenton, and Kingston Penitentiary in Canada are discussed. Guards often are taken as hostages, but generally are treated well. Inmate demands sometimes appear nebulous, and there is the tendency for the inmates to demand media exposure either prior to, during, or in place of negotiating with officials. Most inmates apparently do not want to be involved in riots, but are coerced into them with an "either you're with us or you're against us" argument. Sex offenders and inmate informants stand a good chance of being tortured or killed during riots. Sociological theories of prison riots are compared.

752 Desroches, F. J. "The Treatment of Hostages in Prison Riots: Some Hypotheses." CANADIAN JOURNAL OF CORRECTIONS, 23 (4): 439-450, 1981.

An assessment of the differential treatment of inmate and guard hostages during recent prison riots reveals a greater hostility among the rioting inmates toward inmate "undesirables," e.g., child molesters and informers. During riot situations, traditional mechanisms of social control and deterrence collapse and inmate undesirables become more vulnerable to attack. Also, rioting inmates may restrict their assaults to undesirables since greater risks and more severe reactions would follow attacks on guards.

753 Dodge, C. R. NATION WITHOUT PRISONS: ALTERNATIVES TO INCARCERATION. Lexington, MA: D.C. Heath, 1975.

A collection of 12 articles which provide a broad overview of various schools of thought pertaining to effective rehabilitation of offenders and describe several possible alternatives to institutionalization. An overview of the current correctional system and the trend towards community corrections is presented in the initial three selections of this anthology. Such alternatives to prison as volunteers in probation, wilderness training, halfway houses, job therapy, and intensive probation supervision are explored. The text concludes with a call for a new order of criminology to replace the current system, which has failed to meet the requirements of this age.

754 Drapkin, I. "Prison Inmate as Victim." VICTIMOLOGY, 1 (1): 98-106, 1976.

Violence in prisons that results in inmates becoming victims and the rights of inmates are discussed. The prison, as it is organized and functions, has failed as an institution. A number of common features characterize the prison in numerous books about prison conditions: ill treatment by words or deeds, overcrowding, lack of hygenic conditions, inadequate working conditions and medical services, unsanitary food, drug consumption, restrictions on visits and mail, and sex abuse. Three aspects of the prison are most significant when considering reform: (1) the frequency with which the young and other age groups are violated by other inmates, thereby destroying self-respect; (2) cases of cruel and unnecessary death of inmates suffering from acute diseases; and (3) the state of acute or chronic depression that often leads to suicide or homicide.

755 Ellis, D., H. G. Grasmick, and B. Gilman. "Violence in Prisons: A Sociological Analysis." AMERICAN JOURNAL OF SOCIOLOGY, 80 (1): 16-43, 1974.

An attempt was made to construct and test a causal model of reported transgressions in 29 felon and 26 misdemeanant prisons and among 278 felon inmates in North Carolina state prisons. Of seven independent variables only three--the percentage incarcerated for violent offenses, percentage incarcerated for one year or more, and parole referral date--appeared in both felon and misdemeanant cases. Only age and visits were related to aggressive transgressions at both aggregate (prison) and individual (inmate) levels. A larger proportion of all possible relationships between variables was supported by the data in felon prisons.

756 Flanagan, T. J. "Correctional Policy and the Long-Term Prisoner." CRIME AND DELINQUENCY, 28 (1): 82-95, 1982.

A review of the problems faced by long-term prisoners and their implications for correctional policy are presented. It is argued that since most inmates view length of incarceration as their principal punishment, the conditions of their confinement pose a secondary set of sanctions, and these implicit punishments may be particularly burdensome on long-term prisoners. The author recommends that the administration of prisons containing long-term inmates involve creating institutional subunits based on the unique circumstances and concerns of inmate groups. Long-range programs geared to career processes are suggested.

757 Forst, B. E. "The Deterrent Effect of Capital Punishment: A Cross-State Analysis of the 1960s." MIN-
NESOTA LAW REVIEW,   61 (5): 743-767, 1977.

Building on studies by Ehrlich and Passell, the
influence of the execution rate on the homicide rate was
estimated by controlling for the effects of other
variables and for the reverse effects of the homicide
rate on the sanction variables. The findings do not
support the hypothesis that capital punishment deters
homicides. The increase in the homicide rate in the
United States from 1960 to 1970 appears to be the product
of factors other than the elimination of capital
punishment. Foremost among these are a decline in the
rate at which homicide offenses resulted in imprisonment
and increasing affluence during the 1960s. The apparent
strength of the incarceration rate variable and the
apparent weakness of the execution rate and term of
imprisonment variables as deterrents to homicide lend
some support to Beccaria's 200-year old suggestion that
certainty of punishment deters more effectively than does
severity. The appearance of a strong deterrent effect of
imprisonments on homicides may be the result of changes
in factors omitted from this analysis. And the apparent
weakness of the deterrent effect of long imprisonments
may be caused by the inaccuracy of the term-of-
imprisonment variable, since random errors in the
measurement of this variable will bias downward estimates
of the deterrent effect of the length of imprisonment.

758 Freeman, J. C., (ed.). PRISONS: PAST AND FUTURE.
Exeter, NH: Heinemann, 1978.

A collection of papers focusing on the past,
present, and future of imprisonment. This book
commemorates a convention held in honor of the Howard
League for Penal Reform and its mentor, John Howard. The
historical contributions look at Howard's influence on
the English-speaking world and on the continent of
Europe, and assess his achievement in the light of
present day issues: they cover his work with the Bedford
Prison, his influence in America and on the European
prison system, and his concentration on the day-to-day
details of prison life. The review of present day prison
practice includes such controversial issues as parole,
prisoners' rights, mental health services in prisons, and
the detrimental effect of prison on criminality. Some
radical ideas are presented on social control with or
without prisons, the separation of punishment and
treatment, and the "justice" or neopunitive theory of
penal policy.

759 Fuller, D. A., and T. Orsagh. "Violence and Victimi-
    zation Within a State Prison System." CRIMINAL JUS-
    TICE REVIEW, 2 (2): 35-55, 1977.

    A study of victimization in prisons in North
Carolina was conducted to determine the rate of assault
among prisoners, the causes, victim characteristics, and
possible preventive measures. Three data bases were
used: (1) a sample of records of disciplinary hearings in
ten prison institutions in North Carolina during the last
quarter of 1975--126 assaultive events in all; (2)
interviews with prison supervisors in each of the
institutions; and (3) a stratified sample of
approximately 400 inmates from six of the institutions.
The victimization rates vary markedly by race, age, and
institution. The main precipitating factor causing
victimization is assault. The main factor precipitating
that assault is inmate interaction. The likelihood that
an inmate will become a victim is considerably greater if
that inmate has, himself, committed assault. White
victimization rates are higher than black victimization
rates because blacks are more likely to victimize across
racial lines. Increasing the quantity and efficiency of
supervision is a direct and obvious means for reducing
assault and victimization.

760 Gibbs, J. P. "Death Penalty, Retribution, and Penal
    Policy." JOURNAL OF CRIMINAL LAW AND CRIMINOLOGY,
    69 (3): 291-299, 1978.

    The trend to revive the retributive doctrine in
penology is discussed. The doctrine's perceived merits
are examined, along with possible alternatives to the
retributive treatment of criminal offenders. It is
argued that the Supreme Court's return to the
retributive doctrine is not attributable to a
sensitivity to public opinion but, rather, to doubts
about deterrence theory and the recognition that the idea
of rehabilitation has fallen into general disrepute; and
that this trend can be broken by the creation of new
doctrines or new strategies in crime prevention based on
incapacitation and behavior modification. Retributivists
have failed to recognize that the doctrine really does
not resolve many issues in penal reform. Questions must
still be answered with respect to defining retribution
and determining the appropriate punishment for a given
crime, the seriousness of crimes, the severity of
punishments, and the role of public opinion and judicial
discretion.

302 CRIMINAL JUSTICE IN AMERICA

761 Gibbs, J. P. "Preventive Effects of Capital Punishment Other Than Deterrence." CRIMINAL LAW BULLETIN,
14 (1): 34-50, 1978.

Deterrence is defined as an instance in which an
individual refrains from a criminal act or somehow limits
the commission of such an act because of fear of
punishment. Major nondeterrent preventive mechanisms
include incapacitation and normative validation.
Incapacitation refers to the reduction of an individual's
opportunity to commit subsequent offenses as a result of
the very nature of the punishment. The concept of
normative validation refers to the role of punishment in
maintaining moral condemnation of crime. More
questionable nondeterrent preventive mechanisms include
normative insulation (isolating offenders from former
associates), enculturation (reducing ignorance of the
law), stigmatization, habituation (establishing a
behavior pattern through the threat of punishment), and
prevention through retribution. Punitive surveillance
and reformation, though possible nondeterrent mechanisms
of prevention, are irrelevant to considerations of
capital punishment. Debates over legal punishments and
crime prevention should not be limited to arguments about
deterrence. Anticipated objections to this conclusion
are discussed.

762 Glaser, D. "The Prison of the Future." KEY ISSUES,
2: 42-46, 1965.

The prison of the future will differ from today's
prison if it is designed for goals to evoke in offenders
an identification with anti-criminals and to increase the
released prisoner's chances of achievement in legitimate
post-release activities. Prisons of the future will be
located mainly in metropolitan areas. This urban
location will permit a graduated release of inmates on a
trial basis in order to make home visits, seek and fill
jobs; it will enable the prison staff to know the
influences in the community which will affect their
prisoners. There will be extensive links with community
organizations and increased visiting by friends and
relatives of the inmates. In addition, the prison will
operate industries and services comparable to those in
which there are post-release employment opportunities and
inmates will receive financial compensation. The staff
of the prison will be the treatment personnel. The
personal relationships between staff and inmate will be
used for rehabilitative purposes. To facilitate this
interpersonal relationship, the prison will be small and
diverse in architecture and program. There will be
heterogenous age-groupings so that the youthful inmates
may be better influenced by older unadvanced offenders.
There will be no punishment imposed beyond that necessary

for custodial purposes unless its merit is scientifically
demonstrated.

763 Gorecki, J. CAPTIAL PUNISHMENT: CRIMINAL LAW AND
    SOCIAL EVOLUTION. New York: Columbia Univesity Press,
    1983.

    A review of the conflicting social forces that
affected the U.S. Supreme Court's decisions in Furman,
Gregg, and related cases is provided in an attempt to
account for the oscillating views on capital punishment.
Following an outline of the social evolution of
punishment in Athens, Rome, and Modern Europe, the author
identifies a general tendency toward decreasing severity
of criminal punishments. As societies progress, moral
aversion against crime increases, gradually replacing
fear of retribution as the primary deterrent for
wrongdoing. This process is used to account for the
growth of the movement to abolish capital punishment in
the United States. Declining support of the abolition
movement since 1966 is attributed to the public's
perception of rising crime rates and fear. The author
contends that a renewed trend toward less severe
punishment and support for the death penalty abolition
are possible only if abuses of discretion at all stages
of the criminal justice system were eliminated,
establishing certainty and equity in punishment. Such
reforms would in turn reduce crime since, following
instrumental learning principles, a just punishment would
follow every crime committed. With crime under control,
the public would feel secure with less harsh punishments
available and imposed, leading to a renewed concern for
abolishing capital punishment.

764 Gottlieb, G. H. "Capital Punishment." CRIME AND
    DELINQUENCY, 15 (1): 1-20, 1969.

    The thesis of this paper is that the death penalty
is torture, that it serves no other purpose than revenge,
that revenge is an unconstitutional purpose, and that
torture is an unconstitutional act. To maintain an
institution that sets a barbaric example is to thwart the
civilizing process that holds man's only hope for
survival. The death penalty is the most dramatic symbol
of barbarism present in our national domestic life. Raw
punishment, in whatever form, is no answer to crime. The
appropriate question is how to prevent and cure
criminality--in those already miscreant, in those so
inclined, and in those whose character is still unformed.
The answer to the question must be relevant to the
massive causes and subtle triggers of criminality.

765 Hickey, J. E., and P. L. Scharf. TOWARD A JUST
CORRECTIONAL SYSTEM: EXPERIMENTS IN IMPLEMENTING
DEMOCRACY IN PRISONS. San Francisco: Jossey-Bass,
1979.

An approach to prison reform based on instituting
democratic principles within prison was implemented in
the Niantic Correctional Center in Connecticut.
Successes and failures of the program after eight years
are described. Its evolution from the concept of self-
governing units as rehabilitative instruments to use of
these units as laboratories that not only served inmates
but also explored the inner workings of the prison is
traced. The conflicts between a minidemocracy and the
larger bureaucracy served to sharpen the conceptual as
well as the practical inconsistencies implicit in both
prison management and bureaucracies generally.
Preliminary results of a 2-year study indicate that self-
governing units (cottages) had a positive effect on
female inmates' lives after they left prison. Of the 20
female model cottage graduates, less than 15 percent
returned to Niantic after one year with either a new
charge or for parole violations. Finally, constraints in
instituting a democratic system within the confines of a
prison setting are reviewed.

766 Holt, K. E. "Nine Months to Life: The Law and the
Pregnant Inmate." JOURNAL OF FAMILY LAW, 20 (3):
522-543, 1982.

Holt examines pregnant inmates' problems, lawsuits
to protect their rights, statutes relating to the treatment of pregnant inmates and their offspring, and
proposed guidelines for uniform treatment. Pregnant
inmates' problems include unsuitable work assignments,
required physical examinations performed in unsterile
conditions, inadequate medical care, lack of information
about childbirth and contraception, poor diet, and loss
of custody of the newborn child. Federal regulations
ensure delivery of medical and social services much more
comprehensively than most state statutes, which apply the
general standard of "adequate" medical care and review
each case in custody. Holt suggests that, with the
expected increase in women inmates (and thus
pregnancies), increased litigation is the best way to
compel an examination of pregnant inmates' problems.

767 Jacobs, J. B. "Prison Violence and Formal Organiza-
    tions." Pp. 79-87 in A. K. Cohen, G. F. Cole, and R.
    G. Bailey (eds.), PRISON VIOLENCE. Lexington, MA:
    D.C. Heath, 1976.

This article proposes that prison violence may be
reduced by improving prison management so that the
opportunities for prison violence (location and hardware)
are diminished. Prison violence is often attributed to
the violence proneness of inmates, the presence of
troublemakers, and the prison conditions. The author
calls for the collection of systematic statistics on
prison violence so that patterns in the locations, times,
types of victims, types of offender, and most common type
of weapon may be determined. Such statistics would allow
prison management to identify areas in need of
improvement and to eliminate the conditions (such as
loose scrap metal in prison shops or unsupervised
areas), which provide an opportunity for prison violence.

768 Jacobs, J. B., and E. H. Steele. "Prisons: Instru-
    ments of Law Enforcement or Social Welfare?" CRIME
    AND DELINQUENCY, 21 (4): 348-355, 1975.

Prisons function as parts of both the criminal
justice system and the social welfare system but without
conceptual clarity as to their place in either system.
Prisons are and always will be moral instruments of
punishment. Once it is agreed that prisons punish and do
little more, we must squarely face the questions of who
should go to prison and exactly how much punishment is
due. The answer to the first may be "fewer" and the
second, "much less." Prisons will cure neither crime nor
social and personal disadvantages. It is only when we
view prisons and imprisonments in this type of systematic
context that our attention and resources can be freed to
tackle the complex problems of law enforcement and social
welfare on their own terms.

769 Jay, D. G. "The Rights of Prisoners While Incarcer-
    ated." BUFFALO LAW REVIEW, 15 (2): 397-424, 1966.

If the purpose of imprisonment is rehabilitation and
reintegration of the offender into society, those rights
remaining to a prisoner should be safeguarded. The
doctrine of civil death should have been discarded.
Disability, the penalty of civil death, is no deterrent
and its continuance serves no useful purpose. It has
never helped the family of an inmate; in fact, it creates
still more problems for them. The solution of the Model
Penal Code is preferred: no disability attaches upon
imprisonment execpt for those rights necessarily incident
to execution, specifically denied by constitution,

statute, or order of court. The franchise of prisoners should depend on a more rational ground than the classification of their crime as a felony or misdemeanor, or their incarceration in state rather than county prison.

770 Kimball, E. L., and D. J. Newman. "Judicial Intervention in Correctional Decisions: Threat and Response." CRIME AND DELINQUENCY, 14 (1): 1-13, 1968.

Courts are giving increasing consideration to probationers', inmates', and parolees' challenges of various discretionary decisions by correctional authorities. In general, this intervention is perceived by correctional personnel as undesirable and threatening to agency and professional autonomy. However, judicial review of correctional decisions poses no substantial threat since courts generally ask only whether correction has acted in a reasonable way. Correction has usually responded to the threat of intervention by adopting a defensive position, claiming, under the guise of the right-privilege doctrine, that courts have no right to review agency decisions. This is self-defeating; courts have the last word in all situations where liberty is involved. A wiser strategy is for correction to make changes in certain practices and procedures to persuade courts of the competency and fairness of correctional discretion.

771 Knorr, R. R. "Correctional Innovation and the Dilemma of Change-From-Within." CANADIAN JOURNAL OF CORRECTIONS, 10 (3): 449-457, 1968.

Administering a public monopoly screened from close public scrutiny and with powers exclusively granted on grounds of their expertise, correctional administrators may be inclined to conceal their difficulties. Correctional planning must consider the inmate, elicit his cooperation, and anticipate his problems after release. If the inmate is to learn new ways of dealing with others, he should be given the opportunity to interact with ordinary citizens in an authentic human relationship. Instead of perpetuating the mutual isolation of inmates and the community, the correctional establishment should provide the means by which offenders and their future fellow citizens can deal with each other under ideally mediated conditions. By excluding participation of inmates and the community and by their exclusive claim to expertise, the correctional establishment has neutralized the efforts of those seeking to change it.

772 Knorr, S. J. "Deterrence and the Death Penalty: A
    Temporal Cross-Sectional Approach." JOURNAL OF
    CRIMINAL LAW AND CRIMINOLOGY, 70 (2): 235-254, 1979.

        Studies that attempted to verify empirically
the existence of a deterrent effect for the death penalty
are analyzed, and new empirical research into the
deterrence question is documented. In the present
attempt to isolate, identify, and measure economically
the deterrent impact of capital punishment on homicide
rates, many of the criticisms of prior deterrence
research are taken into account. The analysis is
performed at state and regional levels. Only probability
of apprehension is shown to have a significant deterrent
effect, and that only at the state level. No deterrent
effect is found for the death penalty. The analysis does
lend support to the thought that the presence or absence
of a deterrent effect for the death penalty may not be
demonstrable by statistical means, given available data
and problems in estimation.

773 Krause, K. "Denial of Work Release Programs to
    Women: A Violation of Equal Protection." SOUTHERN
    CALIFORNIA LAW REVIEW, 47 (4): 1453-1490, 1974.

        The thesis of this article is that a state which
offers work release programs to its male inmates is
constitutionally required to offer equivalent programs to
similarly situated women prisoners. The author contends
that failure to offer work release programs to women
prisoners is a sex-based classification which cannot
stand under the rational basis test as modified by the
1971 case of Reed v. Reed or under the compelling state
interest test. Two standards of judicial review of state
action--restrained review and active review--are also
examined. Under the restrained standard of review, the
court scrutinizes a statute only to determine whether the
distinctions it establishes are rationally related to the
purposes of the statute. Numerous decisions upholding
sex-based classifications are cited to illustrate the
judicial deference to state action using this rational
basis test. Under the active standard of review, the
court uses strict scrutiny when groups characterized as
"suspect classifications" are involved, as well as
interests the courts recognize as "fundamental rights."
Judicial decisions indicating a trend toward treatment of
sex as a suspect classification are cited.

774 Lembo, J. J.   "The Relationship of Institutional
    Disciplinary Infractions and the Inmate's Personal
    Contact with the Outside Community." CRIMINOLOGICA,
    7 (1): 50-54, 1969.

    This study compares the disciplinary infractions of
adult male inmates in the West Unit of Apalachee
Correctional Institute, Chattahoochee, FL, who received
personal contact from the outside community to those
inmates who did not receive such contacts. A random
sample of 100 inmates was selected. The study showed no
statistically significant relationship between
disciplinary infractions committed and the inmates'
contact with the community. However, human behavior as
reflected in the recorded disciplinary infractions of the
inmates is a multifactor causation process; therefore the
variables affecting behavior and interaction such as age,
marital status, and the nature of the visit received were
indeed reflected in the whole. The case histories
indicated that visits do serve an important function in
assisting the inmate to adjust and reflected the
possibility that older married men serving a longer
sentence tended to adhere more closely to institutional
regulations.

775 Lockwood, D.   PRISON SEXUAL VIOLENCE.   New York:
    Elsevier, 1979.

    The psychological impact of victims of prison sexual
threats and attacks is discussed, as are patterns of
victim selection, "target" violence, and staff handling
of the problem. The study is limited to sexual behavior
perceived as threatening and offensive by targets of
aggressors. From October 1974 to September 1975, a total
of 107 "targets" were interviewed in the New York State
prisons of Attica, Auburn, and Coxsackie. A "nontarget"
control group was selected, made up of four percent of
the populations of Attica and Coxsackie. Aggressors were
most often young blacks. Victims were whites who had a
generally slighter build than aggressors and nontargets
and who were perceived as having feminine physical and
personality characteristics. About half of 152 incidents
examined involved physical violence, with those
initiating the violence divided evenly in number between
aggressors and targets. Both the prison and the outside
subcultures from which the targets and aggressors came
tended to advocate violence as a primary means of
relieving frustration and irritation. Because
victimization tends to stimulate fear and patterns of
isolation and suspicion, victims continued to be affected
emotionally months after the event. Prison staff did not
usually intervene directly in the sexual harassment that
occurred between aggressors and their targets.

776 Lopez-Rey, M. "The Present and Future of Non-Insti-
    tutional Treatment." INTERNATIONAL JOURNAL OF CRIMI-
    NOLOGY AND PENOLOGY, 1 (4): 301-317, 1973.

The present functional role of probation as part of
an obsolete penal system should be adapted to
sociopolitical considerations presently ignored or
minimized by the "individualistic" conception of the
offender and his rehabilitation. The present image of
the treatment of the offender is in most cases a fiction,
with rehabilitation not its main aim. Sociopolitically
and logically, the aim of criminal justice is simply
justice. As long as the socioeconomic and political
structures (whether capitalist or socialist) of the times
are unchanged, the right to refuse rehabilitation, re-
adaptation, or correction should be recognized.

777 Mabli, J., C. S. Holley, J. Patrick, and J. Walls.
    "Age and Prison Violence: Increasing Age Heterogene-
    ity as a Violence-Reducing Strategy in Prisons."
    CRIMINAL JUSTICE AND BEHAVIOR, 6 (2): 175-186, 1979.

The authors report on a two and a half year project
of transferred older prisoners into the Federal Correctional Institution, El Reno, OK, and younger inmates into
the prison at Texarkana, AK, to reduce the violence at El
Reno. Before 1975, FCI-El Reno was a maximum security
facility for young males, age 18 to 26. It became a
training ground for a primitive type of socialization and
violence was the norm. The FCI-Texarkana prison was a
medium security institution with 90 percent of the population older than 28 and a relatively low level of
violence. Baseline data were collected for a year before
July 1, 1975. Then three stategies were used to make the
age composition at the two facilities more heterogeneous.
In late 1975, inmates were reassigned between the two
institutions on a randomized basis with the major
criterion being age. After this initial exchange, direct
court commitments were assigned to the two institutions
on the basis of age, and routine transfers from maximum
to medium security facilities were again made to one of
these institutions on the basis of age. Before the
experiment began, almost none of the El Reno inmates were
age 28; by February 1977, 36 percent were 28 or older.
The percentages of inmates under age 28 at Texarkana
increased from 10 to 42 percent. This change in age mix
led to a significant decrease in violence at El Reno
(from 6.33 incidents per 1000 inmates to 2.00). Violence
at Texarkana rose from .33 to 1.17.

778 Martinson, R. "The Age of Treatment: Some Implications of the Custody-Treatment Dimension." ISSUES IN CRIMINOLOGY, 2 (2): 275-293, 1966.

The ideology of treatment has gradually replaced the earlier concern with salvation or humanitarianism in corrections. Proponents of prison reform have gained footholds in correctional systems primarily by incorporating new categories of professional staff. As the helping professions entered the traditional custodial facilities, research activities multiplied. "People-changing" has become a skill, a profession, and a moral injunction. As the age of treatment begins to give way to an assertion of the need to transform man, efforts are being made to introduce methods which are in fundamental opposition to the democratic ethic. Sociologists should ask themselves what kind of correctional system is best suited to a democratic society.

779 Megargee, E. I. "Population Density and Disruptive Behavior in a Prison Setting." Pp. 135-144 in A. K. Cohen, G. F. Cole, and R. G. Bailey (eds.), PRISON VIOLENCE. Lexington, MA: D.C. Heath, 1976.

This study was designed to investigate the relation of population size and population density to the incidence of disruptive behavior over a three-year period in a prison for male youthful offenders aged 18 to 25. The results indicated that, in a prison setting, where crowded conditions are chronic rather than temporary (as in laboratory research) and where people prone to antisocial behavior are gathered together, there is a clear association between restrictions on personal space and the occurrence of disruptive and aggressive behavior. However, since the changes in available space correlated more strongly with disruptive behavior than did changes in the number of residents, support is suggested for the theory that there are different affects associated with reducing available space and increasing the number of individuals in a given space.

780 Miller, H. S. "Current Perspectives in Corrections: A Cacophony." LAW AND CONTEMPORARY PROBLEMS, 41 (1): 132-163, 1977.

Issues in the debate over the proper relationship between crime and punishment are discussed. At issue is whether punishment should fit the crime or the individual who commits the crime. Conflicting views and changing assumptions concerning human nature have affected sentencing and correctional policies and their implementation in the United States. Controversy in the field of corrections has focused on rehabilitation and reformation, indeterminate and determinate sentencing, probation and parole, individualized treatment, prison unrest, the prison environment, and the costs of prison. The corrections system is in a transitional stage, in which new explanations are beginning to compete with old ones, but fundamental change will not occur until a new view of the nature of humanity emerges. The notion that, through rehabilitation, punishment, deterrence, the "just prison," or some mutation or combination of these, the correctional system will have some impact on crime. However, it is a pretense to claim that such efforts are by themselves the most effective way to combat crime. Crime prevention requires a truly just society, not only a just prison.

781 Morris, N. THE FUTURE OF IMPRISONMENT. Chicago: University of Chicago Press, 1974.

This publication recommends voluntary rehabilitation prison programs which are not conditions for the length of time in prison. Graduated testing is suggested as a basis for providing increased increments of freedom. Coerced cure that pressures an offender into a program of change whose outcome determines the length of time spent in prison is considered ineffective and unjust. It is recommended that length of sentence and probation eligibility be fixed and separate from performance standards in prison. The intent of such proposals is that participation in rehabilitation programs will then be noncoercive and will build upon the self-motivation of the inmate. Suggested principles for guiding sentencing are to employ the least punitive sanction necessary to achieve defined social purposes and impose no sanction that is greater than that warranted by the most recent crime or series of crimes. An operational design of an institution for 200 repetitively violent criminals is offered in which the proposed principles could be tested in practice.

782 Morris, N. "Impediments to Penal Reform." UNIVERSITY OF CHICAGO LAW REVIEW, 33 (4): 627-656, 1966.

Penal reform in the United States has been a series of compromises between punishment and rehabilitation. Reform of the penal system must go beyond its traditional humanitarian purposes to achieve greater social protection from crime. The theory of deterrence is an obstacle to penal reform, yet we have no definite knowledge of the efficacy of our penal sanctions as deterrents. All supposedly reformative measures should be subjected to critical evaluation by empirical research methods.

783 Morris, N., and G. Hawkins. "Attica Revisited: The
    Prospect for Prison Reform." ARIZONA LAW REVIEW, 14
    (4): 747-763, 1973.

     The current distrust of the treatment model in
penology must be answered and the dangers of abuse of
human rights from assumptions of power for rehabilitative
purposes must be eliminated. A major step in this
direction would be the adoption of these principles: (1)
Power over a criminal's life should not be taken in
excess of that which would be taken were his reform not
considered one of society's purposes. (2) Parole
prediction must be abandoned and replaced with a gradual
testing of fitness for freedom, e.g., work release,
furloughs, open institutions, and halfway houses. (3)
Correctional practices must be based on facts. No penal
experiment should ever be introduced without accompanying
techniques for discovering whether it serves a valuable
social purpose.

784 Mueller, G. "Human Rights and the Treatment of
    Offenders." CANADIAN JOURNAL OF CORRECTIONS, 10 (2):
    352-362, 1968.

     It is inhuman and inconsistent with the precepts of
the therapeutic ideal to deprive individuals of their
freedom in the name of prevention or correction unless
society is prepared to offer a reasonable guarantee of
preventive or correctional success. Moreover, the
greater part of the crime problem can be removed by the
repeal of (1) statutes concerned with political
conformity, the regulation of pleasures and delights, and
the morality of stimulating industry at a time when
idleness is unavoidable; and (2) statutes which deal with
offenses arising out of the breakdown of family life in a
modern society, and with the criminality which
constitutes evidence of society's failure to gratify
justified economic and emotional needs by legitimate
means. Future efforts at upgrading correctional systems
must make use of computer capabilities. This would
involve: (1) the programming of only clearly dangerous
human conduct into definitional elements; (2) the
programming of variable factors, conditions, and
circumstances of an offense in assessing the degree of
offender liability and in selecting the statutory
framework for the imposition of sentence.

785 Nacci, P. L., J. Prather, and H. E. Teitelbaum.
"Population Density and Inmate Misconduct Rates in
the Federal Prison System." FEDERAL PROBATION, 41
(2): 26-31, 1977.

Data from 37 institutions were used to compare
incidence of rule infractions and population density. It
was found that total assaults and assaults on inmates
increased as density increased, especially among younger
inmates. This study analyzed juvenile/youth
institutions, young adult institutions, intermediate-term
adult institutions, and long-term adult institutions.
The relationship between density and misconduct was
strongest in institutions housing young adults. In long-
term adult institutions, crowding may help to conceal
offenses. With prison densities increasing, dangerous
side effects will occur unless alternatives to
incarceration are found, especially for juveniles and
younger inmates who are more prone to violence, and
unless the perception of crowding is decreased.
Suggestions for reducing the perception of density
include lower lighting, partitioned dormitories, low
noise levels, natural greenery, simple spaces, activities
that fractionate time, fewer mass activities, freedom to
be alone, and social homogeneity.

786 Nagel, W. G. NEW RED BARN: A CRITICAL LOOK AT THE
MODERN AMERICAN PRISON. New York: Walker, 1973.

In 1971, a multidisciplinary research team composed
of a correctional administrator, architects,
psychologists, and social scientists visited over 100
correctional institutions throughout the country to
observe and evaluate the current state of the art in
correctional management and facilities. An effort was
made to record the overall effects of the physical
environment on staff, inmates, and the program. The
author contends that a moratorium should be called on all
correctional construction. Billions of dollars are
needed merely to replace and modernize existing prison
facilities. Prison construction should be halted
because incarceration is not the best response to anti-
social behavior. The proposed innovations are based on
the principle that the reintegration of the prisoner into
the community is the goal of contemporary corrections.
Therefore, the criminal code needs to be revised to
eliminate the imprisonment of victimless offenders. The
jail population should be reduced through bail reform and
speedier trials, and alternatives to incarceration, such
as community treatment facilities, must be implemented.

787 Nagel, W. G. "Statement on Behalf of a Moratorium on
     Prison Construction." PRISON JOURNAL, 56 (2): 32-43,
     1976.

     After an introduction which summarizes findings of
various social scientists on the dehumanizing aspects of
the U.S. prison system and a history of calls for reform,
the relationship between imprisonment and reduced crime
rates is examined. Rankings are made for each of the 50
states according to a number of factors: incarceration
rates, crime rates, violent crime rates, poverty level
incomes, unemployment rates, minority population, black
population, demographic factors, police expenditures,
rates of alcoholism, welfare spending, population in
high-crime-risk age-group (15-25), and prison
construction over the past 20 years. Little or no
correlation is found between crime rates and
incarceration rates. Most of the states having the
highest incarceration rates are in the South or Near
South. There is a close correlation between blacks and
incarceration. There is little correlation between state
political philosophy and crime rate, but conservative
states have significantly higher incarceration rates. It
is suggested that prisons do not deter crime and that
incarceration is a function of race, geography, and
political philosophy. On the other hand, crime rates are
closely related to urbanization and poverty levels.

788 Neisser, E. "Is There a Doctor in the Joint? The
     Search for Constitutional Standards for Prison
     Health Care." VIRGINIA LAW REVIEW, 63 (6): 921-973,
     1977.

     The effects of prison health care system on inmates
are examined, and factors in the development of judicial
standards concerning prison health care are discussed.
Problems in prison health care include the lack of
alternative sources of care, the control of all aspects
of life by correctional personnel whose primary interests
and goals are other than health care, and the unusually
extensive use of medical services by inmates. Denial of
access to medical personnel or care, denial of prescribed
treatment, and other correctional requirements that
aggravate or prevent treatment of physical ailments are
the primary effects of the prison health care system on
inmates. There is a need to develop constitutional
standards that address the special problems of health
care delivery and the particular deprivation fostered by
incarceration, yet limit judicial intrusion into prison
administration to the extent necessary to ensure access
to and delivery of adequate medical care.

789 Newman, D. J. "In Defense of Prisons." PSYCHIATRIC
    ANNALS, 4 (3): 6-17, 1974.

    The arguments against incarceration are reviewed.
It is pointed out that even the most avid reformers admit
that hard core criminals could not be handled by
community alternatives or decriminalization. Even
rudimentary attempts to decarcerate have not been
successful because the prison tradition is firmly
entrenched and community alternatives do not exist. It
is also pointed out that prisons exist not only for
"rehabilitation," but also for punishment and to let
society establish its norms. Since prisons merely
replaced overseas penal colonies, banishment from the
community, whipping, and hanging, it is suggested that if
prisons were abolished, society would replace them--
probably with greater use of capital punishment,
vigilante committees, misuse of mental hospitals for
indeterminant holding of criminals and such sophisticated
horrors as electronic monitoring of probationers.

790 O'Brien, K. E. "Tokens and Tiers in Corrections: An
    Analysis of Legal Issues in Behavior Modification."
    NEW ENGLAND JOURNAL ON PRISON LAW, 3 (1): 15-46,
    1976.

    Token economies and tier advancement systems are
clinical applications of the learning theory principles
of Skinnerian operant conditioning. Both systems pose
legal problems in their designation of target behaviors
and choice of reinforcers. The process of selecting
value or behavior patterns for alteration through operant
conditioning can intrude upon traditional First Amendment
rights. Even when a compelling state interest is shown,
programs are limited by the test of "least restrictive
means" required by the Constitution. The Eighth
Amendment proscription of cruel and unusual punishments
is now clearly applicable to correctional treatment
therapies. Token economy or tier advancement systems
utilizing "baseline" or basic reinforcers can violate the
protections contained in the Eighth Amendment when they
make basic necessities of life--e.g., light, heat,
clothing, other physical necessities--the subject of
contingent reinforcement.

791 O'Leary, V., and D. Duffee. "Correctional Policy: A
    Classification of Goals Designed for Change."
    CRIME AND DELINQUENCY, 17 (4): 373-386, 1971.

    The need to study the assumptions that underlie
correctional administration and to examine correctional
change processes systematically is noted. The nature of
correctional goals and the different ways they may be

classified are described. The offender's motivation of behavior within the system is an important criterion in classifying goals. The change strategy typology of Herbert Kelman is described, and the change agent's models of compliance, identification, and internalization are related to correctional concerns. Using these change strategies as a base, four models of correctional policy are developed and described: reform, rehabilitation, reintegration, and restraint. The results of administering a policy questionnaire are reported, with the conclusion that perception of policy may be quite different at various levels in a correctional organization. The relationship between correctional policy and correctional research is discussed.

792 Pederson, W. D. "Inmate Movements and Prison Upris-
    ings: A Comparative Study." SOCIAL SCIENCE QUARTER-
    LY, 59 (3): 509-524, 1978.

A comparative historic study of inmate behavior under varying conditions of confinement is used to test the application of relative-deprivation models of political violence to inmate movements and uprisings. Inmate behavior in World War II Japanese-American camps, Nazi concentration camps, Soviet labor camps, American military stockades, and American penitentiaries demonstrates that the relative-deprivation model is applicable to prison violence. Findings reveal the following: (1) extreme deprivation results in inmate apathy; (2) as conditions improve, inmate interaction increases and rebellion is unlikely; (3) if conditions and expectations rapidly decline, inmate solidarity in opposition to the authorities increases; (4) certain structural categories of inmates are prone to relative deprivation; and (5) there is a temporal relationship between outside events and the development of inmate movements, for example, during outside wartime protests or severe social conflict. Inmate movements are rare compared to isolated, nonservile prison uprisings. The J-curve model of relative deprivation is useful for explaining when and why inmate movements occur by examining the interaction of attitudinal, structural, and temporal factors.

793 Plotkin, R. "Enforcing Prisoners' Rights to Medical
    Treatment." CRIMINAL LAW BULLETIN, 9 (2): 159-172,
    1973.

Summary of case law on inmates' right to medical treatment, and explanation on preparation of the litigation for lawyers who represent inmates. The jurisdictional requirements for bringing prisoners'

rights suits in either state or federal courts are
discussed. Often these jurisdictional problems depend
upon whether the prisoners are held in state or federal
institutions. Court cases which have granted relief to
prisoners who had received intentionally inadequate
medical care are discussed. Lawsuits can be brought as
individual actions, group actions, or class actions. A
class action suit would attack the medical facilities in
the entire penal system. A checklist for use in
acquiring depositions and interrogatories from state
correctional institiutions is provided.

794 Potuto, J. R. "Model Proposal to Avoid Ex-Offender
    Employment Discrimination." OHIO STATE LAW JOURNAL,
    41 (1): 77-106, 1980.

     The plight of skilled ex-offenders encountering
discrimination because of a prior criminal record is
examined; solutions for enhanced ex-offender employment
opportunities are presented. The Model Sentencing and
Corrections Act contains provisions for voluntary inmate
participation in correctional training programs geared to
realistic employment possibilities after release. In
order to decrease recidivism, however, such training must
be coupled with a societal response for equal employment,
presently impeded by a myriad of restrictions against
licensing ex-offenders. Suggestions for eliminating
discrimination include the expungement and sealing of
records and legislative prohibitions against
discrimination by employers, professional schools,
organizations, and unions.

795 Reasons, C. E., and R. L. Kaplan. "Tear Down the
    Walls? Some Functions of Prisons." CRIME AND DELIN-
    QUENCY, 21 (4): 360-372, 1975.

     Although prisons have been repeatedly exposed for
their inherent degrading and dehumanizing effects, their
survival suggests that they are fulfilling four important
manifest functions, in varying degrees: (1) reformation,
(2) incapacitation, (3) retribution, and (4) deterrence.
More significant are eleven latent functions serving
various interests and needs: (1) maintenance of a crime
school, (2) politicalization, (3) self-enhancement, (4)
provision of jobs, (5) satisfaction of authoritarian
needs, (6) slave labor, (7) reduction of unemployment
rates, (8) scientific research, (9) do-goodism, (10)
safety valve for racial tensions, and (11) birth control.
These latent functions, largely unintended and generally
unrecognized, suggest that abolition of the prison may
not be as assured as some reformers suppose.

796 Reisner, S. L. "Balancing Inmates' Rights to Privacy
    with Equal Employment for Prison Guards." WOMEN'S
    RIGHTS LAW REPORTER, 4 (4): 243-251, 1978.

        Constitutional reasons for inmates' right to privacy
    and attempts to synthesize this right with equal
    opportunity for prison guards are examined. In Dothard
    v. Robinson (1977) the U.S. Supreme Court ruled that
    Alabama was not required to hire women as guards in its
    maximum security male penitentiaries. The decision was
    based on the bona fide occupational qualification
    exception to Title VII's ban on sex discrimination in
    employment. However, that decision ignored the issue of
    an inmate's right to be free from observation by guards
    of the opposite sex while undressing, using toilet
    facilities, or being searched. The article discusses
    this right to privacy and examines the court cases in
    which there was court recognition of the right to
    privacy. Since states have no security interest in
    having guards of the opposite sex performing strip
    searches or toilet facility surveillance, equality
    opportunity could be best served by assigning guards of
    opposite sex to work in areas where they would not
    infringe on privacy rights. It is recommended that in
    inmate privacy suits, selective work responsibilities
    should be ordered in preference to absolute exclusion.

797 Schrag, C. "The Correctional System: Problems and
    Prospects." ANNALS OF THE AMERICAN ACADEMY OF POLI-
    TICAL AND SOCIAL SCIENCE, 381 (January): 11-20,
    1969.

        The prison is viewed as an element in the system of
    justice that operates under constraints imposed by the
    broader society. Many of the contradictions observed in
    the prison's goals and in its achievement strategies have
    their counterpart in community disorganization.
    Accordingly, any major improvement in the prison's
    efficiency will probably require a fundamental overhaul
    of both the system of justice and the community's
    normative structure. Such overhaul encounters strong
    resistance from the community and the agencies of
    justice. Most current efforts at prison reform are
    therefore regarded as stopgap measures.

798 Sellin, T. PENALTY OF DEATH. Beverly Hills, CA:
    Sage, 1980.

        The paradoxical status of the death penalty in the
    United States is analyzed philosophically, historically,
    and statistically, revealing weaknesses in all the
    arguments that support it. The concept of retribution is
    the dominant argument for capital punishment. In

practice, however, retaliation is hardly ever realized, since numerous murderers are never caught at all, statistics show that only one-fourth of willful homicides are prosecuted for capital murder, with the likelihood of a death sentence being very small and that of execution even smaller. Moreover, the death penalty is applied selectively. The second major argument for the death penalty is deterrence. Executions in recent decades have become so rare that they could not possibly influence the murder rate. Comparisons of homicide rates from states where the death penalty has been abolished with retentionist states yield no evidence of the deterrent power of the death penalty.

799 Sherman, M., and G. Hawkins. IMPRISONMENT IN AMERICA: CHOOSING THE FUTURE. Chicago: University of Chicago Press, 1981.

This book presents the major arguments for and against increased prison construction as a solution to prison overcrowding and proposes a new policy emphasizing restricted use of imprisonment as a sentence, more inmate programs, and use of construction monies to rehabilitate or replace existing structures. The fundamental aims traditionally defined for the American criminal justice system are reduction of the number of offenses committed, reinforcement of the legal norms of society, and provision of services to people whose criminal behavior stems from unmet personal needs. As a historical overview shows, each of these goals has guided American criminal justice at some period in history. At present, crime control is a central focus of the criminal justice system and of imprisonment in particular. To overcome the prison policy dilemma, the authors propose that (1) linkage of sentencing, prison construction, and prison programs should be undertaken; (2) imprisonment should be the punishment of choice to meet the threat of physical violence; (3) new prison space should be built primarily to replace or to upgrade existing facilities; and (4) administrators should retain existing services while beginning new ones that can be truly voluntary and facilitative. The authors emphasize that this system would incapacitate the most dangerous offenders without requiring abandonment of the rehabilitative ideal.

800 Sneidman, B. "Prisoners and Medical Treatment: Their Rights and Remedies." CRIMINAL LAW BULLETIN, 4 (8): 450-466, 1968.

Although a prisoner forfeits many rights while in confinement, it is generally assumed that a prisoner has the right to receive medical treatment. While state requirements for medical care are usually phrased in a

vague manner, the federal statute specifically mentions
provision for "safekeeping, care and subsistence." The
fact that an inmate has a recognized right to receive
medical treatment is meaningless, however, unless he can
acquire a legal remedy to enforce it. The reluctance of
administration, as well as the prisoner's difficulty in
suing for compensation are barriers against any remedy
for maltreatment. The writ of habeas corpus can serve as
an effective weapon against prison maltreatment. Also,
the Federal Civil Rights Act has been gaining recognition
as an additional remedy for alleged medical maltreatment.

801 Sommer, R. THE END OF IMPRISONMENT. New York:
    Oxford University Press, 1976.

     The failure of imprisonment is inherent within the
institution itself. The existing system of imprisonment
in the United States isolates the inmate from contact
with the outside and immerses him totally within a
criminal society. Imprisonment is costly, inhumane, and
discriminatory. All offenders requiring incarceration
should be given six-month terms, which may be extended by
six-month increments only after new jury findings that
the inmate continues to be a danger to society. Under
this system, the burden is upon the state to prove
further dangerousness. A first step should be to empty
correctional institutions of all those men and women who
have not demonstrated a repetitive pattern of violent
behavior. Replacing long-term incarceration with short-
term detention for all except imminently dangerous
criminals would have ramifications for all aspects of the
criminal justice system. Conditional amnesty would help
many offenders return to the mainstream of society.

802 Sternberg, D. "Legal Frontiers in Prison Group Psy-
    chotherapy." JOURNAL OF CRIMINAL LAW, CRIMINOLOGY &
    POLICE SCIENCE, 56 (4): 446-449, 1965.

     The increasing use of group therapy by prison
psychiatrists, psychologists, and social workers raises
questions regarding the possible infringement upon the
constitutional and civil rights of participating
prisoners. Group therapy, both inside and outside
prisons, has created a host of legal problems which
present laws controlling individual legislation are
inadequate to handle. There seems to be no case law
which defines the rights and duties of group therapy
participants to each other in general questions of
disclosure; if all participants of a group are regarded
as therapeutic agents for one another it becomes logical

to suggest an extension of the privileged communication law to seal all participants' lips in trials and hearings.

803 Sturm, S. P. "Mastering Intervention in Prisons." YALE LAW JOURNAL, 88 (5): 1062-1091, 1979.

This note indicates that court-appointed special masters may increase the effectiveness of courts' monitoring of prison conditions, but that some judicial supervision is still required. Because of the limited capacity of courts to monitor compliance with court orders, special masters are frequently appointed by the judiciary to intervene in prison administration. Masters provide inmates with access to goods and privileges on an impartial basis and serve as a channel for inmate dissatisfaction. Although prison administrators may be limited in their ability to restructure patterns of decision-making, the master's intervention can demonstrate alternative means of control within the parameters of the court decree. The master also provides the court with specific information relevant to implementation of the decree. Although the master serves as a catalyst for change, the remedies are dependent upon interaction between inmates, officials, and the courts. The performance of the master's assignment may create problems between the interested parties and may require the threat of the court's contempt power to be effective.

804 Sylvester, S. F., J. H. Reed, and D. O. Nelson. PRISON HOMICIDE. New York: Halsted Press, 1977.

This book presents an in-depth study of homicides in U.S. state and federal institutions during 1973; data were compiled relative to event, offender, and victim characteristics. The investigation involved the population of all known prison homicides in 1973 which occurred in adult male felon state or federal institutions housing 200 or more inmates; these homicides numbered 128. Research findings of the 18-month undertaking showed that killings are most common among maximum security prisoners with histories of violent offenses and that, contrary to expectations, gang conflicts and racial antagonisms were not the predominant factors in prison homicides. Concerning the prison environment itself -- staff, physical facilities, and penal program -- there was little evidence that the occurrence of homicide is related to the presence or absence of modern rehabilitative influences. A crucial aspect of prison homicide was the determination of the relationship between the victim and murderer. Two types of homicide were identified: those in which there was a single assailant; and those in which there were two or

more prisoners involved as murderers. Similarities
between patterns of homicide in prison and in society lie
in the concentration of homicides within the violence-
prone segment of the population. Differences lie in the
more instrumental or precipitating factors, such as lack
of firearms, unavailability of alcohol, and absence of
family members as potential victims.

805 Szabo, D. "Do Prisons Have a Future?" KEY ISSUES,
    2: 69-80, 1965.

    Contemporary penal institutions are battlegrounds
for opposing philosophies embodied in pressure groups and
representing special interests. There are the disciples
of retributive justice, the proponents of the deterrent
effect of punishment, and those who wish to protect
society by segregation of criminals regardless of the
effects of this segregation. There are those who believe
that only the rehabilitation of criminals can protect
society. The ineffectiveness of penal administration is
the result of contradictions in penal philosophy. The
weight of tradition, structures inherited from the past,
and the survival of archaic ideas make progress slow.
Our penal system is based on the principle of moral
responsibility of the individual, and society is little
concerned with social consequences. As long as this
remains the underlying principle, there can be no
modification of the penal system. If, however, the
principle of social responsibility became the governing
principle, there would be a real functioning of justice.
This collective responsibility would be applied not only
to the perpetrator of the crime, but to the material
reparation of the damage done. This recognition of
collective responsibility must take into account that
there is limited free will in man.

806 Toch, H. "Social Climate and Prison Violence."
    FEDERAL PROBATION, 42 (4): 21-25, 1978.

    This article advocates the creation of a climate
within prisons that will confront and defuse occasions
for violence. Although motives are personal and
attributable to personality traits, the creation of the
right kind of environment in the prison can decrease the
prevalence of violent incidents. Increases in violence
may occur if prisoners are tacitly rewarded by the peer
admiration received when they endure administrative
punishment. Inadvertently permitting prison gangs or
rivals to mix often results in retaliatory fights. It is
recommended that intervention into incidents occur
swiftly after the problems appear. Crisis intervention
teams, composed of senior inmates, chaplains, and
custodial officers should be ready to intervene and

arbitrate disputes to prevent lingering problems.
Support for victims should be discreet, so as not to
stigmatize the victims and make them even more
susceptible to attack. Additional considerations include
the continual updating of official information on group
tensions and personal problems.

807 van den Haag, E. "In Defense of the Death Penalty: A
    Legal-Practical-Moral Analysis." CRIMINAL LAW BULLE-
    TIN, 14 (1): 51-68, 1978.

    Questions concerning the constitutionality, utility,
and morality of capital punishment are addressed, and
common arguments against the death penalty are refuted.
The constitutional defense notes the Fifth Amendment
implication that persons may be deprived of their lives
when such deprivation is carried out in compliance with
due process of law. It is argued that to regard the
death penalty as unconstitutional necessitates the belief
that standards determining what is cruel and unusual have
evolved so as to prohibit that which was authorized when
the Eighth Amendment was enacted in 1868. Such evolution
is concluded not to have taken place. The essential
moral question concerning the death penalty is identified
as whether the penalty is morally just or useful.
Philosophical justifications for imposing death penalties
are noted. The conclusion is that murder differs in
quality from other crimes and therefore deserves
qualitatively different punishment. The failure to
impose the death penalty represents a failure of nerve.
Punishments proclaim and enforce a society's social
values according to the importance attributed to those
values. To refuse to punish any crime with death is to
hold that the negative weight of a crime can never exceed
the positive value of the life of the person who
committed the crime.

808 Vedder, C. B., and P. G. King. PROBLEMS OF HOMOSEX-
    UALITY IN CORRECTIONS. Springfield, IL: Charles C.
    Thomas, 1967.

    Existing literature on homosexuality is reviewed
with suggestions for alleviating this problem in
correctional institutions. It is suggested that
homosexual behavior is a superficial kind of adjustment
to particular situational privations. Many homosexually
involved inmates have their first affair in prison, and
usually return to heterosexual roles upon their release.
The only solution to this problem lies in the abolition
of conditions that foster such behavior through more
widespread acceptance of conjugal visitation and home
furloughs.

809 Vogelman, R. P.   "Prison Restrictions, Prisoner
    Rights."   JOURNAL OF CRIMINAL LAW, CRIMINOLOGY &
    POLICE   SCIENCE, 59 (3): 386-396, 1968.

    Although there have been significant changes in
principles of penology, the old view persists that wide
administrative discretion should be left to prison
officials. This "hands off" policy by the courts with
regard to prisoner rights continues to be applied by a
majority of courts today. During the past 25 years,
however, some courts have recognized that this is not a
satisfactory principle in prisoner litigation, and one
court has stated that "a prisoner retains all the rights
of an ordinary citizen except those expressly, or by
necessary implication, taken from him by law." If the
courts are prepared to define what rights are denied,
rather than leave it to administrative discretion, they
will have to find a balance between prisoner and prison
interests.

810 Ward, D. A., and K. F. Schoen (eds.). CONFINEMENT IN
    MAXIMUM CUSTODY: NEW LAST-RESORT PRISONS IN THE UNITED
    STATES AND WESTERN EUROPE. Lexington, MA: D.C. Heath,
    1981.

    This book is the product of a conference held to
review the state of knowledge about the effects of
confinement in maximum security prisons, particularly
where such confinement is seen as a last resort for
violent, dangerous, and repetitive offenders.
Contributing papers are arranged in topical sections,
beginning with the problems of identifying habitual
offenders and dangerous inmates. The next group of
papers reports research on the effects of long-term
confinement on imates and staff, while papers in the
third part discuss legal issues and sentencing problems
related to maximum security prisons. The next two
sections are devoted to innovative maximum security
prisons in the United States and in Western Europe. The
concluding section of the volume is comprised of a single
presentation offering an overview of issues related to
long-term confinement.

811 Wolfgang, M. E., (ed.). PRISONS: PRESENT AND
    POSSIBLE. Lexington, MA: D.C. Heath, 1979.

    Innovative models of prison reform, based on the
premise that the greatest good is served by incarcerating
the smallest number of prisoners, are examined. The
United States penal system fails to meet the needs of the
American public, which bears the cost of both crime and
punishment. While public attention to the rights and
welfare of prisoners is increasing, the growing

recidivism rate demonstrates the failure of prisons to rehabilitate. Future solutions will come only by investigating new directions for reform. In this anthology of papers by prominent criminologists, one study concludes that deterrence should be emphasized strongly, but another suggests that means of reducing incapacitation costs should recognize the community's changing needs and values. The final article critiques the preceding ideas, and comments on each. All the articles agree that something drastic needs to be done to ameliorate U.S. prison conditions. By depriving inmates of a positive impetus toward goodness, imprisonment fails to rehabilitate prisoners for life outside prison.

812 Young, T. "Eighth Amendment Rights of Prisoners: Adequate Medical Care and Protection from the Violence of Fellow Inmates." NOTRE DAME LAWYER, 49 (2): 454-469, 1973.

The constitutional prohibition against cruel and unusual punishments expands with "evolving standards of decency" to encompass mistreatment of inmates. Although direct physical mistreatment of prisoners has traditionally been prohibited by the Eighth Amendment, only recently has this theory been successfully applied to inadequate medical care and danger of violent attack by other inmates. The early medical care cases offered two principles: (1) a complete denial of medical care to one in need is violative of Eighth Amendment rights; and (2) given medical care, however slight, any denial or inadequacy must be intentional to reach constitutional dimensions. A more modern line of cases, however, has indicated that in the future, courts may be receptive to Eighth Amendment arguments when only inadequate treatment is at issue. Similarly, courts confronted with inmate attacks on other inmates traditionally have relied on a negligence theory in granting recovery.

813 Zalman, M. "Prisoners' Rights to Medical Care." JOURNAL OF CRIMINAL LAW, CRIMINOLOGY & POLICE SCIENCE, 63 (2): 185-199, 1972.

State and federal legislative and judicial remedies available to prisoners complaining of inadequate medical care are described. Further political, institutional, and legal solutions are suggested. Despite the fairly generous position of state courts in recognizing prisoners' substantive rights to necessities such as medical care, procedures for enforcement of these rights are inadequate. The writ of habeas corpus is the method most often used by state prisoners seeking injunctive relief, but this is often denied. For inmates of federal prisons, relief may be granted if the denial of medical treatment amounts to cruel and unusual punishment. The petitioner must also allege that medical care was administered as punishment. Statutory changes can effectively convert what are now privileges into rights, can narrow the range of discretion where abuses have been frequent, and can motivate rule-making and more effective administrative control. Improvement in general prison conditions will also lead to improved medical care by reducing overcrowding, and moving facilities closer to big cities will make available greater medical talent. Further, effective legal representation is necessary to guarantee necessary services.

LIST OF SOURCES

American Criminal Law Review
American Historical Review
American Journal of Corrections
American Journal of Legal History
American Journal of Psychiatry
American Journal of Psychoanalysis
American Sociological Review
American Journal of Sociology
American University Law Review
Annales Internationales De Criminologie
Annals of the American Academy of Political and Social
    Science
Arizona Law Review
Baylor Law Review
British Journal of Criminology
British Journal of Sociology
Buffalo Law Review
Bulletin of the American Academy of Psychiatry and the
    Law
California Youth Authority Quarterly
Canadian Journal of Corrections
Canadian Journal of Criminology and Corrections
Catalyst
Catholic University of America Law Review
Civil Liberties Law Review
Columbia Law Review
Community Mental Health Journal
Contemporary Crises
Corrections Magazine
Creighton Law Review
Crime and Corrections
Crime and Delinquency
Crime and Delinquency Literature
Crime and Social Justice
Criminal Justice and Behavior
Criminal Justice Review
Criminal Law Bulletin
Criminologica
Criminology
Current History
Essence
Ethics
Evaluation Quarterly
Federal Bar Journal
Federal Probation
Harvard Law Review
Hastings Law Journal
Human Organization
Human Relations
Indian Law Journal
International Journal of Criminology and Penology
International Journal of Offender Therapy and Comparative
    Criminology

Issues in Criminology
Journal of American History
Journal of Applied Social Psychology
Journal of Behavorial Economics
Journal of California Law Enforcement
Journal of Criminal Justice
Journal of Criminal Law and Criminology
Journal of Criminal Law, Criminology, and Police Science
Journal of Family Law
Journal of Offender Counseling, Services, and Rehabilita-
    tion
Journal of Police Science and Administration
Journal of Research in Crime and Delinquency
Journal of Social History
Journal of Social Issues
Journal of Sociology and Social Welfare
Journal of Southern History
Judicature
Justice System Journal
Juvenile and Family Court Journal
Juvenile Justice
Key Issues
Land Economics
Law and Contemporary Problems
Law and Human Behavior
Law and Order
Law and Policy Quarterly
Law and Society Review
Michigan Law Review
Military Police Law Enforcement Journal
Minnesota Law Review
Nation's Cities
Nebraska Law Review
New England Journal on Prison Law
New York University Law Review
North Carolina Law Review
Notre Dame Lawyer
Offender Rehabilitation
Ohio State Law Journal
Oregon Historical Quarterly
Oregon Law Review
Overview
Phylon
Police
Police Chief
Police Journal
Police Law Quarterly
Police Magazine
Police Studies Journal
Policy Analysis
Policy Studies Journal
Prison Journal
Probation and Parole
Psychiatric Annals
Psychiatry

Public Administration Review
Public Interest
Public Management
Public Personnel Management
Quarterly Journal of Corrections
Quarterly Journal of Studies on Alcohol
Review of Public Data Use
Rice University Studies
Rutgers Law Review
Science and Society
Social Forces
Social Problems
Social Science History
Social Science Quarterly
Society
Sociological Methods and Research
Sociological Quarterly
Sociology and Social Research
Southern California Law Review
Stanford Law Review
Suffolk University Law Review
Texas Law Review
Theory and Society
Trans-action
Trial
University of Chicago Law Review
University of Pennslyvania Law Review
Urban Life
Victimology
Virginia Law Review
Washington Law Review
Western Sociological Review
Wisconsin Law Review
Women's Rights Law Reporter
Yale Law Journal

The following are existing bibliographies on criminal
justice from the National Criminal Justice Reference
Service:

Alternatives to Incarceration (1979)
Basic Sources in Criminal Justice (1978)
Correctional Staff Development and Training (1980)
Criminal Justice Evaluation (1975)
Halfway Houses (1978)
Issues in Sentencing (1978)
Jail-Based Inmate Programs (1979)
Overcrowding in Correctional Institutions (1978)
Plea Bargaining (1976)
Plea Negotiation (1980)
Police Discretion (1978)
Prison Industries (1978)
Recidivism (1976)
Strategies for Reintegrating the Ex-Offender (1980)
Variations on Juvenile Probation (1980)